OUTSIDER

OUTSIDER

always almost: never quite

∽∽∽

AN AUTOBIOGRAPHY

Brian Sewell

QUARTET

First published in 2011 by
Quartet Books Limited
A member of the Namara Group
27 Goodge Street, London W1T 2LD

A catalogue record for this book
is available from the British Library

ISBN 978 0 7043 7249 8

Typeset by Antony Gray
Printed and bound in Great Britain by
T J International Ltd, Padstow, Cornwall

3

For Gillon Aitken, without whose
persistent persuasion for twenty
years, this book would not, at last,
have been written.

Contents

Acknowledgements

Grudgingly I must confess my dependence on my mother's diaries as well as my own. She was so indefatigable a recorder of our lives against the larger background of events that I know, for example, and knew at the time, that as we were walking from Whitstable to Seasalter on 3 October 1935, Mussolini's armies were pouring over the border from Eritrea into Abyssinia; how many other small boys had the name Haile Selassie on their lips that day, I wonder. She also kept letters – my stepfather's, from which I was to learn how extended and warm his wooing was, and mine when in the Army or away exploring Europe, have lent accuracy to recollection. As I have outlived most of my contemporaries and all my early friends, her diligence and hoarding have been invaluable. So too have been the corrections proffered by Keith Cheyney, the archivist of Haberdashers – the more generous for knowing how much I loathed the school. At Christie's another archivist, Lynda McCleod, seems always to have been amused by my requests for help, as though uncovering ancient history is fun; and Noël Annesley too, doffing his importance there, has generously reverted to his earliest role as my assistant. From below stairs, as it were, Ray Perman and John White remembered things appalling and hilarious of which, at the time I did not know, and our tripartite conversations brought a little helpless laughter into John's life as cancer inexorably shortened it; Ray, I hope, will one day write an unofficial history of the underbelly of the firm. I have also had vital, enthusiastic and unstinting assistance from Malcolm Rudland, musician extra-ordinary and Secretary of the Peter Warlock Society.

Prelude

Michelangelo's autobiography, dictated to his pupil and amanuensis Ascanio Condivi, is not a work of fiction, but of adjustment and correction, a rebuke, as it were, to Giorgio Vasari, his admirer and first biographer, who had in a number of small things offended him – with, for example, suggestions of arrogance, avarice and homosexuality. When, in my last years at school, I read Condivi's account, I took it to be the truth, but as a student at the Courtauld Institute learned that it was not – at least not quite, but was instead as Michelangelo wished the truth to be. This was a warning to be sceptical with the texts of all who write of their own lives.

The nagging to write of mine began some ten years after the Blunt Affair of 1979. 'You must write your autobiography,' said strangers – but these were strangers who had a vested interest in that event and thought that there were facts still to be revealed and spies and quislings still to be unmasked. When friends joined the chorus of demand it was because they thought my recollections of a decade or so in the employ of Christie's, that historic saleroom of the arts, too amusing to be lost and already at risk after a heart attack that had all but killed me and left the organ damaged and erratic. On Anthony Blunt, the friend who had guided so much of my life and even whose last full day was spent giving me a tutorial, so to speak, on drawings by Nicholas Poussin and his imitators, I felt unready to say more; on Christie's I felt that I could not yet tell the truth of my love-hate relationship with the firm without bruising the heels of those who were once my enemies there; and there were, moreover, other matters on which I felt unable to be open, yet if I did not tell the whole truth it would not be truth at all.

On these last, approaching my eightieth year and old enough to be neither embarrassed nor ashamed, I no longer feel the need for reticence. I was the victim of circumstances that used to matter much, but now much less or not at all; they mattered in the Thirties into which I was born and in the Fifties when I was a young man – then I was constrained by the sensibilities of others and governed by the discreet conventions of the day, but in all but one their mattering faded as I grew older and society less hidebound. The exception was the elusive identity, character and temperament of my father which, as my mother, the only living person who knew the truth, grew older, became for me an obsession, the need to know a torment. I am now wholeheartedly in sympathy with those who, adopted, seek their biological parents, and am convinced that nothing should be allowed to impede them. To the question 'Who is my father?' his name and whereabouts must be the immediate answer. I knew only that mine was dead. Now that I know a great deal more of him I am amused by the coincidences of our natures and abilities. If this book was written for anyone, it was for the handful of readers who have shared the anguish and longing of the rootless child.

Writing it has not been easy. I have been both analyst and patient. Decades too late the analyst has at last realised the reasons for so much that happened to the fool – too trusting, too naive, too influenced by his mother's instructions that he should never shake the tree but wait till the ripe fruit falls. If only she had taught him to be pushy, to dissemble, to tell only the considered truth, his life might have been more successful, whether as art historian or scribbler; but she brought him up in the arms of the Roman Catholic church and taught him to be frank (too frank too often) and truthful. Well into the second decade after her death she is still my principal demon, the only one who still affects my life; for much of her legacy I am grateful; at the rest of it I shudder. I have dug deep into indiscretion and some may say that I have dug deeper into prurience; perhaps I have, but again it is for the benefit of readers who are troubled by their private natures and feel that they alone are driven so.

Prelude

I have no doubt that many who admire me – my 'doting elderlies,' as an old woman friend once dubbed them – will be disgusted. So be it – truth is nothing if not whole. From that friend, Mary Debbane, with whom for many years I walked my dogs early every morning, I had no secrets and she was never shocked; the guardian of my sanity in the worst moments of my later life, she is now dead, but she heard it all before she went.

CHAPTER I

Mother

My earliest recollection of my mother is of my looking down on her and recognising fear. I have no memory of looking up at her, of seeing the bodyless head in which analysts who bother themselves with the earliest artistic impulses of the child would have us believe, the great smiling face of the adult looming over the cradle or the pram, but looking down from the not inconsiderable height of an overhanging branch has stayed with me all my life, not because of the adventure of climbing there – that I remember not at all – but for the startling clarity of a powerful emotion that I had never seen before and did not comprehend. The tree still stands in the garden of Cefn Bryntalch, an unlovely Victorian house in Powys recently described by agents selling it as 'innovative for its use of Neo-Georgian style which is worked into the expressive forms of brick vernacular revival' (house agents rival art critics in the meaningless jargon of their propaganda). The stout trunk of the tree bifurcates at ground level, the lesser part leaning at a shallow angle, forty-five degrees or so, over a slope; nothing could have been easier for a toddling infant to climb – and it is so still – but within a few feet, because of the slope below, the drop is perilous. Because I did not understand my mother's fear I could not share it, and was quite content to be where I was when she left me to fetch the gardener, who climbed a ladder, slung me over his shoulder and put me down in safety.

My other early memory of her is the day when, standing in the bath, waiting to be lifted from it and wrapped in a towel, there was a long, long, pause, and then she said, quite ruminatively, 'Just think, you might have been a little Indian boy.' And so I might, I

I

suppose, for she had had an affair with the Maharajah of Kutch and had tales to tell of that benighted Indian province, its windblown heat, its barren sandy wastes and its Great Rann, a salt morass into which its rivers squander rains so rare that they betray the seasons. 'The poorest Maharajah in India,' she said of him, describing the palace in Mandvi, 'but very beautiful.' Was he really the Maharajah, I wonder now, or just a member of the princely family? She could not endure the heat and wind, she said, and less still the other women, and after some months returned to England. In 1994 a television company that specialised in travel programmes asked me if there was anywhere off the beaten track that I would like to go. 'Kutch,' I replied at once, surprising them with my immediacy, 'to the Great Rann, the desert, the inland mountains and the palace at Mandvi, if it still stands.' The researchers, however, typical of all who work in television, misinterpreting a relief atlas in which borders were not distinguished by political colours, took Kutch to be in Pakistan and set about getting permits and visas to film in that country instead of India; too late they discovered their error and we went to the North-West Frontier and thereabouts instead.

My mother had other adventures. She had been to Sarawak at the invitation of some member of the Brooke family, perhaps Charles Vyner Brooke, the last of the so-called White Rajas of the territory, for she maintained a sparse correspondence with him until his death in 1963. She had been engaged to an army officer stationed in the Malay States, as the federated provinces of the Malay Peninsula were then called, but, on finding the climate there intolerable, she broke it off. She had had a more romantic, more emotionally lasting affair with a young man from an Anglo–Chilean family named Bushell in Santiago (I think without going there) who died of tuberculosis, but with whose mother she remained in touch until the outbreak of war in 1939. And she spent enough time in Paris to know it as least as well as she knew London.

Though born in Dublin in 1900, most of her girlhood had been spent in Hampstead, where her father, who had made something of a fortune in developing cinemas, had a house in Fitzjohn's Avenue. Educated at home, with no thought that she might one day have to support herself, she learned to play the violin and cello, later passing her violin to me but continuing with the cello until arthritis crippled her fingers – both instruments, particularly the cello, were very good. She also had some talent in painting and modelling, but her wish to become a student at the Slade School was frustrated by her father, precipitating her first break with him. She joined the workshop of George Frampton, a Royal Academician described in his day as 'Highly accomplished and firmly based on the true principles of his art', and claimed to have played some small part in his marble and granite memorial to Edith Cavell in St Martin's Place – but it must have been very small indeed, for she was only twenty when it was erected and she can never have had the muscles or the technical skill to work in stone. I suspect that she merely coincided with, rather than worked on, what is at best a very dull monument, but being there, perhaps only making tea, was enough to engender her belief that she had contributed to its making. I know only that, holding her hand as a small boy, it was the sculpture at which I was compelled to gaze more frequently than any other.

She then served some sort of apprenticeship with a now forgotten painter of portraits, William Bruce Ellis Ranken (1881–1941), of whose work I have inherited a trophy dated 1923, a large drawing of a nude; it is not, alas, of my mother. This I think came to a disagreeable end, probably sexual if I can judge from her angry response to my probing. She was then taken on by Kate Ruskin Coughtrie, a painter and sculptor so obscure as to be omitted from all works of reference, but who taught her to paint moderately well and to model figures in terracotta – which my mother continued to do late into her life, vaguely in the manners of Rodin and Dalou. Of her early attempts nothing survives – only the ghost of it in the Elfin Oak in Kensington Gardens. This, the stump of an ancient oak in Richmond Park, was first carved with animals and fairy-tale figures by Ivor Inness (another forgotten sculptor) in 1911; by the late Twenties it had fallen into disrepair because the painted figures were as much modelled in Barbola paste as carved, and Barbola, though inherently resistant to water, nevertheless deteriorated if not painted and the paint renewed every five years or so. When, in 1930, the Oak was removed to Kensington Gardens, it was my mother who assisted Innes with the essential repairs, remodelling the deteriorated figures, again in Barbola, one entirely her invention; there was a second restoration after the war, but the next period of neglect was so long – half a century or so – that when they were at last restored again, at the whim of Spike Milligan in 1997, Barbola was no longer in production and the very damaged figures were fully-carved for the first time by craftsmen who knew nothing of their earlier history.

It was through Coughtrie that my mother encountered Sickert, whom she described as an unkempt and smelly old man with a sharp wit. 'Do come again when you need not stay so long,' she thought a fine thing to say to an unwanted visitor, and used it herself until her dying day. Fitzjohn's Avenue is not much more than spitting distance from Camden Town and Mornington Crescent, and I suspect that my post-war boyhood memories of the area, of Bowman's – a furniture shop with aspirations akin to those of Heal's to lead their clientele into the world of Modernism – and to the Bedford Theatre to see Wolfit playing Lear in a Shakespeare season and, later, his astonishingly ham interpretation of Mathias in The Bells, were inspired by her wish to give me, by proxy, a share in events and an atmosphere that she had years before enjoyed.

Through Coughtrie too, there was some contact with relics of Roger Fry's collapsed Omega Workshops, one of whom, a Miss Quayle (known only as Quaylie), had continued the ragged end of the business from a couple of first floor rooms in Dover Street; she was later to prove a stout friend, offering my mother occasional employment in the miserable post-Depression days of the earlier 1930s.

If any of this suggests a young woman of high seriousness, then that is a grave error. My mother had an allowance from her father, and one dress that survived until her death – probably because, as a very short flapper-cum-charleston dress in heavy silver thread, it could not be re-fashioned – was made by Worth and fetched £3,000 at Christie's, suggesting that the allowance had been generous. With boy friends equally comfortably off, she knew the Café Royal, the Café de Paris, snorted cocaine, learned to drive on some young man's Lanchester and had, I think, as much sexual restraint as an alley cat. Put very simply, the Twenties were a decade in which she wantonly enjoyed herself – until she met my father and became pregnant.

For a devout Roman Catholic girl in 1930 – or rather woman, for she was always as old as the twentieth century – this was an appalling problem. My father's solution was to pay for an abortion, as he had in other brief and casual affairs, but this my mother could not accept. She had by then quarrelled so often with her father that she would not turn to him for help, nor to her mother whom she knew would do exactly as she was told; an aunt in Dublin, after whom she had been named, came to her rescue in some small way, and so too did my father's mother, a doughty woman of considerable wealth who, in the first two or three years of my life, let us spend time in her house in Wales (hence the tree-climbing episode that is my earliest memory) and later gave my mother a very small allowance. For this there were several conditions: that the sum, in cash, was to be collected monthly from her solicitor's offices at 5, Norfolk Street, just off the Strand, that I was always to accompany my mother, and that the identity of my father was never to be disclosed to me. The allowance ceased when my mother married my stepfather in 1942 and my grandmother then made a new will in which no further provision of any kind was made for me. In effect, I was wiped from the family's history.

As soon as I was old enough to ask questions, our visits to Cefn

Bryntalch ceased. My grandmother had a grandson, Nigel, born in July 1917, fourteen years my senior and legitimate – though only by the skin of teeth, for the immature and unstable marriage of his parents took place after he was born. He had hardly ever seen his father and as his mother had deserted them, his grandmother had become responsible for his welfare and education and these took precedence over any needs that I, illegitimate, might have. It must be difficult now, well into the next century, for anyone to understand how sullying was the stigma of illegitimacy to both mother and child in 1931, the year of my birth. The blood relationships of the child were far less important than his legitimacy, and if this was not established by marriage, preferably before the event, then the child might well be taken from his mother's arms and despatched to those of adoptive parents or to the anonymity of the orphanage. The unmarried mother was without status; she dropped to the bottom of society's heap and her child might, for ever, be similarly marked for life with a birth certificate that betrayed him, denied him education, profession and, certainly, inheritance.

My grandmother, enough of a socialite to appear in the auto-biography of Kenneth Clark – he of *Civilisation* – would never have wanted any of her friends and peers to know of an illegitimate grandchild. She had, as it were, adopted my half-brother Nigel because my immature and irresponsible father had, almost six months after his birth, married his mother – a girl to whom he was soon referring as a vampire. Delayed it may have been, but it was legitimacy enough for our grandmother to settle on him a private income within months of the marriage and his abandonment by both parents. The difference between us was that by the time I was born, my father had committed suicide and there was thus no possibility of my being made legitimate by a *post partum* marriage.

In 1934 my mother's mother and Aunt Jessica both died, my mother's father having refused all reconciliation to the point of not informing her of either death, and there remained no hope of support, emotional, familial or financial other than the tiny monthly stipend from my father's mother, whom we never saw or communicated with again. We lived in ill-furnished rooms in basements and attics, a few weeks here, a few more there, some of which we left in the middle of the night, whisper quiet, tip-toe treading, wearing as much of our clothing as we could, not bundled against the cold, but for easier carrying, the rent unpaid. We lived – the word suggests some continuity, but this was true only in the wider sense of staying in more or less the same area for years – at worst in Shepherd's Bush, at best, from my point of view because both were so near the Gardens, in middle Kensington and Notting Hill. These, in the 1930s, hard hit by the Great Depression, were more run down than we can now imagine, the houses rarely painted and even the most respectable rarely without lodgers; spare rooms in Eldon Road, where I was eventually to buy a house and live for thirty years, were before and after the Second World War much occupied by the lesser curators of departments at the Victoria and Albert Museum.

My mother may have been something of a prostitute. This is putting it too baldly, but it is the only way in which I can explain why, throughout years of pinching penury, she kept her evening dresses in repair, often undertaking considerable alterations to keep them fashionable, dismantling them to recut the pattern and sewing them together again on a hand-turned Singer sewing machine. She kept her looks too. In her thirties, slim on her near-starvation diet, tall but small-boned, with a fine skin and an exquisitely pale complexion enhanced by rich brown hair, although she always affected a tragic air, subtly shadowing the sockets of her large dark eyes, she looked a decade younger; on the street, with her long legs and stride, men turned their heads for her. When she wore her evening dresses, she looked wonderful.

Always on these occasions Tilly came to stay – Tilly, who never removed her black cloche hat, Tilly who, when bathing me, would never wash me 'down there' (a working-class inhibition, I suppose), but soaped the flannel and then threw it at my stomach with an exultant 'There's a slap in the belly with a wet fish!' Tilly took me to Shepherd's Bush Market to see, standing on wooden crates to give them height amidst the stalls of fruit and vegetables, hucksters selling remedies for almost every common illness of the belly and the skin, constipation, diarrhoea, duodenal ulcers, afflictions of the liver, kidneys and urinary systems, shingles and eczema – this last the most dramatic, for it involved painting the skin in patches of brilliant gentian violet as frightening as any of the disfiguring strawberry birthmarks that were then a common sight. Most haunting of all, wandering among the stalls but selling nothing, was a man in a flat cap that, though ordinary enough in front, was hugely enlarged at the back to contain a monstrous growth on his skull and neck. He was, said Tilly, living on the money paid him in advance by the local hospital in exchange for his body when he died – but then she paid him a penny to doff the cap and show me the pale blue-veined monstrosity that lay beneath.

It was there too that I first heard the word 'bugger' and, some-how instinctively knowing that it was taboo, treasured it until my mother took me to have tea with an old Russian woman who lived in the gloomy basement of a house in Redcliffe Gardens – a White Russian, said my mother, lending a mysterious gloss to the exotic business of being Russian as she outlined the history of the Revolution as though it were a saga or romance. Paris, I then learned, had been full of wonderful White Russians when she lived there in the Twenties. Mrs Frangopoulo, having married a Greek merchant, had been fortunate enough to escape from Leningrad with more than her skin. She had a samovar and entertained me with small black velvet bags from which, having loosened the double-drawstrings, she withdrew her toys, wrapped in scraps of silk, chamois, or crumpled tissue paper – dumpy little animals, smooth and glistening in chalcedony, obsidian and agate (I was enchanted by these names), and a tiny vase of precious jewelled flowers that profoundly disappointed me, when, having been told that these delicate trifles would tremble if I breathed on them, I found that they did so only if given something of a thump. Even now I view the treasures of Carl Fabergé with scepticism rather than delight.

How did my mother know Mrs Frangopoulo? Perhaps through some White Russian contact in Paris. How did she know Paul Nash, with whom one early summer in my life, at four or five, I walked along Lulworth Cove and was given a stone with a hole through it that he found on the beach; how did she know Eric Ravilious and why did she choose, in the 1950s, to buy a house in the village, Castle Hedingham, in which he had lived twenty years before; and how did she know William Coldstream well enough to send me to him for tuition and assessment when I thought that I wanted to become a painter? These three and other artists she could easily have encountered in her years on the fringe of Fitzrovia, as it were, but what possible reason could there be for her knowing Magda Lypescu, first the mistress and then the morganatic wife of Carol II of Rumania? They were in Paris concurrently between 1928 and 1930 and must have established something of an acquaintance then. King Carol was in London on a state visit in 1938, and while the streets of London on a cold and damp November day were lined with crowds entertained to see two kings in an open carriage, my mother and I were having tea in Madame Lypescu's suite in, I think, the Savoy. Again my mother had to explain matters – the word morganatic (wonderful to a boy of seven, with all its implications), and the fact that while Carol was in Buckingham Palace, his mistress was not far away if he wished to come and see her. It was not all that she explained. Madame Lypescu was a heavy woman wearing an ankle-length dress, the colour an intense dark emerald, the material silk, a heavy lustrous taffeta slippery to the touch – and touch it I did, for at one point she bade me climb onto her lap (not an activity that I much cared for, thinking myself too old for such toddler nonsense), and over the slippery cliffs of her thighs the climbing was not easy; I preferred to stand beside her and let her run her fingers through my curls. It was then that I became aware of a confusing smell, both enthralling and repellant. My mother's response to my question, later, was that King Carol forbade Madame Lypescu to bathe too often and that what had so intrigued me was the combination of expensive perfumes with her natural body odour. Once in a while over many years since, when required to squeeze the obstructed anal glands of a beloved bitch, I have been overwhelmingly reminded of tea in the Savoy.

The one element of stability in my haphazard childhood was the cottage in Whitstable to which we often retreated for months on end. Much altered now, its front door then opened onto the narrow street leading to the harbour, along which, in the middle of the day, walked a woman with a basket covered by a white napkin, crying 'Hot pies, hot pies!' Never once did we buy one. Within the front door was the living room; to the left lay the small bedroom, and beyond lay a steep step down into the kitchen in an open plan of sorts, through the rear window of which I could clamber straight onto the shingle beach; there was no bathroom and the lavatory was at the end of a short passage open to the skies. In summer, that it had no bathroom hardly mattered, for we had the sea – my mother swam like a fish and I was so much accustomed to it that my skin glistened with salt; in winter, a zinc bath that hung in the passage to the loo had to be hauled in and filled with water boiled in saucepans and kettles. My mother bathed in my stale water. I learned to wash her back. I became accustomed to her nakedness. It was a useful preparation for the privations of the war.

How we lived – in the sense of paying bills – I do not know. There was enough money to buy bottles of the cherry brandy with which my mother occasionally drugged me to sleep before leaving the cottage for purposes I never knew, and at some point we acquired Prince, a tall white dog with long black ears, whose job it was to guard me. I was sometimes sent to the harbour when the fishing boats came in, to see if, with the sixpence in my hand, I could buy enough fish for dinner and sometimes the fishermen gave me fish too small to sell. I do not remember being hungry, as I do in the periods of intense rationing during and immediately after the war, but nor can I recall anything resembling a birthday treat or Christmas feast, and I suspect that my taste for scrag ends and hocks, for offal, necks and the heads of animals was founded then.

In the winter, facing north, Whitstable could be bitterly cold, and once in a while the sea was silenced by the ice that stilled it, the familiar beach then eerie; then we lived all day in the tiny kitchen, dressed and undressed there, and going to the bedroom was an arctic adventure. The kitchen table was the centre of our lives; on it we both drew and painted and I constructed cardboard castles and stage sets for the tales we read. And the tales? – tales re-told for a child from the Old Testament and the New, from Greek mythology, from Shakespeare and the Arthurian legends, from jiggety Longfellow's Hiawatha and the Wayside Inn, and tales of the origins of stars; what could be more magical than lying flat on our backs on the deserted beach, staring at the night sky, listening to my mother speak of the ancient origins of the Great Bear and the Milky Way? I did not know at the time, and nor did she, that so much of this tale-telling would prove to be a sure foundation for me as an art historian.

Winter and summer we walked to Tankerton and Swale Cliff in one direction and in the other to Seasalter – which I much preferred, for in one of the meadows that we crossed was a discarded, wheel-less, railway carriage in which an old man lived, almost always leaning from one of the windows that were raised and dropped by a broad leather strap, hoping to offer tea to any passer-by who might spend five minutes gossiping. That snug carriage with its smoking stove, worn rugs and collapsing furniture, its smell of coal, tobacco and bacon, was nearer the lives of Mole, Ratty and Badger in the *Wind in the Willows* than to the chill realities of Whitstable, and it was my first experience of envy.

All my memories of Whitstable are fragmentary and disordered, but still sharp. A boy with whom I occasionally played, who lived in a nearby house with a balcony that overhung the beach, jumped from it to show how impossible it was to hurt oneself on shingle – we had just been jumping from breakwaters – and broke a leg; his scream, the shattered limb – his left foot had landed on a sawn-off post beneath the shingle – and the never seeing him again have stayed with me. At the end of the High Street there was a horse trough in which a drunken, old and (as I was later to know) very bad local landscape painter, Dan Sherrin, occasionally chose to lie on hot summer afternoons until sober enough to walk home. Red-sailed barges plying close to the steeply shelving beach at high tide were a constant excitement, and once a year the summer regattas at West Beach were the great event, for in these there were races for six-oared gigs (the rowing boats towed by sailing vessels), for yachts and yawls, and the three-man randan in which the middle rower pulls a pair of sculls and the rowers fore and aft a single oar. Of the swimming races the most thrilling was the greasy pole to which young men swam, then to climb it for the prize of a leg of mutton presented – at least for the regatta of 1938 – by Mr Hadler, the butcher in Harbour Street. The circus too was a summer event, Lord John Sanger's great tent erected on Whitstable Salts, a meadow just to the west of the town, where, among the giant sea-lions and midget ponies, horse-riding monkeys and untameable lions, the star turn in 1937 was Jumbo 'the Elephant Goal-Getter', who challenged the champion goal-kicker of the Whitstable Football Club.

Beyond the town there were jaunts by bus to Faversham and Canterbury. Faversham in winter was extraordinarily bleak; facing north across the Swale to the Isle of Sheppey, the flat land barely above sea level, there was nothing in the view, but my mother made me look at it and see something in its straight horizontal lines, the drab greys and drabber browns, the wide leaden skies and the expanse of white when snow had fallen. 'It's like Siberia,' she said, and told me a little more of Russian history; and ever since, Siberia – to which neither of us ever travelled, though Omsk,

Tomsk and Irkutsk were then engraved on my brain – has for me been Faversham, extended, expanded, magnified. Canterbury and its cathedral, on the other hand, made no lasting impression.

It was on one of these jaunts that we saw pickers harvesting hops and got off the bus to look at them. In retrospect I am sure that this must have been at my insistence, for to have done so seems entirely alien to my mother's nature. In those hopfields we glimpsed a world of poverty and privation of which I knew nothing, and yet I envied these Eastenders down from the slums of London for an annual holiday, the fathers paid a pittance to climb tall ladders and strip the vines of hops, the women cooking over open fires, the children running wild, and all of them living and sleeping in the ramshackle lean-to shelters that they constructed from tarpaulin sheets and timber props. They seemed not to mind, perhaps not even to realise, that a small boy, probably in a silk shirt (silk shirts were to play a part throughout my life) saw them as something between strange creatures in a menagerie and the illustrations of a fairy-tale; my mother, possibly also in silk and almost certainly in unsuitable court shoes, felt compelled to accept a cup of tea – this I recall only for her determination not to let it touch her lips, but somehow to pour it away discreetly without the giver seeing. The impression that this episode made on me, ideal and enviable in the beginning, changed at the outbreak of war when the Evacuation of 1939 and the Blitz of 1940 revealed so much more of the lives of those who lived in the East End. It was, I suspect, the first foundation of the uncomfortable political position, moderately Conservative, profoundly in favour of the Welfare State, that has all my adult life disenfranchised me.

Where was my education in this random and haphazard life? In every conventional sense there was no education, yet I cannot remember a time when I could not read and was not having my curiosity aroused. I know that reading began with the many tales of Beatrix Potter and that my morality and manners were as much formed by the Tailor of Gloucester, Ginger and Pickles and Squirrel

Nutkin as any other early influence, but I was early beyond such children's books and when I was still small enough to perch on the foot of my mother's crossed leg I could read a newspaper propped against her knee. In winter we went often to the little cinemas in Notting Hill, spending whole afternoons in the darkness, sitting through the featured film twice – though as much for warmth as education. It was thus that I saw Disney cartoons when they were still black and white, Popeye and Olive Oil, Mickey Mouse and his entourage, and such more profoundly influential films as Charles Laughton's *Henry VIII*, *Rembrandt*, *Captain Bligh* and *Quasimodo*, and Elisabeth Bergner in *As You Like It*, establishing for me, even at that early age (it was 1936), a canon of blond beauty that I was later to apply to boys.

Shakespeare we encountered too at the Regent's Park Open Air Theatre, but the only production there that I recall with any clarity was the more than faintly ridiculous *Lady Precious Stream*, supposedly a traditional Chinese tale handed down by word of mouth for at least two thousand years, and only then recently translated into English by S. I. Hsiung. This 'Chinese Cinderella', as it was dubbed, had a peculiarly stilted, puppet-like quality, at the same time tippy-toed and shuffle-shod, as dramatic as my Godmother's Willow Pattern china.

Far more exciting for the infant aesthete was the appearance of Ram Gopal, then only nineteen and exquisitely ambiguous, with his Hindu dancers and musicians, at the Vaudeville Theatre in the winter of 1939, soon after war had been declared. What did I make of him? What were the feelings that he aroused? Seventy years later I can offer no answer other than the certainty that some indefinable longing was the consequence. Russian Ballet, seen a month later, in January 1940, left no impression of any kind, but the pantomimes did – those grand, luxurious productions at the Lyceum, the Stoll and the Coliseum, with their revolving stages, flying ballets, synchronised ranks of Tiller Girls, Grand Finales and full orchestras, their rough and tumble sowing in me an undying ambition, never fulfilled, to play the Widow Twanky in Aladdin. In the programme for Cinderella at the Coliseum in December 1939 there was a list of Air Raid Shelters in the vicinity, but in the 1941 programme there was nothing of the kind – by then most Londoners had become quite fatalistic about the Blitz and we took our chances.

That I can document this early exposure to the theatre is largely due to my mother's notes on programmes – 'Brian and Mamma', with the date and the ticket stubs, some of which are for a few shillings, but most are for front stalls at up to half a guinea. How could she afford such extravagance? Half a guinea may well have been more than she spent on rent and certainly more than we ever spent on a week's food. She may, occasionally, have sold a water-colour or a drawing, and equally occasionally she may have played her cello in some small professional capacity, but again and again I am compelled to wonder if there was some less virtuous source of income. Has my headstrong sexual nature been inherited from her? By 1938 the man who was to become my stepfather was much in evidence and taking us to theatres, but before then . . . ?

Other aspects of my education were as precocious. By the time the war began in September 1939 there was not a major museum or art gallery in London that I did not know, and the National Gallery was above all my favourite. We went there always on Connoisseurs' Day when an admission charge of sixpence was imposed to deter the hoi polloi; of this the consequence was that the gallery was all but empty and our conversations bothered no one. My mother's instruction, given in different rooms, was to find the painting that I most liked, decide why I liked it, then to seek her out and return to it to explain my conclusions. It was a simple but effective ruse to make me look and think. My thoughts were puerile. I liked Baldovinetti's portrait of a lady for her Borzoi profile, wiry fair hair and startling blue background; I liked Murillo's *Two Trinities* for its soft colours and its comforting Catholic familiarity; and I was entranced by Botticelli's *Mars and Venus*, somehow knowing that it meant far more than I could see – it was also a painting that gave me much difficulty in explaining my interest to my mother – this at an age when I had not the slightest knowledge of matters sexual and yet was aware of something that I could not define.

When the war intervened and the National Gallery was emptied of its permanent collection, it continued to function with the Picture of the Month, a series of exhibitions that did not shirk the risk to masterpieces by bringing back to Trafalgar Square only unimportant old masters from the safety of the Manod Slate Quarry in Wales, but brought Rembrandt's *Margaretha de Geer*, Hobbema's *Avenue*, Renoir's *Umbrellas* and, above all, Velazquez's *Rokeby Venus*, which was seen by nearly 37,000 visitors. There were also exhibitions of work by such contemporary artists as Sickert and Augustus John, and of War Pictures by Sutherland, Kennington, Ginner, Ravilious, Nash and others of their generation – thus was my interest in pictures broadened. How much did I understand? How certain was I, if at all, that I would at some future point, be able to understand what was beyond me then? To what extent was I beginning to reach beyond my mother's teaching?

CHAPTER 2

Father

Well into my adult life my father was a shadowy figure. That he died before I was born was the answer to my very earliest enquiry, and it now seems odd that I was for so long content with that, but as I had no friendship with other children of any age or parentage until I was eleven, perhaps it was not odd at all. In my young manhood, that is in my twenties, my mother was occasionally careless enough to let slip snippets of information, unguarded in other contexts, and into these I was able to weave recollections of other such morsels and even earlier events, the significance of which I had been unable to fathom at the time. At fourteen, in the summer of 1945, for example, I told her that I had been to Eynsford and was quite bewildered by the incomprehensible fierceness of her reaction – it was as though I had trespassed on some private property exclusively hers, and sullied Eden. My school set up a harvest camp that year – and following years – near Sevenoaks; the war in Europe over, rationing was suddenly even more severe than during it and, as the armed forces had not yet begun to demobilise, volunteers were desperately needed to bring in a harvest more precious that year than ever before, schoolboys an obvious pool of labour. I and another boy were sent to a farm near Eynsford. There, among many more serious activities, we drank cider in the village pub and got mildly drunk. How could so innocent a prank cause such a baffling reaction from my mother? By then, however, I had learned when not to enquire and, as with so many other small mysteries, set the matter aside.

Twenty years later, stricken by the breakdown of my first long homosexual relationship, a breakdown of which my mother's subconscious jealous behaviour had been the principal cause, I determined to tell her of my sexuality and did so in a letter, knowing that this she would read, but that any face to face confession would be so interrupted that I might not finish it, or worse, that the rising tension would lead to a row. She returned my letter with no expression of warmth or understanding, but with only the words 'You are just like your father.' This I could not set aside. I pressed repeatedly for more. She still would not give me his name but the anger of prompted recollection drove her on: she told me that my father had for some years lived in Eynsford with another man who satisfied his taste for being sodomised while fucking his women friends, one of whom she had been. That, I observed to myself, scarcely made me 'just like' him. If she disliked being in bed with two men, she disliked even more being one of two women with one man, which was often the alternative. His response had been to take a lease for her on the tiny cottage in Whitstable that had been the scene of so much of my childhood, discovered by chance when he had fallen into a drunken sleep on the train from London to Eynsford and been carried so much further on, and fuck her there.

Was it in any way a love affair. What did he see in her? She was beautiful; she was undoubtedly random and enthusiastic in her sexual responses; and in her ability to play the violin and cello she may have been professionally useful, for he was something of a composer. What did she see in him? By many accounts his looks were suave – Augustus John described him as tall, blond, pale and handsome, his expression constantly derisive, but their mutual friend Ottoline Morell put him down as 'soft and degenerate'. Was she attracted to him as a man who was sexually insatiable, a man incapable of emotional and sexual fidelity combined? – I doubt if in any way she shared his barely concealed interest in sexual sadism. Or was it that the unsuccess of this melancholy genius, frustrating his career and driving him into a state of dejection from which there could be no recovery, triggered a profound sympathy? One thing is certain – that their sexual interest in each other outlasted his Eynsford years, for these ended in late November 1928 and the conjugation of which I was the consequence must have taken place in mid-October 1930 and probably in his flat in the basement of what is now 12A Tite Street, Chelsea.

I was well into my fifties when, still not identifying him, she confessed the most significant information – that finding herself two months pregnant in December 1930 she had demanded of him some permanent and exclusive relationship, preferably marriage, although at that time he seemed settled with a woman named Barbara Peache, who passed for his wife. He offered to pay for an abortion, £5 the going rate as he well knew, his having paid that sum often enough for other women friends. She, a Catholic, refused, and the next thing she knew was that he was dead, poisoned by gas in the Tite Street flat. She was, I am certain, convinced that she had precipitated his suicide with her demand and bore that guilt for the rest of her life; it coloured her relationship with me and tainted her relationship with my stepfather. Suicide was not the verdict at the inquest. Suicide in 1930 was a criminal act subject to so severe a moral condemnation in all branches of Christianity that no one who had committed it could be buried in sacred ground; in recognising that there was no absolute proof of it in this case, the jury and the Coroner, who recorded an open verdict, performed a great kindness to my grandmother, whose anguish was pitiable, though she put on a brave performance at the inquest. Nigel, my father's earlier (and perhaps earliest) son (there could easily be more of us), remembered her back at Cefn Bryntalch saying that she felt as though she had killed him; seven years later she was still wearing black.

Have I inherited anything from my father? A great deal is known about his life and my impression from the mass of letters and other documentation is that he was obsessed with women and had no interest in sex with men, or between men, other than as an amused spectator. My mother's recollection of his being buggered by Hal

Collins, his friend and factotum in Eynsford, is unique, but I do not
doubt it, for it is not the sort of thing she could have imagined; it
may well have been Hal's initiative and not my father's, drunk – as
both so often were – or not. Who can know? – I observe in passing
that in my long life I have encountered many heterosexual men
who do not care a damn what kind of sex they have as long as they
have it. That he knew how abandoned sodomy can be, there is
evidence enough in the obscene, though not very funny, rhymes
and limericks in which he pilloried his enemies and occasionally his
friends; they suggest a not wholly unsympathetic and far from
condemnatory view of the proceedings, as in

> You'll love to meet the buggered bull,
> Whose little arse-hole's always full.
> He never seems to tire a bit,
> In fact, he simply thrives on it.
> He doesn't stop to pick and choose,
> The customers line up in queues,
> And as from east and west they come,
> He eagerly presents his bum.

If my father was in some sense sexually sadistic – the evidence
for flagellation comes from other sources than my mother – then in
this I am not his heir. Kenneth Clark described him as of a
'combative amorality which made him legendary in the early
Twenties,' and in this too I do not reflect him. If there is such a
thing as an aesthetic gene and it is possible to inherit it, then my
intense response to music may be his gift to me, but it could as
easily have come from my mother, who was entirely responsible
for my hopeless ambitions as a violinist. The one thing that really
intrigues me is that his uncle, John Postle Heseltine, a trustee of the
National Gallery and founder member of the Art Fund, was a
passionate and important collector of drawings by old masters and
that, decades before I knew this, I had, as a schoolboy with ten
shillings weekly pocket money, begun to trawl the Saturday markets

of Portobello Road and Faringdon in search of them, and within days of my fifteenth birthday had bought my first 'parcel' of them at Christie's for 3 guineas – more than fifty drawings at a blow. That drawings were, within weeks of my graduating at the Courtauld Institute, to become my field of professional expertise, was mere coincidence, no doubt.

In July 1986, in Ankara, lying in a bath of cold water, eating strawberries, I came to a conclusion. Petter Kolrud, an old friend and my companion on many Turkish explorations, was with me, sitting on the end of the bath, and we were talking, the subject my misery at not knowing the identity of my father. How could it be that a man of fifty-five could still be so disturbed by such a matter? We were on our way to north eastern Turkey to make an inventory of Armenian churches there; we had spent the day in the city's great archaeological museum and should have been bubbling with excitement; but there we were, in the pale green bathroom of a shoddy hotel, he calming my rage at the cussedness of my mother a thousand miles away. Absurd though it may seem, this was a defining moment. We were to be away for at least six weeks – nearer eight in the event – but throughout them I clung to my new resolve to confront my mother, already in the early stages of dementia. It was the most trying thing that I have ever done, wearing, exhausting, disagreeable and bullying; she prevaricated, dissembled, lied and pretended not to understand. Her defiance astonished me and she held to it to the very end, for it was not to me that she eventually divulged the name – Philip Heseltine, alias Peter Warlock – but to a friend shrewd enough to ally himself with her and agree that I had been heartless and unfeeling.

Once knowing who my father was, an enervating nausea has affected me whenever I have attempted to put flesh on the small bones bequeathed me by my mother. There was first an early memoir by his friend, Cecil Gray, *Peter Warlock*, 1934, given me by his daughter, Pauline. In 1992 his son, Nigel Heseltine, published *Capriol for Mother*, another memoir, ending on a reproachful, even slightly hysterical note in which he seems to discard the two most probable causes of Warlock's death, suicide or a faulty gas tap, in favour of murder by Bernard van Dieren, a slightly sinister older friend and even more forgotten composer, who was not only the last man to see Warlock alive, but was the sole beneficiary of his will, made as long before as January 1920. Barry Smith, a musicologist, contributed a scrupulous biography with *Peter Warlock*, in 1994; more detached and measured in both pace and mood, indefatigably researched, this is likely to remain for ever the authoritative life, though I dare say that the enthusiastic zealots of The Peter Warlock Society, to whom I am deeply indebted, will add bells and whistles when they can.

If I have any opinion on the cause of Warlock's death it is that his putting out the cat – no more than a kitten – with food, at 6.40 in the morning (heard by the woman who lived in the flat above), suggests the suicidal intention of turning on the gas. That in the midst of what must have been a terrible emotional crisis, he cared that much for the animal, I find endearing and perhaps the only thing I understand about the man.

At his death he had no money and seems to have been dependent on the contribution made to the household by Barbara Peache – £200 a year. He had no prospect of work in music publishing, criticism or musicology. His sound but merciless criticisms of composers, performers and writers had dented friendships and made enemies. His assessment of himself as a writer of remembered songs and forgotten choral compositions was, two years before his death, that he had been in error in seeing himself as in any way creative, and as 'having drifted, more or less by chance, into a milieu where I do not belong and can never really belong . . . but how hard it would be to get out of such a groove after being in it for years . . . ' And so it proved – a self-inflicted death the only way, 'that fatal hour,' as Augustus John put it, 'when he put the cat out, locked the door, and turned on the gas'. I was more fortunate and in one way and another realised early that I too had been in error in seeing myself as creative; the only groove from which I have not been able to escape has been writing art criticism for a newspaper.

In the merrier mood of the Eynsford years Warlock wrote a not unsuitable epitaph for himself –

> Here lies Warlock, the composer,
> Who lived next door to Munn the grocer,
> He died of drink and copulation,
> A great discredit to the nation.

Peter Warlock or Philip Heseltine? He began his life as the latter and ended it as the former, 'resolved finally to abandon all further use of the family name'. On his gravestone in the old Nightingale Road Cemetery in Godalming the inscription is intriguingly confused with PHILIP PETER WARLOCK written in equally large letters, and below, in smaller capitals, SON OF COVIE AND ARNOLD HESELTINE, whose grave it also is. It is as Peter Warlock that he is remembered as a composer, as Warlock that he is to be found in reference books. I cannot bear to hear his music, but in my mother's papers, on her death in 1996, I found sheets and sheets of it and, far odder, a catalogue of the North Italian drawings that once belonged to John Postle Heseltine – by Titian, Bellini, Mantegna, Carpaccio, Tintoretto et al – and another, of his thirty-one drawings by Rembrandt.

CHAPTER 3

Stepfather

Of the ceremony and witnesses at my parents' wedding I remember nothing other than the handsome staircase and heavily patterned carpet of the registry office, but my suicidal rage against the event is as clear now as it was then. I could think of no more immediate remedy for what I saw as a monstrous intervention in our lives than, careless of the consequences, throwing myself down the stairs, the more broken bones the better. This plan, however, was defeated by the carpet, thick and soft; no bones snapped, no intolerable pains shot through my small frame, not a scrape or scratch was to be seen – hurt lay only in the ignominy of being set on my feet by the very man for whom I had developed such envious hatred and who, moments earlier, had become my stepfather, or rather, my father.

I, who had for so long been contentedly fatherless, even to the extent of not knowing my surname, now had a father whom I did not want. He was not a stranger – indeed, I had been aware of him for years and had been accustomed to calling him Uncle Robert, a role in which I liked him well enough. We first met on Wimbledon Common, an occasional treat in wilder country than Kensington Gardens, when I was six or seven, an encounter engineered by my mother, I suspect, to see how we got on, for clearly she already knew him. I was lying on my back in long grass that had run to seed, examining the bowed heads above me with some intensity, for they were red against the sky, not green. Was this some optical effect, or were they really red? All these decades later, now living near the Common, walking dogs, I still look for red-headed grasses in late summer; they are never as red as I remember. Suddenly, there he was. He wore tweedy-brown plus-fours and had a dog to match, Flossie, smooth and cuddly, the first dog in my life, though never in any sense mine. Over some years he reappeared from time to time, often in evening dress, and I'd hear my mother return very late or even in the morning. Sometimes he took us both to the theatre; whether he thought it good for me or because the dependable Tilly could not babysit, I do not know, but it contributed to the foundation of a habit that was to flourish in my later schooldays. What, I wonder now, was a boy of seven expected to make of Dodie Smith's *Dear Octopus* in 1938? – whatever it was it lay dormant for nearly seventy years until, in 2004, I saw *Festen*, by David Eldridge, another family drama with undercurrents exposed.

Late in August 1939, the month's very last day, I think, the Second World War imminent, Robert drove down to our cottage in Whitstable and removed us to the safety of his cousin's house near Hitchin. This led to some of the happiest and most educative months of my life, but these were preceded by an immediate tragedy – the death of my dog, Prince. Robert shot him and left his body on the beach for the tide to sweep away. Packed among the suitcases in the car I saw Prince led toward the sea and heard the shot. I did not cry, as I would now, but a cold, hard, vengeful aversion lodged in my memory. There was a brief explanation about war – to me a meaningless concept but not to him, with long experience of the First World War, not only in France but in three of its intriguing peripheral campaigns, Mesopotamia, the Balkans (the Gardeners of Salonica) and the taking of Jerusalem by Allenby. In these he had seen what war could do to civilian populations and, convinced that the Germans might invade at once, Whitstable virtually in the front line, he was determined to see that we were safe. Poor Prince was an impediment; he lived on, however, as a rod with which to beat my father's back, for with every 'What do you want?' for birthday or Christmas, the answer was always 'A dog'. To this his response was that I could have a dog 'when the war is over' – and on the 8th of May 1945, when the war came to an end in Europe, I bought a puppy for half a crown, as white and black as Prince had been, but a mongrel terrier bitch entirely lacking his long-legged pointerish nobility.

In Hitchin we saw much more of Uncle Robert; he came down from London every Friday night, slept with my mother, and returned on Sunday evening. During the week I too slept with my mother – as I had always done – and resented, deeply, my being lifted from her bed late in these weekend evenings and removed to a smaller bed, warmed with stone hot water bottles clad in buttoned flannel jackets, in a distant room. Though I tried to stay awake so that I could object to it, I always failed. To my 'Why can't *he* sleep in the little room?' the answer was another question, shifting guilt – 'Surely you can't be so selfish as to begrudge him the comfort of a bigger bed?'

There was then a long hiatus. In December 1939 we returned to London and for some months there was no Uncle Robert. Nor was there any war. With snow and ice it was a savage winter, but there was food and coal enough and it was no more uncomfortable than any previous winter; in any other year we would have enjoyed its severities in Whitstable, but the town was barricaded behind defences and we were not allowed to go to it. I learned to sing 'The last time I saw Paris' – a silly sentimental song to an unsuitably jaunty tune – and my mother talked of the wonders of the Louvre. In the high summer of 1940, however, the bombing of London began, peripherally and tentatively at first, but in earnest and more accurately by early September. My mother walked with me from Kensington to Kennington, where my godmother lived in an enviable mansion flat decorated in strong blues and yellows, furnished as though it were a farmhouse in Normandy – 'This is where you must come if anything happens to me,' her instruction impressively urgent. When a nearby house was hit by an unexploded bomb we fled, not with clothes or other sensible belongings, but she lugging her cello and me her violin, and when half London was on fire we somehow made our way to Saffron Walden and the house of an old dame to whose son my mother had at some time been engaged. It was from her rooftop (the house had a tower and a winding staircase) that at night we watched the orange glow of London in flames forty miles away.

Back in London, numbed by the persistent bombing, there was a sense that this was how life must be and fatalism replaced fear. In the middle of a summer day, hand-in-hand in Kensington High Street, we were blown by bomb blast through the window of a shop that sold skeins of knitting wool, its window shattered a split second earlier, and there we lay, laughing, among the shards of glass and unravelled miles of wool. One morning we went to early Mass at the Carmelites in Church Street and found it bombed; the Catholic church on the south side of the High Street was bombed too, a great crucifix wedged at an angle across the entrance, seeming to bar entry to the roofless shell. We stopped going to Mass. And then Uncle Robert reappeared. Early in 1942 he married my mother without sacramental ceremony, legally adopted me and changed my name to his. We were an instant family and Uncle had become my father.

My mother and he expected me to believe this. He treated me then as I now treat a rescued dog that must learn an unfamiliar name; as I in my time have said over and over again in a dog's ear 'Your name is Titian,' or Schubert, or Nusch, so he said that my name was Brian Sewell and made me write it in my books. For the first time in my life I was made to realise the importance of a surname; for the first time I had a piece of paper with my name on it, an address and, I think, a number, and the important-seeming words Identity Card. My many protests were dismissed. My mother explained the long hiatus with the excuse that my new father had been working on some secret enterprise in Edinburgh, which may well have been true, but this was a man of whom I had been aware for years as Uncle and I believed neither his metamorphosis into father nor the Edinburgh tale. I was offended that they thought me dim-witted enough to accept these fictions when this was the man who had shot my dog, lifted me from my mother's bed and replaced me there. Never having had a father I had no concept of what a father should be, but I knew in my bones that I was being tricked and taken for a fool.

After my mother's death more than half a century later, I read his letters to her; they revealed an honest and continuing passion of which I never saw evidence in their daily behaviour to each other, a passion so intense that from his offices in Chancery Lane he often scribbled notes expressing it; these, if he caught the 3.00 pm collection, were delivered home later that same afternoon. Others, earlier and longer, suggest that my mother bargained with him on my account, for they contained his promises to see to my education and adopt me so that we all bore the same name, to love me as though I were his son and to ask for no other children. In all this I sense what I sensed at the time – that my mother had nothing more than fondness for him (and perhaps not even that) and that the marriage was the only means by which, at the age of 42 (he was ten years older), in the middle of an exhausting war, she could engineer some security for us both.

I do not know how they managed the sexual side of their marriage; I do not know if my mother was still anything of the sexual animal that I am convinced she had been in her twenties; I know only that in the more comfortable circumstances of Robert's flat, after a tantrum about being given a room to myself far from their bedroom, he agreed that I should have a bed in the small room off it that he used as a dressing room. It was little more than a cupboard containing a lofty mahogany wardrobe and the enormous chest-of-drawers between which and the wall a narrow divan was squeezed; this gave me the sense of being hidden away in a corner, the child's craving for the aedicula perfectly satisfied. But then there were the nights when Robert came into the room and masturbated, an urgent, private, silent, business that had nothing to do with me in my dark corner supposedly fast asleep, but was of intense interest; his technique informed my own.

I had long since clumsily indulged in that solitary pleasure, accidentally discovered when I was six or so, but not disclosed to my mother; how is that young children know when something should be secret? But at eight she found me at it in an unlocked bathroom and uttered the formidable threat 'If you do that, you'll never go to a university.' No more was said then or ever again, and as I had no concept of what a university might be, the threat had no specific meaning and could not be assessed; dire though I thought it must be, it did not affect the practice but confirmed the secrecy; when, eventually, a university seemed well within reach, the threat, though always remembered, I knew to be as false as all the others uttered by schoolmasters, priests and non-conformist busybodies. Robert would have been appalled had he known that he had unwittingly demonstrated the simplest and easiest way to masturbate and, that in doing so, he had encouraged me to outgrow my need to be within reassuring distance of my mother, abandon the bed in the dressing room and develop the parallel world of my own room along the corridor.

There was, I am all but certain, an abortion. A doom-laden atmosphere lay heavy in the flat, my mother in bed, depressed, angry and unfriendly (a very rare thing), Robert pacing about in an equally angry sulk, the bathroom out of bounds. A strange doctor came, grim, unsmiling and, to me, unspeaking. And, indeed, the bathroom was occupied for hours, the moans and cries distressing. For days afterwards, it seemed, Robert and my mother hardly spoke, and then she went away – 'Not well . . . in need of country air . . . ' Later, occasionally, some thoughtless or selfish action on my part was rewarded with the reproach 'You will never know how much I've done for you' – and I associated it with the day the unfamiliar doctor came. There was also, once, a wistful response to my expressing a wish that I had had an older brother – 'Well, you might have had a little sister . . . '

Robert Sewell was a good man, but this for all my boyhood years I failed to recognise. He deserved a son of his own and not a second-hand recalcitrant. Early in his days as my father he came into the bathroom to see me bathe, and enquired if I retracted my foreskin and washed there, telling me of the campaign in Mesopotamia in which he had fought and the importance of genital hygiene in the desert, even if no more than a mug of water could be spared for it – wiser than washing your face, he thought. When three years or so later, I was in the throes of puberty, he asked the simple question 'Is there anything you want to know?' I knew exactly what he meant and answered 'No.' There was, as it happened, a great deal, for the schoolboy confusions of my peers at school, and the dissemblings, cautions and prohibitions of those who dipped their toes in the waters of sexual education were scarcely to be believed, but I did not want to be told the truth by him. I did not want to be touched by him, physically or emotionally, and shrank away from his rare attempts to hug or kiss me.

He tried very hard to be my father. His first gift was a kilt. With the Cameron clan in his recent ancestry and the Cameron High-landers his regiment, it must have seemed to him a useful instrument of bonding. He did not just buy one – that was probably not possible in the third year of the war – but took me to a tailor to be measured and fitted, and I hated him for it. The kilt was never worn and it disappeared from my wardrobe. His second gift was cricket gear. Insofar as he could be fanatical about anything, cricket was his mania, and somewhere in London he found an outfitter who still had a cream flannel shirt, a pullover in cable stitch, white kid boots and enough heavy cream flannel cloth to make trousers for a boy. Though better dressed for it than any other boy at Haberdashers', I had no talent for the foolish game and such perfect clothes for it made me feel an idiot.

Haberdashers' was a gift of a different kind. I was nearer eleven than ten when I became Robert's son, a child of absolutely no formal education and much too much that was informal and pre-cocious. He might have persuaded his old school to accept me – certainly he thought that I should be a boarder somewhere safely away from London – but since my birth my mother had never been separated from me even for a day, and she was appalled by the idea. It is usually the son who does not want to be parted from his mother, but in my case I was attracted by the proposal and would willingly have gone; instead, Robert approached school after school in London and took me to be interviewed, but none would have me without a grasp of any form of mathematics, without the formalities of English grammar – what did I know of algebra, they asked, and could I parse a sentence? Haberdashers' was the last of several possibilities, and there Robert was offered hope; it was by then May 1942 and the entrance examination was to be on the 13th of July – if I went to an approved preparatory school for two months it might just be possible to cram my brain with the essentials of mathematics and grammar.

That I passed the examination in any conventional sense I now do not believe. The cramming took place in a shoddy little dame school where I was mercilessly bullied by two older and bigger boys, the brothers Summerfield, and I am still sickened by recall of their punches to my stomach – one restrained me while the other struck; I had had no experience of boys, knew nothing of fighting, and had never, until then, been hurt. I was utterly bewildered by algebra, geometry, parsing and syntax, and I am sure that Haberdashers' let me in only because it was by then a very run-down school of no reputation and uncertain future, its catchment area largely lower middle-class (more Cricklewood than Hampstead), its pupils the sons of small independent shopkeepers and bank managers with social ambitions, and it needed the fees of every pupil it could get.

Robert let Haberdashers' do its worst. At crucial moments but to no effect he paid for extra maths lessons in both the lower and the upper schools, and he argued my case when the headmaster put me into the Remove and would have had me gone. His own contribution to my education lay in steering me away from the Catholicism early instilled by my mother and into the Church of

England traditions of which he was, largely through his love of English choral music, an uncritical supporter. He looked after the financial affairs of several composers and performers, Benjamin Britten one of them, and took me to the first performance of Peter Grimes in 1945 – an occasion of which I ought to remember more than the Adam's apple and excruciating vibrato of Joan Cross; I hated it. It was his interest in organ music that generated mine and pushed me literally into the arms of Alan Harverson, a young rising star of these great instruments in the 1940s, who taught me all I know of them and also took me to his bed. I cannot imagine, had Robert known of this, what he would have done, if anything, but – though we had never spoken of what schoolboys might do together – I knew of his views on homosexuality from the disgust he expressed when cases of importuning were reported in the *Daily Telegraph*. A little later, when his friend Ian Horobin, Warden of Mansfield House University Settlement in the East End, was tried for homosexual offences – it seems that he urged bigger boys to bugger younger while he looked on and masturbated – Robert seethed with a sense of betrayal by a man whom he had known so long and yet been duped by his dissembling.

With my precocious smoking Robert dealt elegantly and effectively. His view was that I should smoke well or not at all; my smuggled Woodbines he discarded with disdain and we set off for an eminent tobacconist in St James's with whom I am certain he had entered into conspiracy. I was persuaded to choose a pipe and a very mild tobacco called Baby's Bottom was suggested, together with a waxed wallet in which to keep it, and all sorts of pipe-smoker's impedimenta, the expense considerable. At home, with some ceremony, all this was put to use and, encouraged to inhale deeply, I was within moments miserably sick. With permission to smoke whenever I wished, the wish abruptly withered. On discovering my wayward sexuality he could hardly have employed a kindred stratagem; besides, I was determined that he should never know; nor should my mother.

Stepfather

As I grew older, Robert played less and less of a role in my life. He did not share my interest in the visual arts and never once went to a gallery or exhibition with me, but to the Saturday morning jaunts that, as a schoolboy, I made in and out of the then many art dealers' premises in Bond Street and thereabouts, he gave a tacit blessing in that he occasionally met me for lunch, sometimes in a Chinese Restaurant in Wardour Street, more often in Manzi's in Leicester Street because, as he told me, the original Manzi had been one of Lord Leighton's models.[1] He saw to it that I went to the theatre, introduced me to the plays of Anouilh, Fry and Rattigan, and encouraged me into the habit of cycling from school into the West End, there to pay four shillings or so for a numbered stool that secured a place in the queue for seats in the pit or gallery when the theatre opened in the evening – and on it, in St Martin's Lane or Shaftesbury Avenue, I sat and wrote a homework essay.

Robert's passion for my mother cooled after five years or so of marriage and they quarrelled mightily. I broke in on them one evening – I was fifteen – and said something like 'For God's sake, why don't you two get divorced?' – to which the answer came, almost in unison, 'We stay together for your sake.' How like them, I thought, to blame me for their misery. Robert took to politics (perhaps persuaded by Ian Horobin who had been a Nationalist MP in the 1930s and was to represent the Conservatives as an MP before his disgrace) and as a distant cousin of Bonar Law (Britain's shortest-lived Prime Minister) had quite a happy time on the fringes of the Conservative Party in its darkest post-war days. My mother developed a number of pseudo-asthmatic ailments that could only be relieved by weeks in the sea air at Eastbourne or sniffing the mud at Westcliff (then believed to be a sovereign cure

---

1   The dates do not appear to support this: Leighton died in 1896 and the first Manzi premises were established in 1902; it is, nevertheless, possible that a member of the Manzi family had been in London earlier, paving the way. Robert was never a man for tittle-tattle and I am inclined to think that there must have been some authority for his assertion.

for respiratory problems), and it was evident that their lives were falling apart.

There was one cruel event that no one explained adequately at the time and I cannot explain now. Robert took me to the Law Courts one morning and a hearing took place at which I understood that I had the opportunity to reject his adoption and his name. I know that it was painful for him, for before it began he had to tell me himself that he was not my father, and was put out by my response – 'I know. I've always known.' The judge, if that is what he was, put me under extreme pressure with a review of all that Robert had generously done for me, urging me to do 'the decent thing,' ending with the suggestion that as all my schoolfriends knew me as Brian Sewell, that was the name by which I should continue to be known if I wished to stay in touch with them. For a moment my real identity was within my grasp, my real name, my real father, and the gnawing curiosity could end. But I funked it. Exactly as the judge had suggested, rejection of Robert's name seemed too cruel a blow to a man who, to all intents, purposes and onlookers, was indeed my father, but had I known what I was to know later, I would not have hesitated. The anger is with me still.

With an abbreviated birth certificate that gave no indication that I was adopted and sound advice on what I might expect in the army, Robert saw me into National Service – though seeming offended that I had refused his help to get into the Cameron Highlanders. Not a Scot, never seduced by the romantic nonsenses of Scottish history, literature or song, loathing the wail of bagpipes and remembering the rejected kilt, why should I want to join his swaggering regiment? It was at this point that my mother decided that she no longer wished to live in London. He bought her a house in Castle Hedingham and let her go, while he settled down with an air hostess from British European Airways.

Achieved without animosity, this seemed a satisfactory arrangement until he began to die of cancer. Operation after operation, seven in all, weakened him to the point at which nothing more could be done, there was no hope of recovery or even remission, and he was sent to Hedingham to die. He lasted six months and the nursing nearly killed my mother. I was with him for the last few days, with him, indeed, when he died, listening to his apnoea, ready with a soft silk scarf with which to tie his jaw in place when the moment came. Shortly after midnight he opened his eyes for a moment, looked at me intently, and said two words – 'Poor Brian.' An hour or so later he was dead.

'Poor Brian' puzzled me, but before we could bury him I knew why he had said it. A termagant of a woman arrived at the door, demanded entry and said 'All this is mine.' She had with her a rather younger woman and a solicitor with evidence that the one was Robert's wife and the other his daughter. They had seen the notice in the *Telegraph* – a notice intended for his friends, his clients and his regiment, not this – and they had come post haste. She was indeed his wife; she had not seen him for more than thirty years, but there had been no divorce and he had constantly supported her, had paid for the education of his daughter, and had left a will in her favour made many years before. His marriage to my mother had been bigamous and he left her penniless, though as the deeds were in her name, she remained in possession of the Hedingham house, her only asset. Robert's adoption of me, though with the best of intentions, was fraudulent – and my mother knew it.

In his wardrobe I found three live hand grenades from World War I and the pistol with which he shot Prince.

CHAPTER 4

School

Haberdashers' Aske's Hampstead School was housed in a gaunt red brick building designed for it in the last years of the nineteenth century, to which a less aggressively ugly Science Block had been added in 1931. As an institution it had some ancient history in that the medieval haberdashers of London, dealers in beads and buttons, needles and thread, had, having been granted armorial bearings, formed a guild in 1448, late in the reign of Henry VI; Aske, Robert of that ilk, a late seventeenth-century Master of the Haberdashers' Company, in bequeathing money for the education of twenty haberdashers' sons of 'proven poverty,' was responsible for the foundation of the school. By the late nineteenth century, however, poverty had no part to play in the choice of boys to attend, fees had to be paid and entrance examinations passed, and the school was something of a stepping-stone to Oxford and Cambridge for the shop-keeping classes, but Hoxton, the site of the original school, had become a run-down area of slums and shop-keepers were fewer than they might have been – hence the move to Hampstead. This was not, alas, to the jolly Hampstead of the Heath, the fairs, the artists' colony, but to the gloomy northernmost point of West Hampstead, recently developed as a middle class alternative to the new slums of Cricklewood and Kilburn, the local street names Gondar, Menelik and Somali bearing witness to Napier's Abyssinian Campaign of 1868, and Agamemnon, Achilles and Ulysses to a developer with a classical education.

The northern perimeter of the school indeed formed the border with a Cricklewood council estate from which rude boys emerged to mock us for our straw boaters, and access to the school was primarily from the bus and trolleybus routes that intersected at Cricklewood Broadway. Thus it was, in the 1940s, a decade of war and punishing austerity, that Cricklewood was on my map. It was then a nesting-place for European Jews and it was Issy Bonn, an engaging Yiddish humourist on the BBC's Home Service, who dubbed it Cricklevitch and adopted the persona of a local Kosher shopkeeper suffering the hazards of the Blitz. Its most prominent building was a dance hall that seemed to function every hour of the day and we schoolboys in short trousers, already prurient, and more prurient still in trousers long, speculated much over the conjugation of blond factory girls in snoods with the spivs and black GIs who lay in wait outside – wicked stuff for Burra watercolours. The marshalling yards and sidings of the old Midland Railway attracted the Luftwaffe to Cricklewood to drop more than the area's fair share of incendiary and high explosive bombs, and we collected shrapnel on our way to school, a currency to be exchanged for conkers and other treasures to be found in the pockets of small boys – I once swapped what I swore was a piece of fuselage (how could I know?) for a whole doughnut.

I knew haberdashery to be the ground-floor departments of such shops as Barker's, Derry and Toms, and Ponting's in Kensington High Street, associated it with knicker elastic and hat ribbons, and thought it a ridiculous name for a boys' school – not a good beginning. I suspect that some of the masters too thought it an uncomfortable name for a great educational institution, for we were too often reminded that its origin lay with a medieval guild. The school's motto, Serve and Obey, I loathed, thinking it perfect for the tired old things who stood behind haberdashery counters measuring elastic at a penny three-farthings for a yard, but not for a boy who had been taught to think.

In September 1942, on the first day of term, Mr J. F. Cooper, deputy headmaster of the Lower School, despatched me to Form 2B, of which the form master was a mistress, Irene Johnson – we were three full years into World War II and young masters were elsewhere. For me she was the perfect introduction to formal education – that is, largely careless of academic rules and casual with the syllabus. History and English were her subjects, but she had a sister who could sing and with a piano in the room we were occasionally treated to song recitals instead; Irene, it was, who planted an undying love of Schubert in my soul. If she taught us anything of the dynasties of English medieval history, I cannot recall it, but she inspired in me such an interest in weaponry, siege machines and castles, that I was once able to remember the progress of English dominion and decline in France largely through the fate of the castles that were constructed there. As for her conjuring the Crusades, her evocation of Le Crac des Chevaliers in Syria (another castle) was as powerful as her images of Richard the Lion Heart, his Queen Berengaria, and his probable lover, the itinerant lutanist Blondel. Can we imagine any teacher now imprinting images of Le Crac on the eyes and minds of a class of eleven year old boys, or hinting at the particular relationships of men?

She did not stay long at Haberdashers' for the school was no place for free spirits; in the sense that she was both driven and diverted by her enthusiasms she was perhaps very like my mother and I wish now that I had realised earlier just how exceptional she was. I wish too that I had been able to thank her for taking so easily in her stride my odd precocities; on the very first day she put us at our ease by asking each in turn what books we had just read, William and Biggles high among the responses, but when, late in the hour (for we sat in alphabetical order), I rattled off novels by Warwick Deeping, Jeffrey Farnol, Joseph Farjeon and Dornford Yates (whose snooty characters were initially responsible for my passionate interest in beautiful cars), no eyebrow rose and she treated the list as though it were to be expected. These were my mother's borrowings from the local library, and I read them too, avidly engrossed, though having recently re-read both Deeping and Yates, I wonder now what on earth I saw in them – but that is also my response to Trollope, all of whose novels, even the *Golden Lion of Granpere*, I read for pleasure in my later teens.

Irene Johnson also persuaded us to speak, to give short talks on favourite things, a pet or holiday, and again she did not curse me when I chose to go beyond these limits. With Puccini there was a simple life to tell – an unhappy marriage, an almost fatal accident with a car, cancer of the throat, death and a great unfinished work – but with Wagner and the Leitmotiv rage and ignominy were the consequence, for the boy who had agreed to demonstrate on the piano rebelled when I demanded that he find his way through my mother's miniature score of *The Ring*. We read Shakespeare too, performing *Macbeth* text in hand in the shallow empty space before the class, and thus the following year, in the Third Form, were at twelve and thirteen not the least abashed at mounting a full performance of it in the School Hall.

Three things were the cause of abject misery. In English Grammar we were compelled to parse sentences – that is to deconstruct them and name their parts and tenses; but I already spoke and wrote grammatically the English of my elders, instinct and rote my guides, and the exercises merely confused me and, though more often than not my answers were right, they were not based on reason. Even now, earning my living as a scribbler, I still cannot parse and yet I lock horns with editors, propensity and personal precedent the rocks on which I base my argument. But I learned wonderful new things – metonymy, synecdoche, hyperbole and metaphor – and have been in love with English ever since. With mathematics, however, there were no such consolations.

Double Maths, an unbroken hour and a half of it, was the most dreaded entry on the charts of lessons that we were given on the first day of term. Double maths meant ninety minutes of blind incomprehension, of futile struggle with an unintelligible discipline, the letters and language of algebra and geometry impenetrably abstruse, the arithmetical problems absurd – with water leaking at twenty gallons a minute, how many boys must stick their fingers in the dyke if one finger reduces the flow by five eighths of a pint in nine seconds? I could visualise the dyke, the boys, the wind and weather, I could indeed have drawn the problem, but I could not solve it. As for sines, secants and tangents, logarithms and equations, pi and Pythagoras, of these the immediate consequence was the physical shutting-down of my mind and I sat at my desk a hapless idiot, my only achievement – one still with me – the ability to shut my eyes and precisely count against the clock the sixty seconds of a minute. Of the eight years I spent at school at least two, if we string all the hours together, were utterly wasted in lessons on maths, chemistry and physics; my brain was simply not attuned to them.

My stepfather, who could solve finger-in-the-dyke problems as though they were the simplest mental arithmetic, decided that I should have extra maths lessons after school and consulted Cooper, who agreed to teach me twice a week for five shillings an hour, which meant travelling home by bus in the evening rush and in the darkness of the blackout, a small boy often allowed to stand on the upper deck – a privilege forbidden to adults – in the heady atmosphere there of Virginia tobacco, damp cosmetics, sodden rubberised mackintoshes and stale body odours. It was the most extraordinary combination, a smell ranking high above roasting coffee, stinking fish and other street smells of my childhood, seductive and repellant. Extra maths continued until the end of my first term when poor Cooper had to admit that I had shown not the slightest improvement. I had, nevertheless, enjoyed the lessons, for Cooper, a neatly constructed little man, had sat close, his left arm about my shoulders, though often wandering lower; he seemed warm and affectionate in a way that my stepfather was not, and I liked it. I liked the hand on my bare knee and I liked too Cooper's standing behind me, close, after some errand that had taken him from the desk. There was nothing overtly sexual about these contacts, but they were, in today's jargon, inappropriate.

I did not betray Cooper. His moustache bothered me a bit, but to a boy who was at the beastly school only because a newly-acquired and dour stepfather compelled it, Cooper's warm touch was appealing. I sensed – as children do, for they have surprising canniness – that what he did put us both in peril, and said nothing, and it was only my continuing failure to raise the level of my marks in maths that brought an end to our association. The contact did me no harm – I was, I am certain, already queer – but I am convinced that had I told my homophobic stepfather, the consequences would have been appalling, with me, no doubt, consenting to words put in my mouth, the consequence an abiding sense of guilt about sex, my sexuality and my betrayal of a man who gently taught me something about the pleasures of my body, lasting to this day.

Nor did I betray Horace a year later. For a man as hostile to homosexuality as my stepfather to put me into the care of a professional footballer too old to be in the army, was an act of astonishing naivety. I was twelve and showing neither interest in, nor aptitude for, the abominable game of soccer that was compulsory in winter in the Lower School, and I spent most games afternoons either in goal where I froze with inattention and the weather, or enraging the little know-alls in my team by invariably being off-side. Where the hell, I wondered, was on-side, and why was it never where I chanced to be? I was always among the last to be chosen for these ad hoc teams, and the games began with ignominy. School reports betrayed me and my step's response was the same for soccer as for maths – extra tuition. Having found a maths master with embracing arms, he now found a footballer with wandering hands, all too willing to explain some unexpected rules and show me how to play a different game.

This was at a stage in the war when Londoners had become blasé about air raids, were hungry and ill-clad, and our motor cars were all standing on piles of bricks in locked garages, their essential parts removed so that, in the event of a German invasion, they would be useless to the enemy. Horace, however, a red-haired and wiry player for Spurs, collected me every Saturday morning in a

Ford Ten Tourer of 1934, for professional footballers, it seems, were among the very few non-combatants allowed a petrol ration. The Ford was a blandishment quite irresistible to a small boy; never mind the privilege of sitting on the touchline (if that is the term in soccer), and of witnessing the manly mysteries of jockstraps, communal bathing, massaging and horseplay after the games – it was the journeys to and fro that I enjoyed, for the Ford's flapping hood was almost always down, and to rattle windblown from pitch to pitch through the bleak environs of London in that puny little car was exquisitely seductive, even thrilling, for I had to play a part in driving it – without a roof it was subject to extreme flexing over bumps and the potholes that were many and deep as a consequence of the Blitz, and I had always to be ready to grab the passenger door and slam it shut; this, in turn, gave Horace an excuse for grabbing me.

I do not know what happened to Horace after that winter. I dare say that school reports indicated no improvement in the game and that my step thought his pound notes better spent elsewhere. I dare say that Horace became disenchanted with 'my little toff', as he invariably introduced me to his mates, their ribald responses beyond my comprehension; perhaps he found a boy less toffee-nosed and innocent, happier to make mutual the pleasures that he offered – I missed his car more than I missed him. In a subsequent winter Haberdashers' introduced me to the ecstatic pleasures of rugger, a game then mercifully unencumbered by obscure and restrictive rules, fast, furious and indelicately physical.

If other boys had such contacts with adults, they did not speak of them, but in my second year at the school, in the Third Form there was an abiding atmosphere of, at first latent, and then active sexuality, curiosity urged on by changes in our bodies, but cruelly ill-informed by feeble and evasive attempts to instruct us. We were urged to keep ourselves pure for the day when we got married and, above all things, to eschew self-abuse, for the consequences of this evil were blindness, debility and early death, to say nothing of moral turpitude. If one boy knew that the erect penis must enter the vagina to make babies, then swiftly all boys knew – but then what? Adler, the boy who told us this, could only suppose that we then had to pee; we were appalled by the thought. Harry Claff, a handsome curly-haired Jewish boy, nearer thirteen than most of us, was the first to ejaculate and solve the mystery of what really happens when men and women conjugate, for spunk – then the word for it – had never been mentioned in lessons that dwelt on the role of bees in the pollination of plants. Harry could demonstrate several times a day until other boys caught up with him and curiosity in his oddly purple penis waned; then he gained supremacy again by bringing to school the first – and in my day, only – pornographic paperback, from which I recall the mystifying phrase 'the love juices streaming down her thighs'. From then on it seemed that almost every boy was obsessed with the idea and practice of mutual masturbation in the air raid shelters (from which we used to remove the light bulbs), behind the fives courts, in the loft above the school hall, in the swimming-bath cubicles (though they had no doors), in the communal bath after rugger or cross-country running, and at the summer harvest camps some boys knew enough to take matters a great deal further, shading into sexual sadism and bondage, even genital bondage, all of which seemed to come about by instinct rather than instruction.

I am convinced that nothing of this did harm and that if any of us in adult life identified ourselves as homosexual, the many happenings at school were not to blame. When, to celebrate the twenty-fifth anniversary of our leaving school an old boy invited me to dine with a dozen or so of my contemporaries, they were all contented married fathers, whose prinked, perfumed and appalling wives spoke of nothing but their university ambitions for their brats, most of them at Haberdashers'. When conversation turned, by chance, to homosexuality, the condemnations of the husbands were as shrill and vituperative as those of their wives, and, the hypocrisy intolerable, in one of those hushed moments when

43

mutual outrage has exhausted company, I heard myself say, my voice perhaps rather too intentionally audible, 'There is not a man at this table with whom I did not have sex when we were boys,' and left the house. It has always puzzled me that hetero-sexual men have the ability to haul down the shutters on their adolescent sexual experiences and utterly deny them; to me they were unforgettable adventures in revelation, instruction and self-knowledge, too important ever to be denied.

I spent the long summer break of 1944 away from London, sent thirty miles or so north-west to escape the flying bombs of which almost seven thousand were to fall on London and the near south-east between mid-June and early September, when I had to return to school. Leaked intelligence had suggested that some fifty thousand of these first *Vergeltungswaffen* (retaliation weapons) might be despatched, and when the House of Commons heard, three weeks after the engine of the very first cut out, that almost all were falling on London – as most Haberdashers already knew from the long hours spent in the school's air raid shelters – my stepfather explained with some gravity his decision that, for my safety, I should spend the summer in a pub he knew near Mentmore where there was a family of boys. Off I went to learn their country ways. They were far more advanced than young Haberdashers. In the wooded hills above a nearby airfield, watching the movement of planes was varied at the wish of the eldest, at seventeen, waiting to go into the Navy; at will, he buggered his brother of fifteen who, in turn, buggered the next, of fourteen, but that poor boy was allowed only to eye his brother of eleven and mutter 'See what you'll get when the time comes.' I was allowed, indeed encouraged, to watch, but absolutely forbidden to touch or be touched, for this was family business. Do they remember this, I wonder, as they mingle with their sons and grandsons? Newly knowing what could be, intrigued and fascinated by my knowledge, back I went to school, knowing too about scrumping apples, putting my ear to a railway line to tell if a train was coming, and what could be written and drawn in a pub lavatory.

There was one aesthetic adventure. Alone and on a bicycle I rode the long avenue to Mentmore, of which my step had spoken; no one was about, or so I thought until caught peering through slightly parted curtains. It was not quite a twisted ear moment and I must have been coherent in my excuse for trespassing, for I was taken into the kitchen and given tea and cake, and then allowed to peep into a ground floor room or two and see a dust sheet pulled away from furniture, a light switched on near a painting. It was my first experience of a great country house and when, in 1978, I drove Anthony Blunt and Neil MacGregor to Mentmore to view the sale that marked its disposal and dispersal, I realised how sharp my visual memory can be.

In the Upper School I learned to play rugger, though I never quite understood the rules, discovered an unexpected love of cross-country running – it is the loneliness, the self-dependence that is so seductive – and was a reasonable all-rounder at athletics. Confessing to my mother one sports day when my house was weak, that I felt I had to do too much, she pressed a tiny hip flask into my hand with instructions to swig from it if I felt myself flagging. I did, and it made things infinitely worse, legless indeed; I learned later that she had filled it with neat gin. At cricket, the one summer pastime that really seemed to matter at Haberdashers', I was hopeless, never put in to bat or bowl and always condemned to field as long-stop – which at least allowed me to read most of the time. It was Mr Dudderidge, the PT supremo and an Olympic canoeist in the 1936 Games, who at last realised that extreme long sight prevented me from seeing the ball once it left the bowler's hand. Academically I was dogged by failure in maths and science; science I could eventually drop, but maths remained an obstacle. My step resorted to the old business of extra maths tuition when I failed it in the School Certificate exam that was then the equivalent of GCSE, this time by a master more amused by caning than fondling – but still to no effect. Caning I considered the most acceptable of punishments, over and done within minutes and the slate wiped clean; I did not enjoy it but I did not care if the masters did and it had not the slightest effect on my sexual development.

Failing maths, a compulsory subject, meant failing the whole School Certificate exam in spite of distinctions in English and History, and I was put in Form 5R, the Remove as we knew it then, though the current regime at the school (an institution now wholly removed from its Hampstead incarnation) prefers the expression 'Fifth Form Repeaters'. This was the form in which the ineducable were dumped until they left, in which I was both destined for oblivion and bullied. It was a form almost without discipline. One young master, demobbed early for medical reasons, we were told, but of which there was no physical evidence, the boys simply would not allow to teach – uproar greeted the wretched man when he came through the door and drove him out again; after a day on which he wept, we saw no more of him, but as no other master came to take his lessons, we realised that he must have told no one of the state of play, and mayhem was the consequence. Miss Amali Dittrich, a petite and pretty middle-aged Czech who was supposed to teach us French, got much the same treatment: on one occasion I was de-bagged, that is stripped of my trousers and pants – a common jape – and roped to the seat of my desk, helpless to open a book or write a word; as I could not explain what was amiss, she came to see, and discovering my nakedness, let out a little scream and left the room, never to return, more tuitionless periods the consequence.

Dickie, a big and amiable boy, was the ringleader in most of these pranks and it must have been he who decided to go further with the horseplay that had rid us of Miss Dittrich. Off came my trousers and pants again and this time I was tied to the master's wooden chair. Where, I wonder now, did Dickie get so much rope and where had he concealed it? It was stout stuff: it had to be, for the next step was to lower me out of the window to dangle at the level of the Headmaster's room immediately below, that is from the second floor to the first. The odd thing is that I do not remember being terrified, swinging at an awkward angle thirty or forty feet above the tarmac down below, only a determination not to wriggle, unbalance the load and slip from the chair. I suppose the boys did not, mid-morning, expect the Headmaster to be at his desk, but he was and I shall never forget the horror on his face as, alerted by my shadow, he saw me. To give him his due, he thought at lightning speed, put his finger to his lips to silence me and did nothing to alarm the boys above. Not until I had been safely hauled back into the room did he enter it. There were no punishments – it was the last day of term, a common day for tomfoolery, and most of the boys were leaving. Their bullying had been wearying in its frequency, but never as spiteful as the treatment meted out the year before by Murray, who had left. That had been vicious. Murray, older by two years or so, was short, tough, muscular and merciless. He went about with two larger henchmen whose duty it was to secure a victim for Murray's use as a punchbag; first cornered, then dragged in front of him and braced erect to take the blows, I was as often as not that victim and I lived in fear of his repeated punches to my stomach. It was the Summerfield brothers again, but infinitely worse.

There was nothing sexual in Murray's bullying, just the exercise of power and the conscious cold infliction of fear and pain, the exploitation of his stupid henchmen an intriguing gloss. There should be a gentler word than bullying for the behaviour of the older boys in 5R; it was often sexual but there was neither hurt nor harm to it, though the frequency of it was a serious interruption to my attempt to hold on to my hope of eventual academic success. Mutual masturbation had at first been entirely random, urgently performed with any boy or boys willing to join in, but soon selection began to limit it as we became aware of the particular attraction of this boy or that. For some terms Davidson, my closest friend, and I made a common list of desirable partners and, sworn to honesty, compared our respective tallies on the last day to see which of us had had whom and how many times. The third phase was when fierce affections beyond our understanding began to develop, as well as more sophisticated practices. A German-Jewish boy – there were several in my age group who had escaped the Nazis in the later Thirties – for whom I wrote essays and poems in exchange for help with maths, astonished me with an unhesitatingly unsqueamish demonstration of fellatio when we were both fourteen. A year later I was jealously in love with Michael Jessett, a tall athletic boy, and on the night of my sixteenth birthday learned a bitter lesson when he buggered me. My willingness to please him, my romantic wanting it to happen, did little to ease the pain of my inexperience and his urgent clumsiness, but what really hurt – and permanently – was what immediately followed; I was lying on my belly, he withdrew, lit a cigarette, patted my bottom and said 'Gosh that was good – if you were a girl I'd do it again.' It was the end of our friendship. Love, if that is what I felt for Michael, froze; later that summer, at harvest camp, when other boys were holding him down and boot-blacking his scrotum for some perceived offence, I could have helped him, but I simply stood and watched. As mawkish as the silly girl he wished I'd been, I had given him the last remaining shred of my virginity and he had thought it a poor alternative. A successful musician, he married early and had children – what we had enjoyed, almost monogamously, for many months, had not the slightest effect on his adult sexuality.

For me, however, this was a turning-point. I knew that I was irrevocably queer, and so did other boys for whom our common sexual activities had been nothing but a step on the way to hetero-sexual maturity; I had friends at Highgate, UCS and St Paul's, and these too, once all willing partners, were changing, drifting steadily in an adult sexual direction that had nothing to do with boys or men. Occasionally they might oblige, but there was little joy in their grudging consent to these comfort wanks for past time's sake.

From academic oblivion I was saved by the decency of two masters in English and History who saw me through a repeated nightmare of School Certificate and Matriculation examinations taken internally and externally over the next two years, summer and winter, the set texts and periods changing in my favourite subjects, adding to the labour. I was then in the Sixth Form, on a two year course of study for the Higher School Certificate and Intermediate BA that pretty well guaranteed entry to a university, but this was an exam that I could not properly sit without first passing the lower School Certificate. Always in maths, a compulsory subject, I failed, and failed, and failed . . . but after the seventh sitting received a slip of paper with the words 'The examiners have decided to grant you a pass in the subsidiary subject Arithmetic. You may now sit higher examinations'.

The unstinting support of these two masters manipulating the indifference of a school that didn't care a damn as long as fees were paid, together with the patience of a stepfather who never let me see his despair, got me through these most difficult years of my school life, still with no clear notion of how I might want to earn my living. A careers adviser, interviewing me when in the Remove, ignored my interests in art and music and suggested that I might sit the Civil Service exam – 'You won't get into the Foreign Office or the Treasury, but you might just scrape into the Ministry of Ag and Fish.' Had I been at a state school, I would have sunk without trace, yet all these decades later it is into precisely my position, apart from fees, that the state education system, with maths still a compulsory subject, puts thousands of gifted children, wasting their time, obstructing their progress, perhaps wrecking their lives.

I must argue that all children are not equal and are not able to respond in equal measure to equal opportunities. I blame no one for my failure in maths, for I had no aptitude for it, but I do blame those who failed to see that, with figures, I was halted by a mental bloc so solid that I felt it physically. Not even for seconds can I retain a telephone number, the time of a train, the A or B number of a road. I know just enough of pounds and pence, euros and cents, miles and kilometres, to find my way about, and that is all I need – I have no wish to calculate the age of the universe or our distance from the Dog Star, and when Global Warming strikes, the men of Lincolnshire must work out for themselves how many fingers they must poke into how many dykes. My two years of hours wasted in *not* learning maths would have been far better spent on languages, motor-cycle maintenance or the history of art.

I hated most of my schoolmasters. Lewin, the sympathetic English master in the Upper School, I almost loved, and years later told him so. Locke, the senior History master who propped my progress through the Sixth Form, I enthusiastically respected; grave and dry, my quotations from *Alice in Wonderland* at the head of every essay on English constitutional history seemed to amuse him, but he could be cutting – 'A parlourmaid in Ponders End has better syntax,' he remarked of an essay on the *Eikon Basilike* written by another boy. Both men broadened my mind and with Lewin I could be frank about my miseries – though not my homosexuality; of Locke I still have a memento, a characteristic note advising me to read *Mémoires de Louis XIV pour L'Instruction du Dauphin*, but without telling me where or how to find a copy. Keevil, the art master, was friendly but indifferent, useless as a teacher, useless even as a basic instructor, but he let me into the art room without question whenever I was bunking off from maths or science – which, with increasing frequency, I did. Often, when I was in the sixths, he left me in charge of younger classes while he disappeared to tinker with his car, a troublesome Morris Ten of the earlier Thirties to which he had fitted an unsuitably lively Hotchkiss engine.

Payne, a mean-minded little man in polished brogues with steel tips (Blakeys) to heel and toe, failed utterly to teach me physics and was much given to twisting my ears in spite, though he occasionally gave me a small mark for a decent diagram. Through some divine malevolence he was appointed my invigilator when I sat, alone in the school hall, the Higher Schools Certificate examination in Art History – a subject self-taught, not in Haberdashers' syllabus, and therefore examined very much against the wishes of the Head-master, who was convinced that I would fail, though he gave in to my stepfather's pleading. So there we were, the two of us, old enemies, and Payne walked relentlessly up and down, the Blakeys on his shoes clicking hard against the timber floor, the regularity quite maddening. Even so, I was given a distinction by the examiners.

Knight, after bullying me for years, at last tired of the unfair game and pretended that I was absent; this, when he gathered us round his high demonstration desk in the chemistry lecture theatre, gave me unhindered opportunity to fumble in the trousers of other boys and they in mine. There were two masters called Small, the younger a post-war addition to the staff who could be reduced to helpless laughter by the merest whiff of masturbation, but was a friendly soul, inclined to give boys lifts in his pre-war open version of the first Ford Prefect. The other Small, elderly, with rimless spectacles, was an even more spiteful ear-twister than Payne, much given to patrolling between desks hitting boys painfully hard with the flat of a ruler on their bowed heads and necks; to have him behind me was to abandon all concentration on the subject in hand, bracing myself for the blow. And then there was Barling, the rugger-playing Wesleyan Welshman who prevailed on the Head (equally low church) to let him give us religious instruction instead of French; a conscientious objector, he was mistrusted by the boys who, all too often, had to bow their heads in honour of an Old Haberdasher killed or missing in the war. In my day most boys at the school were low church Christians, if anything, and a head-master who was a non-conformist suited their parents' religious views well enough, but Barling's idea of religious instruction was a vituperative rant against Roman Catholicism and masturbation. He drove me into furious defence of the Immaculate Conception and belief in the Transubstantiation of the Host, even into refusal to be taught by him, but when I walked out of the room there was no punishment – even he must have realised that his rabid prejudice was to be shared with converts in his native valleys and could not be regurgitated as religious education.

Worst of all was Callan. It was in the Third Form, when I was twelve that I spent a miserable year under Nat Callan, an English master whom I unreservedly detested. English was a subject in which I was strong – very well read for my age and sustained by an instinctive grasp of grammar – but Callan, nicknamed Nat for reasons now forgotten, though he introduced us to the sonnet and to Keats, pilloried me for my speech in almost every lesson. God knows I had a tough enough time with other boys over the way I spoke – 'You've had elocution lessons,' they mocked, when I did not even know the meaning of the word – tougher by far than any German-Jewish boy with something of Dennis the Dachshund about his English, but to be mocked for it by my English master was incomprehensible. It was Callan's custom to make me read aloud while he stood by my desk, half facing me, his head cocked to one side. Every so often he stopped me and, turning to the class, picked on my pronunciation of a word. 'Sewell says *appreciate* sounding the *c* not as *sh*, but as though it were an *s*. Who else does that?' Not one boy, it seemed – or none was foolish enough to admit it – whereupon Callan, after accusing me of prissiness and affectation, asked 'How then do you pronounce *appreciation*?' And inevitably I was ridiculed for illogic in not sounding the *t* as a *t* instead of *sh*.

These bouts were always humiliating and I always lost. The obvious remedy was to learn to speak as other boys did, but I had little ear for the difference (and still do not, unless it is extreme), and no capacity for mimicry, though I knew and know when I am being mimicked. Besides, there was the problem of betrayal. I spoke as I spoke because it was the way my immediate elders spoke, and to adopt a form of oral camouflage because Callan was so bloody-minded did indeed seem a form of cowardly betrayal. I could not do it. I did not want to do it. I began to skip Callan's classes, spending the hour behind the fives courts or, much riskier, in the lavatories when it was cold or wet; without a watch, this brought other difficulties and air raids occasionally complicated matters. As I could not altogether avoid Callan, I had always to be ready with excuses for absence and having done no prep, and was surprised when, as they grew more and more improbable, he accepted them without question.

I sank from the top to the bottom of the class, but did not care – did not care, that is, until the end of term report in which Callan had written none of the conventions about trying harder, only the brief note 'Is a plausible liar'. I thought I had been implausible. I cannot recall my explanation to my stepfather.

*   *   *

In the Sixth Form I led a small rebellion against compulsory membership of the Cadet Force and the weekly opportunity it offered to a certain type of master and boy to strut and bully. My only support came from my strict Jewish peers who had to be home by nightfall on Friday, the day on which the Force paraded and pretended. Though much my age, they seemed older, wiser and always more adult. Jewish boys were envied for having pubic hair when we had none, for ejaculating when our climaxes were dry, for having jockstraps first, for often being rather good at boxing and rugger, and for being academically brighter. They were not plagued with threats of palsied blindness for their masturbation; they were sceptical, questioning and worldly-wise, and the older boys who looked after the religious needs of the younger every morning, were respected for their gravity. It was these who had the courage to refuse to play the silly war games of the Corps. We were pilloried and punished. One whole day was spent at Bosham in canoes (Dudderidge's idea, no doubt), not canoeing from point to point, but held in a basin where, over and over again, we were compelled to perform the safety exercise of righting a canoe when it has turned turtle – to do that we had to turn it turtle first; the contemporary torture, waterboarding, cannot be much worse. We

were also sent off alone on our bicycles for rides of a hundred miles
or so, from post office to post office in the Chilterns to collect a
note of the next destination; in my case this was once varied to my
having to draw churches and other village buildings, including
Medmenham Abbey, the artificial ruin in which the Hellfire Club
conducted its obscenities – whose wry humour lay behind that
instruction, I wonder? How we did these things on the paltry
rations of the day I do not know, but we had been schooled in
hunger and endurance by five full years of wartime shortage and
the harsh austerity that followed it.

My final year at Haberdashers' was wasted, I was exhausted by
the business of getting, at long last, my subsidiary pass in arithmetic
concurrently with my Higher School Certificate, for which I had
neglected Latin, then an essential for University entrance, and I
had given no thought, nor been given any advice by the school,
as to which university I should try for and what to read when
there. There were too the vague ambitions vested in my painting
and my neglected violin. I struggled to catch up in Latin, daily
spent hours with my violin, played rugger and took rather too
strenuously to religion as a cure for my homosexuality – to join
the priesthood and be celibate and chaste held strong attractions.
Nevertheless I was hopelessly in love with a younger boy, and had
been with another, who had left school suddenly; to neither of
them did I show my hand though it was obvious enough to boys
of my own age, two of whom, Trask and Gaskell, mean-minded
twits affecting an attitude *de haut en bas*, mocked me for it publicly
and with sickening frequency, 're-fuelling' their euphemism for
my supposed sodomy – re-fuelling aircraft in flight, was one of
the technical achievements of the day, and in photographs it
looked remarkably sexual to those who chose to see it so. It was
also a pun identifying the younger boy. I knew, however, as well
as they, that I had not 'grown out of it' – the only reassurance
ever offered in our rare instructions on matters sexual – knew that
it was not a 'phase,' and knew that I could never control it (unless

with the help of God), yet, at eighteen, I vowed that I would never again have sex with a boy.

The school gave me what were called Sixth Form Privileges, but this exalted state brought only the responsibility of tolling the school bell every morning to urge laggards walking from Crickle-wood to put on pace, and the bellringer had to be hauling on his rope some twenty minutes before assembly. Finding this irksome, I climbed into the belfry roof, found that a slim cord linked the rope to the bell and severed it at both ends (most boys then carried a clasp-knife) leaving no trace; the rope then slithered five storeys to the ground. I was never accused of the offence, but nor did my name again appear on the bellringing rota.

I am inclined to say that the school gave me nothing; certainly it gave me no prizes, not even the prize that I deserved for my Distinction in Art and the History of Art, and at my last Speech Day I watched with growing bitterness as others collected their prize books for similar prowess in less recherché subjects. On the last day of my last term I procured a small revenge on the Head-master who, though rumoured to have fathered five daughters, drove a Fiat Topolino, that tiny two-seat work of automotive genius. The Upper School lavatories were attached to the building in a lean-to shack, its wide doors swinging open like those of a garage, facing the recreation field; open, they were only inches wider than the Fiat's length and I persuaded other boys to help me lift it sideways in, leaving its nose in one bank of urinals and its tail in the other. I then went to the school hall and removed the smallest pipe from the organ that occupied the rear wall. I have it still, in a cabinet of curiosities with dogs' teeth, a silver glove stretcher and other memorabilia.

But the school did give me something – rugger, cross-country running, confidence in my body and a dawning awareness that whatever I was to do or become would be determined by my own actions, that on my last day at school I was as alone as on my first. A frustrated act of kindness by my Latin master encapsulated all my years at Haberdashers'; he suggested that I should paint a mural for the Classics Room, above the picture rail, and, inspired by the paintings of John Craxton, I began an idealised strip cartoon of the Odyssey but had not quite finished by my leaving day; when I returned to it, late in the summer break, before the boys commenced the autumn term, I found it obliterated with a coat of distemper. Thus had the school wiped me from its memory.

CHAPTER 5

Intermezzo

As the first of several definitions, the Oxford Dictionary has intermezzo as 'a musical entertainment interpolated between sections of
more serious fare'. Music had begun to dominate my life in my last
year at school and in the following two years proved to be a cuckoo
in the nest of all other possible ambitions. These were to read
History at Oxford, to become a painter and be elected to the Royal
Academy, and to play the violin (as a soloist, of course). The violin
tutor to whom my mother sent me was Max Rostal, of whose
eminence I was unaware. Austrian, Jewish, small, neat, formal and
ascetic-seeming, his voice of memorable timbre, he had settled in
England in 1934 and was about to become, as player and grey
eminence, a profound influence on the performance of chamber
music here. I dare say that in the austere years after the war he was
glad of whatever fees my mother paid him – they cannot have been
much – but in retrospect I wish that he had refused them and not
encouraged me (and her). An uncompromising disciplinarian, he
forbade me to ride a bicycle with my violin slung over my shoulder
and corrected the lazy techniques developed under my mother's
tuition, but seemed not interested in soul – either mine or the
composer's. Soul was above all things what I wanted to put into my
playing, and sometimes I played blind, through tears, moved to
them, I hope, less by my playing than by the beauty of the music; I
am still moved so, tears welling, shoulders shuddering with silent
sobs, breath trapped in my chest. It was my mother's view that a
wrong note here or there was of scant importance compared with
feeling and emotion, and she gleefully played records of Casals,
Thibaud and Cortot to prove her point.

Rostal and I soldiered on for two full years and more and never once did he even hint at what he should – that at best I might play second fiddle in an orchestra and should relegate my playing to the pastime of a competent amateur. My mother could not (or would not) see how weak I was, and nor could I, blinded by dreams, but my stepfather could – yet he said nothing until a few days before I went into the army to do my National Service for two years. Then he put his foot down, asked me to trust his judgement and warned that there could be few things more 'asking for trouble' than for a raw recruit to report to an Aldershot barracks carrying a violin. 'You might just get away with it in a Scottish regiment,' he said, 'but not in a working class mob like the Service Corps.'

Robert was, of course, absolutely right. I tuned the fiddle on short leaves, but there were too many other things to do on 36 or 48 hour passes; I did eventually take it to Aldershot on my first long posting, but when sent on from there, left it at home. After two years of neglect, my need to play it began to seem imaginary and the drive to do so faded. I kept it, tuned it now and then and drew a bow across the strings a little, but never made any serious attempt to revive what skills I may once have had. Now, when I can, at concerts I sit close to the second fiddles and see how expert they are, yet how submissive too, dutiful and unambitious, the soloism beaten out of them. I look at their hands and see delicate fingers with which mine compare as closely as those of an Irish labourer, and curse Rostal for not diverting my ambitions to the trumpet. Within weeks of my mother's death I took my violin to Christie's to be sold. It had been far more her dream than mine.

To become a painter, on the other hand, was more my dream than hers, and without my mother's pushing me into the arms of William Coldstream I might just have achieved it, for as well as my Distinction in Higher School Certificate, I had already had a ghastly picture shown in a mixed bag exhibition at the disreputable Cooling Gallery in Bond Street (a girl feeding a swan, nauseating rubbish long since destroyed), and with a pseudo-Expressionist painting of an *Absinthe Drinker* had won Third Prize in the nationwide School-children's Exhibition that was still an annual event when I began work as a critic. This was noticed by the *Daily Worker*, reproduced and praised as a piece of social comment on a decadent capitalist world, all the more remarkable for coming from a would-be public school. I should have had no difficulty in getting into an art school, but my mother, ever one to exercise influence and pull strings, sent me to Coldstream. What were the strings in this case? Why Coldstream, I have wondered since, now supposing that, though she was older by eight years, they must at some point have tumbled into bed together and that in enlisting his help with me she was forcing him to pay for his casual concupiscence; if this is the case, then it was probably in 1933 when he shared an exhibition, also at the Cooling Galleries, with Henri Enslin du Plessis, an amiable self-taught painter from South Africa, a handful of whose paintings my mother owned and with whom she was still in contact well into the 1970s.

I found Coldstream inscrutable, unsympathetic and seemingly incapable of warm enthusiasm for any other painter's work. Under his tutelage my romantic talent withered. I am not sure that this is true, for precocious ability is often nothing more than mimicry, and adolescent flare can fizzle to ashes in early maturity. True or not, it is what seemed at the time to happen and, within a year or so, Coldstream had convinced me that my technique was meretricious. I liked thick paint; I liked the accidental effects of colours mixed on the canvas rather than the palette; I liked the brave demonstration of the sweeping stroke and sacrificed the accuracy of drawing for the impastose gesture with the loaded brush: Coldstream liked none of these things and sought to tame them, though it now surprises me that he expressed no sympathy for the urban subjects that so often pleased me – the smudged smokey views of London from Parliament Hill, now long lost, and the dark leaden skies and thick yellow sunlight that still combine to lend theatrical magic to the Thames – for he was himself at his most accomplished (least contrived, perhaps) with the metropolitan railway station and the smirch of industry, dubbed 'Squalorscapes' by his friend Graham Bell. My recollection of the chill of our relationship is painful, and I still wonder whether, had Bomberg been my master – I am the same age as Auerbach – I might now be earning my living as a painter instead of a critic; nevertheless, I am convinced that I am a better critic for the experience.

Coldstream could do nothing to a canvas without a haberdasher's tape measure, a ruler and a plumb-line with a weight to chart his unsteady course across it, and he had the mentality of a haberdashery assistant, measuring everything minutely and costing it to the nearest farthing. To remind me of these years I have kept one canvas painted according to his methods, a dry and diligent piece of self-portraiture, pale in tone, tentative in touch and a shrewd imitation of all his mannerisms. As Professor at the Slade School for more than a quarter of a century, 1949–1975, he was to be the most major of major influences on the course of education in art schools throughout the land, on ministers and academics too, and I have no doubt that the long-term consequences of his power as an authoritative committee man have been disastrous – early in his career, the critic Geoffrey Grigson foresaw that this might be so and attacked him as cunning, a racketeer who would take bread from the mouths of better painters, a toady, a snob and with a foot in every camp. He even had a foot in the Courtauld Institute where I became a student concurrently with his later random lessons on the craft of painting – he had known Anthony Blunt, its Director, since at least 1938; I was from time to time grateful for the existence of the back stairs there that enabled me to duck out of his way.

He was rumoured to be extricating himself from an affair with one of the older students, Phoebe Pool, whom I adored. She had been an occasional student with the Euston Road painters in the late Thirties and had fallen in love with him then, but for him it was a thing of inconstancy and liability to which her response was a generally miserable demeanour, her considerable intellectual brilliance dimmed, dulled and disabled by incurable melancholy. To those who chose to speculate they made a strange pair, for Phoebe was a tall but stooping bag of bones, with glasses, a hearing-aid and twin set after twin set, and Coldstream we knew to have been dubbed 'Walking Death'. After almost a decade of struggle with clinical depression Phoebe achieved a brilliant BA in 1957 and followed it with a PhD two years later, her thesis so good that her examiners suggested its publication as a book.

Further bouts of depression delayed this until 1962 and it was achieved only with the persuasion and assistance of Anthony Blunt in writing the captions to the illustrations. The publisher of *Picasso, the Formative Years* then insisted that his name should precede hers on the cover; in his foreword Anthony made it clear that the text was 'entirely hers,' and privately deplored the presentation of the book as primarily his. Nevertheless, without his collaboration the book would never have been finished, for Phoebe was by then so deep in pathological depression that putting in order a pile of photographs and writing lucid notes on them, was quite impossible. Her condition inexorably worsened and, in rational intervals, suicide appealed as a logical end to it: in November 1971 she was killed by a southbound train at Bounds Green station on the Piccadilly line. When told of it, Anthony broke down in tears, and was still in tears when he told me. By 1984 Coldstream was in the grip of senile chorea, and death followed in February 1987. My mother, though by then slipping into the vagaries of senility, cut a notice of his death from the *Daily Telegraph* and tucked it into her diary.

*   *   *

As for Oxford and History, these were no more than ought-to aspirations inspired by rivalry with other boys at Haberdashers' whose paths through the school had been smoother and more rewarded than mine – the prefects and the prizewinners – but the truth was that I dreaded the prospect, a dread engendered by other boys encountered there competing for a place. I cannot recall which friendly soul sent me the slim pale green prospectus for the Courtauld Institute, but when it reached me one morning in the high summer of 1950 I raced on my bike to Portman Square (where it then was) and, to my surprise, was sent to a tiny office on the second floor overlooking the garden. There I found Charles Clare, the silver-haired, pipe-smoking, warm and kindly Registrar, who said that my Higher School Certificate was enough to let me in and that I could come in October. So ended my unwilling flirtation with Oxford.

Charles, who became a friend and remained so long after his retirement to the Isle of Wight, should not have let me in. It may seem odd, so many years later, for me to have blamed Max Rostal for my wasted years as a would-be violinist and William Coldstream for my failure as a painter, and now to make Charles responsible for what was to be another failure, but this is what it was and he, not I, knew how academically tough the Courtauld had become after a shaky beginning as an unintended finishing school in the 1930s. I was nineteen, but still a boy, absurdly sophisticated in some respects – an habitué of Covent Garden Opera since its reopening in 1948, of Christie's (where I had already bought several parcels of prints and drawings for the minimum bid of 3 guineas – pocket money for six weeks), and of Bond Street art dealers too, none of whom took amiss the regular Saturday morning visits of a curious schoolboy propping a bicycle nearby – yet I was bewildered, overwhelmed indeed, by the sophisticated adult company of the older students among whom I found myself. Most were post-graduates with an Oxford or Cambridge degree in another subject intending to do in two years what I would do in three, and for the men among them, National Service was a thing of the past and some had even been in the real army in the last stages of the war. Among these, the Students' Common Room was no place for an immature and untravelled boy from a school that had in no way prepared him for the complexities of an academic discipline that it did not teach. These older students already knew Rome and

Florence; some had lodgings within walking distance, and for others money seemed never to be in short supply – Delia Dawnay, for example, later to marry Oliver Millar (Blunt's successor as Surveyor of the Queen's Pictures in 1972), flew to Madrid for a long weekend to see the paintings there by Velazquez when he was the required subject of an essay. Michael Jaffé, dapper in even casual clothes and dominant in every conversation, Cecil Gould with KUNSTFORSCHUNGEN writ large on the files he always carried, Francis Hawcroft, John Shearman, John Steer, John Golding, Ronald Alley, Christopher White, Reyner Banham, Jennifer Montagu, Sheila Somers and Michael Kitson (of whom more later) were among the subsequently professorial grandees who overwhelmed not only me but the handful of other school-leavers beginning their first year as undergraduates.

The art history that I had taught myself had been no more than the ability to write essays of some small stylistic elegance, poetic insight and occasionally wry interpretation. These pale reflections of Walter Pater might have served me well as a student of English at Oxford, but as art history they were undisciplined rubbish; they had nothing of Pater's broad intellectual weight and far too much of his literally flowery language – 'powdered all over in the Gothic manner with a quaint conceit of daisies,' he wrote of Botticelli's *Birth of Venus*, and I fell in love with him. That half sentence is the Calais engraved on my heart and I repeat it to myself when now I fall – as occasionally I do – into Dear Reader mode, recalling the schoolmaster who once rebuked me for my purple passages. The first essay required from me by my first tutor, Peter Murray, a dry young stick who could have made a dull business of Michelangelo and Leonardo, was on Filippo Lippi, an ideal painter for the quaint conceit of daisies treatment, and he got it; Anne Hewlett, a fellow new student, reminded me this year, fifty-eight years after the event, of Murray's appalled response – 'Well, that's the first time in my life that a student has written an essay without a single date.'

Outsider

Art history, I discovered, depends on dates, the *terminus ante quem* and the *terminus post quem*, the dates of death and birth, the dates of commissions and the dates of their completion. It also requires at least a reading knowledge of German, Italian and French, and Dutch and Russian might be useful, as might ancient Greek – Latin was taken for granted. An art historian must be a plain historian too, aware of the whats and whens of Kings, Emperors and Popes; to be confronted with the Guelphs and the Ghibellines of early Italian Renaissance politics when all my history at school had been either English or European as it affected England, was to realise that distant memories of Richard the Lion Heart and Le Crac des Chevaliers were not enough; to be told to read Ludwig Pastor's monumental *History of the Popes* in the original German, was to realise at once what provincial little mice we undergraduates were. There were too the international ramifications of banking and trade and their influence on patronage, the effects of plague, famine and wars of religion might have to be taken into account, and it was often very much a help to be aware of philosophy, medicine, music and literature. Art history, it seemed, opened doors on every aspect of history and culture, for art never stood alone.

And no teenage undergraduate in the first year had ever been anywhere. This was long before the institution of school trips abroad or any form of foreign travel was encouraged, when allowances in foreign currency were restricted to the cost of one night in a decent hotel, when few had cars and European railways were still disrupted by damage inflicted in the war. At home, rationing of all essential foodstuffs was still in force and we none of us had any idea of what might confront us across the Channel. And so we had not crossed it and this put us at a crippling disadvantage.

*   *   *

There was another element of confusion – my attachment to Alan Harverson – and this was indeed the frivolous intermezzo between boyhood and manhood, leading nowhere. With increasing frequency Alan had taken me to his bed in my last years at school – as a man taking the initiative he did not count as one of the boys I had forbidden myself to woo; physically I found him not in the least attractive and enthusiasm cannot have been much in evidence in my cooperation, but in his late teens a boy is carried along by the responses of his body and, in terms of good manners, to have rejected his physical expressions of fondness would have been, I thought, a wretched reward for his countless musical generosities. To a wider audience Alan is, perhaps, still remembered for mastering the organ of the Albert Hall on the last night of the Proms from the late 1940s well into the 1970s, and for a handful of recordings of exquisite performances of music by Mozart and Bach in the 1960s. I remember him most for the musical madness to which he introduced me in the austere post-war years, a schoolboy already in thrall to the range of music to be heard on the BBC's then new Third Programme, suddenly exposed to the glories and subtleties of the organ – Bach, Pachelbel, Widor, Fauré, Reger and Messiaen. Here was a man who with music transported congregations from the dreary sameness of Church of England ritual and made Matins and Evensong glorious occasions, who restored a sense of exaltation to Christmas jollity, to whom the services of Easter were moments of profound belief.

His base was a church in Cricklewood where the parish priest, William Bulman, big, bluff and wonderfully sensible, was an old friend of my stepfather. When I 'got religion,' as they say, Robert saw to it first that I was confirmed in the Church of England in a mass confirmation service at school, for in spite of being a Christadelphian (an American sect that rejects the Trinity and believes every word of the Bible to be inspired and infallible), the Headmaster had appointed a School Chaplain from the bells and whistles department of the C of E, and then made sure that Bill Bulman took me under his unperfumed wing, thus manoeuvring me away from my mother's dormant Catholic influence – how odd that having neglected my soul for some years, and their own souls for that matter, Robert should now engineer this small Protestant victory. Bulman, however, a priest who thought the distinctions between Rome and Canterbury mere matters of semantics, politics and ornament, opined that my baptism as a Roman Catholic and my confirmation in the English church were not incompatible, gave me a Latin Vulgate and suggested that if I was serious about becoming a priest I should think about learning Aramaic (what, I wonder, would my Christadelphian headmaster have said, had I demanded that?), and then decide in which denomination to confine myself, for serving both was, for the moment, quite impossible. When, troubled by uncertainty in the matter of the Transubstantiation of the Host, I bearded him in his study; after some exegesis he summed up his response with 'My boy, you must bring everything to the bar of your own judgement.' This was not helpful: I wanted authority that would either confirm or confound my misgivings about this beautiful and terrible belief, and got instead a gnomic utterance that had no clear meaning for a boy of sixteen. It was, nevertheless, the wisest instruction ever given me. Understanding dawned soon enough and that simple sentence has ever since been my guide in politics and social responsibility; in religion it proved eventually to have been the first insidious blow of scepticism against the received faith that might have been a comfort.

With Bulman's support, Alan formed the St Gabriel's Singers in which, to the accompaniment of organ, harp, cello and fiddle, the fine voices of young professionals sang music then strange and rare. One of them, Heather Harper, then unknown, he let loose on Purcell's *The Blessed Virgin's Expostulation*, a prophetically operatic piece, but the career of another, Dorothy Bond, a protégé of Thomas Beecham and a pretty girl of extraordinary promise remembered now only for having sung the role of Olympia in his 1951 film of *The Tales of Hoffmann*, was cut short by a fatal car crash a year later. There were many more for whom the ad hoc

Singers were a stepping stone for a long professional career, but there were stalwarts too who offered the bright young things the solid backing of experience, among them Primrose Ballard, a formidable contralto, and Mignon Fressard, the harpist, who took me to her bosom and stayed a friend until her death in the 1970s.

Like Dorothy, Mignon was one of many figures who played no important part in my life, made no difference to its progress or direction, and yet enriched it mightily. She was not French, but her husky accent had so long been part of her Piaf reinvention of herself that it rang true. Nor was she Mignon; she was Gladys Adams from Newcastle who long ago had had a French lover whose pillow name for her was Mignon and, ever the northern realist, she knew that as a musician she would go much further with his name than with hers. She played the very largest of harps and seemed waif-like at its strings, for years transporting it in an old Austin Ten with all but the driver's seat removed (there were no hatchbacks then), painted a uniquely bilious yellow so that she could always find it at a glance. In St John's Wood, a stone's throw from Dorothy, she lived in an enviable dead-end mews in which every cottage was occupied by musicians – the cacophony of heaven on a summer's day. She left me her Bechstein, a grand in white lacquer.

Alan not only played organs, he knew about their workings. One midwinter soon after the war, still in his early twenties, he somehow got permission to go to a still very ruined Germany to seek out what baroque instruments had survived in the British Zone, and, close to the Walker family, he persuaded those redoubtable builders of peculiarly British organs to take inspiration from German models of the eighteenth century. He wanted his Bach to sound as it had sounded to Bach himself, crisp and clear, not clouded with rich Victorian confusions, not to be mistaken for Stainer and Stanford, and in designing modern organs – as he did – he had to know how those he most admired were constructed. The immediate consequence of his first German journey was his ingenious specification for the organ at St Gabriel's, rebuilt in 1948–49, an instrument intriguing enough to become almost the property of the BBC so constant was the Corporation's use of it.

With Bill Bulman at the wheel of his ancient Vauxhall 14, priest and organist set off, summer after summer, to explore the cathedrals and organs of France and Italy – this in the days when the travel allowance was only £25, but such a trifle would never have deterred Bill who, a contented comfortable man of substance with an unambitious contempt for bishops and archdeacons, quietly paid for the Singers and the new organ without drawing attention to his generosity. The energy of friendships with other organists formed on these journeys, Fernando Germani of St Peter's and Jeanne Demessieux of Nôtre-Dame among them, resulted in their coming to London, where they not only played the organ at St Gabriel's, but gave spontaneous recitals on every interesting instrument on which they could lay hands. They and Alan played for the sake of playing, experimenting and responding each to the other's challenge, and late one night, in a deserted Westminster Cathedral, Alan and Jeanne had so many stops out that the organ died with the unforgettable groan of a great beast. And my part in this? It was to pull out the stops and turn the pages – my role again in 1954 when, on an organ not designed by Alan, his help was enlisted by the engineers brought in to improve the poor acoustics of the Royal Festival Hall; for days on end we ranged through the pipes and stops from *vox angelica* to *bombarde* – alas, as we all know, to have no remedial affect on that cheap and shoddy building.

A generous teacher and a major player in the spirited revival of interest in organs and organ music after the war, Alan, never pushy, was too soon overtaken by far less able organists, less ingenious and musical, who rarely recognised how much they and their profession owed him. When, in 2006, I was asked to write a brief obituary for the insignificant Lives Remembered column of *The Times*, it was not published, yet thirty-six column inches and a photograph had been devoted to his pupil Lionel Dakers three years earlier – but then he was a Coldstream in the world of organists.

Alan did not usurp my mother as a musical influence – that would have been both unwise and impossible – he simply worked with her. While she opened my eyes to opera at Covent Garden, he took me to concerts and recitals and, of course, exposed me to choral music and the organ – formidable competition for essays on Filippo Lippi, Brueghel and Jan Steen required as a student of art history. At the Courtauld Institute an oddly disturbing episode jogged my sexual relationship with him. Leaving it late one after-noon in May 1951 at precisely the same moment as a man whom I had several times seen leaving both Anthony Blunt's study on the first floor and his chill quarters in the attic, we fell into step and he suggested a drink. I refused, at which he insisted on buying me a milk shake in Baker Street; we sat on high stools at the bar, turned towards each other, drinking something sweet and pink through straws while he went through the performance with which he hoped to fascinate me, while I contemplated the egg on his tie and savoured the tobacco on his breath. A day or two later he waylaid me and invited me to dinner, after which he inflicted the traumatic experience of taking me to his 'club,' which was not in Pall Mall, but in some cellar haunt where I was more or less compelled to dance with him – more food stains and foul breath, and an over-whelming discomfort at the very idea of doing such a thing. I fled. And so did he – within a few days Guy Burgess was headline news in every paper. There cannot have been a student who had not seen him in the Institute; there was not a student who did not suppose the Director to have been in some way involved in his flight with Donald Maclean, yet none of us was dismayed, appalled or outraged at the thought – we simply took it in our strides. This was 1951 and not one single journalist rang the doorbell at 20 Portman Square.

The brush with Burgess did appal me in another sense: were seedy clubs, food droppings and sloppings on my clothes, the empty chatterings of seduction, and mephitic breath, what I in middle age, would inflict on pretty boys? Celibacy seemed ever more attractive.

Espousing the comforts of religion as an instrument of change in what I knew to be my sexual nature, and even that done clumsily as a Catholic born but, for the past decade, not a Catholic bred, I lacked the courage to break with Alan; to do so without hurting his feelings required an external agency beyond our control. One was within reach. Failure haunted me; as though failure as a painter and musician, were not enough, I sensed impending failure as an art historian, the poorest of degrees ahead of me (and what use could that be?); and then Robert, in the summer of 1952 delivered the blow that really broke me, not so much in his admission that he was not my father, but in yet another failure on my part, the failure to grasp the opportunity to demand to know – no matter what the cost to Robert and my mother – who and what I really was. I talked to Charles Clare, suggesting that if I left the Courtauld Institute at once to join the army for my unavoidable two years of National Service, the break would conveniently run from September to September, fitting with university terms; if during these two years I decided that I wanted to return, would the Courtauld accept me and would it allow me to start from scratch, taking the full three year course again? To both questions he answered yes, and then, eyes twinkling, offered me this encouragement – 'You know, you're not as hopeless as you think.' The wasted years of my intermezzo were concluded.

CHAPTER 6

National Service as a Squaddie

In my young days boys were prepared for life by dancing lessons and National Service, and of the two I much preferred the latter. Oh the misery and discomfort, the crippling sense of inadequacy engendered by the hours spent in the compelling arms of a corseted dancing mistress learning the quickstep, the foxtrot and the tango – to these the ingenious bullyings of strutting Warrant Officers and corporals proved infinitely preferable.

What did I learn from National Service? I learned to shoot with a cold accuracy that surprised the men who taught me. I learned to ride a motorcycle and to drive almost everything the Army had on wheels. I learned to pitch a tent and dig a trench and wriggle at a snake's pace on my belly. I learned, if I did not already have them, the habits of neatness and economy. 'Any fool can be uncomfortable,' said one of my instructors, a Captain in the Gloucesters, lately wounded in Korea, and I learned from him to make silk purses from sows' ears. These were practical things that have stood me in good stead, but the less definable things have served me even better. In the intimacy of my platoon it was as though we had sworn the marriage vow to obey, serve, love, honour and keep each other in sickness and in health. We learned lessons in loyalty and interdependence that wove the platoon together; we learned self-reliance and the generous exchange of our modest capabilities; we learned that the strength of a group of men is the strength of the weakest member and that the weakest can be made stronger with forethought and support. With modesty and squeamishness abandoned I learned that compliance is not an easy option, but often the only option in a particular set of circumstances – that one can, and sometimes must, do things about which one has almost overwhelming intellectual and moral reservations, or that are deeply offensive to one's taste. I think I learned – it was never put to the test – that there was nothing that I would not do, that needs must when the Devil drives. I believe this still to be so, though my choices now might be significantly different. I learned too, that separation from my dog was more painful than separation from my parents.

Most of a lifetime later I am so burdened with moral baggage that I have perhaps lost the ruthlessness the Army taught me, but for decades I believed that my two years of National Service had done me far more good than my three as an undergraduate, my eight at school and twenty on my knees in church. National Service revealed depths and darknesses in my soul that I was grudgingly glad to know were there; if I am now capable or making worthwhile moral judgements it is because I was for two brief years a soldier of sorts, not because I am an art historian, a lapsed Conservative, an agnostic Christian.

Only a fool could do two years National Service and resent it as a waste of time. Its benefit to society was formidable. It removed every young man in the land from the unemployment pool for two full years and paid him a mean pittance while training him in essential societary skills, often teaching him a trade that made him readily employable on his return to Civvy Street. It removed him to an almost closed society, monkish in its way, disciplined and orderly, and taught him to manage his indiscipline and disorder, anger and sexuality. Bullying, brutality, intimidation and fear were among its training tools with raw recruits, victimisation too, but even these had their educative purpose and were the stimulus of resources of resilience that had not been tapped before.

The entirely independent decision to enlist was my first indication of maturity. Early in September 1952 I took a specified train to Aldershot. The repeated advertisement for beer along the railway track, 'You are now entering the Strong Country' seemed as weightily portentous as the 'You are now crossing the county boundary' with which Beatrix Potter threatened Pigling Bland. On arrival, my brief experience in the School Corps immediately proved useful – I knew how to clamber into the back of an army truck.

I am not certain that as it swung through the barracks gate I murmured 'All hope abandon, ye who enter here,' but in essence that was the response of all of us. We were puny, skinny boys, half a century ago, a wartime generation brought up on short rations, shorter still in the bleak post-war years, and none of us was overweight, none of us had a beer belly. We were inclined to be obedient, for we came straight from school, apprenticeships and jobs without much promise. We were not independent and most of us were bound by apron-strings to mothers who had taught us nothing of the 'girly' domestic skills required by the Army, nothing of fending for ourselves. Very few of the lads had regular girlfriends or were married, and the rest of us knew of sex only by proxy or fumbling with other boys – never to be admitted in these circumstances. But we had neither time nor opportunity for sex, we were imprisoned, or so it seemed, and convinced that the Army cooks put bromide in our tea to undo our sexual appetites; only the regular creaking of an iron bed might indicate that one of us was on the way to orgasm, but most of us were so exhausted that sleep was more important.

We were the Army's property, to use and abuse as its minions thought fit in what was called Basic Training, the weeks of spirit breaking, humiliation and belittlement, degradation and indignity, insult, outrage and affront that seemed to have no connection with courage, heroism and nobility, the great abstract virtues of the military life of which I knew from a French set book at school – Alfred de Vigny's *Servitude et Grandeur Militaires*. We were taught that every moment of the day and night our bodies and souls were not our own but in the common ownership of every officer, commissioned and non-commissioned, from the single stripe of the lance-corporal to the dizzy height of the half-colonel, the loftiest rank that we squaddies would ever encounter. We were to march, drill, run and jump when ordered, sleep, wake and ablute when ordered, and even the emptying of bowels and bladders could be done only when ordered.

Time was not ours – that too was Army property and NCOs were mean with it; things that would have been better done in five minutes had to be done in three, and if done badly, punishment was the consequence. Punishment was always out of all proportion to the misdemeanour; for the merest trace of Brasso polish on the back of a buckle on a gaiter six feet below the sergeant's eye, madness, mayhem and the wanton destruction of hours of scrupulous work preparing kit were immediate. Lance-corporals pretended to be terrified of corporals, corporals of sergeants, sergeants of sergeant-majors, and all used that terror to justify the terrors that they, in turn, on us, inflicted; all had the ability, within a millisecond, to puff to twice their size and turn the rainbow colours of a baboon's backside. To a callow youth who had never suffered worse than six strokes of a cold schoolmaster's cane, and suffered those unseeing, the nose to nose aggression of the purple swollen face, the spray of spittle from the open mouth, the screaming volume of the insults and the orders were a monstrous and terrifying phenomenon – and worst of all was the business of having to shout back, repeatedly – 'louder!' the most dread command – 'I am a prick, a poofter and a pile of shit, dear Corporal!'

There were tears too. Tears broke the tension induced by long hours of irrational discipline, futile punishment, wretched discomfort and the unrelenting exaction of obedience. I saw no one in my intake break into tears before an NCO, but in bed, in darkness, sobs of misery were sometimes audible, the tough little East End bruiser next to me the real surprise; he had strength, stamina and street-vicious responses, but sewing on a button was for him intellectually beyond the gender barrier and not something he could or would do. It had, nevertheless, to be done and he saw it as some sort of self-emasculation. A boy in another section, fastidious, pernickety, uncooperative, gave no help to his mates, got no help from them and probably deserved the blackballing that they, exasperated, gave him; it was cruel – a scrotum boot-blacked raw with new Army brushes is no joke, and with showers permitted only once a week, not much could be done about it. The poor kid fled the barracks to demand sanctuary of the Fathers at Brompton Oratory, but a fat lot of good that did him when they informed the Military Police. We were told that he had been sent to Colchester, to the Army prison there, a Hell beyond the Hell of Dante. It was thus, unconsciously, that we learned to be Stoic philosophers.

Had any of this ill-treatment any point? It did not seem so at the time. It went so far beyond the calculated spite of schoolmasters and prefects that it was beyond comprehension. Why shout when conversational exchange would better do the trick? – but conversation between the high and low is not the Army's way. Why waste time with mindless punishment when more time for a task would have let us do it well? Why bully when explanation would give us understanding? Why exhaust us? Why, worst of all, seem to offer us a moment of conciliation, an inkling that an NCO is not all brute, and then, in some sense, betray us? We were learning when and whom not to trust, yet what surprised me later, after Basic Training – and in isolated cases, during it – was how reasonable senior NCOs could be when not in the Army's public eye. We learned immediate obedience, though some of us had qualms that obedience to the idiocies of barracks NCOs might kill us in Korea, Malaya, Aden and the other theatres of war to which we might be sent. And eventually we realised that Basic Training was exactly what the Army claimed for it – the business of breaking us down in order to build us up again as more self-reliant mentally and stronger physically than we could ever have been without it.

Swiftly it dawned on the sensible among us that we must play the Army's game. If we were told that heaps of coal must be painted white with blanco, then white we painted them; with razor blades we scraped the crystalline deposits from urinals, and with Brasso we polished the heads of nails in floorboards, for this was the off-with-his-head world of Alice in Wonderland. My own particular intellectual crisis came with bayonet practice – the blood-curdling yell and then the plunge into the belly, never the ribs because it might be difficult to withdraw. Could I do this to another boy? That question was impossible to answer, and this was not the moment for debate: all that was required of me was pretence, the pretence of stabbing a sack of straw hanging from a gibbet, a charade that was not, in itself the moral dilemma; that I would deal with if and when it confronted me on a bleak hillside in Korea or the steaming forests of Malaya; only then would I know the answer in an adrenal rush of fear or in the cold logic of survival that I was beginning to discern in myself.

Army life was regulated by the ten minute smoking break every two hours or so. 'Who doesn't smoke?' asked the corporal in charge of our first attempts at rifle drill, and on finding me the only squaddie in the platoon without nicotine-stained fingers, stood me at ease and then instructed the other twenty boys to prop their rifles against me while they smoked or dashed away to pee – this in a chill October morning. Next day I produced Woodbines and matches bought in the NAAFI overnight as evidence that I had joined the smokers. 'You're learning,' said the corporal, and chose another boy to be the prop. I took to reading in these breaks, swiftly transported to saner worlds for a few moments, but these were not to last: a recruit was supposed to have nothing in his pockets other than the customary essentials and, in his left breast pocket, his pay-book, the slim passport-like record of his identity, next-of-kin and pay, but I also had the Penguin edition of a novel by Evelyn Waugh in the opposite pocket of my battledress – unwise on a day when the first parade was to be taken by a Warrant Officer, a senior NCO of the most impressive kind. Inspecting the length of our hair, our shaving skills, our boots and uniforms, when he reached me he tapped the Penguin pocket with his pace-stick – a hefty thing of timber and brass resembling an enormous pair of dividers, with which, swaggering and dexterous, he measured stride – and so quietly that the boys on either side could not comprehend, said 'Wog, Woof or War – which is it?' 'War, Sir.' 'Don't bring it on parade again.' It was a reproach as effective as any scream of rage and a thousand times more intelligent, for it immediately engaged my respect and would have engaged my loyalty had we ever found ourselves in a situation that required it. From this episode I also learned that I had no privacy, that I had not only been observed reading, but that the observer had been close enough to read the cover of the book and mean enough to report it – a spiteful lance-corporal, no doubt, not literate enough to pronounce Waugh's name, hence Wog and Woof, and intent on getting me into trouble.

Almost every minute of our lives was regulated, but from time to time the frantic pace was disrupted by a medical inspection for athlete's foot and its equivalent in the crotch, by the requirement that we should donate blood, at the sight of which, frothing in the bottles, a surprising number of supposedly tough boys fainted, or an interview with a Personnel Selection Officer. My PSO was as hapless as the careers officer who had interviewed me at school: in the RASC (the Royal Army Service Corps as it then was, almost the very bottom of the army heap, the Shit Corps), the two careers it offered were either as a driver or a clerk, neither of interest to a boy besotted with music and art. He decided that a few minutes with an army psychiatrist might be helpful to us both, and I was ushered into the presence of a captain in a neighbouring office. 'Which of your parents do you love best?' he asked. Surely better, I thought, as I have only two, but answered 'Neither,' sensing danger in both directions and disinclined to disclose my bastardy, my rage against my stepfather, my ignorance of my real father and my determination to cut my mother's apron strings. He did not ask me if I might be queer, the question that I most feared, knowing that to tell the truth would wreck my purpose in serving my two years away from home and London. On his advice the PSO decided that I should become a clerk and the Army then taught me how to type – for which skill I have ever since been grateful; it also tried to teach me rudimentary accounting – as conceptually confusing as trigonometry.

I cannot now recall quite how many weeks we spent in Basic Training – two, perhaps, in coming to terms with the brutality of army discipline in Buller Barracks, and another six in the comparative harmony of Willems. We were given occasional short breaks, often with no warning, of which only those who lived in the South-East could take advantage – and even they were hard-pressed to get home and back within 24 hours. So little time meant only that we had a Sunday free of church parade and could sleep all day if we chose. Resisting surrender to homesickness, I slipped away to nearby Fleet where Alice Denne, a friend of my mother who grew Rhodesian tobacco in her conservatory and rolled her own cigars, fed me as though I were a civilised being and not a ravening animal. She had an almost professional knowledge of seventeenth century Dutch still life painting and part of the seriously important Assheton Bennett collection of such things hung on her walls.

Ten or so years earlier an elderly man had knocked on our door in the hope of selling the small wares in a tray hanging from his neck – matches, boot laces and other necessaries from which street hawkers then made a wretched living, and my mother, sensing something amiss, something gentlemanly in the shabbiness, had hauled him in, fed and watered him, questioned and lectured him, and given him money enough to return to the family home, the prodigal brother returning to his sister, Alice Denne. That was the benign, unselfish, practical side of my mother's nature.

With a 36-hour pass from noon on Saturday to midnight on Sunday, real civilisation became possible. I could be in Waterloo early in the afternoon – but then what? From late November until the beginning of March 1953, the Royal Academy mounted one of its great winter exhibitions devoted to Dutch Painting 1450–1750 – 644 paintings, and the great Gallery III hung with

Rembrandts alternating with Cuyps, perhaps the most memorable hang in all my lifetime; this was where I spent every hour of leave that I got, except for the very first of my passes, shortly before it opened. On that occasion, in heavy boots and prickly uniform because no new recruit was allowed to change into civilian clothes, unappealingly naked of hair about the ears and neck, I walked to Covent Garden and spent a guinea on a seat that evening in the stalls circle – twenty-one shillings of the twenty-four that were a squaddy's weekly pay, gone at a stroke. Then I walked to the National Gallery to kill time with old friends, the last of them the Arnolfini Portrait by Jan Van Eyck, that immaculate description of a medieval reality with its convex mirror (of which David Hockney was one day so mistakenly to make so much) and oriental rug, the dog and the discarded shoes, the shutters and, behind the hinge, the crack through which we see the garden. Engrossed, I was almost unaware of the grand old man in black cloak and fedora, the only other being in the room, until he came near and asked 'Who do you think those two people are?' I gave him the obvious answer 'Giovanni Arnolfini and his wife,' to which a histrionic 'No!' was the retort, 'they are Jan van Eyck and his wife.' Then to my 'You've been reading that silly book,' he responded with a triumphant 'Reading it? I *wrote* it.'

The old man was Maurice Brockwell, a curator and historian of art long before art's history became an academic discipline in Britain, of a generation for whom it was enough to write well of whimsical ideas, the silly book his slim volume *The Pseudo-Arnolfini Portrait*, published that year, 1952.

My confusion and embarrassment were put to rest with his inviting me to lunch at the Athenaeum the following day. I explained that I had to be in boots and battledress, but he would not accept refusal and so it was that I found myself not only in his company but that of two painters too, Alfred Munnings and Stanley Spencer. Munnings questioned me closely on the conditions of the National Serviceman, went through a range of appalled reactions, though he must have seen things far worse during the First World War, and said that he would write to my commanding officer – quite the last thing this squaddie wanted and I had to be, I think, rude, to put him off. Stanley – as I was instructed to call him – a tiny man who had spent most of that same war in the Balkans (one of its most intriguing campaigns) in unrelentingly grim conditions, showed no interest in my misfortunes, nor, indeed, in any of our conversations' drifts, and at one point slipped from his chair, I think onto his knees, until his eyes were level with the tablecloth, and then began to adjust the relative positions of the salt, the pepper and all other permanent occupants of the vast white waste, much as Poussin and Gainsborough must have arranged the miniature landscapes that informed their finished paintings. This, Brockwell and Munnings ignored, while I felt as Alice felt at the Mad Hatter's Tea Party, 'very much confused,' the discussion of art as wayward and inconsequential as the Dormouse's disquisition on drawing.

Maurice became something of a friend until his death in December 1958, though he had little respect for the Courtauld Institute and sorely tried my loyalty to it. He lived in Earls Court, in a mansion flat that had seen much better days and which, after the death of his wife early in 1952, gradually descended into near squalour. It was his wife's death that led him, lonely, to play ancient mariner in the National Gallery, and I wonder how many other young men he waylaid – not that he had any interest in young men other than as an anxious tutor. He had outlived all possibility of income; his long curatorship of the Cook Collection of old masters had ended with the outbreak of war in 1939 when he was just short of seventy, and his indefatigable research into the quibbles of the history of Netherlandish art can never have made money for him, any more than they added weight to his reputation as a scholar. What little he had was depleted by what his Times obituarist described as his 'interest' in horse racing. The Athenaeum quietly 'forgot' his subscription, but his landlords finally forced him out of his flat and his last months were spent in The Charterhouse. Of his lifetime of scholarly research papers – mistaken though so many of his assertions were – not a trace remained for those few of us who, on his death in 1958, thought they might be worth preserving.

*   *   *

Our basic training and our corps training complete, someone somewhere in the hierarchy decided on our fate. Given posting application forms on which we were to list our three preferences, boys who were homesick, or had girlfriends, or were even married, hoped to be sent to units in the British Isles; some suggested the safety of Germany and Egypt, but no one asked for a posting that involved active service; in the event, the whole platoon was posted to Korea where British casualties were known to be heavy and winter conditions terrible. Other platoons were sent en bloc to Egypt. Before we were despatched on embarkation leave we were lectured on the weather, clothes, food, conditions, the state of the campaign, leave (in Japan, for us), the political background and what we would experience in the long confinement on a troopship. For the last of these lectures the whole intake was gathered to hear a Brigadier give us instruction on matters sexual – the horrors of syphilis in particular, the treatment for which had us squirming in our seats – did the Umbrella, I wonder, really exist, or was this instrument, inserted into the urethra, then opened as with the spokes of an umbrella and withdrawn, scoring its inner wall to make it bleed, a myth to make us shy away from penetrative sex? At this and tales of the sores and smells that lurk in a Gippo prostitute's vagina there were vague murmurs of distaste, but a sound far more audible and general was that of in-drawn breath when the lecture ended with an admonition to avoid sex with any natives anywhere, 'but if you *must* have it, take your best mate round the back of the barracks and bugger him.'

For me and a handful of others, however, the someone some- where had second thoughts and decided that we might, perhaps, be what was dubbed 'officer material'. With my school record I had not thought of it myself, but there were boys in my intake who had been to a public school and spent years in a Cadet Force, or who simply had a high opinion of themselves founded on class, all of whom thought they should be officers. I was taken off the Korean draft, for which I had already had a week's embarkation leave, and returned to Willems Barracks to await a War Office Selection Board, or WOSB (always spoken of as a Wosby). For some weeks we were astonishingly well-treated: we were nothing more than raw privates, yet we were paired off in small rooms that gave us more privacy than I ever had as an officer cadet, and our sole duty was to read the daily newspapers with which we were supplied and make ourselves aware of the world and its events. There were odd parades to sharpen our drill and occasionally an officer appeared to tell us something of what to expect at a WOSB and how to pass it but, set apart, as we were, it was a deliciously idle few weeks. Boys were called quite randomly to their WOSBs and, whether they passed or failed, disappeared either to a working unit or to Mons, the great officer training unit for the aspiring middle-class dullards of the RASC and the really well-bred boys who had joined the Cavalry.

I shared a room with Eric Biddle, a grammar school boy from Stoke-on-Trent, short, wiry, tough, quick-thinking and intelligent, politically to the left, and perhaps the one boy in our batch who should have become a subaltern, but did not; I dare say his Potteries brogue let him down and, far too honest to pretend, he may not have shone in the WOSB atmosphere, which was very Junior Common Room, but I have no doubt that in command of men, their respect for him would have been far greater than for any of the strutting coxcombs who became the baby officers of the RASC in my time.

One night, when we were both in our beds, reading, two regular army corporals came stamping into our room with all the authority of those who are on official business. Eric, in pyjamas, but given time to put on boots, was hustled off on some specious errand that we neither of us understood, and the remaining corporal unceremoniously buggered me. Much bigger, much stronger, unrelentingly purposeful and with the authority of rank, he just got on with it, my yelps, if any, muffled by the pillow, his entry eased with the spit I heard him hawk. Done, he did not gloat, did not taunt me with proposals that I had asked for it or enjoyed it, offered no reason for it, but merely warned that if I did anything about it, 'they' would not find him, but they'd make bloody sure that I'd never be an officer.

He was, of course, absolutely right and it had been a shrewdly calculated rape. I had not, wittingly, seen the man before and the only thing I knew about him was that he wore corporal's stripes. What would I say if I reported the matter to the Battalion Guard Room, where I would find only National Service amateurs, and what would be the consequences? There could be no WOSB while the Military Police established the facts, and if any of them were to ask if I were queer or had had homosexual experience, that would certainly put an end to my National Service. And what had I lost? – not my virginity. I went to the loo, excreted the evidence, tidied my bed and pretended to be asleep when Eric returned. His explanation next morning, confused and vague, could have been interpreted as evasive, but if he too was buggered – which I doubted, knowing him to be a fighter – he revealed no more to me than I to him. The episode worried me: did I *look* queer, did my behaviour (the term body language had not then come into use) betray me, did the care I took not to look curiously at other boys indicate to the knowing that I was indeed queer? I wonder now whether there was some kind of buggers' network between barracks through which NCOs could exchange likely lads in perfect safety, for later experiences, out of the army, were to suggest that regular soldiers often had a taste for sodomy, or were tolerant and obliging for a fiver, as long as no one accused them of being queer.

As it happened, within a few days we were deprived of the comforts of this interlude and were posted hither and yon, to

Shorncliffe Camp in my case, near Folkestone, where perhaps a dozen of us, waiting for our WOSBs, were put to some use as RASC clerks – it was then that I learned that in the army, rum, whiskey and stout were medical supplies of which the nearby military hospital's store had constantly to be replenished. The rum we had an immediate chance to try when the great surge of the North Sea swept into the English Channel at the end of January 1953; within a week of transferring from Aldershot we were waist deep in the ice-cold sea at Hythe, shoring the defences there with sandbags, rum reassuring us – or so the sergeant thought as we swigged it from what may have been a demijohn, but few of us had any stomach for it.

Shorncliffe was a wretched posting – a run-down barracks so under-manned that we were compelled to stand guard every three or four nights, snatching only scraps of sleep, and were rarely spared for a week-end pass. What hours we had off duty were mostly spent in bed in our chill barrack room, but once in a while we went into Folkestone where there was a cinema enlightened enough to show foreign films – it was there that I saw Kurosawa's *Rashomon* and was so enchanted by its revolutionary approach to narrative that I went again, alone, to feast on it. Some trouble with my right foot developed – an enraged toughie (my fault, my words) from the East End had, booted, stamped on it, unshod, in the first few days at Aldershot, and the swelling caused then occasionally flared in later months; the medical officer decided that I should go to hospital and have it X-rayed and drained. As hospital for in-patients was regarded as, technically, a posting to another unit, I had to take with me all my documents in a sealed envelope, and these, easing the envelope open before the clerk's spittle had dried, I read as I limped on my way. They were few, and only one was of interest – the report of the psychiatrist in Aldershot who had asked me the which-do-you-love-best question: his conclusion had been that I was emotionally unstable and on no account should I be sent anywhere near a front line. No document was ever torn into smaller shreds nor thrown to the winds over a larger area. Was it, I wondered, the reason why, while other boys were called to their WOSBs, I had been left to rot in idle postings? There had been a flurry of hope on 15 February 1953 when I had been told to report to a WOSB on the 18th, but it was cancelled two days later, with no reason given.

I had two more months to wait, but at last I reported to a WOSB on 15 April, feeling far from well. That I was in the early stages of mumps may well have contributed to my passing. I remember very little of the tests – car tyres suspended from ropes played some part in one that was performed under my command, and I gave a brief lecture on the absence of sexual imagery from Pre-Columbian Mexican sculpture, inspired by either Roger Fry or Aldous Huxley (or perhaps both), to which the supervising officer responded with 'I can't help feeling I've had my leg pulled, but it makes a change from how to look after a horse.' In spite of the headache and swellings in uncomfortable sites or, as I believe, because of their dulling effect on my behaviour, I was competent enough in the tasks through which the army distinguished the able from the incompetent, and was sent on the home leave that was the bonus for passing. My mother's diary records that at 4.00 pm on the afternoon of 17 April 1953 I returned home from my WOSB with a temperature of 104.2 and collapsed. Mumps was diagnosed. Her entry for the following day reads 'Brian very ill indeed. We must get his temperature down.'

Three weeks later – that is after fifteen wasted weeks attached to Shorncliffe Camp – I reached Mons, dumped my kit and went in search of Keith Fowler, another boy who had endured the Shorn-cliffe doldrum, who had arrived a fortnight earlier. I found his barrack room and walked towards him with arms outstretched to hug him, only to be rebuffed – he was happy to shake my hand, but not to be embraced. There was nothing sexual in my gesture, nor was there anything sexual in my affection for him, but in parrying my action quite so sternly he suggested that he saw it so and needed to demonstrate to all who might be watching that he wanted nothing of it. It was another lesson in the need for restraint and dissembling, another lesson in the fragility of friendships formed in adversity.

Mons I found a long hard slog. The aftermath of mumps affected my energy and stamina, and, seeming to develop an allergy to dust and pollen, I feared that this might become serious enough for those in charge of me to decide that I was unfit to stay in the army – the very last thing that I wanted. It was infantry training all over again, but with a seriousness that far exceeded our experience as raw recruits, and as we crawled and crept and ran and lay concealed and still on the dry heaths of Aldershot, I wished for the cold and damp of autumn that had made tolerable our first attempts in this pretence of war.

It was tough and unrelenting by day and riven by snobbery at night, for the elite young Cavalrymen rarely mixed with the rag, tag and bobtail of the Corps. We were far from equal – young subalterns of the RASC might command one arm of the support on which the tanks and armoured cars of these unhorsed striplings must depend, but we were scarcely distinguishable from the proletarian masses of our men. We shared taxis into town; they drove in and out of camp in 3-litre Bentleys by the dozen – indeed, I suspect that every example of this car, all 1,600 of them built between 1921 and 1927, was at some point in its life in the hands of an Officer Cadet at Mons, as *de rigeur* as the tweed jackets, tight cavalry twill trousers and flat caps that were their off-duty uniforms. Boastful and braying, few made good companions for boys from grammar schools or the wretched in-betweens like Haberdashers' and we were promptly pigeon-holed by perceived background and speech. Not obviously from the one group or the other, I was very much the odd fish and occasionally made to feel it. I valued greatly the friendship of three boys of one caste, John Peile, with whom I am still in touch, Nigel Hensman and Tegner (Christian name forgotten), with whom I am not; of the other caste I can recall none and nothing.

National Service as a Squaddie

In adversity we all pulled together well enough. Was Coronation Day an adversity? It seemed so at the time, for officer cadets were destined, with ordinary soldiers, to hold back the crowds. Preparing for it took quite a slice out of our training and humiliatingly returned us to the status of squaddies, bullied on the parade ground by day and in the barrack room by night, to achieve levels of perfection in drill and dress matched only by guardsmen Trooping the Colour. 'You will not faint.' This, above all other instructions for Coronation Day, I recall, not in such simple terms, but at extraordinary volume and quite twice the length when embellished with the sexual threats and swearwords customary in army life. 'You will not faint' – but I had an unaccountable tendency to faint, not yet discovered by army doctors, when standing still too long, and never knew quite how long too long might be; Coronation Day was not the most suitable day on which to reveal this frailty. To avoid the faint we had been taught to shift our weight imperceptibly from heels to toes and back again, to wiggle toes and clench our buttocks and breathe deeply, even to divert our minds and concentrate on sex, booze, leave and other pleasures, without losing our grasp of the matter in hand.

We fell into three categories. The least competent and most fortunate were given five days Coronation Leave and sent home. The rest knew what was expected of them – a day of patient endurance and longsuffering, a day on which there could be no customary ten minute break every two hours so that we could smoke a fag and empty our bladders, a day on which, indeed, if needs must, we were told, we must pee where we stood, within our trousers and down into our boots, a day that would not end until the applauding crowds had cheered the Queen, subsided into anti-climax and gone home. This group was to be unexpectedly divided. The day began the night before, bulling best boots yet again and pressing knife-sharp creases into uniforms that grated raw the skin of inner thighs. An hour or two of wakeful sleep was all we had, and then the sluice of cold water and the scrape of razor blade, the attempted emptying of obstinately unready bowels, the rush of breakfast, soggy bacon swimming in grease, eggs fried crisp as biscuits, tinned tomatoes a luke-warm slop, thick wedges of white bread and quite disgusting tea, laced we thought with bromide to unman us, the bitterness of leaves caught in our teeth cutting through the sweetness of the milk and sugar. And then the rush of detailed dressing, the rush of inspection, the rush of being marshalled hither and yon, the day just dawning.

Many of us did indeed stand in the drizzle and pee in our boots, damp without and sodden within, but for others the day for which they had prepared so diligently and long came to an early and bathetic end – they were superfluous and their day of duty was converted into useless leave, useless because, in best bib and tucker on a day when all London's useful functions had come to a stop, there was nothing to do but return to Aldershot.

*   *   *

'Cushy' is the army's word for the weeks that cadets, having graduated from Mons, spent in an RASC barracks in Aldershot learning specifically to be its subalterns. An inglorious but necessary Corps, its officers were expected to be as much clerks and drivers as their men, and much of the training was fun, for in theory we should, on a motorcycle, have been as nimble as a despatch rider, and at the wheel of an articulated truck (that is one with a universal joint amidships linking it to a trailer that doubles its bulk and capacity), as able as any professional trucker. We learned the lore and practice of the convoy, which could be of thirty vehicles at regular intervals and slow, perfect for devastating attack from the air, or of three, each driver properly briefed and capable of reacting individually to emergencies, much faster and safer. Both were, of course, subject to the ten minute smoking break – not the easiest thing to fix when on the road during a military exercise; later, in the real life of the army, we were to learn that many of our men (still boys in late adolescence) regarded these as breaks for masturbation as much as a cigarette, for they found the rattling, vibration and bucking of the old Austin and Bedford trucks that were their workhorses a source of irresistible prostate stimulation. Of this the blind-eyed army must always have known, but no word of it was ever spoken. We drilled as much as was essential to see us through a passing-out parade without disgrace, and the Senior Under Officer – that is, theoretically, the most promising of us, but in fact the most physically beautiful (and young May was both beautiful and imposingly big) – learned to do things ceremonial with a naked sword.

Like ordinary soldiers we slept, polished our boots and brasses, and had our being in a barrack room – only the SUO had a room to himself and his sword. Our evenings were often free and I sometimes slipped away to see Alice Denne, but more often went to a local pub to learn to drink a pint like a real man (I have loathed draught beer ever since), or just lived the simple life of the barrack room at ease. There was some talk of sex, most of it uncertain, but two of us went into town and found it – or so they said. One, a graceless, pushy lout with heavy spectacles, who was to overturn his Singer Nine (an open tourer) and never be seen again, gave us a blow-by-blow account of orgasm between the breasts of an Aldershot trollop – shocking to boys who knew nothing of the norm, let alone such deviations from it. Another, far the oldest of us, a sometime apprentice in the Austin factories in Birmingham and a heavy smoker of the kind who holds his cigarette within the shelter of his cupped hand, had been ordered to get rid of the ungentlemanly nicotine stain that kippered his palm – and he did, overnight, by, as he told us with the air of one used to such things, fingering the vagina of another trollop to make her juices flow. Astounded, most boys responded with a 'Yuck' or 'Ugh,' but I, having a decade earlier read Harry Claff's filthy paperback, already knew of these juices and was inclined to believe that they might indeed have that peculiar property.

On the evening before our passing-out parade, bulling boots and pressing trousers for the last time (we would soon have batmen for such chores) – a corporal strode in and told me that I was wanted by the Commanding Officer. Another corporal, another rape? But there were a dozen witnesses. He was insistent – my state of dress (I wore nothing but a towel) was of no importance and shirt sleeve order would do – and thus, unkempt, I followed him. With the CO was the Captain from the Gloucesters who had been father and brother to us throughout the later stages of our training to be subalterns, a man who had striven to teach us that there was more to this small authority than strut and swagger, that we had a duty of respect and responsibility to our men, that we were part of something infinitely larger than ourselves, and on the CO's other side sat the psychiatrist whose report I had torn to pieces months before. Of this, the CO explained, a copy had just been brought to his notice. The meeting was entirely informal; they sat at a table and I sat with them in a what-have-you-got-to-say-for-yourself debate. Panic turned to ice-cold calm. I argued that having got to within twelve hours of being commissioned without anyone noticing my supposed emotional instability, I had proved the psychiatrist wrong, that I was a first-class shot with the Bren and every hand-held weapon, that there was no army vehicle that I could not drive and the workings of which I did not understand, and that were I to be returned, sans commission, to my old unit in Shorncliffe, the army would have wasted the considerable cost of training me to be something that only one man had said, on the basis of only a very brief interview at the very start of my National Service, that I should not be. I was then sent out to join the corporal. Minutes later I was recalled to be told that the general consensus was that I should be commissioned the following morning. General consensus? Did that mean that the psychiatrist agreed with this decision? I dared not ask.

CHAPTER 7

National Service as a Subaltern

Shortly before we were commissioned we completed posting applications. Germany would have been best for me, for though still largely in ruins, its museums and galleries were slowly reopening and perfection in the language would have been a very useful accomplishment, but the army had the reputation of being cussed in these matters – better not to ask for what one wanted most, for then there was a better chance of getting it. I ruled two lines diagonally across the form and wrote between them ANYWHERE ABROAD. I should have written ANYWHERE AT HOME, for when my posting came, it was to Aldershot and to the very Willems Barracks where I had my basic training as a clerk. And there I went, though I immediately applied for an alternative posting, this time just anywhere.

At Willems I spent my time sorting out the problems of recruits – the desperate need for leave when learning of a girl friend's pregnancy or of a single mother too ill to care for younger siblings, pleading the good character of a soldier when some civil offence caught up with him, even pleading it before a formidable Court Martial when an inexperienced youth had rashly answered back or refused to perform a degrading punishment. The most difficult case was a contemporary at Haberdashers' who had failed his WOSB and been returned to Willems as a despised dogsbody private, to be mocked for his failed ambition by every junior NCO. He broke down in tears when I told him that I had no power to persuade the Board to reverse its verdict or put him through the tests again. I did not remind him of how lofty he, as a prefect and a cricketer, had been with me at school, and how, though we had often had our hands in each other's trousers, he had later scorned me for my homosexuality, but I dare say that he remembered well enough, may even have sought to exploit part of this recollection, and attributed my refusal to help him to something approaching vengeful malice. It was not so. I knew enough of the army's way to be certain that there was nothing I could do for him, not even put my arm round him for old time's sake in a gesture of hopeless comforting (as was my inclination); nor could I rebuke the NCOs in charge of him without betraying the misery of this interview and thus making things much worse for him.

I had to wait till mid November before my alternative posting came – and then it was nothing more abroad than Blandford Forum, one of the jewels of Dorset, to a training battalion where boys learned to drive and then moved on. I, thank God, was given a working platoon of experienced drivers whose duty it was to provide support for other regiments and we were as often as not out on convoy or playing some ancillary part in exercises on Salisbury Plain, Thus it was that I sometimes found myself joyriding in tanks and other armoured vehicles, or cheek by jowl with the big guns of the Artillery. I am deeply grateful for these experiences, for from them I gained some small insight into the daily life of the soldiers of the front line, know something of the heat, noise and discomfort they endure, the sound and fury, so to speak. Have any of our masters in the House of Commons now, such knowledge?

There were many lighter moments. In the early hours of a bitter cold night exercise, Salisbury Plain made magical by frost and moonlight, my dependable Corporal John drove me away from the hostilities to a refreshment van parked on the A303, and introduced me to the luxury of the bacon sandwich – two slabs of white bread thickly buttered, with long hot rashers projecting inches beyond the crust, held firmly in both hands, to be eaten leaning forward to prevent the melting butter from running down the chin and onto one's uniform. I still try from time to time to replicate the experience, but it is not a thing to do alone and somehow neither the bread nor the bacon ever seems to match the original. Returning from another exercise, driven by my fat sergeant, an indolent and evasive man for whom I did not much care (he boasted of a mistress in Crewkerne to whose bosom he too frequently repaired when on duty – but then, with a wife in married quarters on the camp, only when on duty could he go to her), chased a plump piglet along a winding lane. Fearing for its life, I stopped him, stopped the tilly (the army's pet name for a small flat-bed carry-all truck covered with a canvas tilt), gave chase and caught it. But what should a young subaltern with a muddy piglet wriggling in his arms then do? We found neither farm nor farmhouse, nor any evidence of pigs by sight or smell, and were nearing camp when the sergeant said that he would drop me at the officers' mess and then take the piglet, now deeply asleep on my lap, to the police station in Blandford. I believed him. I thought that rescuing the piglet had been my good deed for the day. By extraordinary coincidence there was suckling-pig for dinner in the sergeants' mess a few days later – the officers' mess, full of envy, wondered how this could be?

For my unreliable fat sergeant, Corporal John, another regular soldier living in married quarters, was more than compensation; knowing, usefully devious (but always on my side), his experience, wisdom and guidance kept me out of trouble with pernickety senior officers and, in always seeming to know what was about to happen, he, I and the platoon were always a jump ahead. The platoon, though entirely of National Servicemen, was almost permanent and when a boy reached the end of his two years his leaving did not disturb our equilibrium. Introducing myself, I told them that I was no more interested than they in the idiocies of army discipline and we struck a bargain, so to speak – that as long as they kept themselves and their barrack room reasonably tidy, that would be enough for me, that I'd even tolerate the Windsor knots they tied in their ties, but when they were to be inspected by the Company Sergeant Major or some other hierarch, they must not let me down. They never did, and on my last night as a National Serviceman, they gave me in a local pub a send-off that I took to be not mere ritual, but an expression of genuine affection. They were mostly rough and tough, incipient teddy-boys, and yet their immediate superior, their fellow National Serviceman Lance-Corporal Organ, contrastingly gentle in manner and softly spoken, managed them very well. I was very lucky to have the support and loyalty of John and Organ – other subalterns in the battalion seemed always to be at odds with their NCOs, the jumped-up second lieutenants thinking that mere rank gave them superiority, their war-torn sergeants and corporals knowing every one of them to be a jackanapes. I was lucky too to have such decent men under my command; only once did I have misgivings, but they were premature. Expecting a replacement driver I was notified that a Private de St Croix was on his way. With such a name, I thought, he must be of ancient Catholic lineage, his ancestors Crusaders, Plantagenets, Angevins, even the Norman knights and courtiers of William the Conqueror; and if that were not enough in the wretched circumstances of an RASC training camp, with such a name he is probably a public schoolboy who has failed a WOSB and now feels as disgraced and shamed as that unhappy boy from Haberdashers. In the event, Private de St Croix was nothing of the kind, but a tiny, undernourished and very pretty Cockney boy from the East End who, on announcing himself as Private Deesty Croiks, could not understand my laughter at such a d'Urberville moment.

The months passed easily at Blandford, the winter lightened by playing rugger again, for the battalion at first and then a little further up the line, and once in a very rough game against the Navy. On my first reporting to the Commanding Officer he had quizzed me to see what sort of new puppy had joined his pack, and I had given a rather diffident answer about my skill, as a hooker; two or three weeks later, the battalion's hooker injured, again with diffidence I volunteered to take his place, and as it was only an hour before the game began and no better offer had been made, I joined the team. Somehow the chemistry was right, the game flowed wonderfully and equally and both sides shone. Before I could get my boots off a messenger from the CO told me to report to him at once and filthy as I was. 'You told me that you were not much good at rugger. That was not true.' I muttered something about not blowing my own trumpet, but the CO, determined to be disagreeable about my modesty, called in his adjutant and told him to make me duty dog for the next week.

The duty dog – a term new to me – turned out to be the officer responsible for the camp and all its works for every hour of the day. Confined to camp, he had to be up at six in the morning and was rarely in bed more than five hours earlier. It was his duty to inspect the guard, the fire precautions and the kitchens, to check the state of every barrack room, the lavatories and ablutions (as the washrooms were called), to ensure that any prisoners were properly cared for and properly employed (this meant such fatuities as blancoing the stocks of coal and cutting the grass round the sergeants' mess with a pair of nail scissors), and being present in the mess hall to deal with any complaints there might be about the food. The duty dog himself was the only man who might dare to comment adversely on the achievements of a sergeant in the Catering Corps and his assistant cooks – my comments on his boiled cabbage and his tinned tomatoes brought a response just short of mutiny. It was a useful experience and a valuable chore, for it meant that no tap ever dripped for want of a new washer, no lavatory cistern ever malfunctioned for more than the time it took to report it, and no door squeaked. It was not on my watch that a barrack room burst into flames (every building on the camp was made of wood), but because of the system of the duty dog, the blaze was extinguished long before the local fire brigade arrived and not a boy was hurt. Every business and institution in civilian life should have its duty dog – were it so, then faxed messages would not be mislaid by newspaper offices and the lavatories of national museums and galleries would never stink like middens (as they occasionally do).

Apart from rugger, the winter pleasures of the mess had been entirely unknown to me – billiards, snooker, table tennis and forms of poker played with dice as well as cards that always ended with the loser having to swallow whatever concoction of alcoholic drinks the winners could afford, poisonous blends of Benedictine, Calvados, Tia Maria and rum perhaps, stirred into half a pint of warm brown ale, the game halted until the last drop was drunk. There were the hazards of the Mess Night too, the formal occasions when we temporary subalterns wore Service Dress, our best kakhi uniforms, and all the married and other older regular officers at the head of the table donned a dark blue uniform of tunics bedizened with chain mail and tight trousers with a broad red stripe, spurs clinking at their heels – it was the wretched RASC pretending to be heroes of the cavalry reaching back to Rupert of the Rhine. We ate, we drank, we passed the port and toasted with grave formality, but on retirement to the drawing room, off came our jackets and the games began. 'Are you there, Moriarty?' was usually the first, the ice-breaker to let loose the vicious brute, the question asked of one officer by another when both, blindfolded, their left hands clasped in an unbreakable grip, lay on the floor with, in their right hands, hefty clubs of close-rolled newspaper. To the answer 'Yes,' the asker then thwacked his weapon where he thought his adversary's head might be. This response was not necessarily immediate; the asker might wait to hear the sound of breathing or a faint shuffle on the carpet, for these could confirm that the answerer was stretching as far away as he could (though the sane man knew that it paid to be as close as possible, where, though more likely to be hit, the blow must be enfeebled by proximity), and the longer he waited the more certain of accuracy he might be; most, however, gambled on the quickest response. The Adjutant, the CO's right hand man and executioner, big, handsome and, we youngsters thought, far too much of a gentleman and too intelligent to be in the RASC, was strong enough with his left hand to twist the forearm of his opponent, forcing him onto his back and thus able to thwack him across the face rather than the back of the skull, splitting a lip or bloodying his nose. We thought this a punishment for some small episode of recalcitrance or cheek that had not merited an official rebuke or penalty; if it was not – and we could never quite be sure – then it was calculated sadism. Was it coincidence that the winner of each bout was judged by the viciousness of his successful strikes rather than their number?

With the departure of the CO, usually well before midnight, High Cockalorum, the roughest game of all, brought these evenings to a close. Eric Partridge, the High Priest of all enquirers into the vernacular, has it that this began as a schoolboys' game, a nineteenth-century variant of leapfrog in which one team of players presents a chain of backs and bottoms achieved by tucking their heads between the legs of the boy or man in front and gripping his thighs, while the rival team tries to break the chain or collapse it with their accumulated weight, by each member taking a long run from behind, leaping along its length as far as possible and holding his position against all attempts to shake him off. Often rougher than any rugger scrum when played by adult men, minor injuries were common and more serious mishaps not at all unusual; these, in official terms, were passed off as 'sustained by 2nd Lt Dobbin in pursuit of his duties'.

Most young subalterns acquired cars – not the 3-litre Bentleys so common at Mons, but equally old Austin Sevens, a rather distinguished Riley Nine (an exquisite small car in its day), a Vauxhall 14 drop-head coupé from that marque's last years of reputation for fine engineering, and mine a very ordinary Morris Ten of 1934, bought as a reliable runner for £30, my gross pay for six weeks or so. And reliable it was for a while, until early one morning on Salisbury Plain, returning from a stolen evening at Covent Garden, the float chamber of the carburettor stuck, neat petrol poured onto the exhaust system, and when I halted the car it burst into flames. I walked back half a mile or so and thumbed a lift; when my Good Samaritan drove past the car, still burning, he slowed to a stop and we ran back to see if anyone needed help, but there was, of course, no one, just an old car burning, dumped, complained my Samaritan. Corporal John asked if I had removed the number plates and, on learning that I had not, at once drove to the carcass and removed all evidence of ownership. I became the passenger in other subaltern's cars, or took to stealing away alone on an old BSA motorcycle, big, heavy and utterly reliable at a steady mile a minute, bare-headed and shirt open at the neck until I ran into a bumble bee, the impact so hard that it was, I thought, like being shot in the chest – and then the sting began to affect my ability to breathe. It was the discovery of a frightening allergy.

I took no long leaves and few weekend passes once the winter of 1953–54 was at an end, wanting to consolidate the separation from my mother and my new sense of independence and to have some continuing benefit from it in my coming years as a student. I was not alone in this, for other subalterns too saw some benefit in escape from the cloying pleasures of home. One of us chose always to spend his leave at Porton Down as a guinea-pig for a cold cure, a wicked deception thought by most of us to be connected with poison gas or nuclear radiation – this on the grounds of gossip in the camp – but he was a Scot, and as payment was to be had for this, he would not listen (but then he would not listen when we told him that introducing Scottish sword-dancing to the mess would be an utter failure). For the rest of us the sea was within reach at Bournemouth, where we might swim, see a film and end the day with dinner away from the formality of the mess; a little more adventurous, we might scamper south to Lulworth Cove, walk across meadows to the sea, swim and then feast on lobsters cooked by an old fisherman with a hut just off the beach. We explored the Piddle villages in the valley of that river, the Tarrants and the Hintons, and we wandered further to Bath and Wells,

Salisbury and Wilton; it was not quite a posting to Germany, where an early Volkswagen might have borne me to Cologne and Frankfurt, even to Munich and Bavaria, but Blandford was not exactly barren of cultural delights.

Early in September 1954, my two years complete, I left Blandford, but not without regret. There had been a suggestion that I might stay on for a third year, upgraded as a regular, and I was sentimentally tempted to do so, but I knew that National Service had done for me exactly what I hoped – it had cleared my decks of clutter. Now I yearned neither to play my violin nor to paint pictures; I had proved to myself that I could be celibate and, through abstinence, could suppress my homosexuality; and I had learned that I could, with a touch of Jesuitical casuistry, unostentatiously maintain my religious observance in the conflicting quotidian circumstances of army life. To have achieved all this and then imperil my new equilibrium by staying on in the army – for one year, perhaps another, seduced by the temptations of rank – might well clutter my life with other enthusiasms and responsibilities from which it would be even less easy to escape. I felt, moreover, compelled to respond to the overwhelming siren call of the Courtauld Institute, older, wiser and far better read than in my first incarnation there, a man rather than a boy.

I was not completely cut off from the army. Transferred to the Reserve, I had to report to the Duke of York's Barracks on King's Road, Chelsea, on Tuesday evenings and play soldiers for some hours, and for the first two summers there was a fortnight's camp with all the discomforts of army life in the field. This meant renewing acquaintance with the open latrine, sharing a long pole on trestles with any other officer who chose to empty his bowels concurrently, a lugubrious embarrassment, screened by draped sacking from the passer-by; it involved the pretence that an officers' mess in a tent should be almost as formal as in some historic barracks surviving from the eighteenth century; and worst of all, I was deprived of coffee (to which I had long been addicted) – the only alternative the disgusting tea that was brewed at every opportunity, the bucket of water, the quarter pound of tea-leaves, a pint tin of sweetened condensed milk, an extra pound or two of sugar, all brought to the boil over a fire of twigs. These were holidays as active and healthy as any bought now at vast expense and they were wonderful fun (how odd to have such a reaction when, at school, I had hated the annual field days); on one I added to my reputation for overturning things (when running an urgent errand for my CO at Blandford I had rolled his Austin Somerset on an icy corner) by testing too far the limits of a Gipsy, Austin's poor and transitory response to the Land-Rover; on another, a sergeant enthralled us with photographs of a hefty whore with a white mouse emerging from her hirsute vagina.

These jaunts with the Reserve should have continued for at least five years, but Suez intervened. This was the moral moment that I had mistily foreseen when learning to use a bayonet. I and many others in the Reserve were instructed to report for duty. I refused. I thought Eden's handling of the Suez Crisis indefensibly illegal and immoral, doubly so in its concurrence with the Soviet invasion of Hungary, and wrote so in a letter of resignation and refusal to my commanding officer in Chelsea. I delivered it myself and watched him read it. 'You realise that this means a Court Martial?' was his response. He did what he could to persuade me not to be so bloody-minded, so self-destructive and even said that if I allowed him to destroy the letter not another word would be said of it, but I sensed uncertainty in his tired old arguments for loyalty and obedience, hearing in them an echo of the unthinking motto of my school, Serve and Obey no matter what (the perfect admonition for Germans under the Nazis), and I stood my ground. He sent me home to wait. And wait I did, for years suffering repeatedly an absurd but mildly disturbing dream of discovering my army uniform to have been destroyed by moth – as, eventually, it was. I heard nothing until 2006 when, in response to an article written on the half centenary of Suez, I received some two dozen letters from others in the Reserve who had done the same and been sent home to await the consequences. They too had heard no more of it. I assume that up and down the country there were so many rebels that, after the international political disgrace of all involved in the Crisis, the army authorities felt that nothing could be achieved by hauling us all before Courts Martial. Our punishment was to be left in ignorance, knowing only that a Damocletian sword might strike at any time, and to be informally excluded from the Reserve, never knowing quite what our status might be if the Cold War became hot. Never again did I set foot in The Duke of York's Barracks as a soldier (now that they are Charles Saatchi's Gallery they have again become my haunt), never again did I enjoy a field exercise, never again did I wear my uniform. My only memento of army service is not, alas, de Vignyan *canne de jonc*, but the army issue clothes brush that was every squaddie's indestructible friend, stamped 8881, the last four digits of my army number; it is still my friend, for no brush inherited from my fastidious stepfather is one jot as effective in removing the hairs of a blonde bitch from the shoulders of a plain blue overcoat.

In my year as a subaltern my lessons were very different from those learned as a squaddie who had discovered a steely core within himself and knew that if needs must, there was nothing that he would not do. I learned that the officers above us were poor stuff, the best of them Captain Rigby and Captain Macnamara of the REME who knew more about engines than Henry Royce – but both had risen from the ranks and were wry in humour and respect; the worst of them, Captain Le Rougetel, in command of the company of which my platoon was part, was a hapless muddler whom subalterns could reduce to panic, hysteria and, very nearly, tears. Haunted by the prospect of compulsory retirement in early middle age, there was about all these left-overs of World War II, the hang-dog air of the professional soldier at the bottom of the heap, there because that was a fair estimate of their worth. My fellow subalterns could be broadly divided into two groups –

middle class boys who took their tasks to be a serious responsibility and were determined to get more out of National Service by putting more into it, and middle class boys who were, with little reason, uppity, relished the opportunity to swagger, and who were often quite gratuitously unpleasant, even bullying, to the young soldiers in their charge. It was never pretty to witness, in the accents of the grammar school, young 'gentlemen' echoing the caricatural abuse of their sergeants. In the RASC the third category of subaltern was never to be found – those born and bred for sacrifice, valiant, dauntless, unhesitating and expendable, the brave and beautiful always driven to the front by rash notions of duty and example, there to be killed off. Subalterns of that kind we knew only as the cavalry cadets with whom we had, for a few weeks, rubbed shoulders as a commonality at Mons.

Today's society is much poorer without National Service. It was a great force for good in society. Within the divisions of rank it sowed seeds of social cohesion across class barriers and was an instrument of mutual benevolence much more than a class–ridden autocracy, its fundamental philosophy close to that of the welfare state. Society has, alas, so altered in the four decades and more since National Service ceased, that it could never be re-instituted; were we to attempt anything of the kind and make it subject to the same implacable discipline, the political correctitudes would smother it at birth and the young would, *en masse*, refuse to serve. For me it was the most important period of my education and, looking back on it, I see that it gave a firm foundation to my social attitudes and politics. It taught me never to trust those in authority, never to despise those without it. It confirmed William Bulman's injunction that I should bring everything to the bar of my own judgement.

*   *   *

What part did my mother play in these army years? She sent me a parcel of long woolly underwear, Chilprufe the marque, when the first winter came. Hoping for chocolate biscuits, fruit cake or other treats that might be shared with my immediate mates, in a rage I sent it back and broke an apron string. Her diary records every one of my snatched visits to the Royal Academy and Covent Garden, her anxieties over the episodes of mumps and pseudo-asthma, and the gift of a trip with her to Paris confidently arranged to fill the eight full days between my passing-out as a subaltern and my first posting. We flew there. Flying to Paris must now seem unremarkable, but in 1953 it was almost adventurous, particularly as the plane flew low and slow enough to count the cows and cathedrals on the way. At fifty-three, my mother, with not a hint of grey in her chestnut hair, was mistaken for my elder sister and behaved so; wholly in command, in the very street off the Rue de Rivoli, in the very hotel in which she had lived, it was as though Paris was her daily beaten track and quite unchanged in the quarter century or so since that had been the case. It was a marvel of a week – the Louvre, the Opera, Versailles, the lamb chops, *tete de veau*, custard tarts and wine astonishing to those accustomed to the austerities of still-rationed post-war London.

The only mishap was my fainting at the Opera during the first act of Boris Godunov with Boris Christoff in the role – not some genteel fit of the vapours, but a proper, deeply unconscious faint. I recovered in the corridor, breathed the night air in the interval, returned to my seat and fainted again. Back in the corridor, dragged there by far from sympathetic Frenchmen who forebade me to make a third attempt to hear Christoff, we slunk away. I had fainted before – at school, usually after games or swimming, in church and even in the street – but these faints were dismissed as growing pains, or not enough breakfast or too long on my knees; once I fainted at a bus stop in Edgware Road, toppling others in the queue like ninepins, I was told, then to be swept off in an ambulance to spend twenty-four hours in a Paddington hospital, mystifying doctors – and it was not until decades later, after a heart by-pass operation, that the frequent blackouts that followed it were attributed to a vaso-vagal syndrome that had probably been present since my birth.

'Have you a history of fainting?' my cardiologist enquired. I replied that I had not, but when I thought about it, found that I could recall what had seemed unaccountable faints throughout my life, as far afield as New York, Ankara and Rawalpindi.

After our return from Paris – in my case with smuggled books from the Olympia Press, Miller's Tropics, Gide's Corydon and Wilde's Teleney among them, more literary than Harry Claff's seminal paperback and rather less astonishing, and a handful of educative photographs retrieved from the undusted top of the wardrobe in my hotel room – my mother's authority faded again. She had from the very start of my National Service been ready to accompany me to the opera on a stolen evening – these were times when even Callas as Norma did not fill the house and on Saturday 23 June 1953, with tickets bought that afternoon, we saw her with Joan Sutherland and the greatly underrated Giulietta Simionato – but these excitements ended abruptly when the Morris died. By the time my National Service ended my mother had a son who was determined to maintain a not unfriendly distance from her, to be a prop only when necessary and to maintain the financial independence that his small income as a subaltern had given him.

*   *   *

And what of sex these past two years? Celibacy was a partial state for me, and sanity lay in sex with my imagination and my hand – easier as a subaltern than as a squaddie denied privacy. If sex became the subject of conversation it was always ribald or downright filthy enough for all to join in the general laughter – most of us were virgins and we knew it, no matter how bold the pretence to be Don Juan. I kept a condom in my wallet, its outline polished in the pigskin for anyone to recognise, but it was my only lie, for no one ever asked if I was queer. In the army I would never have admitted it. There were boys who almost broke my resolve to be celibate, among them a cavalry cadet at Mons with whom I fell asleep in the back of a truck after an exhausting exercise, an RASC cadet with whom I sensed that there had perhaps been a this-can't-happen moment, and a doe-eyed and hopelessly stupid servant in the mess at Blandford who probably had not the slightest notion of just how pretty he was, but they were few. On one of my days as duty dog, inspecting empty barrack rooms, in one of them I found two squaddies naked on a bed, oblivious; for a moment I thought to slip away without disturbing them and then chose the alternative, for had I been any other officer or NCO, all hell would have been let loose. I have never seen such scared rabbits as when I tweaked the toes of a projecting foot. 'I don't care what you do, only that you don't get caught' – and walked away to check the taps and chains in the ablutions.

In a training battalion sex was not a major problem among trainees – they were, for the most part, too exhausted to do anything more than talk about it – but Blandford was also a working unit with soldiers who might spend the best part of two years there, and for these and those in charge of them there were at least the problems of non-specific urethritis and gonorrhoea. Our Medical Officer, a National Serviceman, gauche, inexperienced and hopelessly lugubrious, kept a store of ET Packets (what, I wonder, did ET stand for?) – condoms with lubricant – that were free Army Issue, but available only on application, and none of my men was prepared to report to the RAMC sergeant and signal his intention to go into town in the hope of a random fuck. When a man in my platoon had NSU or the clap, the MO always told me, and it was then my duty to address him and all his mates on this sensitive matter, informally and casually, as the man of the world that I was not; they knew that I was much given to giggling over matters of high seriousness and, with blank-faced frankness, could reduce my admonitions to farce. Their alternative ploy was to pretend innocence, not knowing the word condom, the slang terms French Letter and Johnnie quite strange to them, their function incomprehensible. In frank mood they argued that condoms deadened the sensation (their word for orgasm), that wearing one they might

not achieve orgasm at all, that the business took too long and that
they might have to finish it off for themselves. There was, among
them, an obscure lower class prejudice against masturbation, based,
I think, not on any of the Padre's occasional and always oblique
and querulous references on Church Parade to the abomination of
self-abuse – keeping oneself pure for one's wedding day the great
ideal – but to some notion that it was a halfway measure only
suitable for boys, and that real men abstained from it to reinforce
their fucking.

The only lecturing the subalterns got was from the wives of
regular officers when these charmless harridans were brought in
from married quarters for sherry before lunch on Sundays. Their
only conversation lay in fierce questions about girl friends and our
intentions to get married; it was far safer to invent a girl, to describe
her every detail, than to be unattached, though I occasionally
found it difficult to recall quite what I had earlier said of my
Dulcinea. In the absence of these ghastly women the topic of
gossip in the Mess was as often as not the affair of Lord Montagu of
Beaulieu and his friends and catamites. This had begun in August
1953 with accusations of buggery with two boy scouts and was
mightily reinforced with similar accusations in a second case, this
time with a pair of admitting and consenting adult airmen, both
having taken place in a beach hut in the Palace grounds. The trial
in the first matter fizzled out – one of the scouts, too knowing,
told too rich a tale – but early in January 1954 its details were
greedily recalled when Edward Montagu, his cousin Michael
Pitt-Rivers and his friend Peter Wildeblood were all arrested for
sexual offences committed with the airmen well over a year earlier
and, significantly, months before the scouts came into play. This
second trial, for more than half a century known as The Montagu
Trial and notorious as a tipping point in the long slow change in
the attitudes of society and the law to homosexuality, ended on
24 March 1954 with all the defendants sent to gaol (the airmen
were prosecution witnesses).

National Service as a Subaltern

As Beaulieu was on our doorstep, so to speak, these matters were of more than national interest, they were intensely local; moreover, Montagu and his friends were scarcely older than the battalion's subalterns and the airmen could as easily have been its soldiers. For three full months we spoke of the second trial and the supposed offences with apprehension, awe and dread; could any of us nurture affections or desires that cut across the barriers of rank so carefully maintained in the army or betray the barriers of class outside it? It was unthinkable – except that I had thought it, and with the pretty private who played servant in our Mess. We subalterns were, on the one hand, dutifully appalled, and on the other as dutifully amused by the cruel and brutal humour of the jokes and riddles with which the Mess was awash – the heterosexual imagination is remarkably filthier when the homosexual is the victim of its jibes. At these we guffawed, and I, ashamed of joining in, felt myself to be a pusillanimous little shit. It was all very well for me to play the celibate, but I knew my nature and knew too how easily my celibacy would have evaporated given a Beaulieu opportunity. The legal and social penalties loaded onto Edward Montagu were the harsh punishments of the day, though had he and his friends been of lower social status they would undoubtedly have been harsher; for me they were a terrifying warning.[2]

2 See Lord Montagu of Beaulieu: *Wheels within Wheels*, Weidenfeld and Nicolson, 2000. Peter Wildeblood: *Against the Law*, 1955, republished 1999.

CHAPTER 8

The Courtauld Institute

In so far as sex can ever be the last thing on a young man's mind, so it was with me when I returned to the Courtauld Institute in October 1954. I was fortunate to have this second chance, for I knew that my first had been utterly wasted through my immaturity, through the many diversions that so frequently interrupted study, and through my failure to recognise, at first, the high seriousness of art history as an academic discipline. In my defence, however, I must argue that when that recognition eventually dawned, it was the most powerful instrument in my decision to cut short and start again. The Institute, physically tiny in its home in Portman Square, was capable of managing a student body of only thirty or forty at a time, which meant a very small annual intake of undergraduates – in 1954 it was a dozen – and on my previous performance its decision-makers would have been perfectly justified in taking the view that, while all other applicants for places might be brilliant, they knew very well that I was not. Why then accept me? Much affected by their decision, I was determined to reward them with, at the very least, hard work and loyalty. In this I was particularly supported by one fellow student.

A very different animal from the callow boy of my first incarnation at the Courtauld – a young man now, confident and capable, the perfect example of one for whom National Service had brought extraordinary benefit – in Jill Rigden I found my perfect match. Much the same age, born in Abadan in April 1932, where her father had been a power in the politics and management of Anglo-Persian arrangements over oil, thus providing a background that lent strength to her natural confidence (some students thought it bossiness, and later, that is exactly what it became), she came to the Institute after three fruitless years at St Martin's School of Art. Like me, having profited from the practice of painting, she had abandoned it. We had no particular ambition to become art historians in any conventional sense – that is toilers in museums or teachers on the lower slopes of Academe – indeed, Jill's plans were completely unformed and mine were gradually hardening in the notion that I should become a priest, a vocation in which some serious knowledge of the ancestral arts might be peripherally useful – but swiftly both of us were moulded, wholly and completely, by the Institute.

Twenty Portman Square was the perfect ivory tower for a course of study that, though well established in Germany, Italy and France, had scarcely been acknowledged in England. Here the history of art, its criticism and connoisseurship, had always been a field ploughed by amateurs with literary ambitions anxious to reiterate their received and conventional opinions in prose often more suited to light romantic fiction. Built on the north side of the square for the widowed Countess of Home (pronounced Hume) in the later 1770s by Robert Adam, it was a great house in small for the woman nicknamed the Queen of Hell, with seven wonderfully decorated rooms, the magical staircase at its core ingeniously shifting its axis from narrower north-south to shallower but wider east-west between the ground and first floors, making the house seem larger and lighter as one climbs it. Confined within a cylinder, lit by a glass lantern in its delicately plastered dome, a straight free-standing flight of thirteen steps divides at the thirteenth into wings that cling close to the curved walls; from ground level, perspective dictates that these appear to rise more steeply than they do, as though they are the wings of a great bird on the point of taking flight. I can think of other, grander, staircases that offer as pressing an invitation to climb, but none for which the words wing and flight are more precisely and poetically applicable; even on a drab winter morning the light and lift of this staircase exalted my spirit after half an hour cycling through the fog. Students in my last year as an undergraduate, thinking to offer entertainment more amusing than the annual garden party given for the staff, thought to perform the daring obscenities of *Lysistrata* on these stairs, but could neither muster enough heroic women nor find space enough in the hall below to accommodate the audience.

In the years just before Home House became the Courtauld Institute, it had been the private residence of Samuel Courtauld and his family. With other acts of munificent generosity he had transferred his lease to house the fledgling athenaeum and in my first incarnation there it seemed that he and his family were still the occupiers and we were mischievous squatters for the day. This was occasionally reinforced by the appearance of Courtauld's daughter, Sydney, wistfully drifting through the pretty rooms, settling longest in the Blue Room on the second floor, her old bedroom hung with hand-painted Chinese wallpaper. Her husband, R.A. Butler, was rumoured to have seized much of Sam Courtauld's furniture when the takeover took place, but there was still enough of the heavy mahogany to give a flavour of his occupation. To the fury of Anthony Blunt, Butler proved the rumour true in 1959 when, five years after Sydney's death, he married Mollie Montgomerie, the widow of her cousin Augustine Courtauld, and made new (and successful) demands for more of his former father-in-law's furniture. Only once before, when defending me from André Chastel's public vituperation over some point of seventeenth century scholarship, had I seen him trembling with cold rage. When I asked why he had given way to Butler, he simply said that he had to; I have since wondered how much Butler may have known of Anthony's then hidden life.

By 1954 the house seemed less a home with a pervading air of domestic wear and tear. The library had grown (and continued to grow) and the faded grandeurs of Adam's exquisite interiors inexorably disappeared behind racks of iron shelves painted a grim khaki green, the files of glass slides and other evidence of functions essential to an institute of academe. The most prominent of these abuses, in the sense that it was open to all passers-by and adjacent to the Students' Common Room, was the marble bathroom on the second floor, a place of homage to the dreams of Alma-Tadema, but roofed with glass and so cold in winter that the chill oozed from it to cleave the warm air of the antiquated central heating system in the passage outside; in it there was just jostling-room for the mittened secretaries to perform, like animals in a menagerie, the daily drudgeries of a university department. We students wondered how the wealthy Courtaulds could ever have tolerated such extravagant discomfort.

Every inch of the house was occupied by books or people. Blunt held state in the first floor ante-room overlooking Portman Square, his rare and esoteric painting by Antoine Caron, a painter then 'enjoyng a rather exaggerated popularity' – as he put in 1953 – but now again forgotten, over the mantelpiece; on either side of it he kept much of his extraordinary collection of original source books from the seventeenth and eighteenth centuries, and to these we had immediate access during his tutorials on Philibert de l'Orme and François Mansart, the two French architects to whom he was attached emotionally as much as mathematically. Johannes Wilde, his *éminence grise* and deputy director, revealed the mysteries of Titian and Rubens in the Etruscan Room overlooking the garden, an interior of such daring imagination and intense colour that Cézanne's *Card Players* over the mantelpiece seemed dulled to a Sickertian sludge (though the cold north light may have had something to do with that). Immediately next door, Elsa Scheerer, their shared secretary and the dragon who protected them and ordered their lives, chain-smoked and typed and tele-phoned in a tiny octagonal ante-room as prettily decorated as the interior of a Georgian sewing-box.

Margaret Whinney, fondly nick-named Dame Margaret, maid of all work but the third power in this land and the high priestess to whom girl students took their emotional as well as academic troubles, occupied a bleak room above Anthony's, her secretary

The 'magical staircase' the core of 20 Portman Square built on the north side
of the square for the widowed Countess of Home in the later 1770s by
Robert Adam – the home of the Courtauld Institute

The north front of Home House and *below* the door to the music room, the main library.

squeezed into a narrow slot of a space that had been a lavatory (the Queen of Hell had evidently not been prepared, for all her Jamaican sugar millions, to pay Adam to decorate rooms that her admirers would not see). Charles Clare kept his Registrar's notes and accounts on the backs of envelopes in the pantry next to the service lift, and students crowded in what had been the second north-facing bedroom, dominated since his death in 1934, by the collection bequeathed by Roger Fry, the most pontifical, vain-glorious, grandiloquent, superficial and, unfortunately, influential of all English art critics. We ate our sandwiches and drank our tea in the company of Sickert, Bonnard and Vanessa Bell, an African fetish figure and a mask, and by the door our touching farewells wore away the patina of a substantial bronze by Renoir. In two glass-fronted cupboards flanking the fireplace were his examples of ancient and ethnic pottery that, for reasons traditional but never understood, the students' President and Secretary were required once a year to wash; I shall never forget the horror of feeling an unglazed pot of Assyrian antiquity dissolve into a muddy sludge slipping from the fingers of my left hand.

Lectures were given in the former ballroom, paintings by Fra Bartolommeo and Camille Pissarro at risk from careless shoulders, illustrated by old-fashioned monochrome glass slides of which thousands were stored in the neighbouring reception room, Cézanne's *Lac d'Annecy* its most glorious embellishment. Only in the basement were students deprived of Sam Courtauld's paintings, but the only reasons for being there were to read bound volumes of *English Homes*, a serious architectural supplement to *Country Life*, use the dedicated loos in the chill and moulering cubicles under the garden paving, or to be bound on some errand to the Winkles, the caretaker and his wife. Winkle, a heavily-built old sailor with all an old sailor's wiles, stoked a fiery boiler big enough to accommodate Shadrach, Meshach and Abednigo, and occasionally changed a washer, replaced a sash-cord, or refixed a rod on the slippery threadbare carpet of the servants' staircase that the students, the lift forbidden them, were compelled to use (down this I found that, with feet rigid at an angle of 45 degrees or so, I could, as it were, ski at great speed if wearing shoes with well-worn leather soles). He gave the impression that nothing was beyond his skills and yet, with a snail's sense of immediacy, did very little. Mrs Winkle's only evident responsibility was the provision of tea for staff and students every afternoon and for both she baked delicious cakes, though never quite enough. If ever we bumped into her she responded to our greetings with complaints about her feet – and well she might, for within her rumpled stockings and slippers down-at-heel, they were as much distorted by excrescences as any pair of Jerusalem artichokes or roots of ginger. Never throwing away anything that might be useful, the Winkles lived in squirrel squalour beyond imagining until a favoured student was allowed a glimpse.

The Winkles and the discomforts of Home House were the farcical elements in a serene comedy. The house was so beautiful inside and out that chaining my bicycle to its railings seemed an act of worship, an uplifting prelude to the activities within, and to climb the stairs and find my way to my adopted table in the far corner of the music room – the main library – was as improving a ritual as any in *The Magic Flute*. I am convinced that Robert Adam's architecture, mathematically Mozartian (three months apart their deaths) was a significant contribution to the aesthetic sensibility of every Courtauld student and to the rapid establishment of the Institute as briefly the greatest school of art history, not only in England – where it had no competition – but in the post-war world. It was not always so. Its pre-war reputation was as a finishing school for well-to-do girls (the boys were few) and no early survivor is left to deny the belief that the Institute closed for Ascot Week. With staff and director drawn from other academic disciplines, teaching was flawed by the amateurism of their interest in art history, and by 1936, that is within four years, London University, to which it was affiliated, had concluded that its academic standards were embarrassingly poor. The following year, its first Director,

W. G. Constable, resigned to take up a career as Curator of Paintings at the Boston Museum of Fine Arts and gain celebrity as the first blind man to become the world's premier authority on Canaletto. Poor Canaletto: Constable, known worldwide as W. G., even after decades of delving into the differences between prime originals, contemporary copies, variants, versions, later imitations and downright forgeries, still could never tell t'other from which, and J. G. Links, who sought to make sense of the confusions that rendered his two volumes of Catalogue Raisonné almost useless, proved only to be another over-affectionate amateur without the necessary eye. Their combined efforts are of value only to the art dealer happy to gull the collector into believing that he has bought an original backed by the as yet unreplaced expert opinion of Constable and Links. Constable was succeeded as Director by Tom Boase, an Oxford medieval history don who knew even less about the history of art. That the Institute was not closed was due to his shrewd reorganisation of its degree courses and his invitation to scholars from the Warburg Institute to teach them.

How can I describe so wonderful a thing as the Warburg in a single paragraph? Aby Warburg was a German art historian whose interests lay as much in the history of ideas, science and such more popular forms of culture as ritual, folk memory, astrology and magic. In 1926 his formidable private library in Hamburg was converted into a public research institute, Die Kulturwissenschaftliche Bibliotek, but, as Warburg (who died three years later) and most of his assistants there were Jewish, it was moved, lock, stock and barrel, to London in 1933, to settle under Collcutt's Tower in the old Imperial Institute; it was incorporated into London University in 1944, there to become a beacon of scholarship of an arcane kind without precedent in British academe, Ernst Gombrich its most celebrated luminary.[3]

3 For a sympathetic evocation of Warburg himself, his scholarship, his madness, his 'Hamlet-like psychology', his manic depression and his genius, one should turn to Bernd Roeck: *Florence 1900, The Quest for Arcadia*, Yale University Press, 2009.

The Courtauld Institute

Anthony Blunt, so far self-taught as an art historian, 'never', as he observed at the time to Gertrude Bing (the most undeservedly forgotten of the Warburg's early staff) 'having had any training in *Kunstgeschichte* at all . . . ,' joined it as general editor of its publications and began work there in September 1937; his next step was to offer the Courtauld Institute his services as a teacher, hoping for a permanent post. In March 1939 he was appointed the Deputy Director there, but with the advent of war Home House was closed for two years – and might as well have been closed for six. From the autumn of 1939 all the functions of the Institute fell into the hands of Margaret Whinney; it was at first evacuated to Guildford Technical College, but she and the few remaining students returned to Portman Square late in 1941 and bumbled on into desuetude. In 1940 only two students graduated, only one a year between 1942 and 1944, and fourteen in all before 1947, the first year in which graduates might reflect the influence of Blunt.

In April 1945, the war a month from its conclusion, Anthony was appointed Surveyor of the King's Pictures, succeeding Kenneth Clark; he also set about the task of re-opening the Courtauld and organising an academic year to begin in October. When Tom Boase returned from a posting in the Middle East in August, it was for little more than a year as Director; he resigned his post early in 1947 to become President of Magdalen College, Oxford. Anthony was at once appointed his successor and began the task of transforming the underfunded, academically obscure and scarcely reputable Institute into a school of art history that would rival, equal and surpass all the schools of *Kunstgeschichte* and *Kunstwissenschaft* long established in Germany and central Europe. When he moved into the rambling flat in the attic that was his post's most desirable perquisite, Home House became the place not only where he lived and worked, but had his being, and the house provided the perfect atmosphere for both the man and his academic ideals. Anthony was later to claim that he could not imagine the Institute in any other setting, and I cannot imagine it under any subsequent director – with the exception of Michael Kitson (of whom more later) who was not appointed to that post. It was a Cambridge College in small, utterly civilised, hung with masterpieces, dedicated to the cultivation of aptitude and intellect, ideas and reason, in a field so far from a precise science that most panjandrums of London University could comprehend neither how great a gift the Institute had been nor the great gifts it might bestow – that is with the exception of Lionel Robbins, long a professor at the London School of Economics, already recognised as great and good, whose chairmanship of the Institute's Management Committee was a step on the way to trusteeships of the National and Tate Galleries. Physically as tall as Anthony but twice his weight, with a hint of the working-class bruiser about him, Robbins was unaccountably as besotted with him as the half-dozen aging spinsters of the Institute who unreservedly and unrequitedly adored him; the cynic might mistakenly attribute this to Robbins' undoubted social climbing, but to me it seemed the honest devotion of the dog. With considerable cunning he acted as Anthony's protector from enemies and detractors within the machinery of the University.

Under Anthony's wing the Institute attracted the greatest scholars of the post-war years. Lectures, seminars and tutorials were given by Demus, Grabar, Kurz, Buchthal, Wittkower, Gerson, Van Gelder, Clark, Pope-Hennessy, Ettlinger, Gombrich, Frances Yates, Greta Ring and a host of other international luminaries, many of them drawn to London by some business with the Warburg Institute with which the Courtauld shared a learned journal, the association lending it formidable academic respectability worldwide. For students the atmosphere was as forcing as a gardener's hothouse, as puritanical and conditioning as a monastery (and as chaste), encouraging in most of them minds closed to any career that did not involve the further pursuit of art history.

Over three years the syllabus covered the Renaissance from just before Giotto to just after Michelangelo, a long period of English art that spanned either from the Dark Ages to circa 1550 or from

1550 to the then present day, and a special period that could be Byzantine, Romanesque, Gothic or any post-Renaissance century. With luck the courses fell – as they did for me – in that order, locking together chronologically so that when the special period came in the third year, the student was most experienced and mature; the only flaw was that we were at our least mature when confronted with the Renaissance, the foundation stone of all that followed in western art, and had to make sense of not only Leonardo and Michelangelo, Raphael and Titian, but of Jan van Eyck and Roger van der Weyden, Bosch and Brueghel, Dürer and Holbein, the Schools of the Danube and Cologne. This syllabus provided a sound frame for any independent work the student chose to do – one who had specialised in the seventeenth century had no difficulty in tackling French Impressionism, for he was already aware of at least its bare bones from working on the New English Art Club and the Camden Town painters in his English year, nor in making sense of Neo-Classicism, for its antique sources were the same as those of the Italian Renaissance and the classicising branch of the Baroque.

That these were still the early years of the Institute makes Anthony's performance in his first decade as its Director (1947– 57) all the more extraordinary. He was, I am certain, talent- spotting. He could be distant with unpromising students, and enthusiastic, warm and generous with others. Never did I see him be unkind to one, with the exception of an American who, as the Professor of Art History at a very minor far provincial university, had chosen to spend a sabbatical year taking the Courtauld's undergraduate course in seventeenth-century art as a refresher; irredeemably dim-witted, he knew less than any of us, understood nothing and, as he could speak not one word of any continental European language, determinedly employed Churchillian mis- pronunciation. With him, Anthony did indeed lose patience. The professor, nicknamed The Ladykiller for his smarmy response to any woman within reach, lasted less than a term, and, feeling himself to have been gravely insulted during a tutorial on Borromini, left, taking with him the bossiest of the secretaries in the marble bathroom. Anthony was perhaps not displeased when students fell away at or before the end of the first year – of the dozen in mine, only six survived to take finals – for he was interested only in teaching those who might one day, even perhaps very soon, be members of a spreading Courtauld team, as it were, capable of holding every academic, administrative and curatorial post open to the art historian. For all sorts of reasons I was never to be one of them, but within weeks of my graduation he did not hesitate to shunt me off to University College to deliver in his stead a couple of lectures on Poussin, and to the University of Birmingham to unburden myself on the rest of seventeenth-century French painting. John White is a much more serious example of Anthony's fast-tracking a student – working for his PhD when I was in my first incarnation at the Institute, he achieved his doctorate in 1952, was immediately appointed Lecturer and was my first tutor there when I returned in 1954; my recollection is that Anita Brookner lectured us on Greuze while she was still working on her PhD; and Michael Kitson, six years my senior and my fellow BA student in 1950–52, was, between 1954 and 1957, one of the triumvirate of tutors who formed me as an art historian.[4]

Of these the first was Johannes Wilde. It was under his guidance that we were introduced to the greatest figures of the Italian Renaissance, yet he never once expressed impatience with the naivety, stupidity, laziness and incompetence of raw and jejune students so evidently drowning in the deep end of art history; the worst rebuke he ever delivered to any of my contemporaries was to John Acton, speaking nonsense of a Titian in the National Gallery – 'But Mr Acton, have you *seen* the painting?' That it was a

---

4 Of all these fast-tracked students, the most well-known now is Neil MacGregor, whom Anthony is reputed to have described as his most brilliant pupil.

rebuke when he said to me, again in a tutorial on Titian, 'Mr Sewell, you like dogs, I believe?' and then produced from a drawer in his desk photograph after photograph of Titian's dogs, from mastiff to muff-warmer, I was uncertain at the time and am so still, preferring to think of it as an instruction to enjoy the simple pleasure to be found in looking at paintings, or to share the private pleasures of the painter himself.

It was Johannes who taught me that though I must be 'humble before the facts,' art history is not merely the disciplined recounting of dates and documents, but an adventure into the spirit and humanity of man, and if I have any further insights into the work of Leonardo, Titian and Michelangelo, they spring from his profound sensibilities as well as from his immaculate scholarship. Tall and stooping, his hands a-tremble, his quirkily poetic English slow in delivery and heavy with the accents of Budapest and Vienna, his demands of us as first-year students were patiently formidable and, occasionally, gently humorous. He published very little, and the students who loved his gentle presence and infinitely subtle mind have only the texts of his lectures on Michelangelo and Venetian painting to support their fragile recollections.[5] In the course of many moves I have lost every essay and lecture note I wrote as a student and have no record – and scant recollection – of what, in my third year, he taught me in tutorials on Rubens, Rembrandt and Jan Steen; later, immediately after graduation, he was persuasive in his attempt to steer me towards Rubens as a subject for my PhD. As for the one northern artist with whom he dealt in my first year, Pieter Brueghel, extending my knowledge deep into the study of prints and drawings, the loss of these notes I regret more than any other.

'This veritable High Priest of *Kunstgeschichte*', as Peter Kidson, one of his earlier English apostles, put it – brought to the Courtauld

---

5 Michelangelo: *Six Lectures*, Clarendon Press, Oxford, 1978; *Italian Drawings, Michelangelo and his Studio*, British Museum, 1953; and *Venetian Art from Bellini to Titian*, Clarendon Press, Oxford, 1974.

the traditions, wisdom and practice of art history in German-speaking Europe. When Blunt brought him to the Institute in 1947 and appointed him Deputy Director the following year, he not only introduced the most important factor in the extraordinarily rapid growth of the international esteem in which it was held until Anthony's retirement in 1974, but made amends for the suspicion and mistrust that had led to Wilde's internment and deportation to Canada as an enemy alien during the war.

With Johannes we students felt that we were given the purest distillation of ideas and scholarship, and after his lectures and tutorials I felt much the same as I did after choral Mass, though communion with him was founded on demonstrable fact; in this faith did play a part in that, though Johannes encouraged us to reconsider the received wisdom of authority, we preferred to exempt him from such scepticism and enquiry, to accept his teaching as gospel, and believe.[6] The lectures and tutorials of Kitson and Blunt, the second and third of my triumvirate, were entirely different; both felt hesitantly spontaneous, even spasmodic in the sense of having seen in a photograph or a slide on the screen, something not in their notes but so important that it must immediately be discussed, leaving the remainder of the planned lecture undelivered. Anthony might recover enough to end with the suggestion that he would return to the original theme in the next lecture, but Michael either lapsed into silence after well over-running the declared hour, or mumbled a half-hearted 'Well, I'm sorry not to have finished, but if any of you . . . '

In tutorials, which both of them treated as open-ended – they began at 2.00 pm, paused at 4.00 for Mrs Winkle's tea and cakes, and then drew on until almost 7.00, when the Institute closed – if there was much more to be said, then we continued the following

6 For evidence of the devotion of his students see special editions of the *Burlington Magazine* in his honour, June 1961, and in his memory, March 1971.

day. Tutorial groups were very small – four at the most in the first year and perhaps only one in the third – and it was wonderfully exciting for students to be in lively exchange with such minds. In my last year, in a tutorial on François Mansart (one of Anthony's extreme enthusiasms), I made a casual observation that intrigued him, and within minutes groundplans and elevations had spread from the table to the floor and he was urging me to write a note for publication in the *Burlington Magazine*. I didn't, it wasn't, and I now have not the slightest recollection of what it was that so excited him. Anthony it was, of course, who steered me towards Poussin, the great *peintre-philosophe* who was his abiding love, and then opened my eyes to Vouet, La Hyre and Blanchard, to Georges de la Tour and the brothers Le Nain, and to such comparatively minor figures as Vignon and Stoskopff.

It must seem odd to the outsider that Claude was not one of Anthony's enthusiasms – too romantic, perhaps, and insufficiently philosophical and mathematical – but Michael Kitson had the perfect sensibility to deal with so poetic a painter. Claude, he wrote, 'is not a painter who offers instant sensations, . . . one of the great introverts in the history of art . . . his art is subtle, elusive; . . . subjective, it invites a subjective response.'[7] It is a wry thing that instead of becoming the world's acknowledged expert on the man, he was usurped in this by one of his Courtauld pupils, Marcel Röthlisberger; Michael was far too modest ever to nurture such an ambition and far too sweet-natured to be envious of Röthlisberger's success, but to the onlooker it was evident enough that his laurels had been snatched from him. Perhaps, if he had not been quite so conscientiously burdened with teaching at the Institute, his primacy with Claude might have been maintained. In his address at Michael's memorial service in 1998, Neil MacGregor described

7 *The Art of Claude Lorraine*, introduction to the exhibition catalogue, Arts Council 1969, reprinted in Michael Kitson, *The Seeing Eye* (a collection of his criticism), Mnemosyne Press, 2008.

him as 'the outstanding scholar critic of his generation, perhaps indeed of the century . . . a man not just respected, but loved . . . of unfailing courtesy of manner and seemingly inexhaustible generosity of spirit.' I recognise how closely, but far more clumsily, I have unconsciously followed him as a writer, and it is in part to him that I owe the range of interests that have enabled me to be a jobbing critic, for with him I tasted not only the divine elixir of Claude but the small beer of Wilkie and Mulready and the large beer of Turner. With Wilkie, Michael led me to the quotidian art of nineteenth-century Germany and an abiding interest in the Schools of Düsseldorf and Munich to which Picasso was attracted before he thought of Paris – but to open such doors is the way of the intelligent art historian.

CHAPTER 9

Student Life

My friendship with Jill Rigden lasted with much the same intensity – domination on her part, submission on mine – until her death in 1998. We were at once brought together by being put in the same tutorial group under John White whose duty he deemed to be to teach us method. This he did so aggressively and so much to the exclusion of any aesthetic excitement we might have experienced, that Jill dragooned the two other students in our group into supporting a minor rebellion. I, having said nothing of my earlier years at the Institute, when Peter Murray's mantra 'Students are the lowest form of life here' was too often heard, was content to let her lead it. We bearded him in his room where, standing himself, he kept us on our feet while Jill expressed her opinion that method could be taught in twenty minutes and be reinforced as we went along, and that what we wanted and needed more than his forensic examination of every shred of documentary evidence, was expanding familiarity with the works of art themselves in some sort of orderly framework. Warming to her attack, she asserted that we did not want to be bogged down with such obscurities as Tino da Camaino and Arnolfo di Cambio, on whom we had unprofitably wasted two tutorials. John White, tall, elegantly dressed and, I think, aghast at the assault, suddenly flung himself onto the settee behind him, a gesture that reduced us all to laughter, not because it was absurdly dramatic (though it was), but because the ancient bearskin that concealed the settee's rents and exuding stuffing could not stand the sudden strain and exploded into a cloud of loose hair that set us all wheezing and sneezing. No better device could have been conceived to ease the tension and, to give

John his due, subsequent tutorials were infinitely more instructive and enjoyable.

It was probably Jill who proposed that some of us should drive to Italy in the Easter break of 1955, though it could equally well have been the result of conversations in The Gondola, a coffee bar in Wigmore Street to which she and I repaired for a sixpenny cappuccino almost every morning. Soundings among other students whom we thought serious resulted in a party of six, for which Jill's tiny pink Austin A30 was too small and for such a journey my very large but very pre-war Wolseley might not be reliable. To our surprise we found that, so early in the season, we could hire a new Vauxhall Velox for £5 a week, with two bench seats and a gear-change lever on the steering column, and a hefty roof-rack for most of our luggage.

With my mother, who was always anxious to know my where-abouts, I left a sheet of paper pompously headed *The Grand Tour*, listing the main cities on our itinerary with approximate dates between 24 March and 1 May 1955, and the names of the students with whom I was to travel – Jill, Margaret Lake, John Acton, Alton Jenkins and Giles de la Bedoyère, to whose name I added the note 'Lives in Wimbledon with his father, who is editor of *The Catholic Herald*' in the belief that if anything was amiss at home he, of all people, would be able to trace us in Italy. Alton, American and the oldest of us, was far more practical and used American Express offices as places from which to pick up mail – to the rest of us this seemed astonishingly worldly-wise.

We stayed in Youth Hostels and very cheap hotels of a kind that lasted into the early Seventies but can now no longer be found. For emergencies we carried a one-man tent that I had kept from my army days, knowing that by lowering the ridge-poles and stretching the outriggers, the four boys could just squeeze into it, leaving the car's bench seats for the girls. Only once were we enough wretchedly situated to use it; making our way over the hills to Rimini by a very minor road on which our speed was little more than walking pace, darkness overtook us and we camped for the night. We should have reconnoitered, but we simply pulled off on a flat patch under trees, sure that we were in uninhabited territory; but we were not and our awakening in the morning was terrifying – men with shotguns shouting in a dialect none of us could understand (though we recognised the tenor of it) hauled us from the tent, while others hammered on the locked doors of the car. For a minute or two, rape and murder seeming imminent, we were seriously scared, but our repeated apologies (and perhaps the fact that there were six of us, six witnesses to any intended crime) eventually calmed the men and they bundled us and our baggage higgledy-piggledy into the car and sent us on our way.

Within an hour we reached the coast road and turned north, Rimini almost in sight, and were astonished to encounter road-racing cars whistling past us towards the south. Then we were chased by a police car and forced off the road. On its very day we were on the course of the Mille Miglia race, and as all lateral roads had been closed we had to explain how we had got there – down a farm track, it seemed. We were then cautiously conducted into Rimini and spent the rest of the day minutely examining the Tempio Malatestiana, a gothic church dedicated to the poverty and piety of St Francis, reconstructed (but unfinished) as an almost pagan temple commemorating the depraved Sigismondo Malatesta and Isotta, the illicit love of his life.

The first Youth Hostel of the journey, in Rheims, stank everywhere of urine, and boys were separated from girls only by filthy blankets hanging from a rope across the room. In Dijon we found lodgings with a family who fed us on bread and lentil soup (it was Friday and in Lent) and then put the four boys in one vast bed in which we were all savaged by bed-bugs. In Switzerland the hostels were clinically clean, but by then we all had lice; the eyebrows of the female pharmacist in Basel to whom we sheepishly explained our trouble – seeing that we were six – could not have risen further. Years later, by then working for Christie's, after a week in

Paris inspecting paintings offered the firm for sale, I caught crabs again and, even more sheepishly, went to the august chemist in St James's Street; there, however, crabs were not a matter for stricture and disgrace, and the response of the man behind the counter when I fumblingly apologised for the nature of my errand was a hearty 'Oh don't you worry,' and, holding up a bottle of white liquid, 'all my gentlemen come to me for this.' Really? – I wondered; all those eminent gentlemen in White's and Boodle's?

That we reached Milan in the early hours of the morning was the consequence of an hilarious confusion over trains through the Simplon Tunnel, for at Brig we put the car on the right one to Domodossola, but, after a drink in the station café, ourselves on another going God knows where. As this added hours to our journey and we were far too late to find our sort of hotel open, Jill decided that in Milan we should spend the rest of the night in the baths of the main railway station. I fell asleep in mine and awoke in tepid water to find a fierce concièrge in a white apron shaking my shoulder, while my companions looked on my nakedness as the sons of Noah did on his. In Florence we stayed in the Piazza Santa Maria Novella where, in the Pensione Santa Lucia, the famiglia Brogi gave the girls a small bedroom and, for the boys, abandoned their living room with its great ceiling beams and frescoed decorations – it was the *gran salone* of a small palazzo – and added four truckle beds to the furniture. It was an act of extraordinary kindness, for it gave all six of us room to sit and read, write, talk and play, at Jill's insistence, Canasta.

We had been advised by older students to stay, in Assisi, at the Convent of the American Nuns; a plump and ruddy nun opened the door and, before I could ask for rooms, welcomed me with 'Gee, if it isn't little Lord Fauntleroy,' followed by a gale of laughter. In Venice too we had good fortune, again advised by older students, in finding an apartment on the Giudecca – then the city's least visited quarter, working class and down at heel – in finding an apartment occupied by a penniless Englishwoman, a lost soul who retreated to her bedroom and let us have the run of the rest of it. In the Fifties, for the benefit of workers, the ferry across the Bacino to the Riva degli Schiavone was free if boarded before eight in the morning, and as we were by then in a penny-pinching state, this was a useful discipline in rising early to get on with our art history studies – though we hardly needed it, for the objective in undertaking the journey was the single-minded business of putting flesh on the bones of what we had seen in poor quality coloured reproductions and the monochrome photographs and slides with which lectures and tutorials were illustrated.

The great benefit of the car was that we could see things invariably missed when travelling by train – thus it was that we saw the quirkily beautiful cathedral at Laon, Claus Sluter's *Well of Moses* in Champmol and his *Weepers* (touching embodiments of grief) in the museum in Dijon, *The Miraculous Draught of Fishes* by Konrad Witz in Geneva and the Holbein drawings in Basel. Jill and I were alone in looking at these last and we became increasingly uneasy with what seemed their lifeless quality – that is until one of the warders, understanding our chatter, haltingly explained that they were facsimiles and took us to a curator; she, enthusiastic soul, opened the solander boxes in which the real things lay. For both of us it was a lesson, partly in essential conservation, but more in the need always to question everything that rouses a misgiving. A mesh of scepticism through which to filter what he sees, is the art historian's first defence against the excitements, delusions, assertions and deceits of his peers, for without informed scepticism, he is their dupe.

There were benefits too in the journeying itself, for the laden Vauxhall with three of us on each bench seat, luggage under our feet and more cases on the roof nullifying the few aerodynamic features known to the designers of its body, was most at ease when lolloping along at less than fifty miles an hour. This let us look at landscape, let us see, for example, what Konrad Witz had seen on the journeys between Basel and Geneva that inspired him to paint a topographically accurate view of the Lake in 1444, that most of us believe to have been the first portrayal of a real landscape in the centuries of the Renaissance. In Italy the physical changes in land-scape between the valley of the Po and Tuscany, Tuscany and Umbria, Umbria and the Marches, lent us insight into the political rivalries of the Renaissance, the frequent journeyings of artists between the influential centres of painting, sculpture and archi-tecture, the discovery and development of aerial perspective, and the conscious use of observed landscape as the setting for a martyr-dom or crucifixion. At another level there was the thrill of cresting the hill at Fiesole or San Miniato al Monte, thence to look down into the great bowl of land in which the city of Florence lies, or of following the winding road from Arezzo to Borgo San Sepolcro to see Piero della Francesca's *Resurrection* and his *Madonna del Parto* at Monterchi; to see Assisi, Siena, Orvieto and Todi from a distance was to experience beautiful astonishments. In the Fifties, Italian towns and cities were much as they had been for centuries; they had no urban fringes, no crass and jarring new developments outside their ancient city walls, and we drove into them with the insouciance of those who know that they will have no difficulty in parking, for every town square had spaces dedicated to the cars of tourists. We parked within yards of Leonardo's *Last Supper* in Milan, Giotto's Arena Chapel in Padua, the Palazzo Diamante in Ferrara and the great church of San Petronio in Bologna; such feats are now impossible.

Alton, Jill and I did the driving; Giles, the Dormouse of this party, had a license but only once was he allowed to take the wheel, so hideously crunching were his attempts to change the gears. Alton drove like every American, relaxed, angled against the door, one hand on the wheel. Jill accelerated hard and slipped the clutch so much that by the time we reached Milan it had to be relined. By the grace of God there was a General Motors garage in the city and by dint of using Opel parts the work could be done within a morning – and that morning provided me with what remains the most exhilarating drive of my life, though I have since driven much faster. Just as I settled down to read a book for a couple of hours, a mechanic took pity on me: a Gullwing Mercedes 300 SL had just been delivered from Stuttgart and he was required to take this exquisite paradigm of aerodynamics for a test run; would I care to come, he asked. He put a clipboard of data in my hand, saw me into the passenger seat, and off we tore, up the autostrada to Como, ticking off the kilometres in seconds, to chuck it about on the corniche to Bellagio, and then race back to Milan through Monza. For that experience, the two seats snug and low, with no room even for a lapdog, the roar of an engine reaching 6,000 rpm with every single revolution of it communicated to the cabin, a mile a minute reached within a twinkling (in eight seconds I know now) and a speedometer calibrated in too few kilometres to outdo the ambitions of the needle (we beat 200 kilometres an hour, more than twice the Vauxhall's maximum without a load), I have ever since been grateful. When, in the spring of 2005, half a century on, I again witnessed the Mille Miglia, no longer a race but an endurance test for geriatric machinery, no fewer than twenty-four Gullwings were paraded, and they looked as thrilling, beautiful and astonishing as ever.

When the Vauxhall was on the move over a long distance, one of us read aloud from an odd assortment of books on which, to eliminate duplicates, we had agreed. We took pocket editions of Berenson on Italian painting, Blunt on Italian artistic theory, Burckhardt on Italian civilisation and other necessaries; the only outsider book that I can remember was a slim volume of poems by T. S. Eliot brought by John Acton, that, had it included *Old Possum's Practical Cats*, I would have stolen and thrown away, but this he knew by heart and could not be persuaded that a crowded Vauxhall was no place for his thumping, gesturing, booming delivery, much too often repeated. As semi-outsiders I took as many essays as I could find by Aldous Huxley, for among them I knew his subversive interpretations of El Greco, Brueghel, Vermeer and Conxolus, and with these I hoped to sow seeds of sedition. I also took Bocaccio's *Decameron* and this proved a suitable companion for our only languourous day in all the weeks we were away; it was Good Friday, a day on which every museum in Florence was closed and half the citizens were on their knees at Tenebrae, a beautiful melancholy service of Holy Week that had survived unchanged since the Middle Ages but was to be changed after 1955. Had I known that this was its last unmodernised year, I too might have spent the day in church; instead, finding what we could for a picnic, we drove out into the countryside and lay in the sun, quaffing Chianti and listening to unexpurgated tales of love, lust, deception and murder.

From the very beginning of the journey, though in the evening we ate proper dinner, picnic breakfasts and lunches were the order of the day – bread, 200 grams of mortadella and 200 of cheese, fruit, wine and water; looking back, I am astonished that six young adults could be content with so little, but in England we were still accustomed to the frugalities of post-war rationing and seemed unable to take advantage of the casual plenty that was everywhere in Italy. There were occasional extravagances; in Milan, after the episode of the baths, we were tempted by the little dishes of trippa Milanese that stood on the counters of coffee bars; in the shade of an arcade in Bologna we lunched on saltimbocca that we could not sensibly afford and drank Lambrusco; and in Mantua, as a breakfast delicacy with great bowls of milky coffee (an addiction for which, if necessary, I would go hungry) we were given a dish of fritto misto, dredged from the lake, the waiter said, that had in it as many infant newts and frogs as minnows. In Florence, in the shade of Ognissanti, we bought glasses of wine from an old man carrying flasks of red and white Chianti on a yoke, dunking the glasses in a bucket of water, and in this simple thing sensed some direct connection with the Quattrocento, imagining that just such a peasant in a yoke was there when Donatello installed his homage to the handsome boy, *St George*, in one of its several external niches. In Assisi, at the end of a long day trying to make sense of who did what and when in the too extensive decoration of the upper and lower churches – a viral obsession for John White and other students of his generation at the Courtauld, for whom the answers have proved more elusive than the solution of the last theorem of Pierre de Fermat – we came upon a man roasting a whole pig; into generous cornets of rolled paper he sliced slivers of flesh and crackling from it, and then plunged his arm deep into the carcass for a handful of chopped onion and sage – that his hands were filthy mattered not at all as we sat eating on a wall with the sunset plain stretching to the west beneath us. Again we felt the past, felt that we were doing exactly what had been done six centuries before by the painters of the frescoes in the gloomy lower church after a day of mixing plaster and clambering about on scaffolding to illuminate for an illiterate peasantry the life of Christ and the miracles of St Francis. And in Venice, tempted by the warm spring sun as we got off the boat from the Giudecca, Jill and I broke away from the others, sat on the Riva degli Schiavone and drank the viscous hot chocolate that is unique to La Serenissima before taking off for our duties among the city's churches – a small event of which the sentimental recollection years later and after Jill's death, brought me to unquenchable tears.

What were the qualities in Jill that so affected me? At first it was perhaps the sense that at the Courtauld we were both in the same boat, that we had both wasted too much time on ambitions that were will-o'-the-wisps and that this, the Courtauld, was a now or never opportunity to make something of our lives. We were both adults with some sense of financial security in that Jill's rich father gave her an allowance, and I, having spent my army savings on a handsome car – a Wolseley 25 of 1936 – had volunteered it and my services to a nearby chauffeur-driven hire service and thus earned money at weekends as a standby minicab driver, occasionally very well tipped if not well paid. We had, in addition, the grants that were then given to almost every university student. And we both had interests beyond the walls of Academe – though mine, apart from motor cars, were largely connected with the visual arts. Even when I was in the army I had, whenever possible, continued to trawl the art dealers of Bond Street, and I now took Jill with me to share the rich and various experience to be gained there. We went, too, to the auction houses, and in the week of the Rees Jeffreys sale at Christie's in November 1954 – that is very early in our relationship – I dragged her, John Acton and Alton Jenkins to see his *Portrait of Derain* by Matisse, so convinced was I that this beautiful picture would be bought by an American collector or museum, never to be seen again (it was, however, bought by the Tate). Apart from the Winter Exhibitions at the Royal Academy, this was not a period of blockbusters, and as the Tate, the National and National Portrait Galleries were impoverished and somnolent, we depended for enlightenment on the annual exhibitions of the Edinburgh Festival brought south by the Arts Council, on the occasional small shows mounted by the Arts Council in their elegant premises in St James's Square, and on what art dealers were prepared to show us. We depended particularly on Colnaghi's, Agnew's and Matthiessen's, but many smaller dealers, working from rooms on first and second floors, were sources of intriguing backwater knowledge and Jill became almost as voraciously enquiring as I.

The Italian journey cemented our relationship. Of the group, Jill and I were the most greedily determined to see everything, to buy the slim limp catalogues bound in pale blue paper published by the *Ministero della Pubblica Istruzione*, with monochrome illustrations the size of postage stamps crowded four to a page (in 1955 no one had thought of vastly expensive encyclopedic catalogues) and to collect the blurred post cards offered by the churches. We were unflagging. For John Acton cigarettes were the most important things in his life – he never had more than one hand available; Alton was languidly and beautifully at ease with himself and had no sense of urgency; young Giles was far more theologically than art historically interested in what we saw and had the makings of an earnest dilettante constantly diverted by irrelevances; only Margaret shared anything of our imperturbable high seriousness but was too often inclined to drift and dream. On our return Jill and I were as loosely connected with them as before.

One morning early in the Summer Term Jill came to me in the library and, in more peremptory tone than usual, commanded me to accompany her to The Gondola at once – 'I have something to say to you.' Not until we were there would she give me an inkling of what it was and then said, without preamble, 'David proposed to me last night.' I knew of David – David Allibone – an ambitious young solicitor with whom she had been involved for some time, and asked if she had accepted him. 'Well no. I need to know what you intend to do.' I had never thought of Jill in such a sense and wondered what on earth had given her the impression that marriage was even a remote possibility. But for carrying her over my shoulder across a piazza near the university in Padua and dumping her on the roof rack of the Vauxhall – it was after dinner, we were both a little drunk and I was driven on by the applause of students, one of whom began to sing La Donna e mobile – we had had no physical contact of any kind and the only sexual trigger to disturb my celibacy of many months had been no thought of her, but a moment in the youth hostel in Basel when, sleeping on the top bunk, I had looked down to see Alton in the lower, serenely and a-sexually beautiful and had longed to touch so sculptural a face. I fumbled my reply, aware that to blurt that I had never thought of marriage might be insulting, and at the same time unwilling to let slip that I was queer. A day or two later, with carefully prepared delicacy, The Gondola was witness to my telling Jill that I had plans in which marriage and children could play no part, that priesthood was my intention. Within a year or so she married David and was eight months pregnant when we sat our Finals in June 1957.

What was this haunting intention to become a priest? What was the source of it? It was partly a resolution of my theological uncertainty as a boy, a rejection of the low church banalities preached at Haberdashers', a recognition that if I believed any of its infallibilities, myths and miracles, then I must believe all – there must be no Church of England halfway house and I must be a Roman Catholic, reason utterly and comfortably suspended in belief. Such a surrender was an attractive proposition, simple, uncluttered and unquestioning, sans argument. It must also have been a response to my homosexuality, offering the comfort that no one would question the unmarried state of a priest in the camouflage of a cassock, and I was convinced that prayer would protect me from any temptations offered by altar boys, servers or other priests, for I had managed to be abstinent, at least in deed, since the rape in Aldershot – and in that I had been the mute object and in no sense a responsive participant. I attended occasional retreats; at these I observed other young men who, from indications to which I was scarcely attuned – excessive piety and a superstitious response to the slavery of ritual, perhaps – I thought might be similarly troubled; what, I wondered, might be the temptations of the seminary? From a letter received in June 1956, it is clear that I had by then taken official steps to train for the priesthood and been accepted as having a vocation; the writer advised me that, though recognising the need to work for my degree at the Courtauld, I should also make time for close study of the texts of the Bible and Apocrypha, and make a start with elementary Greek and, by extension, Aramaic. I did nothing of the kind. With the year of my special period by then immediately ahead – Rubens, Rembrandt, Velazquez, Caravaggio, Poussin, Claude, Bernini and the vast landscape of the Roman Baroque – how could I turn my mind to a dead Semitic language and give it precedence?

In the summer break of 1955 I immediately had work to do. Frederick P. Bargebuhr, a professor at Iowa State University, was in London to work on a paper to be published in the Journal of the Warburg and Courtauld Institutes and required a research assistant. That he had given me the job I again had Charles Clare to thank, though Charles knew perfectly well that, apart from my command of English, I had not the slightest qualification for helping Bargebuhr, whose subject was eventually whittled down to *The Alhambra Palace of the Eleventh Century*.[8] It is a measure of the man that to an article 45 pages long he appended 22 pages of notes, and that tucked into the offprint that he sent to me 'With much appreciation and a cordial good-bye,' were nine more foolscap pages close-typed with corrigenda and addenda that had escaped publication.

When he returned to America his final version of the paper was at least twice as long. In broad terms the subject was the interaction of Jewish and Arabic cultures in Moorish Spain late in the first millennium, its emphasis primarily on gardens, water, fountains, sculptured lions and poetry, but as Bargebuhr was a scholar who could never jettison a notion, no matter how peripheral, on all these matters he was likely to leap as far back as the Chaldeans for a precedent, or forward to demonstrate the continuing influence of Arabic culture in Spain in the eighteenth century – the last of his published footnotes is, absurdly, a quotation from Théophile Gautier.

It was on the poetry that he wished me to concentrate. In Arabic and Hebrew, Bargebuhr was as accomplished as in his native German, but his English was profoundly flawed. After tidying the main text to make it less excruciatingly unreadable, the tedium of re-typing it with all Near Eastern accents added by hand quite maddening, it was my duty to render the poetry into rhyming verse. Whether or not the verses rhymed in Arabic and Hebrew, I could not tell, but he was determined that they should in English. He translated them into German; I then translated the German into English and wrestled it into forms that not even William McGonagall could excel, but he had neither ear nor eye for scansion and was happy when it rhymed. Much of this was done in the Warburg Institute, within earshot of Joseph Trapp, later its Director,

8 *Journal of the Warburg and Courtauld Institutes*, Vol. XIX 1956, Nos. 3–4.

trying his renowned good humour to such a degree that he found a lightless cupboard in which to sequester us. When the paper was at last published I wondered if he, as one of the Journal's six editors, had taken revenge by slashing the length of Bargebuhr's prolix text and abandoning my rhymes in favour of direct translation.

In the early Sixties when I had Rubens on my mind and still nursed the faint hope of academic scholarship, I was, I felt, the only visitor to the Warburg to be greeted by Trapp with a scowl. If I learned not to be noisy in libraries – a thing I already knew – the more useful lesson was the importance of diligence in copy editing and proof reading, though I did not realise it at the time; I also learned not to be disappointed when not thanked in print for working as a dogsbody – such acknowledgements are of great value to those at the bottom of the heap.

My second year at the Courtauld, the year devoted to English art, passed in an unrewarding blur; apart from Hawksmoor and Vanbrugh I could raise little enthusiasm for English architecture and none at all for the tombstone stuff of English sculpture; in English painting, only Reynolds and Gainsborough, Constable and Turner, really raised their heads above the Waters of Oblivion, though, cussedly perhaps, I developed affections for John Singer Sargent, Wilson Steer and Sickert, Gilman, Gore and Ginner, academically sound enough to find, immediately on graduation a year later, employment as a lecturer on these painters at the Tate Gallery. In many ways this English year proved to be the most useful preparation for working in Christie's too, for with 1550 as its *terminus post quem* and the then present day as *terminus ante*, it covered every kind of English painting and watercolour that most frequently appeared at auction. It dealt with Van Dyck, his predecessors, imitators and influence, and concluded with Bomberg who was then still alive. The most tedious subject on which I was compelled to write an essay was English portraiture between Kneller and Reynolds (the one was born in the year that the other died, 1723), but a nodding acquaintance with Knapton, Dandridge,

Pond and Hudson, despairing though I was in making it, proved invaluable three years later – invaluable too because my tutor was Ellis Waterhouse, whose encyclopedic capacity for facts, visual memory and extraordinary range of scholarship (it began with El Greco in 1930 and ended in 1981 with a comprehensive *Dictionary of British Painters*) ensured that he taught us of these pygmy face-painters with a mischievous sense of proportion. It was the beginning of a slightly *de haut en bas* friendship for which I was devotedly grateful when arguing the rights and wrongs of attributions rashly made by directors of Christie's who could hardly distinguish a Gainsborough from a Sawrey Gilpin. When cataloguing in Christie's vaults I put all sorts of things aside for his almost weekly visits and his question 'Anything for me to see?' – and was constantly astonished by how many dull obscurities he had already seen, often decades earlier; his notes on anything he thought should interest me he sent on post cards from Birmingham written as soon as he reached home, his handwriting so small that I could never read it without a magnifying glass – so short-sighted was he that he removed his spectacles to read and held books and papers only squinting inches from his eyes.

Our other guide through the long tedium of English art was Margaret Whinney, determined to ensure that we thought Inigo Jones a match for Palladio and Wren the equal of Bernini; she was a dry and diligent teacher, rarely able to infect us with her enthusiasms for Nollekens, Colley Cibber and their ilk, but her knowledge of English architecture and sculpture was profound; only Vanburgh and Hawksmoor, however, survived her teaching to become my enthusiasms too. We suspected that when the three-year syllabus was devised, all that was left when the male grandees had secured their roles was what none of them wanted, and the drudgery fell to her. One other field was left, fifteenth century Netherlandish painting, and this too she taught ploddingly in annual lectures; only in one small particular did she ever communicate excitement and that was the tale of her sitting with

Jan van Eyck's *Ince Hall Madonna* on her knee and what a thrill it was to have this exquisite tiny masterpiece in her hands before it was exported to Australia; but when it was lent to an exhibition in Bruges in 1956, there to be damned as at best a poor copy and at worst a fake, this pretty nonsense had to be dropped from her narrative. Some of us thought her severe and humourless – and I still cringe when I recall the crushing severity of her rebuke when I duped John Acton, writing an essay on Wren's City Churches, with St Bridget's, Bun Street, the great architect's only use of the Tuscan Order in conjunction with a circular groundplan. John, always late for tutorials, was very late that day, and blurted out as his excuse, his fruitless search for any trace of it. In truth she had our interests at heart, and her warmth could always be glimpsed behind the severity of her gaze over the top of her horn-rimmed spectacles if one looked hard enough. Generous with her scholar-ship, which was unrivalled in the backwaters to which she was committed (John Summerson, her friend, colleague and Director of the Soane Museum, dared to describe her English sculpture as a daunting subject, inconveniently scattered and not of an inspiring kind),[9] she had no vanity.

The solid grounding that she provided in so many aspects of English art was enlivened by tutorials given by Oliver Millar and Michael Kitson. For Van Dyck and his contemporaries we went to Oliver's offices in St James's Palace where, as Deputy to Anthony Blunt as Keeper of the Queen's Pictures, he did much of the donkey work and was the perfect courtier. Over tea and biscuits he painted Van Dyck as a romantic and Lely as a lecher, but the most daring thing he did was to point us toward the Earl of Rochester as representative of an aspect of court culture usually ignored by art historians. Dame Margaret would never have done that. Michael Kitson thrilled us with his insights when cramming the armatures

9 John Summerson, *Obituary of Margaret Whinney*, Burlington Magazine, 1975, p. 732.

of Turner and Constable into our minds, and an example of the scrupulous discipline with which he constructed these is the chronological study of Constable in the years 1810–1816 published in the Warburg Institute in 1957, on which he must have been working when teaching us.[10] The other Constable, the truth to nature painter turning into one whose deliberately dramatic and restless landscapes are as much the consequence of his experience as a professional painter as of his, at first, aesthetically uncluttered seeing eye, ran side-by-side with his chronology, but did not appear in print until 1976.[11]

With Jill this English year had forced a parting of the ways, for she had chosen to study the centuries before 1550 to ensure a firm grounding for the Gothic art and architecture that was to be her special period. Of the others on the Italian journey, Alton had returned to America, never to be seen again, Margaret had completed the diploma course that lasted only a year, and Giles had disappeared to take up a monastic life as a schoolmaster and the writer of appalling doggerel; only John remained, dreadfully addicted to his cigarettes, much diverted by the cinema and other frivolities of popular culture, and notorious for unhelpfully never completing an essay until almost too late. Willy-nilly this meant closer contact with other students formerly in other tutorial groups and with some in their third year compelled to share tutorials in English art with us because their numbers too were reduced by premature departures. This was the regular pattern. For the third year students there was some advantage in that they spent only two terms on English art, the third a period of concentrated revision, but a more serious disadvantage in that, though they had had in their second year three full terms on their special period (as I and

10 *Journal of the Warburg and Courtauld Institutes*, XX, No 3/4 1957, reprinted in Kitson, *The Seeing Eye*, 2008, p. 130 .

11 Kitson: *The Inspiration of John Constable*, Journal of the Royal Society of Arts, CXXIV, November 1976, reprinted in *The Seeing Eye*, 2008, p. 152

my peers would not), they were then not yet at their peak. On first year students we, in our second year, gazed with mature amusement – so many of them seemed so young, as indeed many of them were, school leavers as naive and hapless as I had been in my first incarnation, yet among the girls were Juliet Bareau, soon to become an (and perhaps the) authority on Goya, and Wendy Dimson who, as Wendy Baron, became unarguably the authority on Sickert, and among the boys there was Robin Chanter, later Librarian at the British Institute in Florence.

Hearts stopped when Robin first walked into the Students' Common Room. Tall, slim and languid, at twenty-six he astonished us with his beauty and unconscious elegance, the immaculate suit of fine greenish tweed marred only by the urine drippings of a man wearing boxer shorts and careless when emptying his bladder. All his trousers were so stained, but nothing else distracted our eyes from his beauty, and he was indeed the embodiment of all that is now implied by the cliché Brideshead. He was mysterious in the sense that we knew of him as 'protected' by an older man with whom he lived in Italy. Evidence of the protection lay in everything about him, his London lodgings within short walking distance, his clothes, the smart little Fiat in which he commuted between the Courtauld and Florence, his command of half a dozen European languages and his careless arrogance towards, not only his fellow students, but the grandees of the Institute at whose feet he had come to sit. Among the dowdy sparrows of the student body this peacock did not long perch – 'a spell,' as he later put it without definition. To put the record straight, in his mid forties he fell in love with a young woman at the British Institute, married her and fathered five children, Bacchus, Athene, Artemis, Aphrodite and Demeter. I treasure his memory, not only for his beauty, but for his active interest in curtailing the wholesale slaughter of birds migrating over Italy, the annual mindless pleasure of Italian hunters – the last care to be expected of him when he was a student.

The long summer vacation brought me an extraordinarily well

paid job. Several of us depended on vacation jobs to supplement our grants and I had already worked in factories making condoms and sanitary towels, and as a night watchman in Covent Garden Market, then still in the neighbourhood of the opera house. Compared with the mockery and mimicry I suffered from the women in the factories, vicious in their sour humour, the marketeers were genial and much like old hands in the army when confronted with raw subalterns; they treated me to more mugs of tea than I could ever drink. This new job, however, was not one in which old clothes, clumsy sandwiches and ribaldry played any part, for it was the task of conducting a very small group of American tourists round almost every museum, gallery and distinguished country house between Aberdeen and Arundel, round London, Paris and Rouen. They were four wealthy women who had answered an advertisement in a magazine devoted to antiques; the magazine had expected many more and sought to cancel the expedition, but these women had paid their deposits and were threatening to sue. They were to have been accompanied from New York by a Mr Fixit (their term) and an American expert on antiques, but instead, through Charles Clare, whom the magazine regarded as the Mr Fixit of the Courtauld Institute, got me, on Charles's instructions masquerading as a junior member of staff.

In some ways a year spent studying English art and architecture was the perfect preparation for such a jaunt, but these women were serious collectors of silver, porcelain and furniture – subjects of which I knew little – who wanted to be taken to public collections and to centres where they might add to their own; these they believed to be Aberdeen, Bath, Leamington Spa, London and Paris, and they also, and particularly, wished to visit the factories of Stoke-on-Trent. All this had been arranged from New York and my duties were to follow the schedule, check them in and out of their hotels, solve any problems that might arise there or in purchasing antiques from dealers, and conduct them round the houses and museums. For me this meant a crash course in hallmarks and factory marks, for the only expertise I could reasonably claim was recognising the difference between the blue and white porcelains of Caughley and Worcester, my mother's mild enthusiasm. Days spent in the silver collections of the Victoria and Albert Museum gave me some grounding in that field, and to the collection of china there, formed by Charlotte Schreiber, I owe knowledge enough to mask my ignorance. Even so, I expected my four charges to be formidably knowledgeable and to unmask me sooner or later. As for the country houses, thank God for Margaret Whinney and all the architecture from Inigo Jones to John Soane that she had crammed into my head, was my thought.

I went to Southampton to collect them from the France, a ship that was to make several journeys to and from America before I put them back on her in Le Havre some six weeks later. On the train to London I got something of the measure of them. The leader of this pack of widows was Renata Buchanan Cameron Duncan, Magna Carta Dame and Daughter of the Revolution, constantly reiterating her claim of ancestry from 'one of the barons who wrested the Charter from wicked King John,' from all the Scots that ever were and from the early English colonists. Majestic in gait and proportion, all her dresses were made with what she called 'a window-box front' so that she could clip a slim wedge-shaped vase of water between her breasts for which one of my many unofficial duties was, every morning, to find posy flowers (not easy in Stoke-on-Trent). Profoundly deaf, she had brought with her another Daughter of the Revolution, Mrs Renshaw, very much her side-kick and as mute as Mrs Duncan was voluble, but accustomed, it seemed, to tuning the hearing-aids that Mrs Duncan wore in both her ears. Mary Sowell, a sweet woman from Alabama with neither quite their wealth or social standing, was also deaf; her only minus point was her insistence that, in spite of the different spelling of our surnames, we must in some sense be related. Fourth, youngest and most vigorous was Peg Heller from Charleston, South Carolina, whose husband's fortune lay in the lowly manufacture of screws and files and other engineering bits and bobs, and whose amused contempt for the pretensions of the Daughters was already well-developed.

We were in the last carriage of a long train, with a stack of heavy luggage for which, when we reached London, I needed a porter with a cart. My instruction to 'Stay where you are while I fetch help,' too softly spoken, was neither heard nor heeded. I felt Mrs Duncan immediately behind me as I dismounted and, turning to warn her of the considerable gap, was dismayed to see her about to transfer her weight onto a foot that was poised midway between carriage step and platform edge. Daughters of the Revolution survey the world with their noses in the air, taking no account of what is at their feet. Flinging myself forward I was just in time to get my forearms under her armpits, but I could not hold her weight and we were nose to nose as I sank to my knees and she slid into the gap until her feet were on the track. She screamed mightily. Mrs Renshaw joined the screaming but could not leave the carriage without standing on Mrs Duncan's head. Other First Class passengers gathered round us, the train's guard blew an alarm call on his whistle, porters came running, and Mrs Duncan, cut off at the level of her window-box, the flowers and water of the silver vase tipped about her bosom, a surreal and potentially ghastly phenomenon, became astonishingly calm. She also proved to be immovable. When a bedizened station master arrived, she had exactly the right words with which to put an end to the confusion – she simply bellowed 'Who do I sue.'

Men got down onto the track and heaved her from below while others hauled her from above; retrieved, she was carried off on a stretcher to a waiting ambulance. Only at that point did the other women leave the carriage, Mrs Renshaw to run after her; Mrs Heller, who had seen enough over Mrs Renshaw's shoulder to know that she should tread warily, dismounted safely enough, but then there was another scream and we all turned to see that meek, mild and stone deaf Mrs Sowell had replaced Mrs Duncan in the gap, without the benefit of my slowing her descent. Taken away in another ambulance, she proved to be much more bruised, scraped and shaken than Mrs Duncan, whose clothes had borne the brunt of her misadventure. For the magazine employing me I had to write a detailed report of the calamity, and the compensation claim initiated by Mrs Duncan, in which I was included as in some sense responsible, dragged on for months.

Their tour began the following morning, but when I reported to their hotel, the women were in no mood for the scheduled antique hunt. Feeling that I ought to do something easy and nearby, I took them to the National Gallery where my party of four grew to forty or so as strangers became hangers-on, one of whom, when we had finished, approached Mrs Duncan who all the time had hung on my arm, and asked 'Tell me madam, where did you get your guide?' Mrs Duncan's immediate response was the clearest possible warning of what was to come – 'Get him? We bought him.'

With the rape of Portobello Market done, every shop in Church Street Kensington inspected, Chrichton's (specialists in silver) stripped of every trifle made by Hester Bateman or Paul Storr, with Syon, Osterley and Kenwood explored and with envious homage paid to the silver and ceramic treasures of the V&A – with a wink from me to Charlotte Schreiber – we took an overnight train to Aberdeen, were met by a Humber Pullman limousine, and began the tour in earnest. We had tickets for the Braemar Games, of which I recall only brawny men in kilts tossing cabers of increasing weight; was there, I wondered, some element of phallic boasting in this ridiculous competition? I wondered too why we were there at all, but the answer to that riddle came when the leader of the pack found shops in which to buy plaids in the three tartans whose names she bore. Our hotel there was the bleak and turretted Scottish Baronial Castle, Craigievar, where we were entertained to dinner by its boastful, libidinous and Gaelic-speaking Laird, William Francis Forbes-

Sempill (Forbes to be pronounced Forbiz, he insisted), the 19th Baron Sempill. Penniless, he was reduced to entertaining rich Americans for cash, but it amused him too; my rich widows he drove up the narrow winding stairs of every turret, not to see the changing view, but with the purpose of pinching whichever of their bottoms was before him and within reach, though all were in their sixties. He gave them exactly what they had paid for – to be treated as old friends in an ancestral setting; he had a piper on hand, wore a kilt in the Forbiz tartan, broke into Gaelic, Lallans and Old Scots, and switched unnervingly from *dix-huitième* courtesy to medieval boorishness. At me he winked as to his conspirator.

And a conspirator he perhaps was in a quite different sense. One of the most distinguished long-distance solo aviators of his day, internationally as much honoured for his pranks as for the high seriousness of his prowess (he was the kind of man who could, and did, park his seaplane on the Thames when asked to lunch at the Savoy), he had been responsible for the development of the Japanese Air Force in the mid 1920s. Loyalties engendered then were to bring him suspicion and opprobrium when Japan entered World War II. To get and keep this high-ranking officer in the Naval Air Services out of trouble, he was deprived of his post in the Admiralty and transferred to one in Canada for the rest of the war. If, indeed, he had spied for the Japanese, he was not paid for it and, always short of money, his paying guests were what kept the roof on Craigievar.

As we drifted south I began to realise how little my four charges knew; their seeming indifference to Kenwood and Syon I had attributed to the uncertainties of an unfamiliar country, its food, water and strange customs (they never did become accustomed to driving on the left), but at Mellerstain Castle, on our way south from Edinburgh, a house by Robert Adam with some claim to be among the richest of his interiors, I saw a truth revealed. They were indifferent. They knew nothing of architecture and could not respond to it even with simple awe. They knew something of their small enthusiasms but did not want to learn anything of the wider culture to which these scraps belonged, and if they could not buy it, saw no point in looking at it. Their curiosity was limited to the age of a church, the height of a tower, the name of house and its occupants as the Humber ambled past, and to such unanswerable questions I learned that any answer served me better than a hapless 'I don't know,' for Mrs Duncan's response to 'Don't know' was a spiteful 'Why don't you know? – knowing's what I pay for.' The women grew fractious. There was a wearying sameness about their days – breakfasts that none of them wished to eat, coffee that if available at all was never to their liking, loading the Humber, the 'Oh, you're in my seat' squabbles, another country house of little interest and another provincial museum of even less, a prim country hotel for lunch, village antique shops to be inspected and another railway hotel in which to dine and stay the night. The Revolutionary Daughters always left me to get their luggage to the car, while they settled into the wide and deep rear seat, leaving the jump-seats for the others; at first I sat with the chauffeur, but Peg Heller soon usurped me, preferring his male company; in a jump-seat, Mrs Duncan could jab her finger in my back.

In Stoke-on-Trent we stayed in a red brick hotel designed for more prosperous times and yet again there were complaints about the rooms and having to share with unknown men the bathrooms and lavatories at the ends of gloomy corridors; I had to console the motherly receptionist accustomed to commercial travellers who might bathe once a week, with whom Mrs Duncan had been viciously cantankerous. I dreaded dinner, dreaded having to see her again so soon, and was last to reach our table in the otherwise empty dining room. Mrs Duncan's mood had changed; she was, as usual, holding court but her tone was affable. I later discovered that she had returned to the reception desk with an offer that could not be refused – no other rooms on her corridor would house a man, and a 'Private' notice was hung on the bathroom door. The ancient waitress brought us lentil soup. Mrs Duncan, gesturing to make a point, caught her spoon in the cord of her right deaf-aid and ripped it from her ear; that it described a wild parabola and fell into her soup was enough to provoke a giggle that I might have been able to suppress had she not then used her spoon to retrieve it, popped it into her mouth, sucked it and plugged it back into her ear, hardly pausing in her narrative. The giggling then became the helpless laughter that no effort of will can stop and I was well and truly in disgrace.

By the time we reached Paris it was clear that the women had lost all interest in museums and great houses, flea-markets and *antiquaires* – they wanted to shop for clothes and perfumes. Diligently I saw them for dinner and outlined the programme for the morrow, but they wanted nothing to do with any of it; instead, as they spoke no word of French, Mrs Duncan and her side-kick demanded that I accompany them. This I refused on the grounds that Peg Heller and Mary Sowell, who had formed something of a bond, might want to stick to the schedule – but they did not and were happy to explore shops on their own. This left me to do my duty – as I saw it – alone, and without them I followed the programme for which, months before, they willingly had paid; the appointed Cadillac limousine drew up at the hotel door, I climbed in beside the driver, and off we swept to Versailles and Malmaison, Fontainebleau and Anet, a very useful preparation for my next year of study at the Courtauld. The driver taught me where and what to eat, where and how to find a prostitute *de cinq à sept*.

It was after one of these jaunts, spiritually and intellectually lifted, that I decided to skip dinner with my charges; instead, in the little streets behind what is now the Musée d'Orsay but was then our hotel, I bought a picnic – snails and salami, a custard tart, fruit, bread and wine – and took it to my attic room in the eves over the grand facade. It was a tiny room, fit only for the servant that I was, with a single chair, a table on which one might just have fitted a game of patience, and a dry bidet – that is one not connected to any plumbing; its one touch of luxury was a rouge marble fireplace.

I had just pulled the table and chair to the window so that I could sup in the setting sun, the picnic laid as best I could with only a penknife and a tooth glass, when Peg Heller knocked on the door, Mary Sowell behind her. 'What are you doing for dinner tonight?' 'Having a picnic,' I replied. 'Have you enough for three?' Her response to my firm negative was to call room service and order more things to eat and more things with which to eat them.

My scholar gipsy evening suddenly became rather jolly. Peg sat on the chair, Mary on the bidet, the basin of which we had stuffed with a folded eiderdown, and I sat on the bed; we drank too much and laughed too much, and Mary, rocking on the bidet, rocked a little too far, fell backwards from it and hit her head on the fireplace. For some moments unconscious, she groggily recovered when dowsed with water and slapped by Peg, who then took her off to be put to bed. I had just finished tidying my room – the snail shells made a gratifying clunk on the spreading glass canopy far below – when the door opened. I assumed that Peg had come to report on Mary's condition, but she had not; instead, she closed the door and stood with her back to it, her arms widespread, and froze me to the bone with 'I'm old enough to be your grandmother, but I'm going to bed with you.'

And so she did, after a fashion. I had no wish to tell her that I was queer, and it says something of the weakness of young man's will and the overwhelming strength of his sexual triggers, that she so easily had her way with me. I remember more clearly than all else the interruption of pleasure when her diamante spectacle frames occasionally plucked a pubic hair; as for the rest of it, what we did was entirely determined by Peg and she seemed well enough pleased by it. She stayed in touch for several years, sending cookies that are peculiar to South Carolina, accompanied by letters so explicitly pornographic, so minute in detail, so far – I believed – beyond the imagination of a woman, that I was appalled by them. These letters were, oddly enough, the first things ever to make me consider the possibility of death: what, I wondered, would my mother think were I to die young and she to find them? Decades later, during the Blunt Affair, another elderly woman, Elsie Crombie – a friend to both of us – used to conclude our telephone conversations with 'Do you think MI5 is listening?' With the preamble 'Then let's give them something worth hearing,' she could launch into the most extended and extraordinary phallocentric fantasies.

The last night for my American charges was spent in Rouen where they were foolish enough to think that they could experience Monet by watching the cathedral dissolve into successive brush-strokes of Impressionist colour; Mrs Duncan was particularly high-pitched in her disappointment and would not be hushed, but worse was to come. In the Grand Hotel de la Poste, grand in name but not in comforts, she outdid herself in shrill recrimination at the reception desk and in the dining room, there explaining to an incredulous waiter that ladies do not eat the dark meat of the chicken and she must have only breast. In the morning she called me to her room; a towel was draped over the bidet – 'Look,' she commanded, and I did. In it lay the emptyings of her bowels. It was perhaps her revenge for my (everything not to her liking about the tour had been my fault) having made her spend the night in yet another room with a distant lavatory. Quite what she expected of me I did not know and did not ask. I simply said 'Perhaps you should call the maid,' and walked away. At Cherbourg I saw the women to their cabins on the France and said my farewells – coldly to the Daughters of the Revolution, almost affectionately to Peg and Mary, and then, for the crossing to Southampton, climbed to the windy upper deck where they were unlikely to find me. For some years my attitude to all things American, particularly American politics, was coloured by my having been a slave to Mrs Renata Buchanan Cameron Duncan; I am still reminded of her every time I see posy flowers suitable for her window-box front, and every time I eat the leg of a chicken.

*   *   *

Outsider

For my last year, the year of the seventeenth century, my dedicated subject, I saw even less of Jill, closeted with Christopher Hohler, a gothic expert of demonic quality with the appearance of a middle-ranking army officer disappointed not to be commanding a brigade. She was now married and set up in a gloomy rambling flat in Emperor's Gate and the morning coffees in the Gondola, reduced to an occasional pleasure in our second year, now fell away altogether. David Allibone was fiercely ambitious as a solicitor and Jill, on the rare occasions when time could be spared from her gothic duties, talked of her new interest in solicitory matters – she eventually became a formidable magistrate; she was, moreover, swiftly pregnant, heavily so when she sat Finals. For me, work was more intense than ever. My tutorial group was often of only two with a second year student, Francine Sorabji, having to endure my growing sense of urgency and pressure. Other students in her year had long since rechristened her Francina and pronounced it as though it were Italian; this she suffered well enough, but I have often wondered since whether I made life unbearable for her with my constantly driving on impatiently. Two or three years my senior and taking a second degree, she had every right to be impatient with me – moreover, she came from a distinguished academic family and Sorabji is a name that may still echo in the corridors of Oxford and Anglo-Indian history. Warm, enthusiastic, enquiring and old enough to be motherly (she was to marry another Courtauld student, David Irwin, a then emerging expert on Neo-Classicism – 'God knows what they see in each other' said Anthony Blunt), she seemed driven by an infuriating innocence, and wide-eyed with wonder, was too easily wounded by my occasional superiorities. We were the beneficiaries of an extraordinary level of teaching, not only from Wilde, Blunt and Kitson, but from such visiting luminaries as Gerson and Van Gelder, who inspired me to spend my last vacation before Finals in Holland, looking at Rembrandt, Hals, Vermeer and all the little masters – another exercise to prove of great significance when I joined Christie's a year later.

Within the Courtauld there was one more tutor, often forgotten, to whom I owe a great debt, Philip Troutman, who was responsible for opening my eyes not only to Zurburan, Ribera and Velazquez, but to a host of minor masters, and to seventeenth-century Spanish sculpture and architecture, tying it all to the economics and politics of the day. Desperately shy and inhibited by the worst of stammers, he sometimes fell into long silences and had to be coaxed out of them by our proposing hypotheses to which he could respond with nods or shakes of the head that then released his tongue. Sometimes we were compelled to suggest alternatives and ask for his silent assent to one of them; but if jollying him along like a car with a hiccupping carburettor was the price of access to his remarkable sensibility, shrewd eye and intuitive intellectual response, it was worth the stumbling effort that we had to make.

Small though the undergraduate student body was, by tradition it had to have a President from the third year and a Secretary from the second. My election was a case of giving it to the least unwilling of half a dozen survivors none of whom wanted to take on anything that might interfere with Finals nine months away. The secretary was Juliet Bareau, now international scourge of Goya scholarship, scrupulously competent and wonderfully unselfish in carrying out the chores. Neither post was burdensome – our only prescribed duties were, once a year, to wash Roger Fry's pots and organise a garden party for the staff, but there was some pressure from younger students to give them something of what they understood real university life to be, even for affiliation with the Students' Union at University College far away in Bloomsbury. I thought the Courtauld Institute no place for beer and skittles. Instead, in Laytons, a newly-opened (and short-lived) restaurant in nearby Manchester Square, its wine-shipping owner happy to quote a bargain price, a handful of us gave dinner to an eminent guest content to return with us to Home House and the other students and informally debate some peripheral aspect of art history, or simply talk about his life. The willingness of John Sparrow, Warden of All Souls, connoisseur, collector and lively homosexual, I can understand, but why Gombrich should have given us such a bonus beyond his lectures and tutorials, giving us glimpses of the Warburg Institute before it came to London, I cannot imagine, unless it was his passion to open intellectual doors. Among younger worthies we entertained Richard Wollheim and A.J. Ayer, philosophers less than a generation older than ourselves, peripherally interested in the visual arts; they seemed, then, whimsical, even foolish, and, in our field, not as intellectually disciplined as we. Decades later, Wollheim became something of a celebrated writer on art, but his ingenious thinking was never better than the cockerel brilliance of the clever Oxford undergraduate who cannot see. And then there was Vice-Admiral John Hughes-Hallett, Conservative MP and uncle of Richard Hughes-Hallett, one of the few survivors of my year; he proved contemptuous of the arts – 'no use to any man'; his own enthusiasm was for cycling at furious speed on a lightweight machine with dropped handlebars and sixteen gears. Richard also proposed that we should invite his cousin several times removed, Lord Raglan, author of *Jocasta's Crime*, to discuss incest and other anthropological aberrations, but to this the student body strenuously demurred. A decade or so later, when Richard told me that he was infatuated with a spotty adolescent boy, I wondered whether raising the question of incest had been a covert way of introducing the subject of his particular subsection of homosexuality – it was not a subject ever discussed in the Common Room and I doubt if anyone thought Richard queer, but by the time he and I were talking freely about it he was too far down the road of mania and melancholy ever to recover.

One significant external event disturbed our ivory tower. At more or less the same time as my personal crisis over the invasion of Suez threatened to disrupt my life, the Hungarian Revolution of October 1956 occurred. Of this, one consequence was that two of the some 190,000 refugees who fled into exile, knocked on the door of Home House. They were an unlikely pair – George, short, sturdy, hirsute and uncouth, and Ursula, pale, ethereal and blonde. The bare bones of their story was that, as students of art history, they knew of the Courtauld Institute and of Johannes Wilde as a fellow Hungarian, that in making for Vienna on foot, George had come upon an exhausted Ursula and had half dragged, half carried her to safety over the Austrian border, and that with some help from the British embassy, they had made their way to London. The Courtauld, though sympathetic, at first rebuffed them – it was late in the first term of an academic year, there was no measure of their academic level, they had no money on which to live and no means of paying fees, and their command of English was too wretched for them to understand any lecture or tutorial. Had their visit not coincided with the afternoon break at which the whole Institute halted for Mrs Winkle's tea and cake, in which a despairing Charles Clare dumped them in the Students' Common Room, we might never have known of them. Their sudden presence inflamed my anger over Suez and how this folly had utterly wrong-footed the British in the arguments we should have had with Russia over the invasion of Hungary, and I felt that the Courtauld, the beneficiary of so much middle European scholarship, should be the last place to turn away these refugees.

By the grace of God Jill was there and we went at once to Charles with the proposal that were the students to stump up enough money to feed, clothe and house the pair, the Institute might cover their fees. The decision lay with the Director, was his answer. I do not know how it was squared with the authorities of London University, but squared it was, and Jill, Joan Seddon – a brilliant student of conservation in the Technology Department – and I each contributed £75 to a fund administered by Charles. As most other students were as poor as mice we kept this largely to ourselves and refrained from rattling the begging-bowl in the Common Room.

Ursula did not long need our financial, or any other, assistance. George was inconspicuous – apart from flooding a bathroom and bringing down a ceiling in the house where Joan lodged in Pembridge Square – and must have left the Institute early, for his name does not appear in any list of graduates at the Institute. Ursula did not graduate until 1961, four and half years on, by then married to Kenelm Digby-Jones, briefly a fellow student who, of ancient lineage (with an ancestor at the Court of Charles I painted by Van Dyck) and considerable wealth, was for her a giant step on the ladder of English society that she had, from the very beginning, been determined to climb. The girls at the Courtauld were awed by what they saw as her strange beauty – for Francina Sorabji particularly, it was as though a Botticelli Venus had walked in – but the boys were less convinced that her lofty and wide brow, long and straight blonde hair, wide-set pale blue eyes and extraordinary pallor amounted to beauty and thought the combination weird. Coldly arrogant and boastful, she soon lost our sympathy, and if we remember her for anything other than her looks, it is for her repeated claim that this famous painting and that celebrated masterpiece had once hung in her mother's bedroom in the huge castle on the vast estate that she, an only child, should soon inherit from her brutal drunken father – there was not a girl in the Institute who did not at some point mimic Ursula's throaty utterance – 'Zat voss in my muzzer's bedroom . . . '

Kenelm Digby-Jones was, as Robin Chanter before him, an adult student of twenty-seven putting in 'a spell' at the Courtauld, but in the hope that it would lend some gloss to his ambition to be an art dealer, not for the sake of scholarship. How old was Ursula? As old as Dracula, perhaps, and old enough to make a bee-line for a possible husband. To all other male students she responded with contempt, dismissing us both as poor and as wilting homosexuals – an accusation that she could neatly spit. After her death in 1981, her then brother-in-law, the painter Timothy Behrens, pieced together from her journals and other papers, a biography[12] the first years of

12   Timothy Behrens: *The Monument,* Jonathan Cape 1988 .

which, if not entirely fictional, are so embroidered and embellished, as well as simply wrong, as to be laughably preposterous. That Ursula became a student at the Courtauld through a chance encounter with Blunt in 'the History of Art Department at Oxford' (and where was that in 1956, I wonder), that he immediately 'put her through a searching test' and found her 'grasp of both artistic and historical concepts exceptionally mature,' was enchanted and whisked her away to Home House, there to become 'very fond of her . . . his favourite pupil,' with the expectation of an academic career for her, is the stuff of a romantic novel. The only fact of any interest among the fantasies of Ursula's life was the bloody manner of her death, messily self-inflicted in Khartoum in 1981, after a prolonged and painful infatuation for a Sudanese policeman for whom she was nothing more than a trophy blonde. As one of her contemporaries at the Courtauld put it when I told her the news – 'I can't feel sorry for her – she had such a marvellous time while it lasted.'

She haunts the Institute still. At a gathering of 'Early Courtauld Graduates' – crocks and crones still capable of reaching it in April 2009 – her name was on the lips even of many who had not been her contemporaries. Deborah Swallow, the Director, asked me if I had known her and what sort of girl she was. Half succubus, half siren, the creation of Edgar Allan Poe.

*   *   *

It may have been the arrival of George and Ursula, and the financial troubles of another student, an older post-graduate who had come late to the history of art and was very promising (indeed, eventually a professor), who could not, without help, have completed his studies, that enriched my simple pupil-professor relationship with Anthony far beyond the enthralling tutorials from which I learned an academic discipline of wide enquiry that suited me so well. The affairs of the Student Common Room had occasionally to be discussed with him, and I also had to confess the difficulty into which I had precipitated myself over the Suez Affair and the possibility of a Court Martial – just in case Military Policemen came knocking on the door.

One morning he came to my desk in the library. 'Oh good – you're wearing a jacket.' Why his surprise? I always did, and a tie. It demonstrated how little he saw if seeing was not essential, how distracted and unaware he generally was. 'I'm off to the Palace in ten minutes and thought you'd like to come.' And to Buck House we went to re-hang a painting just returned from restoration. What then happened was so akin to the action of Alan Bennett's play of 1986, *A Question of Attribution*, that I wondered if some palace worthy told him the tale thirty years after the event, suitably embroidered. The Queen did indeed come in and find us; I was up a ladder straightening the picture and Anthony was yards away directing me. She and he began a conversation and I stayed where I was, above them but with my back to them, my nose only inches from the canvas, wondering what the Devil I should do. I stood stock still for what seemed many minutes, though it was probably only seconds before Anthony told me to come down, but with my feet on the carpet and having turned to face the Queen, I still did not know what to do. Bow? – but to what degree between a nod and a Japanese kow-tow? Clasp my hands behind my back? Reach out to shake hers? Join in their conversation or be mute? Later in the day I had no recollection of what, in my confusion, I had done.

*   *   *

In the Easter break I went to Amsterdam with the one friend I had retained from school, Malcolm Tomkins. Never in any sense sexual partners, the subject never raised in conversation, our friendship was based on a common intellectual frivolity with matters that most boys then treated with reverence – the Bible and English literature among them. Far better at it than I, at sixteen he began to send pieces to *Punch*; the difference between us was that I would rather have been as good as Keats, attempted to be so with pastiches and failed, while Malcolm was content with polished witty mockery. The pity of it is that he came from a background that neither believed in what he did so well, nor would support him in his doing it, and taking the advice of the school's careers adviser, he sat the Civil Service examination for a job that drained the mischievous spirit from him. He married early and spent his honeymoon in my mother's house in Castle Hedingham; he died early too, oblivion the consequence for a modest genius who should have been remembered for his wit.

Not much interested in paintings, he was patient enough with me in the Rijksmuseum – even a literary man can stomach Rembrandt and Vermeer – but found other things to do when I took trains to Utrecht, Haarlem and other centres of Dutch art. For me this was the consolidation of insight and understanding that can only be stirred by photographs and reproductions. It was all very well for Johannes Wilde to suggest that I might, after graduation, work on Jan Steen, as he did after I had written a more than usually hard-won essay on the man, but not until I went to Holland and saw more of his paintings than I could in England, did I fully recognise their beauty, complexity and scale. It was all very well for Johannes to expound on Rembrandt and for me to know and love the paintings in the National Gallery, Dulwich and Kenwood, as well as to have spent so many hours with others in the great winter exhibition of 1952–53 in the Royal Academy, but to stand in front of *The Night Watch* was to see and understand a development in the history of art as explosive, disruptive, essential and revelatory as Leonardo's *Last Supper* or Signorelli's frescoes of *The Last Judgement* in Orvieto.

In the last weeks before Finals we were left to revise in anxious peace – no tutorials to attend, no essays to write. We sat our examinations scattered among a thousand strangers being examined in other disciplines, in a vast room in the old Imperial Institute, separated only by a corridor from the Warburg Institute where the accumulated wisdom of its staff would have answered all our questions of whatever period. Knowing that, after several retreats in the past year or so, my vocation as a priest had been recognised and that I should soon be a student of theology, I was in an utterly fatalistic mood. I said a short prayer – 'Dear Lord – let me get the degree that I deserve' – and did what I could with the first examination paper.

I wonder now what my examiners made of my handwriting; my essays I always typed because my broad-nibbed and heavy-pressed longhand was often impossible even for me to decipher, but without a typewriter and with haste and desperation playing their part, every page they had to read must have been a cat's cradle of unruly scribble. It has not much changed and recipients of my letters occasionally return them with the note 'Translation please.'

At the midday break we found Michael Kitson on the steps outside, there like an anxious parent waiting to sweep us off to lunch in a nearby restaurant – a gesture of extraordinary kindness that steadied us for the afternoon session and prepared us for the morrow in that he had shrewdly shown us where we could eat for a modest sum on any other full day of examinations. The last exam was in the morning and, farewells to the others done, I took myself to the cinema to clear my mind of all anxieties – two films in quick succession in neighbouring houses. *Boy on a Dolphin*, with Sophia Loren and Alan Ladd, was a pretty piece of highly coloured romantic nonsense that did nothing for my sudden sense of emptiness; nor did the unrelieved pessimism, the certainty of perdition, of Henri-Georges Clouzot's dark thriller *The Wages of Fear*, though it seemed enough of a masterpiece to be worth sitting through a second showing as, long ago, one could. Or was it that, as long as I stayed in a darkened cinema, I was not compelled to confront what had to be done next?

CHAPTER 10

A Second Intermezzo: 1957–1958

For three years I had been studying to become an art historian of
sorts – much longer if my first two aborted years at the Courtauld
and the two more of serious intention during National Service are
taken into account – and these had been years of increasingly
monkish devotion to this academic discipline. It was still June and
there were only two certainties in my life, the Viva that was very
soon to come and the theology to which I was to be devoted in
October, an even more monkish discipline. I suffered what can
best be described as withdrawal symptoms; the last weeks of term,
revising for Finals, and Finals themselves, had masked the absence
of the drug – but now I needed a lecture on Michelangelo, a
tutorial on Rubens, an essay to write on Bernini, I needed to sit at
the feet of Wilde and Blunt and to go on learning. I began to
realise that with art history I had become addicted to a powerful
drug with which Latin, Greek, Aramaic and theology could not
compete; I wanted to consolidate what I already knew, not venture
into disciplines in which I should be a neophyte.

This misgiving I could not confess even to my parish priest. Nor
could I confess a second misgiving, released by the first. This, of
course, was sex. With a seamless and immediate transition from art
history to theology I might have kept the lid on this bubbling
cauldron, but with three months between, sex seemed to rip into
my mind and, let loose – for the time being – from obligations to
my future priesthood, I experienced what I can only describe as
intellectual rape by the idea of sex. Thought, desire, need – all
were inescapable and ever-present in my mind, but I had become,
in spite of adolescent experience, shy, secretive and inhibited – the

vow of chastity that I had made to vanquish the demon had done a terrible damage that I could not easily undo. Because of it, over the next twelve months or so, a handful of small incidents that would have been trivial in the life of any normal man, assumed absurd importance in my sexual reconciliation with myself.

My way of dealing with withdrawal from student life could be described as funk, or, as I thought it, as weakening the addiction by diluting the drug. I asked the Professor of Technology at the Courtauld, Stephen Rees-Jones, to take me on as an unpaid dogsbody-cum-student for three months. The technology of paintings, their conservation and restoration, had been a basic weekly course in our first year. I had had it twice, but in my first incarnation the course had been under Helmuth Ruhemann in the room set up for him as a studio on the main floor of the National Gallery (then still recovering from the damage caused by the war, with more paintings on storage racks than hanging); Stephen's teaching was close to home in the Institute's Department of Technology established in every nook and cranny of the mews cottage that formed the north wall of the garden. They were very different teachers.

That there was a Department of Technology is one of the unsung master-strokes of those who founded and funded the Institute. The English tradition of restoration was wholly amateur and unscientific, the rare best of it done by failed painters with some capacity for subduing their own instincts in favour of those of the artists whose work they were employed to restore. Damaged edges were trimmed from canvases, with even whole sections cut off and discarded (Glasgow's Giorgione, *The Adulteress*) is an example, though this may have happened before the canvas came to Britain – a former owner, Christina of Sweden, was notorious for trimming pictures to fit spaces on her palace walls); what was left of the originals was then ironed with an unreliably hot iron onto a supporting canvas, the adherant the sort of animal-based glue used by makers of furniture, and lesser wear and tear to the flattened paint impressed with canvas grain, liberally overpainted. The cracked and parting panels of paintings on timber were often skimmed until wafer-thin and then they too were glued to canvas. These processes, in many cases, did irreversible damage. Much continental conservation was not much better; a number of paintings in the National Gallery that passed through the hands of esteemed Italian and German dealers in the nineteenth century have, through restoration, the aesthetic qualities of that period (at the risk of reopening old wounds I point to some lesser pictures in the Mond Bequest) – but it was, nevertheless, in Germany that science began to influence the business.

When Ruhemann, in the forefront of the debate and internationally known for his work in the Kaiser-Friedrich Museum in Berlin, fled Nazi Germany in 1933, within a year he found willing employment in both the Courtauld (with which he stayed until Home House closed in 1940) and the National Gallery. He believed that cleaning should be thorough and thrust small swabs of solvent into our hands, bidding us to swab and swab until we were through the accumulated dirt and varnish and the bright nakedness of the paint layer was revealed. If our swabs were eventually tinged with colour – as they were from Botticelli's *Adoration of the Kings* (the tondo version NG. 1033) – he was not in the least perturbed, for his view was that what came off could as easily be put on again. This he proved with Vermeer's *Lady seated at a Virginals*, to whose unconvincing forearms he added substantial touches of improving and more brightly coloured paint (removed in 1965).

Here was a man who talked to us of painters who subtly adjusted tone and colour with glazes so fine as to be fugitive at the first touch of solvent, of glazes that might post-date the first fine varnish, of scumbles of translucent delicacy, and yet it seemed not to trouble him that these he had, if not removed, disturbed and disrupted in his determination to reach unarguably original pigment – but then he also told us that if we scrubbed the most obstinately tenebrous Rembrandt long enough, colours as vivid as those of purblind

Monet would emerge. Ruhemann's work on a handful of National Gallery paintings during and after the war, when revealed to the general public in an exhibition in 1947, raised a controversy that has never since quite died away; his contract was nevertheless renewed by the Trustees in 1948, 1951 and 1953.

Stephen Rees-Jones, though only half a generation younger than Ruhemann (born in 1909, against the other's 1891), was so infinitely discreet in his treatment of paintings that I felt compelled to ignore (I could not forget) all that I had been taught in the National Gallery. He had been with the Institute since 1935, an unobtrusive, indeed almost invisible, presence until, appointed head of the department in 1951, he succeeded Ruhemann. He had come to the Institute as a scientist with an MSc in the application of X-rays and other forensic techniques, and his approach to conservation was that of the tender nurse rather than the bruising charwoman. His views on restoration were evidence of rare insight and sensibility, for he recognised that his science could never be enough in itself and must be the tool of feeling and perception. He put me in the care of Joan Seddon, one of his established students, a fine-boned, fragile-seeming beauty with a fine enquiring mind, two years my senior and long since an expert in relining canvases, stabilising panels, tinkering disconnected fragments of paint into position, making moulds of canvas grain, analysing paint and developing techniques for seeing the invisible. She went on to do great things, none greater than her restoration of Mantegna's *Triumphs of Caesar* in the Royal Collection; these nine canvases almost three metres square were so overpainted and dirty that they were all but impossible to read when, in 1962, she and the far more boastful John Brealey began their campaign of discovery – in both the current and obsolete senses of that word. It lasted twelve years and, as is the way of these things, to the woman fell the drudgery, the credit to the man.

Those who put their difficult pictures in Joan's hands will not be surprised to learn that the Mantegnas took so long. Strict scruple dictated that she should solve problems rather than, for convenience, bury them in haste, and that science and aesthetics should have primacy over the commercial concerns of any art dealer wise enough to trust her; private owners were often dismayed to find that her enquiring interest in an obstinately warping panel and its separating gesso ground outweighed any obligation they might suppose she had to finish and return their paintings – her record for treatment was fourteen years. Sensitive restorer, probing and pragmatic scientist, she was for a while president of the British branch of the International Institute of Conservation. As she was also, to her bones, a painter, her landscapes unconsciously akin to the private works of Degas, her nudes influenced by Coldstream, though she was not his pupil, to her restoration she brought a painter's sensibility – not her own, but in some inspired sense, that of the painter on whose work she was engaged. She could be a Quattrocento Florentine, she could be Rembrandt, and she was herself as often as she could be – but not often enough, for the wounded patients in her studio were always on her mind.

There were other siren calls – her related instincts as a collector and a gardener. As a student living in one room she nurtured Alpines, tiny glaucous little things on every ledge. As a young professional in a flat above the Moti Mahal restaurant in South Kensington, the fumes of curry blended with those of acetone and white spirit in her studio, but the Alpines flourished in her bathroom. With marriage to Gerald Griffith they moved to new quarters on Kew Green, and they were with her still at Wellbrook Manor in the last decades of her life. There gardening took over and her ambitions grew to rival Repton in the distances and Jekyll round the house, and the bantam hens that enlivened her tiny patch in Kew metamorphosed into sheep of rare breeds that played a Thomas Sidney Cooper role in the long view from her windows.

She had collecting in her blood. Her uncle, Dyson Perrins, was a celebrated collector of illuminated medieval manuscripts, but Joan was passionate about too many things ever to be so constrained.

She was a voracious magpie, accumulating with Gerald more drawings and paintings than they could ever hang. Their shared interests were Modern British – Gilman, Ginner, Clausen, Maitland, Lucien Pissarro – but Joan was far the broader in her taste and could be as thrilled with unattributable portraits and drawings by esoteric old masters if she discerned in them some peculiarly convincing quality.

She was a rescuer, a nurturer, a healer in her way; these abstractions embrace all her interests – in works of art damaged and discarded, in plants and trees (from nurseries she often bought the saddest specimens), in the cats she rescued, and in Titan, the gelding whom she rode, fearlessly, without a saddle. The long muscles of her thighs were iron hard and she was as proud of them as of her work on the Mantegnas.

'Can you afford to buy a damaged canvas?' Joan asked, 'if you can, then nothing is at risk and you can be let loose on it.' And so I did, for five shillings in Portobello Road – a sunset coastal scene with an elegantly wrecked ship and rescued figures in the foreground, in the manner of Vernet, with a big H-shaped rent in the centre, fragments of paint still clinging to the loose breakaway threads. It was a tough old thing and it survived my clumsy attempts to reline it, mend its wounds, clean and restore it, and a year or two later I sold it at Christie's for 300 guineas, gleeful in a profit that seemed a measure of my competence, but the real benefit of this crash course in conservation was not this profit, nor the skills that I could later (even more profitably) put to use, but the change from acquaintance with Joan as fellow student into an intense friendship that lasted exactly half a century, until her death in July 2007. I cared for her Alpines whenever obligation compelled her to leave them. I took her to dinner the night before her wedding and comforted her for the miseries and anxieties brought about by Gerald's sudden confession that he suffered from epilepsy. To comfort her mother, in hospital stilled and silenced by a stroke, I smuggled in my whippet, Hecate – and in her eyes never saw better evidence of the healing effect of animals. I helped, after their deaths, to empty her parents' house in Cheltenham of their extraordinary accumulations – her father had been an eminent aviator before and during the Great War. I was with her when, at dinner with Joe McCrindle, many of whose collection of paintings she had cleaned, a young American curator scoffed at her claim to have ridden bare-back – up came her skirt and there indeed were the long hard muscles of her thighs. With no other woman friend was my life so closely interwoven, not even Jill, whose ventures into multiple child-bearing, the mysteries of magistracy, lake-digging, viticulture and other virtuous pursuits suitable for the wife of an increasingly eminent solicitor, drove us apart for twenty years or so, though we lived within short walking distance of each other.

*   *   *

Working with Joan, an experience that chanced to be one of the most useful in preparation for what was to become my career, was a diversion from the preparatory studies in which I should have been engaged. When, immediately after my Viva, Anthony Blunt took me on one side and said that I must, not should, embark on a PhD and not (though he did not put it so crudely) waste my time with theology, I blurted out some of my misgivings about my intention to become a priest – and the first of many lunches in his attic kitchen was the consequence. Only a really wretched cook could over-grill lamb chops and under-boil potatoes. Only Anthony could blindly tolerate the subdued squalor achieved by the ancient Irishwoman who cleaned his flat, short, squat and moustached, her ten-to-two feet dragging in short shushes along the linoleum in sheepskin slippers, her voice a throaty growl in the accents of west Kerry, a trail of dropped cigarette ash from room to room proof of her hoovering presence there. Above the kitchen table hung a large coloured reproduction of Poussin's *Kingdom of Flora*, a painting that he had not seen since before World War II and that he thought he might never see again.

He asked for ideas. I said that I had not expected to continue with art history and had made no financial provision for it – in brief, I had not applied for a grant in the next financial year. He ignored this and returned to ideas. I said that I thought the activity and influence of Rubens in France still had to be explored – but that this would require money and long absences from England; an English subject might make life easier and I fancied resurrecting Alma-Tadema. At that, horrified, he said that no one at the Institute could supervise me (though I am certain that Michael Kitson could have done so) and that I would have to do it under Tom Boase, his predecessor and the only man he could think of with the requisite knowledge of late Victorian art. I drove to Oxford to see Boase and was the victim of a crushing interview; he assured me that nothing of any interest could be said of Alma-Tad, that nothing remained to be discovered and that I would waste my time – and then put forward the suggestion that Andrew Geddes (1783–1844) was a marvellous portrait painter well worth investigation, and that if I agreed to him as the subject of my PhD, he, Boase, would be happy to supervise me. At this point Boase had not quite finished the typescript of his English *Art 1800–1870*,[13] of which the preface is dated January 1958; in this, Alma-Tad appears in one sentence, Geddes in two.

If of Geddes I knew anything, it was his small sensitive portrait of David Wilkie painted in 1816 – and that only because Michael Kitson had shown us it in a tutorial on Wilkie – and his vague position as almost an amateur in English circles dominated by Lawrence and Scottish dominated by Raeburn, a portrait painter with ambitions to paint histories. In the various libraries of the Courtauld I could find nothing to confirm Boase's opinion that he was a worthy subject for a PhD and angrily refused his proposal, my anger pretty fierce because I remained convinced that Alma-Tad was a worthwhile subject. Geddes remained uninvestigated

13   Oxford University Press, 1959.

until 2001 and even then the diligent catalogue of an exhibition at the National Gallery of Scotland seemed the stuff only of an MA thesis.[14] That Boase was in error with Alma-Tad has since been made clear by several serious books (to one of which my contribution was not acknowledged), a major exhibition[15] and, particularly, by the serious interest in him developed by the London art market;[16] had he allowed me to write my thesis, I would have been the first in this field.

At much the same time I was offered a job by Peter Brieger, Professor of Art History at the University of Toronto, who had two years earlier completed his *English Art 1216–1307*, Volume IV of *The Oxford History of English Art*, edited by the ubiquitous Tom Boase, and was in England seeing it though the final stages of production. He sought me out because he needed someone to teach, particularly, the seventeenth century, but able to fill gaps in other fields. An immediate leg-up into academe, with a salary significantly higher than I could expect in England, was an almost overwhelmingly attractive proposition, and it forced me to confront the issue of my training to become a priest – with the curious consequence that I decided to delay the latter and refuse the former. I liked Brieger and felt very comfortable with him for, like Johannes Wilde, he was not only grounded in the severe academic disciplines of German art history, but had far wider interests than might be expected from a man whose English reputation was restricted to medieval English art and architecture; by chance he also knew and liked Joan Seddon's uncle Dyson Perrins, as much for himself as for his distinguished ancient manuscripts. But Canada seemed too remote – I knew no one there, no one even on the continent other than Peg Heller and the Magna Carta Dames, and it would

14 See Helen Smailes, *Andrew Geddes, a Man of Pure Taste*, 2001.
15 *The Van Gogh Museum,* Amsterdam and the Walker Art Gallery, Liverpool, 1997.
16 See the sale of the Allen Funt Collection of thirty-five important works by Alma-Tadema, Sotheby's Belgravia, 6 November 1973.

have meant deserting my dog, Penny, who had just re-entered my life. With the exception of the first, all my previous lives had been in ready-made societies – school, the army and the Courtauld – and among the values of these experiences lay the adjustments that had to be made if I was to be part of them. All had in their very different ways immediately offered the comforts of companionship (even if only in adversity); of Toronto, however, of which I knew nothing, I feared the probability of loneliness.

I also felt compelled to examine what I had thought my spiritual vocation. Examined and interviewed in retreats over a period of years, I had the comfort that others too had perceived a vocation, but my own certainty was weakening. To reinforce it I had taken to attending Mass in the middle of the week as well as Sunday, as though a double dose of piety might compensate for, or reverse, a decline in conviction. I wanted to believe the miracles and myths, particularly of the Transubstantiation of the Host, for I found them beautiful and I was so often emotionally touched by the evidently unquestioning beliefs of others (and am so still) that I doubted my own doubts. I had long taken refuge in observance, in ritual and custom, in the music of the church, its bells and whistles so to speak, but now, in stripping the great celebrations of Christianity of their pagan clutter and examining them as verifiable events, reducing them to the unembellished simplicity of a verdict that declared them true or not true, I discovered a scepticism that no will to believe could reverse. I felt impertinent, even blasphemous, and the improbability of what I had once fervently believed became impossibility – and that done, what was left? I felt that I should close my mind to such thoughts, pull down the shutters on this creeping agnosticism, and return to the comfort of unquestioning belief that I had enjoyed throughout my childhood and adolescence, but I could not make that leap, and until I could, I knew that I must not take the next step towards priesthood. Besides, what should I do as a priest? Would I be content with the Seven Works of Mercy? Was it not every man's duty, not just that of the priest, to feed the hungry, give drink to the thirsty, clothe the naked, harbour the stranger, visit the sick, minister to prisoners and bury the dead? Were these injunctions even peculiarly Christian rather than the common decencies of every civilised society? And if I turned from the Seven Corporal to the Seven Spiritual Works of Mercy, then praying for the living and the dead, forgiving injuries, bearing wrongs with patience and comforting the sorrowful seemed universal responsibilities, and this left converting the sinner and instructing the ignorant as the only possible priestly duties for me – an ignorant sinner – for the last work of mercy, counselling the doubtful, I could not even do for myself.

As if this were not enough, I had too to contend with the increasing pressure of sex and its conflict with piety. I could no longer persuade myself that masturbation was no more than an assisted bodily function, a purging as natural and necessary as the emptying of bowel and bladder – 'Think no more of it,' my parish priest once said, 'just as you think nothing of going to the lavatory' – for unlike these, it engaged my imagination in fantasies that could not be dismissed and which, in their focus on other men were in violent conflict with the state of grace that I profoundly believed essential to achieve before attending Mass. These fantasies made nonsense of ideals of chastity and purity. No amount of prayer banished them or reduced the frequency of their storming through my mind, and even the boys and young men who carried cross and thurible in procession were the subjects of speculation, encouraged by memories of the mutual masturbation I had so frequently enjoyed with other pubescent altar boys while our priest was preaching from the pulpit.

*   *   *

Within a month of Peter Brieger's offer, running out of money, I was to reconsider Canada. In the 1950s there was a scheme for sending fit young men to remote camps there as lumberjacks for stints of a year, the pay ridiculously high to compensate for isolation and primitive conditions; with free accommodation and food part of the deal, I could return to London with enough in my pocket to live on comfortably for at least two years if I spent nothing in Canada on booze and wild women, so to speak. Surely a lumber camp could be nothing like as harsh as the conditions to which National Service had accustomed my generation? And then it occurred to me that this too was perhaps another indication of funk – that fleeing as a newcomer into yet another closed society was a way of avoiding responsibility for myself. Joining a lumber camp might seem brave and purposeful, but might it not unwittingly be just one more monkish thing to do after school, army and university, and an even more foolish choice than a seminary for a young man muddleheaded about sex.

Anthony introduced a hiatus to the confusion by offering me work at Windsor Castle, cataloguing the architectural drawings of Carlo Fontana and his workshop, kept in the Royal Library there. There was to be no payment, but the experience would be useful and prestigious and I would have the opportunity to browse at will through the rest of that mighty collection. There was some urgency. The catalogue had first been commissioned from Arnold Noach, Professor of Art History at Leeds, as one of a series of volumes in which all the important drawings at Windsor were to be published; many of these were begun, at Anthony's invitation, during the war, providing a serious purpose for many eminent scholars whose galleries and museums were shut and who had scant opportunity to teach, and at least two had been completed by the end of it, with others following in the late Forties and early Fifties. Noach, how-ever, had been diverted by other responsibilities, had done pitifully little work and produced nothing that could be published, even with what Otto Kurz, the writer of another volume, described as Anthony's 'Socratic midwifery, patience and perseverance,' though some of his material was eventually incorporated in the final text.

The Windsor drawings by Fontana are a formidable cache of material by a long-lived (1638–1714) Roman architect and engineer (both structural and hydraulic) trained by Pietro da Cortona and Bernini, and in some sense their heir – it is a tragedy that his most ambitious and imaginative projects were not realised, particularly his new town plan for the Vatican with a piazza behind St Peter's. His plans and elevations throw light on many important seventeenth-century buildings, sacred and secular, functional and decorative, permanent and transitory, primarily in Rome but also in Urbino, Naples and Prague, ranging from St Peter's itself to a prison for young criminals. This last, a *Casa Correzionale* attached to the Ospizio di San Michele, pioneered the concept of single cells with individual sanitation. To me these drawings were a treasure trove, an extraordinary insight into the workings of a fertile and inventive mind. Excited by my first skirmish with the fifteen volumes in which they were bound, I went, as a matter of courtesy to see Noach, whose qualifications were far weightier than mine, hoping for his blessing. I was not given it. Instead, he proved spiteful and ungenerous; he broke the first appointment, leaving me an unapologetic note to read when I reached his home, and on the second, berated me as though I had engineered his usurpation and refused all help. He had not even done the basic chores of measuring and identifying the medium of each of the 783 drawings, nor had he grouped them by subject with an index to the volumes, but had been diverted by the problem of distinguishing the hand of Fontana himself from the hands of his two main assistants, Alessandro Specchi and Nicola Michetti – an almost pointless exercise when it is evident that they (and every other assistant) conformed to a common workshop style.

Windsor was, to put no fine point on it, fun. The writers of other catalogues, John Pope-Hennessy for example, wrote forewords that suggest it to have been what Hogarth might have described as 'a self-regulating community of equals' and a place of earnest industry; and so, no doubt, it was, but my two immediate bosses there, Sir Owen Morshead, Royal Librarian, and Aydua Scott-Elliot, Keeper of the Prints and Drawings, both had a mischievous sense of humour. Aydua, 48, bespectacled, iron grey hair drawn sternly back and long of skirt, was a bottomless pit of Royal Library gossip that reached far back into the nineteenth century. She should have written these tales herself, but as a royal servant could not, and I recall only a handful, of which the first was of pornographic drawings by Leonardo da Vinci.

There was once, it seems, in the 1870s, a plan to publish in facsimile every one of the Leonardo drawings in the Royal Collection of which there were hundreds, indeed far the largest single group, and many more lay undiscovered on the versos of sheets laid down. There was, however, a moral hiccup: a dozen or so were of what are now called homo-erotic subjects that could never be put into the public domain by the Royal Collection, yet, as these drawings were by a man esteemed as 'the most universal genius of all time' they could not be censored or suppressed from a publication that was to be declared complete, even to the slightest scrap. It was decided that as the drawings had not been documented in any way, not catalogued, not numbered and certainly not photographed, the offensive sheets could be discreetly lost or even stolen from the collection. A German visitor was then invited to examine the collection. Was this the Professor of anatomy whom we know was to assist in publication? Was he from the Berlin press chosen to print the facsimiles? – German printers were far ahead in this then new technology. Or was he, as Aydua averred, a Leonardo scholar as much suspected of homosexuality as celebrated for his scholarship? Whoever it was, after his visit, the then Royal Librarian found that the unpublishable drawings had conveniently disappeared.

The ambitious publication nevertheless fell by the wayside and when Edward VII succeeded Victoria in 1901 it was decided that every drawing should be stamped with his collector's mark – a discreet oval bearing a crown and the initials ER VII. This means that were the stolen drawings ever to reappear, on the market or in some other collection, they could never be identified as having once been in the Windsor group. One sheet is possible – I must

argue probable because of its claim to an unbroken German
provenance back to the 1860s (then a little vague) recently rediscovered in a private collection in Germany; it is of a young man
posing as an angel or John the Baptist, with a substantial erection,
foreskin drawn back, the large testicles hanging low in the scrotum,
on blue paper identical with sheets in Windsor. It is not by
Leonardo but by an immediate imitator – but that is true of many
drawings in Windsor.[17]

There is no doubt that the intended publication reached an
advanced stage, for Carl Ruland, a Royal Librarian who left the
Royal Collection in 1870 to take up a post in Germany, wrote eight
years later to enquire the fate of 'the Leonardo negatives or Stones'.
An earlier letter refers to the half-dismantled state in 1869 of the
volume in which the Leonardo drawings had been safe for centuries,
with the remarkably prescient 'it might become dangerous too, to
let so many hundreds of leaves and fragments of leaves remain quite
loose; there it is lucky that nobody gets easily access to these
treasures'.

Windsor became the rock on which I spent every day other
than those few occupied by earning my living. I was grateful for
odd jobs that offered payment, for the garage man who had passed
me, as a student, the work that he could not handle as a chauffeur,
had gone up-market, and my twenty year old Wolseley no longer
suited him. The Arts Council asked me to translate the introductions to catalogues of small exhibitions shipped in from France,
of which the second – by René Huyghe, once one of the most
distinguished (and, during World War II, gallant) curators of the
Louvre, but by 1957 more all-purpose cod-philosopher, pseud and
first holder of the Chair of the Psychology of the Visual Arts at the
Collège de France – proved untranslatable. When I confessed that
his elusive language and slippery ideas had utterly defeated my

17 This was published usefully and at length by Carlo Pedretti, *The Angel
in the Flesh*, in Achademia Leonardo Vinci. Vol. IV, 1991, pl. 11.

attempts to render them into English, back came the response that
this was always so and I must write something of my own, but with
a high-flown touch that would pass as his. Years later, Jonathan
Griffin, poet, diplomat and Director of BBC intelligence during
World War II and a much superior linguist, confessed that he too
had much the same experience when commissioned to translate
Huyghe's psycho-spiritual ramblings. Lectures on Poussin at Senate
House interrupted Fontana for days – the lectures themselves were
short enough, but their preparation, as I was treading on Anthony's
territory and I assumed that the job came to me at his prompting,
had to be scrupulous; they were later repeated at Birmingham
University, doubling the fee. And then came God's gift, as it
were – work on the Royal Academy's Winter Exhibition, *The Age
of Louis XIV*, scheduled to open on 4 January 1958 but far behind
in the preparation of the catalogue – and yet again I had good
reason to be grateful to the army for teaching me to type.

Work on Fontana skidded to a halt. Aydua Scott-Elliot and I
drew dust sheets over the volumes on my desk, ordered my papers
and locked the door of my room so that nothing could be disturbed,
and for the next two months or so I abandoned the riches of Italian
baroque architecture for the pell-mell thrills of working on an
exhibition that brought me into the closest possible proximity
with, not only Poussin, Claude and Georges de la Tour, but with
dozens of seventeenth-century French painters of whose names I
knew, but whose work I had had no opportunity to see.

I was, however, deprived of a rich source of sexual speculation,
for at Windsor my concentration had often been disrupted by the
sight and sound of the young soldiers guarding the castle. At the
Courtauld there had been almost no such reminders of my
suppressed sexuality – almost, for Alton Jenkins had come near to
breaking my resolve in my first year, and in my last, Juliet Bareau,
on a day spent exploring Stourhead and its Claudian garden, had
brought with her an aristocratic Italian boy in his late teens of a
dark animal beauty that I found impossible to ignore – Saint

Augustine would have understood, even forgiven, the desire that he roused in me; but at Windsor the reminders were continuous. Then, on a late autumn evening, I received a jolt that was impossible to ignore. It was my custom to drive to the castle, but once, having travelled by train instead, waiting near Paddington station for a bus to take me home, a teddy-boy asked me for a light. It was my own fault for I had been covertly – though not quite covertly enough – looking at him and his codpiece prominence in skin-tight jeans. 'I don't smoke,' I said, and 'I don't want to,' he replied, 'I was just asking.' And then he made so blunt an invitation that my panicked brain stumbled into instinctive refusal. Later that night I called myself a fool.

Could I ever have settled down with a girl? It would have been easier, indeed easy, because expected and conventional, and occasionally I thought of it and the possibility of children. A life with Juliet Bareau would have been fun with a fiercely intellectual side to it, and she was slim and boyish enough in looks almost to bridge the sexual attraction gap, but I doubt if I could ever have matched her imperturbable aplomb, her command of every situation, her stern social grace, and I was pretty sure that she was shrewd and worldly enough to know the truth. Baby Helen was none of these things; the younger of two Helens among the students, she was warm, funny and affectionate, and on a trip to Waddesdon, picnicking, she had taught me how to roll downhill. She, I thought, was too sweet and unsophisticated to suspect my homosexuality and would far too easily be hurt if she discovered it. But I should have been wholly honest with myself, recognised the flaw and known that it could not be remedied with heterosexual deceit. I should have made a pass at Juliet's Italian boy, at a soldier in Windsor, or at the Paddington teddy-boy – but I was not yet ready for such undisguised adventures.

*   *   *

The Age of Louis XIV proved to be a full-time occupation in the sense that, until it opened to the public, I spent not a waking hour of any day on anything other than it and the quotidian essentials. I have always believed that this inspired and instructive exhibition was conceived by Michel Laclotte, a young art historian with the General Inspectorate of French Provincial Museums, rather than by any of the many older worthies thanked in the preface to the catalogue and happy to take the credit for it. Initially my task was only to translate Michel's catalogue, but I could not resist adding odd observations of my own and notes that I thought might help the general reader rather than the art historian. It was my first experience of compiling bibliographies and the histories of owner-ship and previous exhibitions – a chore that to this day I regard as essential if paintings and their variants and copies are not to be confused. That this detailed clerical information is now almost always omitted from exhibition catalogues results in the concealment of contrary opinion and disputed authenticity. Of this the Royal Academy's Winter Exhibition of 2004, *The Genius of Rome*, was a deplorable example: of the fifteen canvases included as by Cara-vaggio, seven were not, yet the visitor was left wholly unaware of the controversies surrounding them, and the reader of the catalogue had to dig very deep into dissembling texts to discover here and there the rare admission that even the curator had her doubts.

Working on the exhibition was not only an invaluable experience in terms of the practicalities of such an enterprise, its logistics too, but I learned that whenever credit is to be claimed, art historians and panjandrums descend like vultures. The British had no case for doing so – the idea was French, the scholarship was French and every loan was French – but still they came to poke their noses in, the august editors of *The Burlington Magazine* and *Apollo*, Benedict Nicolson and Denys Sutton, the considerable collector and maverick art historian Denis Mahon and every scholar with an axe to grind on any aspect of seventeenth-century painting, and particularly on Poussin. The French were worse by far. Michel's immediate boss

he climbing tree in the
rden of Cefn Bryntalch

he author's mother
ged thirty-four, after
anishment from Cefn
ryntalch

My mother aged twenty-three, when working with Kate Coughtrie

My mother at the time of her involvement with Heseltine / Warlock, far the most beautiful of his mistresses, most of them dumpy little frumps

Philip Heseltine as Peter Warlock, 1926

Robert Sewell, the author's stepfather, sketched by Eric Kennington

The author, winter 1934

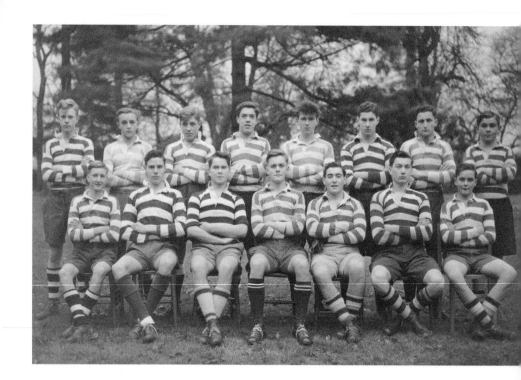

Haberdashers' 3rd XV,
autumn 1947: the author
fifth from left, back row

Haberdashers' 7-a-side
winning-team, 1948: the
author far right, back row.
Note the extravagant
contrapposto

The author at the Courtauld Institute, summer 1957, at the conclusion of his Finals

Johannes Wilde, Deputy
Director of the Courtauld
Institute and its greatest
professor

Joan Seddon in the summer
of 1957, when the author
was her 'pupil' in the
Technology Department of
the Courtauld Institute

The author at Christie's, May 1960, Peter Chance in the rostrum, Patrick Lindsay on the left

Above left: Anthony Blunt in 1962, with Velazquez's *Baltasar Carlos as Hunter* (Prado)

Above right: Claudio Corvaya, a lesser Lampedusa leopard in 1963

Left: David Carritt, William Mostyn-Owen and the author at Christie's

From the *Weekend Telegraph Magazine*, June 1966.
Experts were asked how they would spend £200 buying art.

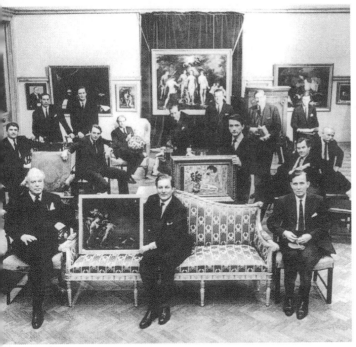

David Carritt seated
with the Rubens
Modello, which was
sold at Christie's in
November 1966
and is now in the
Cincinati Museum

A story of deceit o

How a trusted
official at the
British Museum
bought a small
masterpiece for
£50 after first
rejecting it as an
appalling daub

**Brian
Sewell**

Polidoro's
sketch
for his W
to Calvar
altarpiec
"a 16th
century
anticipat
of Picass
Guernica"

National Gallery

POLIDORO Caldara da Caravaggio is not exactly a household name, even among art historians, let alone among sane men on the Clapham omnibus. One must search lexicons, encyclopedias and indices under all three possibilities, Polidoro and Caldara and Caravaggio (taking care not to confuse him with his namesake, *Michelangelo Merisi da Caravaggio*, painter of dim shadows and bright boys), to find him worth only a column inch or two, or even altogether absent.

Short-lived and with most of his major works destroyed, total oblivion might by now have been inevitable had he not been so much admired by such great later masters as Annibale Carracci, Domenichino, Poussin, Rubens and Pietro da Cortona, his influence on them evident, and had he not left a large number of drawings made, not as preparatory stages in the development of paintings, but as entirely independent works in their own right. These indicate an unfettered and idiosyncratic mind, an imagination dark and never genial, in which borrowings from Raphael, Michelangelo and the dramatic traditions of Netherlandish and German art are blended and moved on into Polidoro's own independent territory. His work was, indeed, a vital link between the high Renaissance and the high Baroque, between the emotional extremes of mannerism and the restraints of 17th century classicism.

His working life was short. Born in c.1500, in the Lombard town of Caravaggio, near Bergamo, Polidoro was in Rome by 1518, working as a builder's labourer in the Vatican — as Giorgio Vasari, his almost contemporary biographer has it, carrying hods of lime for masons. When Raphael and his assistants began the decoration of the new loggias of the papal palace, young Polidoro attached himself to the most able of them, by imitation taught himself to draw and "learned the art of painting so divinely well that he was judged ... the most noble and most beautiful intellect among their number".

Vasari, born in 1511, did not know Polidoro, who died in 1543, but he knew at least three of his contemporaries under Raphael —

Giulio Romano, Perino del Vaga and Giovanni da Udine — all of whom must have given him information for his biography and we cannot therefore dismiss the tale he tells as romantic nonsense.

We must accept that a powerful genius lay dormant until he was 18, that he became a painter, "not by long training, but by Nature", and that in his peers' esteem he earned "an honoured place among the most exalted spirits". If further proof of the near immediacy of Vasari's biography is needed, we should turn to its end for the lively account of Polidoro's murder; he was stabbed and strangled in his sleep by an apprentice and accomplices who stole his money. The apprentice suffered the torment of having his flesh torn by red hot pincers and was dispatched by being quartered.

I raise the ghost of Polidoro, cut off in his prime, because the National Gallery has just acquired its first painting by him. The gallery has nothing by the associates with whom he worked under Raphael's direction and this picture throws light neither on them nor on his own early work, work that is all but lost. It is a later invention, sombre and tenebrous, painted in Sicily, whither he had fled when German troops sacked Rome in 1527, settling in Messina after a year in Naples.

His Roman work was almost entirely secular or mythological in subject, his Sicilian work religious — but religious with the fervour and intensity of a man who had undergone some sort of

revelatory experience under the influence of Spanish mysticism (Naples and Sicily were then a Spanish dominion). Of this, Vasari says nothing, but Polidoro's life and work in the Sicilian years, 1528-1543, were beyond his reach and he writes in detail of only one painting for all those years, but in such a way that we must assume he did not see it — "executed with much excellence and very pleasing colour" is not exactly an informed reaction to a major altarpiece that, though it was carried in triumph through the streets of Messina and was revered as thaumaturgical, is a dog's dinner of a picture and a Dutch dog's dinner at that, for it is more like a bad Scorel than The Road to Calvary by Raphael, of which the National Gallery's new picture is a recollection.

IT is a preparatory sketch, some 30in by 24in, for an altarpiece measuring 10ft by 8ft. Though the third of three attempts to resolve a complex composition and haunted by Raphael's treatment of the subject in an altarpiece of much the same size then hanging in a church in Palermo, 150 miles away, Polidoro's sketches and the painting are very different in figure scale, lighting, perspective and, above all, finish.

The altarpiece could almost be mistaken for a bad painting by a bad Dutch painter, laboured, orderly and meticulous, but the sketch reveals the turbulence of Polidoro's mind, the haste with which he worked, the many alterations and re-thinkings, the inclu-

sion of almost too many su
sidiary ideas, the brushwo
clumsy in its hurry to reflect
change of mind, the paint cloud
in its colour by a dirty palet
space and perspective (both line
and aerial) discarded. The tu
bling composition is anchored
the red cloak of Christ, triangul
beneath the weight of the mass
cross, the only patch of colour
the procession of figures. On t
right, an armoured soldi
restrains a woman, one of t
lesser Marys, perhaps, and, on t
left, the movement is halted by
Veronica holding the cloth wi
which she will wipe the blood a
sweat from Christ's face. Behi
Christ is a bald man blowing
trumpet into the Saviour's ear
cruel motif completely chang
in the final altar), and before hi
is a ragged executioner hauli
on a rope about his neck (a mo
later much reduced in violence
The traditional group of the V
gin fainting at the sight
Christ's torment is relegated to a
afterthought in the middle d
tance.

The contrast with the ha
remembered altarpiece i
Raphael is telling: his is a work
didactic clarity, the violent figur
statuesque and documentar
these characteristics are reviv
in Polidoro's altarpiece, but in h
sketch we have a crowded conf
sion of responses, impetuous ar
urgent, headlong and capriciou
Picasso's Guernica, which we
through nine stages of simila
development.

For this remarkable rarity, th
National Gallery has just paid th

he road to Calvary

...e of Philip Pouncey, a former ...ty keeper of prints and drawings ...he British Museum and former ...stant keeper at the National Gallery, ...not inconsiderable sum of £500,000, ...hich £80,000 was contributed by the ...onal Art Collections Fund.

...r Pouncey's ownership I can offer ...e explanation. In 1959 the painting ...sent for sale to ...stie's, where I was ...new boy at the bot-...of the heap in the ...ure department. ...of the rules of the ...se was that every-...g of Italian Renais-...ce interest must be ...wn to Pouncey, then, ...9, widely respected ...n expert in the field ...by the firm, as its ...llible consultant. ...catalogued the pic-...e as an indubitable ...doro, drawing atten-...to the altarpiece ...en and now in ...odimonte, Naples) ...which it is a sketch, ...igh very different in ...od and clarity. ...ncey disagreed, his ...nediate and very ...ng reaction that it ...an appalling daub, ...esquely unrefined ...with nothing of ...doro's qualities to ...mend it; I was com-...ed to concede and, ...ply labelled Polidoro ...hout reference to the ...rpiece, the picture

Philip Pouncey: admired

'Pouncey stole from me some small credit as an art historian and, by deceit, stole from the painting's owner'

...lot 71 in the sale of 19 June 1959. ...e bidding stopped at 48 guineas ...40) and the picture was bought by ...Dent, a dealer notorious for buying ...es unconsidered and disdained by ...r dealers. The sum was so much ...r than I had expected — a tenth of ...annual income — that I immediately ...ed him if he would sell it on to me. ...n't do that, my boy. I bought it on ...mission." Ten years later, by which ...e I had left Christie's and Pouncey ...become a leading director of ...ieby's, he asked me to dinner and, as

a pre-prandial treat, showed me his treasures. Of these the most astonishing, the most shocking, indeed, was the Polidoro over one of his many mantelpieces. I did not stay for dinner. I did not speak to him again. It was he for whom Dent had acted on commission.

After all these years I do not care that £50 has become £500,000, but I care with anger not one whit reduced that Pouncey stole from me some small credit as an art historian, stole credit from Christie's, a firm that trusted and admired him, and, by deceit, stole from the owner, Christie's client. Of course someone from the National Gallery should have seen it on the walls at Christie's — Pouncey, indeed, its assistant keeper for 11 years, must at once have known what a valuable addition to the national collection it would be and should have gone, hotfoot, to Trafalgar Square and bruited it about, but he did not and kept it for himself.

It is now the centrepiece of another of the small exhibitions in Room 1 that the National Gallery sometimes does so well. Its companions are the two oil sketches that preceded it, a group of drawings that demonstrate his skill and imagination as a draughtsman, and a portrait belonging to the National Gallery since 1876, which has been catalogued as Italian School, Florentine School, Rosso Fiorentino and now as Polidoro and a self-portrait to boot. Alas, neither Raphael's Road to Calvary nor Polidoro's altarpiece lend logic to these smaller things.

● *National Gallery, Trafalgar Square, WC2. Daily 10am-6pm. Admission free. Until 7 December.*

Polidoro's Way to Calvary altarpiece in Naples: "a dog's dinner of a picture and a Dutch dog's dinner at that"

The author's art column in the *Evening Standard*, Friday, 12 September 2003

Arts & Reviews

Spot the difference: The Sleep of Arthur at Avalon, more than six metres wide and nearly three high, on which Burne-Jones was still working on the day before his death in 1898. It has not been exhibited in the UK since 19

Can you see anything wrong with this picture?

Our critic reveals the secret history of Burne-Jones's huge last canvas, on temporary display at Tate Britain

PAINTINGS OF THE WEEK
BRIAN SEWELL

WHAT is in effect the National Gallery of Puerto Rico is closed for renovation. This startling information must be of little interest in London, but for the advantage taken of it by Tate Britain which, for some months, is to offer refuge to two of the gallery's most important British pictures, Lord Leighton's **Flaming June** and **The Sleep of Arthur at Avalon** by Edward Burne-Jones. Flaming June has some claim to be the picture that reversed public distaste for High Victorian art in the mid and later Sixties, and Arthur at Avalon has been described by the director of Tate Britain as its painter's "last and greatest work". Last it unarguably was, for Burne-Jones worked on it the day before his death on 17 June 1898, and the canvas still shows signs of unfinish, though his assistant, the loyal and attentive Thomas Rooke (never credited) must have tinkered it into saleable condition. The old boy's greatest work, it certainly was not: less of a composition than a stiff, stilted and staged tableau, it has nothing of the invention, energy and bravura of The Perseus Cycle with which it overlapped; nevertheless, it is worth more than a passing glance.

More than six metres wide and nearly three high, initiated in 1881 as a commission for the library of Haworth Castle, the home of the painter's friend, George Howard, this vast canvas was to be for Burne-Jones what Parsifal — which took twice as long to complete and was also a last work — was to Wagner: a too personal, spiritual and emotional exploration of himself and a romantic mythological past with which he identified himself to the extent of self-portraiture as Arthur. It is sentimental, anguished and morbid; it reeks with the odour of sanctity; and just as a recent critic described Parsifal as "a bit of a pill ... staggeringly pretentious", so the sane man might say of this picture. It underwent more significant re-composing than even Picasso's Guernica, and became the ageing painter's obsession so much so that Howard released him from the commission so that Burne-Jones could paint it for himself without constraint.

"I'm not in good spirits about Avalon," said the old boy to Rooke in 1897, exactly a year before his death, "it might turn out no more than a piece of decoration with no meaning in it at all, and what's the good of that? I shall have to ... go at it with more fury." But then, within weeks of the first brushstroke in 1881, he had asked himself: "Why did I begin

Flowery detail: by collaborative hands

it?" Two months before his fatal h attack he complained that he mus ish it without any expectation of a and one month later he demar larger brushes, "thumpers and wh ers", so that he could paint faster. still he did not finish it.

In the winter after his death, Ar at Avalon was first seen by the pub a memorial exhibition. It was su quently sold to Charles Goldman, a lector who in 1929 offered to sell it t Tate; when the offer was refused, he it instead. There it was last exhibite 1933, the centenary of the pain birth. It remained on loan until Λ 1962, but at some point, probabl August 1939 when the Tate evacuat paintings in preparation for the Se World War, it was removed from stretcher, rolled, and put into a stou some half-metre square and tl metres long. In that it stayed un turbed until 1963, when Goldm heirs consigned it to Christie's, w I was then working, for inclusion sale by auction on Friday 26 Apri

The box containing the canvas not delivered until the previous Fr 19 April. From a small black and w photograph I had to concoct a c

CONTINUED ON: PAGE 3

'Lying on cushions on the canvas Joan began work at the top, and I, on my knees, began at the bottom on the easier business of repairing the flowers'

CONTINUED FROM: PAGE 37 ▶

...gue entry for a picture that no one ...d seen for 30 years and played no part ... the then available literature; it was ...us with particular interest that I ...atched its arrival in the lofty ante-...om, the unscrewing of the lid and the ...yriad spiders that scuttled from the ...x. The vast canvas was then gently ...urolled on the floor, obstinate in its ...rvature, and the mass of webs and ...er arachnid detritus removed from ...How could we display so large a ...nvas without a stretcher? As a ...pestry on a tapestry bar, I decided, but ...t one in the house was six metres ...ng and another had to be procured. ...th the canvas tacked to it by the raw ...ge that had formerly folded over the ...ginal stretcher, it was hauled up ...e wall with a dozen of us supporting ...o ensure that the inevitable inverted ...rvature was kept as open as possible. ...worked. The canvas, however, was ...ich weightier than any tapestry.

CHRISTIE'S chairman, Peter Chance, then came in to see the masterpiece. Demure, a pink and silver man, short, stout and erect, he strode to ...very centre and within a pace of it; ...that moment the weight of the can-...s began to tear it from the bar. Poor ...ter reached to press it against the ...ll, but the avalanche could not be ...pped, the canvas ripped away, curled ...ward and enclosed him in its vast-...ss. Instead of standing still, he pan-...ed, fought his way out of the belly of ...s whale, dishevelled, and the canvas ...face down, a crumpled heap.

...he one thing that must never be done ...h a painted canvas is to roll it face in, ...t that is more or less what happened ...ts it we saw the consequences — ...ed it we saw the consequences — ...ked paint lay thickly on the floor, the ...ole width of the canvas where flow-...fill the foreground, the area of heav-...t initial impact, was extensively ...maged, and the widespread random

damages elsewhere reflected the chairman's efforts to escape.

I called Joan Seddon, old friend and Courtauld Institute contemporary, a distinguished conservator of paintings then working on the restoration of Mantegna's Triumphs at Hampton Court. We had until 9am on Monday morning, when the picture was officially on view — some 30 working hours, we thought — in which to camouflage the damages. Lying on cushions

on the canvas Joan began work at the top, and I, on my knees, began at the bottom on the easier business of repairing the crudely painted flowers. Thirty hours were not enough and we worked through the night on Sunday.

During the week of the sale not a word was said by anyone. Did no one notice how much of Arthur at Avalon had been damaged? And if they did, did they assume that the damages were old? When the painting was bought by

the museum in Puerto Rico, it was relined, cleaned and stretched before being framed and installed in a specially constructed room — did none of the experts responsible for these procedures not notice how much of the paint was new? Or were all the damages stripped and re-restored without a word to the new owner? Looking at the painting now, 45 years later almost to the day, under the uneven glister of a patchy varnish, I could identify very few of

Joan's interventions, but was appalled by the crude quality of the irises, bluebells and forget-me-nots — is any one of them by Burne-Jones himself, or are they all by one of the 20 assistants he once had, by Thomas Rooke, by me and subsequent restorers?

■ *Tate Britain (020 7887 8008; www.tate.org.uk) is open daily, 10am-5.50pm, and until 10pm on the first Friday of each month. Admission free.*

The author's art column in the *Evening Standard*, Friday, 2 May 2008 showing *The Sleep of Arthur at Avalon*, by Burne-Jones, 18 sq metres of unstretched canvas catastrophically damaged a week before its sale at Christie's in April 1963, restored over that weekend by Joan Seddon

The staff of Christie's. Patrick Lindsay, Peter Chance and Guy Hannen in the front and the author in the third row.

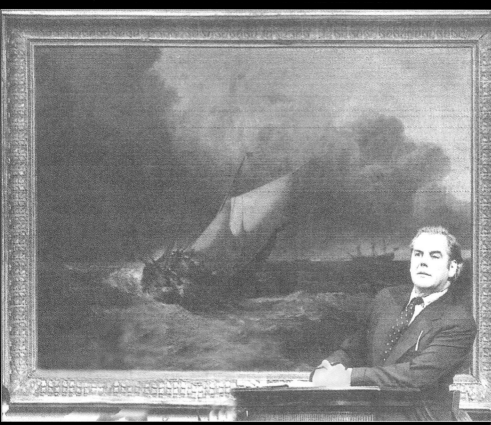

Patrick Lindsay auctioning *Turner's Dutch Boats in a Gale* (*The Bridgewater Sea Piece*)

(whom he adored), Jean Vergnet-Ruiz, had every right to be there as Inspector General of the *Musées de Province*, for they had both worked, separately, for years on forgotten paintings in neglected provincial museums until Michel was appointed to the same office. Sharing their research put them in a very powerful position when the time came to lend an over-arching national order to the country's heritage of paintings of all kinds, and that the museums and galleries of Dijon and Tours, Strasbourg and Toulouse, Lyons, Lille, Colmar and the rest of far provincial France are so fine and logical is entirely to their credit. The only other presence who deserved to be let loose in the Royal Academy was Jacques Dupont, the Inspector General of *Monuments Historiques* responsible for many loans – wonderfully suave, benign and mischievous; the sort of Frenchman who cherished English tailoring and bought his umbrellas at Briggs, he was amusingly contemptuous of his supposed peers, some of whom were merely on the bandwaggon, but others were vain, aggressive and consumed with amour-propre. René Varin, Cultural Counsellor to the French ambassador, to whom all French art historians felt compelled, it seemed, to be obsequious, was particularly odious.

Michel and I lived and breathed this exhibition. I was constantly astonished by his range and depth from the factual nuts and bolts of art history, to extraordinary leaps of perception, whether we were dealing with the matter in hand or drifting towards Trecento Italian primitives and nineteenth-century German Romantics. This was the practical application of art history, the purpose of the discipline, and of it I had had not the slightest glimpse as a student at the Courtauld. Barely two years my senior, the courage of his connoisseurship and his willingness to challenge received knowledge were wonderful examples for me to follow. Born in 1929, a schoolboy in Paris throughout the German occupation of 1940–44, the Louvre emptied of its masterpieces by René Huyghe (then its chief curator of paintings), Michel had cut his teeth on the provincial museums that were later to be put in his charge, precociously planning their reorganisation. When, after the war, both Huyghe and the paintings returned to the Louvre, he thought Huyghe's quixotic new hang appalling and was bold and shrewd enough to say so and be noticed. Vergnet-Ruiz was utterly seduced by his scholarship, connoisseurship and enthusiasm, as well as by his practical abilities. Later, as successor to Huyghe, Michel virtually reinvented the Louvre, and later still it was he who lobbied for the conversion of the Gare d'Orsay into the astonishing gallery of nineteenth-century art that it has been since 1986. I too was utterly seduced. From Michel, more than from anyone at the Courtauld, I learned to respect the seemingly dry disciplines of cataloguing – so much more systematic and diligent than interpretation (which can be, and so often is, whimsical); without the basic structure of his draft catalogue entries I doubt, for example, that I would ever have become curious about Cardinal Fesch, the half-brother of Napoleon's mother who, profiting from his nephew's exalted position, amassed a collection of some 16,000 paintings, many of them masterpieces, including Leonardo's *St Jerome*, now in the Vatican. Alas, he also accumulated so much rubbish that at his death in 1839, grouped by size rather than by school or attribution, his pictures were hastily dispersed by auction at the rate of a hundred lots a day.

In embellishing Michel's catalogue there was no point in disrupting the literary flow by claiming credit, but in one observation on Georges de la Tour and Caravaggio suggesting the possibility of the Frenchman's presence in Rome, Michel, thinking it important, inserted the words 'Brian Sewell points out that . . . ' Anthony, reading the proofs, then told me that he had made precisely the same comment in the course of a lecture at the Courtauld in 1953, but when I reminded him that I was then in the army and could have no knowledge of that lecture, and, moreover, that in his book of the same year[18] he appeared to argue

18 Anthony Blunt: *Art and Architecture in France*, 1953, p. 177.

against La Tour's having journeyed to Rome, he generously agreed with Michel that I should be given the credit. Now, of course, I believe that he should have had it, and that had he published it, the idea of the Italian journey would be much more widely accepted. A further indication of this journey may lie in the similarities between La Tour's *Woman with a Flea* (Nancy) and Caravaggio's very late *Martyrdom of St Ursula* (Naples, Banca Intesa), which the Frenchman could only have seen in Genoa, where it was sent before the paint was dry, and where it remained until 1832. This is not the place for me to launch into the connections between the courts of Genoa and Lorraine that offer further support for this hypothesis.

As there were press and private views for which we had to prepare immediately before the exhibition opened to the public on 4 January 1958, work was unrelenting – we were, amongst other things, preparing a second edition of the catalogue while the first was being printed, and it is to this second edition that interested scholars should refer. Even so, we snatched a day to dash to Manchester to see the exhibition of paintings by old masters with which the city was celebrating the centenary of what has some claim to have been the greatest exhibition of art and artefacts ever mounted – altogether more than sixteen thousand of them – in the Manchester Art Treasures Exhibition of 1857, as it is now fondly known (its proper title is *The Art Treasures of the United Kingdom*). Otherwise ours was a daily slog, often of twelve hours, breaking only for quick snacks in the Kardomah Café on the other side of Piccadilly – neither of us had money for fine food and could not afford even the Academy's own restaurant, then run by Fortnum's. Kardomah was a chain of slightly superior caste, a significant step up from a Lyons tea-shop and further still above the tea-shops run by the ABC (the Aerated Bread Company) where tinned sardines on toast cost a penny less if the toast was not buttered; Kardomah coffee was almost good enough to be drunk by a Frenchman without complaint. The only other breaks were the interminable formal lunches that the Academy offered to French visitors who used them to berate Michel and me for our perceived incompetence and to further their own aggrandisement – with very few exceptions French art historians old enough to be my father were pernickety, bickering and boastful.

Exhibits reached the Academy over a period of days, the thrill of uncrating them almost erotic in the slow foreplay of unscrewing cases and stripping away the packing to see, at random, parts before we saw the whole. Last minute adjustments to some catalogue entries had to be made, canvases had to be inspected and given minor cosmetic attentions by a conservator from the Louvre (from whom I learned a good deal in terms of desperate camouflage), and when everything had been delivered it was clear that we must make changes to the proposed hanging plan. On this the Academicians had their own ideas: they propped the pictures against the walls of every gallery in hangs based on size, shape, proportion, colour, tone and balance. As interior decoration it looked fine, but in common art historical sense it was disastrous and made nonsense of Anthony's lucid introduction to the show in the first pages of the catalogue, a room by room account of the contents of each, with the reasons for their being there. This they had done on the day we spent in Manchester. We knew that this was their intention, but to our misgivings their response was of the 'there, there, now don't you worry your pretty little heads' kind, and the loftier 'we always do it' kind, and when pushed, the 'bugger off, it's our exhibition, not yours' kind. Anxious to see what they had done, though it was late in the evening when we returned to Euston, we took a cab straight to the Academy. Michel was appalled. Off came our jackets and the heaving to and fro began. I warned him that the Academicians might be furious, but he responded that they were more his paintings than theirs and he would hang them as he wanted. It was early morning before he went to his hotel and I to my bed, and early when we returned to the Academy next day, for he wished to be there before any Academician could undo our work and be ready, physically, to defend it.

It was also on this long day that I made a fool of myself with Michel. Small and spare and, with hair *en brosse*, very French, he was not immediately attractive in any physical sense, but working so closely and so intensively with him, talking in an increasingly fluent mixture of French and English (for each of us was at first equally hesitant and un-idiomatic in the other's language) that enabled us to reach far beyond art and the exhibition that had brought us together, I had grown fond. Washing our hands after re-arranging the paintings, exhausted, I sighed. I did not know that I had, but he asked directly 'Why a sigh so deep?' and, remembering the boy at the Paddington bus stop, I seized the opportunity, though only in words. Michel laughed, dismissed my longing as 'a craving for *chaleur* – you are like a puppy-dog – you will grow out of it.' Except for the *chaleur* he sounded like all the adults who had lectured and hectored my generation on matters masturbatory and sexual – grow out of it, indeed. Though we remained friends for some years before the intensity of our careers pulled us apart, there was never a further mention of the subject.

Once the exhibition had opened I returned to Windsor, intending to slave there until all the preliminary chores were done. There was more gossip from Aydua, including a tale about the princely Hanovers that, twenty-five years later, had a sequel. As relief from Fontana – who could be tedious – I worked my way through drawings by painters, accumulating knowledge from the writers of catalogues already published, training my eye and memorising images, ways of thinking and manners of drawing in the hope that I might recognise them as readily as handwriting, sometimes daring to argue against an attribution or even authenticity. When I expressed misgivings about Leonardo's *Masquerader on Horseback*, that was to question Kenneth Clark's authority and I was severely slapped down; yet after half a century I still hold these doubts, now even more strongly. Alone with the Windsor drawings, studying at as slow and as pensive a pace as I chose, holding them to the light to see the nature of the paper and acquaint myself with watermarks, turning them to see what might be on their versos, deciphering inscriptions and committing to memory a basic lexicon of collectors' marks, was a more intense experience, slower and therefore more instructive than, white-gloved and always watched, was to be had by working my way through the solander boxes of the British Museum, the Albertina or the Louvre. Valuable beyond measure, it turned interest into passion and established a firm foundation for what was to become expertise.

At precisely the point when – though the basic chores were still by no means finished – I was beginning to see how the catalogue of Fontana's drawings (to be published by Zwemmer) should, perhaps, take shape, work was again interrupted; the British Council asked me to catalogue the British loans to *Die Welt des Rokoko*, a Council of Europe exhibition opening in Munich on 15 June 1958. In this Anthony had no hand; it was, admittedly, the immediate consequence of my work on *The Age of Louis XIV*, but not at his prompting – the decision to ask me was made by John Hulton, then head of the Fine Arts Department of the Council. The British loans were, with the exception of two Venetian canvases by Canaletto, British, and they included silver and porcelain – how wonderful, I thought, be so soon rewarded for suffering the tedium of the Courtauld Institute's English year and my confrontations with Hogarth, Gainsborough and Reynolds, and never had I thought I would be grateful to have experienced my frantic preparations for, and experience of, my weeks of antique-hunting with the American grandmothers. Necessary discussions brought me into contact with all sorts of experts and museum grandees – the tyro confronted by the tyrant in the case of John Pope-Hennessy, then Keeper of Sculpture at the V&A, a monster to so many but kind enough to me, probably because I roused in him nothing of the sexual interest that governed so many of his contacts with budding scholars, young men now eminent art historians, particularly in American museums and universities, whose first step on the ladder of preferment was taken on their knees before him, facing one direction or the other.

Another grandee was Francis Watson, then Deputy Director of the Wallace Collection, who knew as much as any man about Rococo art and artefacts; a sometime Registrar at the Courtauld (1934–38), he was kindly inclined to all Courtauld students, though very few chose the eighteenth century as their special period (was Anita Brookner alone in this I wonder?), and with me he shared his knowledge with enthusiastic frivolity as well as depth – I loved him for his dottiness and for keeping (so it was said) eighty-seven cats. Charles Oman too, father of Julia, the stage-director, and father-in-law of Roy Strong, was kind, but in a lordly, lofty, distant way, as though he were a saint disturbed in contemplation; Keeper of Silver at the V&A, he prevented me from making an ass of myself in territory of which he was undoubtedly the king. Most of all, however, I enjoyed my brief contact with Roger Hinks, the now forgotten luminary of the Warburg Institute who, as blameless Assistant Keeper of Greek and Roman Antiquities at the British Museum, had been more or less driven into resignation by claims made, largely by the press, that the Elgin Marbles had been harshly overcleaned. I cannot now recall the matter on which I consulted him – he was never a *dix-huitième* specialist and Caravaggio was about as modern as he got – but he seemed to know something about everything and expressed his knowledge with wonderful clarity; an amiably ugly man, he made – though I did not recognise it at the time – what might be described as an intellectual pass.

Working on the Munich catalogue was another formidably useful experience. The formula of each entry was laid down by the editors in Munich and I had simply to follow it; my occasional attempts to add a little interest were savagely cut back and nothing distinguishes my entries – but that is, perhaps, because, as the Chairman of the Planning Committee, Eberhard Hanfstaengel, acknowledged in his Preface, I 'gave valuable assistance in correcting the English edition

. . . '. Behind this simple statement lies a tale of pure panic. When the proofs of my catalogue entries were sent me for correction, they bore not the slightest resemblance to my typescripts, but were nonsense in some German-flavoured pidgin-English of the kind used by Denis the Dachshund and Englishmen making tired anti-Nazi jokes. It transpired, after at first fruitless telephone calls to Munich and a sickening sense of disaster at having my name attached to such gibberish, that the editor, Arno Schoenberger, unable to read English, had been given rough translations by assistants who had then mislaid my typescripts and, rather than confess the loss, re-translated them. When I demanded that all evidence of my par-ticipation be removed from the catalogue, the Munich editors realised that the whole of the English version might be as flawed, agreed to reinstate my text (of which I had two carbon copies) and asked me to revise the various translations into English made by Germans from the French, Italian and German originals. What had begun at a leisurely pace giving me time to do ten times more research than necessary, ended uncomfortably at a frantic gallop, but the long-term benefit of looking at British art in the broader context of the Enlightenment, the Age of Reason, was that I experienced a quiet revelation and my scorn for English art as a student, reflecting the view of Roger Fry (a Courtauld panjandrum if ever there was such a thing) that 'ours is a minor school . . . not altogether worthy of (British) civilisation . . . ,' evaporated. Work on that exhibition sowed in me the seeds of a belief that Hogarth, Ramsay, Gains-borough, Reynolds and Wright of Derby, with young Lawrence at its end, are in their various ways the equals, even the betters, of the more esteemed European painters of the century.

I was still working on the Munich catalogue when William Martin – Bill, as he was always known – head of the picture department at Christie's, approached Anthony, whom he had known as a young lecturer at the Courtauld when he was taking a post-graduate diploma course there, to see if I would like to join the firm and work as his assistant. He had noticed the scrupulous diligence of the Royal Academy catalogue (more Michel's than mine) and thought that I could lift the quality of those produced by Christie's – the man who had since 1919 been responsible for the basic entries in the catalogues of sales was about to retire, and it was the perfect moment for the department to introduce new blood. Anthony, it seems, told him that he had never had a student interested in so wide a range of painters – thinking of Alma-Tadema, no doubt – and put us in touch. I had been slipping into Christie's since I was fifteen or so and was intrigued by the idea and the possibility of a regular income that would lend stability to my life – I had already learned that the free-lancer is flush with money one month and on his beam ends the next. 'You'll like Bill,' said Anthony, 'but you'll loathe Patrick Lindsay, the other director in the picture department.'

Bill took me to lunch at his club, the seedy and bedraggled Oxford and Cambridge. At the bar he ordered mild and bitter for both of us; not much at my ease, my heart sank at the demand, for mild and bitter was 'a man's drink' that I had suffered in the army and detested, but instead of beer we were given sherry, a blend of Bill's own devising, half cream, half amontillado. I saw the point of it neither then nor a thousand sherries later. He nodded to a painting hanging behind the bar, the subject almost impossible to discern beneath the coating of nicotine. 'What's that?' 'George Morland,' I replied, 'though in that state it's impossible to say if it's really by him – most are not.' After lunch at one of those beastly communal tables at which conversation must be had with strangers after introductions that cannot be heard, we spent an hour in his office, a rather grand room on the first floor looking onto King Street. 'What's that?' he said again, this time of a small bust length portrait propped on a chair. 'Caroselli,' I answered – which was right, but – as with the Morland – not particularly clever. 'Is it, by Jove? I knew it was a good picture.' That was typical of Bill – an unerring natural eye for quality and no scholarship to back it, 'Bloody good – we must look into it' so often his accurate but lame response. I learned not to know the answer sometimes so that he'd not look a fool in front of Patrick Lindsay (who really was a fool without an eye), but would tell him later in the privacy of his room. His course at the Courtauld had done him no good, and his only relic of the misspent year was his ability to mimic cruelly the high-flown voice and manner of his contemporary there, John Pope-Hennessy, talking about Domenichino to the barman of the local pub in an attempt to seduce a bit of rough – such a seduction might, just might, have been managed by another student talking of Michelangelo (of whom even a barman might have known), but not of Domenichino, a then deeply unfashionable painter of the seventeenth century unknown even to his fellow students, but not by the preposterous John.

Bill's practical art education had been in Christie's at the knee of his father, Sir Alec Martin, a formidable and ridiculous old fraud whose wilful ignorance over decades had done Christie's reputation great damage. This Bill knew, and now that Old Alec (as he was known) was about to retire, thought he might remedy, but Old Alec, a man of immediate attribution where paintings were concerned and intransigent refusal to consider even the possibility of an alternative, had a disciple in the form of Patrick Lindsay, second son of the Earl of Crawford and Balcarres who had for many decades been the friend and ally of Old Alec in many enterprises. Following Alec's example, Patrick believed aristocratic ownership to be proof of authenticity – a Reynolds the property of an Earl must be a Reynolds, a Gainsborough the property of a Duke a Gainsborough – and it never occurred to either of them, though Alec must have known of the substituting activities of Joseph Duveen (the most conspiring of dealers), that an ancestor impoverished by wagers and women might have bequeathed a later generation an inheritance of copies. Bill, the only one of the triumvirate with an eye yet always the last to be asked his opinion, might murmur his characteristic expression of doubt in these circumstances – 'I suppose (with emphasis on the second syllable) it's right' – but, only momentarily exasperated, they always ignored him. To witness the three of them in discussion was always a reminder of the Mad Hatter and the Mad March Hare with Bill inevitably the Dormouse.

Alec Martin had joined Christie's in 1896 as, in his own words, 'a lad about the house', when he was twelve. The eighteenth of twenty children living in a workman's cottage in Yeoman's Row (now a very smart South Kensington address), the son of a shopkeeper who sold oil for lamps, he was a very pretty boy, small (as he remained), with golden curls. As the lad at Christie's he caught the eye of both Hugh Lane, then building his formidable collection of Impressionist paintings (now in the National Galleries of Dublin and London), and Claude Phillips, art critic of the *Daily Telegraph* and first Keeper of the Wallace Collection (1897–1911), both notorious homosexuals attracted by what Francis Watson was later to describe, ingenuously, as Alec's 'natural sunniness of nature'. Bill, who never outgrew the prurience of adolescence (at Oxford he and his friends had conducted experiments – in the bath as well as bedroom – to test the flammability of farts), was fascinated by the notion that his father had been buggered by these men. It is certain only that they were profoundly influential in furthering his career and that what education he had was largely at their hands. Neither, alas, ever persuaded him to drop his cockney accent or adopt manners that were not ingratiatingly obsequious to the grandee and the bullying of the rough-tongued termagant to everyone else – even to his family. Bill was cowed by him and still called him 'Daddy', and to Claude Phillip Martin, his youngest son, Alec was so mercilessly cruel, both physically and mentally, that the boy spent most of his adult life in a nursing-home of sorts. The tipping point for his sanity occurred when he was fourteen, when, having disobeyed his father's instruction (as a punishment) not to ride his bicycle, Alec, in a terrifying tantrum, smashed it; a portrait of Claude Phillip (named after his godfather, his father's early patron), painted by Sickert at much the same time and inscribed 'To our dear Alec,' catches something of the boy's pathetic nature – it is in the Tate Gallery with equally telling contemporary Sickert portraits of his parents.

To his dying day Alec dropped his aitches. Our first words were exchanged after another lunch with Bill, this time in Overton's, St James's, where he was evidently well-known, again offering me no choice but simply ordering for both of us 'Jellied eels and the Widow'. I hated the tasteless eels and the widow turned out to be Veuve Cliquot. 'You have to meet my father – he's still in charge until the end of the season and has to decide.' Fortified by the Widow, Bill knocked on his door. Seconds passed before we were commanded to enter and even then Alec did not look up but continued to write a letter – he rarely used a secretary for anything other than a letter of acceptance or rejection, both of which began with 'We have now carefully examined your picture and . . . ' – these his secretary could write for herself, for the catalogue note of every rejected picture was scrawled with a huge N (for No), and those of accepted pictures concluded with a note of the proposed reserve. Eventually Alec paused; then Bill stepped forward and said 'Daddy, this is Brian Sewell.' Alec, still sitting, pen in hand, in preposterous wing collar and watch-chain, peered at me through his rimless spectacles and more seconds passed in silence until he broke the stillness of the tableau with 'We know you've no social connections, but if Willy wants you, 'e can 'ave you.' Nothing else was said, no wishing well, no handshake. He resumed his letter and we crept from the room.

My last sight of Alec in Christie's was late on a Friday afternoon, descending the main stair to go home just as some poor soul had reached the reception desk – always known as the Front Counter – with a painting he thought by Hogarth. Ridley Cromwell Lead-beater, the silver-haired, pink-cheeked and carnationed panjan-drum of the Front Counter, scuttled to the bottom of the stairs holding the picture high for Alec to see – 'Gentleman says it's by Hogarth . . . ' Alec, with not the slightest slowing of his step, immediately replied 'T'aint 'ogarth. I'm off to Ro'ampton.' The 'gentleman', an unrecognised lord, was none too pleased and his painting proved to be a decent variant of *The Rake's Progress*.

Back in Bill's room, he sent for Patrick, who took a good ten minutes to appear. The job Bill had offered me was as his personal assistant, and though this description was to some extent to shield me from Patrick's bullying, it meant, nevertheless, that I would be much in contact with him and, in hierarchical terms, his inferior, for he was a partner in the firm and for me ever to be his equal would take at least a decade and involve an impossible level of investment. There were, Bill explained, a hundred shares in the business, all held by partners who were not necessarily directors or auctioneers, though the latter were all partners. Were a new partner to join the board, others would have to be persuaded to relinquish, for a price, a share or two, sometimes a half-share; power on the board was established by the percentage of shares held by each partner. Who owned what was never disclosed outside the partnership.

There had been, early in the year, the most formidable upheaval in the firm. The Chairman, Robert Wylie Lloyd, millionaire industrialist and collector – his Turner and other English water-colours, Swiss aquatints, Chinese lacquer and Japanese swords he bequeathed to the British Museum (the watercolours on condition that they should only be exhibited to the public for two weeks in February, when daylight in London is at its weakest) – had retired at the age of ninety and then, in April, died; and Alec, at seventy-four (but far older in his business attitudes), had been unseated as managing director and forced to agree to retire in July at the conclusion of the 1957–58 season (Christie's then adhered to the Court Seasons and closed from late July until well into October and from mid-December almost until St Valentine's Day). Lloyd and Alec had a weekly meeting every Friday afternoon in the former's limousine as it was driven to Alec's house in Roehampton and then on to Lloyd's weekend retreat. This, weirdly, continued in my day: I knew of it only because of my interest in cars and had noticed Alec being shown by the chauffeur into the rear of the very rare landaulet limousine body built by Grosvenor on a Vauxhall 25 chassis in 1937 or so, a huge car doubly obvious in the attention-seeking Art Deco combination of cream and coffee brown. A coachbuilt big Vauxhall seemed so eccentric a choice (unless the owner knew something of the marque's early history as a maker of great cars), that I remarked on it to Bill, and it was he who told me that Lloyd had left instructions for the car to be at Alec's service until the day that he retired. Did Alec, he wondered, tiny in the cavernous passenger compartment, commune with Lloyd's ghost, cursing the young Turks who had ousted him, confessing sins, perhaps?

There was one sin − of carelessness, if nothing more. Late in 1957 a tiny unframed painting on copper was taken by one of Christie's Front Counter staff to Alec's room for his opinion. He immediately recognised the composition as one popularly known as *The Small Tobias* by Adam Elsheimer, and asked for the owner, Mrs Margery Green, to be brought up. It was, she explained, a family heirloom, traceable back to Dutch ancestors who, in the seventeenth century, had settled in Norfolk as drainage engineers. Alec in turn explained that he too had a version of the painting[19] and would like to compare them; as he had also, until very recently, owned a major panel from Elsheimer's celebrated altar *The Finding and Exaltation of the True Cross* (The Frankfurt Tabernacle, Städel Museum) and this, in his opinion, was enough to elevate him to

19 Both were listed as copies by Keith Andrews, a respected authority, in his *Adam Elsheimer*, Aberdeen University Press 1977, p. 150, Cats. 20g and 20h, Alec's given the provenance as passing from Claude Phillips to Lady Martin. Andrews was unjust in describing the Green version as a copy for he had not seen it − even the best of the half dozen known versions he described as only a 'contestant' with some claim to be the prime original.

the rank of expert, to this Mrs Green agreed. She was given a receipt with the disappointing insurance value of £500 and watched Alec slip the little panel into the drawer of his desk with 'It will be quite safe there.' And so it should have been – and to be fair, Christie's porters, who never recognised the fragility of paintings, were the last people to be trusted with an unframed sheet of painted copper some 12 by 18 centimetres – but it was not. Mrs Green never again saw her Elsheimer, but still had the frame to remind her of her lost inheritance and, until her death in 1999, fought an obsessive but wholly justified campaign for its recovery. Alec could never explain its loss and was widely believed, even by Bill, to have pocketed it.

Alec was not in any serious sense a collector. The dreary brown interiors of his house were sparsely hung with prints and memorabilia rather than frame to frame with masterpieces and offered no evidence of an excited sensibility, yet, over decades, he bought paintings, certainly by the hundred and possibly in thousands. Enquirers into provenance who check Christie's records in the original books kept by the auctioneers and sales clerks will find an astonishing number of purchases by 'Whitehead' over so wide a range as to suggest a dealer rather than a collector. Whitehead, however, was Alec's *nom-de-vente* for himself, and Whitehead bought so much that he was privileged to have a room for his purchases below stairs at Christie's to which two loyal porters, Jock and Les, barred access even to Bill. The contents of this room were from time to time removed to a store thought by Bill to be somewhere in Shepherd's Bush and nothing more was seen of them. Even on Alec's death in 1971 they remained in obscurity, and Bill, who was eventually to fall on hard times, never succeeded in tracing them.

It was on this old man's implacable certitude that Patrick Lindsay modelled his behaviour – not on his treatment of his family, nor on what may have been dealing on the side not in the best interests of Christie's, nor on his foul language – the *fucking* this and *fucking* that of his abuse of junior staff and porters. He showed scant sign of being amused by Alec's juvenile humour – Titian's Latin signature was always pronounced Titty Anus and painters whose names were variants of Cock (and there were many) or could be wrestled into a resemblance of arse or arsehole, were greeted with ritual sniggering, and to the innocent question 'Where was this found?' the expected chorus of response was 'Up the back passage of (for example) the Duke of Devonshire.' But, like Alec, Patrick was resolute in his refusal to pronounce any foreign name with even the hint of a French, Italian or German accent, and though he knew from the upheaval that had unseated the old monster that Alec had been, commercially, a disastrous influence on Christie's fortunes, he chose to become, as it were, his master's continuing presence.

When Patrick, not easily biddable – least of all by someone he despised, as he did Bill – at last deigned to respond to his summons to come and meet me, it was with overwhelming presence. Bill was short and stout, I short and slim, and Patrick was magnificent, his considerable height and bulk enlarged by crutches and a leg in plaster – the consequence of a skiing accident at Klosters or Davos. That was Patrick in a nutshell – he did not just break a leg, he broke it where some Prinzessin von und zu was there to kiss it better. Again there was no welcoming hand, but for that the crutches may have been the reason. Startlingly erect of carriage, he dwarfed me, and my sense of being contemplated by a giant was enhanced by his short retroussé nose, the perfect instrument for expressing his disgust for everything beneath it. He knew what had to be known about me – school, army, Courtauld, Windsor and the Royal Academy exhibition – and within minutes had made me aware of his absolute supremacy. I already knew his father to be the eminent and, in the old art establishment, ubiquitous Lord Crawford, but now I learned that he had Eton, the Scots Guards and active service in Malaya, Oxford (Magdalen – where he failed to finish), and a brief apprenticeship to Bernard Berenson with which to trump all that I had to offer Christie's, and he had been a partner since 1955. This was the man who within four months of my joining the firm was to give me lunch at White's, making an absurd fuss over the colour of the legs of partridges – grey when they should have been pink, and it was the second day of September (the shooting season opens on the first). The purpose of his hospitality was not, however, to show off – as at first I thought (the fuss was Patrick's natural bullying behaviour) – but to attempt to poison my loyalty to (and increasing affection for) Bill Martin, whom he described as an 'ugly little toad,' How could the Honourable Patrick Lindsay put me in such an insufferable position?

*   *   *

There were things to do before I did my first day's work for Bill on Monday 5 May 1958. He knew of my obligation to complete the Fontana catalogue and had promised that I could work only a four-day week for him and spend one full day at Windsor – four days a week for £400 a year; if there were any unforeseen problems with the Munich catalogue (as there were), I could take leave to settle them. I argued for Mondays to be spent at Windsor, and Bill for Fridays; but Friday was traditionally Christie's day for selling pictures (Wednesday Sotheby's, Thursday Bonham's) and for everyone in the picture department it was the busiest day of the week, for there were always last minute crises over reserves and bids, or pictures damaged when taken down from the walls, stacked in the passage behind the 'Great Room,' removed from the stack to be held up by a porter at the moment of sale, re-stacked in another part of the passage, and roughly handled when a buyer known to tip wanted to collect a purchase during or immediately after the auction – and when all that was done, the remaining pictures were bundled down to the store-rooms below. In the process of being sold by Christie's a painting suffered more casual and careless handling than in all the putting-up and taking-down of a domestic life of several centuries. Moreover, as the pictures in one Friday's sale were removed, those for the following Friday were brought up and hung, some wrongly identified – some three hundred and fifty pictures moved by a handful of porters. Friday was never the day on which I could be absent, for the appalling rate of casualties – canvases scraped and punctured, panels split and the corners of carved and moulded frames shattered beyond repair – required the presence of someone who could apologise and offer remedy.

With my promised Fridays I had also offered Aydua Scott-Elliot alternate Saturdays at Windsor (the others to be spent at Hedingham mowing my mother's lawn) and we had worked out, if not a schedule for the completion of the typescript, a point at which to aim – some time in 1963, five years away. Over those years, however, my mother became increasingly frail (or so I thought and she pretended), my Windsor duties were neglected and by 1963 Fontana had all but fallen by the wayside. To my chagrin, Anthony, convinced that I could never finish the catalogue as long as I remained at Christie's, then transferred the commission to the (he thought) steadier hands of Allan Braham, an ex-Courtauld student working at the National Gallery, an altogether more lenient employer. Allan, working in collaboration with Hellmut Hager (later to become Professor of the History of Art at Pennsylvania State University), did indeed complete and publish the catalogue – but not until 1977, fourteen years later.

I had also to find somewhere to live. When my mother left London I had taken to living inconspicuously in the flat that my stepfather shared with Elizabeth, their friend, his mistress – an uncomfortable arrangement that with the promise of a monthly salary could be remedied. I answered half a dozen advertisements in the personal columns of *The Times* in which young men and women constantly sought others with whom to share flats that they could not afford, and thus it was that I spent the late spring and summer months of 1958 with Peter Hunt in Barons Court. I had his flat largely to myself, for he spent most of his nights in the bed of one or other of the two girls who shared the identical flat above – he came home, shared supper, played the same Brahms symphony every night and then disappeared upstairs – I can recall every bar of that symphony. On one of the rare occasions when he slept in his own bed, it was because the mother of one of the girls had come to stay – and she, of course, came down to sleep with Peter. Realising that their vigorous preliminaries must have wakened me, they asked me to join them, and in the spirit of enquiry, I did. If Peter realised that he, rather than Edie, was the object of my fondling, never a word was said.

The only friend from my army years with whom I had stayed in touch, came to spend a weekend. A rowing man, with what in the 1930s might have been described as conventional aquiline good looks, he had been at Brasenose, Oxford, while I was at the Courtauld, and we had seen each other often in a hearty sort of way, deceitfully on my part when it came to mutual confessions on matters sexual. Not very bright, on graduation he had secured a traineeship with Coates, a cotton manufacturer in Paisley, but it taught him nothing other than to hate Scotland and the cotton trade. His purpose in making the journey to London was to pour out his miseries, and I was easily led into pouring out my own, for my suppressed homosexuality had become so onerous that I too needed confession and the counsel of a friend. The visit had its consequences. Max encountered Edie, slept with her, made her pregnant, married her and found a job in London – and then I destroyed our friendship in a rage at what I took to be his betrayal of all that it should have meant. His marriage to Edie swiftly ran into difficulties that he thought insuperable. Early in January 1959 they came to dinner and quarrelled furiously, Max striving to draw me into the row as an ally; then he decided to attempt divorce, and as she was blameless he blithely told her that he was queer and wanted to spend his life with me. Only after they had separated did he tell me. I felt used, sullied by the lie. I was fond enough of Edie to value her trust in me and not to want her hurt, and on my own account was wounded to find that my confession, uniquely entrusted to a man I thought my friend and for whom I had never harboured even a speculative thought, had been exploited to his advantage. Worthy of Iago, it was my first experience of perfidy.

CHAPTER 11

Christie's in 1958

Of Christie's public face I knew the entrance hall, the slow-rising and welcoming stairs, the ante-rooms in which pictures were displayed and the great octagonal room in which they were sold. Of its private face I knew only the rooms occupied by Alec and Bill Martin, particularly Bill's with red damask on the walls and more of it for curtains, a huge desk and a handsome eighteenth-century bookcase with almost empty shelves; I cannot recall the carpet on which he and Alec's secretary, Beatrice West, were rumoured to have been discovered by his father in sexual embrace. Of Christie's workface I knew nothing when I entered the building on Monday 5 May 1958. Bill was not in his room, but as I turned away from the door I caught a glimpse of him, with Patrick, far away in the octagon; by the time I had sidled past the bulky furniture always displayed on the narrow galleries flanking the well of the stairs, he and Patrick were walking towards me across the central ante-room. 'Oh Brian, come and look at this,' he said, returning to the octagon. I followed his glance towards a large painting hanging above the bar on the west wall – 'What is it?' 'An El Greco,' I replied, 'a later version of the Dresden picture.' In this I was in error – it is much closer to a version in Parma, but of this I did not know. 'Oh Gawd . . . ' was Bill's response.

The painting had been hanging on view only since mid-afternoon on the previous Friday (the premises were closed to the public over the weekend) and yet, within half an hour of opening on Monday there was already a buzz of anticipation. Of this the porters were first aware – as always – and seeing dealers gathering like flies, they had reported the interest to Bill. Somehow the painting had slipped unrecognised past Bill and Patrick and been catalogued under an unconvincing and unconvinced attribution to Veronese – unconviction frankly indicated by the omission of that painter's Christian name, then an ancient shorthand in English auction houses for we don't know, we don't care, the painting is a poor thing but it vaguely resembles Veronese; the inclusion of the Christian name indicated authenticity, and an initial – P for Paolo – suggested that the attribution was uncertain but the painting had some merit. It transpired that Alec knew the owner, George Smith-Bosanquet, and had, as a favour, promised to catalogue the picture himself and see that it was swiftly sold; this he had done without reference to Bill who had meanwhile replaced him as head of the picture department and thus bore the brunt of the row that followed. I am certain that had Bill seen it, though he might not have recognised it as by El Greco, he would have gone into his 'Bloody good picture . . . we must look into it' routine – which meant, with old masters, that it would not have been included in a sale until Ellis Waterhouse had seen it.

Ellis was one of a small handful of art historians, museum curators and respected dealers on whom the picture department depended for expert opinion, some of them unreliable because the interests of the businesses or institutions they served were greater than any friendship they felt for Christie's – and all that Christie's ever offered for their knowledge was a word of thanks (and hardly even that from Patrick). Ellis Kirkham Waterhouse, however, born 1905, at Marlborough a friend of Anthony Blunt, two years his junior, was a man of independent means only interested in scholarship. He had worked at the National Gallery for three years from 1929, then becoming librarian at the British School in Rome until resigning in 1937 to work on the following year's Winter Exhibition at the Royal Academy, *Seventeenth Century Art in Europe.* World War II he spent first in the Macedonian and Greek campaigns, then with Military Intelligence from Cairo to the Caspian, and in 1945, in the last stages of the war, by then with the Monuments, Fine Arts and

Archives branch of Allied Military Government, he was responsible for culturally important buildings, museums and collections in Belgium and Holland. On crossing the Dutch border he ordered the arrest of Han van Meegeren, the notorious forger of paintings attributed to Vermeer, whose role as their painter he had suspected as early as 1937 (though given no credit for it). He had been a brilliant Director of the National Galleries of Scotland for three years but could not tolerate the, to him, insufferable social conventions of Edinburgh, and had returned to academic life as Professor of Fine Arts at Birmingham University, and Director of the Barber Institute there. An undemanding post, it offered him freedom enough to become himself.

The essential Ellis was the independent seeker after truth, the man to whom every scrap of information might contribute to the solution of a mystery, not only of attribution, but of the uncertain history of a painting as either the prime original or as a later variant, and he was as indefatigable in his investigation of the backs of canvases and their stretchers as of their painted surfaces, pushing his glasses over the crown of his skull and short-sightedly peering from a distance of three or four inches. Sometimes he would only hum and ha, offering no answers – this, I suspect, he did to reward Patrick's impatience – but on his return to Birmingham he sent me postcards in minute handwriting, not only identifying the pictures that Christie's had for sale, but drawing attention to variants seen before the war in Poznan and Plovdiv (he played a vital role, after the war, in the restitution of looted works of art across the whole of Europe), often supplying details of provenance that might have taken me months to discover. The wry twist is that he had a lifelong interest in El Greco and, in 1927, at the age of twenty-two, after months spent in Spain, began (and continued) work on a monumental monograph that was never completed; and it was he who brought to the Royal Academy exhibition in 1938 El Greco's forgotten masterpiece in the collection of the King of Roumania (now in the National Gallery, Bucharest), the enormous *Adoration of the Shepherds*. Ellis, of all English art historians, was the man to whom the 'Veronese' should immediately have been shown.

Bill should have ordered the El Greco's removal from the sale, but as its owner had consigned it more to Alec's care than to Christie's, the old monster had to be informed of events and he, eying me with evident malevolence as a trouble-making little busybody, obstinately resisted this sensible course. Instead, a note of the revised attribution was pinned next to this very distinguished painting hanging among comparatively worthless others – the sale so unimportant that its unillustrated catalogue could not have drawn foreign buyers to London – and on the following Friday Agnews paid 35,000 guineas for it at the auction. This then very substantial sum made headlines in newspapers, but the mishandling did Christie's memorable damage. It was soon reported that Agnews had sold the painting to the New York collector Charles Wrightsman for double their outlay plus another £100,000.

Later that morning Bill took me to see Christie's new chairman, Peter Chance. His real Christian names were Ivan Oswald, and the staff always spoke of him as IOC, but among his friends he was known as Peter, and he was indeed the rock on which the new, young, thrusting and successful Christie's was to be built – though each course of bricks rose very, very, slowly. Sturdily built, about my height, he was a pink and silver man, a middle-aged *Rosenkavalier*, pink of complexion, silver of hair and often of suit, prinked, perfumed and immaculate, his bearing military, given to doffing his overcoat as he climbed the stairs each morning and handing it to Roy Davidge, the clerk in charge of reserves, commissions and the preparation of the catalogues that auctioneers used during the sales, who invariably 'happened' to be there to hang it for him. I warmed to Peter and to the very day on which I left the firm he was affectionate; never once did he undermine or bully me and, had he had his way, I would not, years later, have resigned. To my surprise he claimed that it was he who had asked Anthony to suggest a new recruit, instructed me to introduce whatever changes I thought would help to bring the picture department into line with current practice in the exhibition and museum world and to come to him if ideas for change were frustrated. Apart from Bill, he was the first director of the firm to offer me his hand and wish me well. 'Call me Peter' were the last words of the interview.

Bill next took me to what was to be my room – a small, dark, cramped box of a room, one of a pair on the west flank of the main entrance, convenient for those working on the Front Counter who might wish to show me a picture brought in by a client. Already occupying it was John Hancock, clerk to the picture department, in his mid-thirties, quiet of manner, wry of humour, and soon to play much the same supportive role in this new life as Corporal John had in the army. He was one of the small handful of men whom I have known to be of absolute honesty, reliability and scruple. He had developed an unscholarly instinct for nineteenth-century paintings and over the next few months acted as my cautionary guide through backwaters of markets I did not know existed, 'Are you sure you want to reject this?' his gentle way of suggesting that I might have made a mistake. He was also a shrewd judge of the dealers to whom we had in some measure to kow-tow, as clear-sighted over the great Agnews and their ilk as over the crooked little runners who too duped their clients and were themselves occasionally duped.

Behind a second desk sat Vic Heather, the man whom I was to replace but who was not to retire until the end of July, three months away. As much a dropper of aitches but not quite as old, he had been Alec's man since 1919, travelling with him to take dictation when an inventory or insurance valuation of paintings in a country house was required, yet in all but forty years he had learned nothing, had developed nothing of an eye and – it seemed to me – cared nothing for quality, beauty, rarity or the history of art. Paintings were a commodity as tedious as any other and, wearing a brown cotton overall, he catalogued them for four hours every morning and then, returning to our room, banished

John and me while he gulped doorstep sandwiches and a flask of tea and, that done, lay back in his chair, hands folded over belly, and fell into a snoring sleep that could be heard as far off as the Front Counter. The only thing for which I have to thank him was his valuable description of the working practices of Hercules Brabazon Brabazon, a prolific painter in watercolour and gouache much admired by John Singer Sargent, whose assistant he had been as a boy.

Brabazon was discovered at the age of seventy. Rich enough always to winter abroad, this friend of John Ruskin, Arthur Severn and James Holland – and much travelled with them (and other watercolourists) – held his first one man exhibition in 1892, when he was indeed seventy. A sell-out, it created a seemingly insatiable demand for more, and in his considerable house, Oaklands, near Sedlescombe in Sussex, he set up a painting room with trestle-tables in a ring against the walls. On these it was the job of Vic Heather, a local boy of twelve in 1900, to place, at random, sheets of coloured paper, blue, pink, beige and white, the rectangles vertical or horizontal and of different sizes – again at random; he then mixed paint in glass pots and laid out sticks of charcoal and a range of brushes. When HBB came in he first made a few indications of a composition in charcoal on several sheets, and then with a pot of colour in hand, wandered from one to another painting the skies, the trees or some other salient feature until, concurrently, a dozen compositions, landscapes and copies of old master paintings became recognisable, while Vic washed brushes and replenished pots. After a long break for lunch and a nap, HBB reappeared to sign and inscribe the day's work – HBB Ischia, HBB Tangier, HBB Hyderabad, HBB Velazquez, HBB Rembrandt . . . Vic then stored them alphabetically by place or original artist with hundreds of others in solander boxes. This Vic had done until 1905, the year of Brabazon's last exhibition and the year before his death at eighty-four. What Vic had done between 1905 and 1919, when he joined Christie's, I was never told, but he was profoundly deaf without a hearing-aid and I wondered if this had been caused by some hellish experience in the Great War.

It was Vic who introduced me to the picture warehouse and the art of cataloguing Christie-style. 'Why 'aven't you worked on the Front Counter?' he asked, 'Everybody works on the Front Counter before they join departments, even the directors . . . ' To this there was no answer that could please him. In the cavernous storerooms stacked with paintings yet to be catalogued or already sold, I was introduced to Jock and Les, the two porters in charge of paintings up to the point of sale – Jock old, frail and given to lunchtime drinks and afternoon confusions, Les younger, but as tiny as a boy of twelve. Between them they struggled to keep the stacks in order and not to damage frames, but I hated the sessions when Bill and Patrick came to check the latest intake and Vic's (and subsequently my) cataloguing, and Patrick, always impatient and far stronger, let them lift big pictures without offering a hand. Both, in their way, were patient and loyal saints.

Vic was far from a saint, though sorely tried; if he was bullied by Patrick, he bullied Jock and Les. I thought him belligerent, resentful and uncooperative, but I dare say he felt threatened by a young whipper-snapper in a suit suggesting other ways to do his job – 'Now look 'ere sonny, I've been doing this for forty years . . . ' But he scarcely looked for signatures, could not be bothered with inscriptions on stretchers or the backs of canvases, and to anything he saw but could not understand he omitted reference. I was, for the first week, expected to stand behind his shoulder and observe, but when I saw something that he did not want to see, he hurried on and would not hold the picture back to take a longer look at it; if I protested, he switched off his hearing aid. When, at last, I was allowed to catalogue, I tried to make some very simple changes – to group previous owners, literary references and exhibitions under the simple words provenance, bibliography and exhibitions, but provenance was a term that neither Patrick nor old Alec recognised and at bibliography they laughed. The suggestion that we should use metric measurements for sales important enough to attract dealers from the continent was also ridiculed. But to some small extent I got my way within weeks, for in the first sale of old master drawings over which I had limited control – the Skippe Collection – I was allowed to use the terms collections, literature and exhibited and even, in brackets, to introduce the metric measurements that are precisely accurate with small sheets of paper.

It did not occur to me that Vic's was a forlorn situation. Within the month I had made superfluous his dogged four-hour stints of cataloguing, and yet, every day he was in the office or the warehouse expecting to work out his time and to train me in the model that he had for so long followed, only to find that I was rebellious and wanted to overturn the rules by which he worked. I should have been more sympathetic, but I could not like the man. We were there to do exactly the same job and the overlap was intolerable; it was to produce a basic catalogue entry, based on supposedly thorough examination, for every one of the five hundred or so pictures that were delivered to Christie's every week, either in bulk at the back door or singly at the Front Counter. Pictures accepted at the Front Counter were always seen by me, Vic, Alec, Bill or Patrick, even by John Hancock and our initials noted on the receipt; for these to be rejected on further examination was very rare. The much larger intake at the back door was never inspected and sorted on arrival, and as rather more than half these bulk deliveries were of pictures too wretched to be sold by Christie's and were thus automatically passed on the Bonham's – 'Nil nisi Bonham' a frequent quip of Bill's – there seemed to me little point in spending half our time producing catalogue entries that could only be for Bonham's benefit. I wanted to apply an immediate vetting system to large deliveries, but this was refused by Patrick who insisted that he must see everything; even so, unofficially and by degrees, and with the connivance of Jock and Les, this is what I did.

It was not comfortable to know that I was trammelled by blind custom. Peter Chance had made this clear, but not quite clear enough to prepare me for the weight of opposition to any change that I might, on his instruction, try to introduce in order to improve the picture department's performance. A bruising encounter with Alec revealed the entrenched autocracy of the old guard. When Jock and Les drew from the stacks a rare and beautiful still life of glasses in a basket, I knew at once that it was by Sebastien Stoskopff, a Strasbourg painter of the first half of the seventeenth century, but the accompanying correspondence between its owner, Senator Maguire of Dublin, and Alec, suggested that it was by Jan van Huysum, a baroque Dutchman of the second half – an absurd attribution, quite inexcusable. I catalogued it with the enthusiasm of discovery – an almost physical pleasure – wrote a note on its relationship with other examples in date and style (Stoskopff was all but unknown beyond the walls of Strasbourg), and bounded up to Alec's room to tell him the great news. 'Stoskopff?' he said. 'Stoskopff?. Never 'eard of 'im. That picture is by Jan van 'Uysum. That is what I've told Senator Maguire and that is what 'e wants to 'ear from us. I will write and tell 'im.' And so, tossing my notes into the waste paper bin, he did; he also wrote a new catalogue entry that was later supported by Patrick and shrugged off by Bill with a 'Never mind, my boy'. I sent a photograph to Michel Laclotte and a copy of the catalogue so that there could be no confusion over the lot number. I also wrote to Philip Hendy, Director of the National Gallery, for I felt that so rare a thing should be on its walls, but it was outside his narrow range of interests (Renoir's grotesque women, clothed and naked) and he did not have the courtesy to reply. The painting eventually returned to France and recovered its identity. Years later, long, long after old Alec should have ceased to be his model, I was to have much the same experience with Patrick who had urged a friend to send for sale a handsome full length portrait of a young man. I catalogued it as by Lemuel Francis Abbott, even though Patrick's notes indicated that he had told the owner it was by Joshua Reynolds and would get her a Reynolds price. I also put it aside for Ellis to see, for unlike most Abbotts the sitter's anatomy did not much deteriorate below the waist and I thought it a better example of his work than any in the National Portrait Gallery. Patrick, however, was obdurate, adopting the stance that as he had said it was by Reynolds, then by Reynolds it must be, developing eventually into the 'I am the director of the picture department and you will do as you are told' stance. It wasn't worth a battle and he had his way – but to every enquiry about the painting I responded with the truth and it was, after its failure to sell, returned to its owner.

Even before the end of May there was another crisis of the El Greco kind in yet another undistinguished sale. It was perfectly reasonable for lot 111 on 30 May 1958 to have been catalogued by Vic Heather merely as an Italian painting by an anonymous painter, but it was beyond reason that its quality had not been recognised and that it had not been set aside for Ellis to see. The subject, *The Flight into Egypt*, composed of the Holy Family, its donkey and a playful putto, at evening in the last horizontal shaft of dying sunlight, dramatic in its chiaroscuro contrasts, is cramped within the dimensions of the canvas, its energy made explosive by the close containment, a steep diagonal running through the group. Caravaggio haunts it, but the colour and the sentiment are too sweet for him – even so, St Joseph's forearm, central to both the movement and the canvas, should have jolted the perceptions of all who vetted Vic's catalogue description. I was astonished when I saw it and went at once to Bill. 'I thought for a moment that it might be by Ribera,' he said, 'but it so obviously isn't that I didn't press the point.' 'It's Milanese,' I opined, 'by one of those tenebrous painters of the kind that were around when Caravaggio was a boy – but this one is later and the influence is reversed. Shouldn't we withdraw it and start again?' To this the answer was that its value was too low for such a bother, and Bill wandered off.

And so did I – or rather rushed off to the Courtauld Institute

where, in old Robert Witt's collection of photographs and reproductions I found enough to confirm my hunch that the painting
might be a late work by Cerano, the most important painter in
Milan in the first quarter of the seventeenth century – the similarities
were strong, but the painterly qualities of the Christie picture
seemed so infinitely superior to everything with which I could
compare it that I was not wholly convinced. The only explanations
for the difference were either that it was by another hand, power-
fully influenced by Cerano, or that it was entirely autograph and all
the larger public works in churches against which I had tested it
had been executed by inferior assistants. Was this enough for me to
be insistent with Bill on Monday morning? I decided that it was
not and spoke instead to Philip Troutman who had just finished a
tutorial, running very late, as usual – but as he too was hesitant, I
did nothing to remedy the matter. The afternoon before the sale,
Denis Mahon, the distinguished independent art historian on whose
research, connoisseurship and wisdom almost all current scholarship
in seventeenth century art is founded, and a formidable collector,
came to see me, said it was by Cerano and asked me to bid for
him – up to 150 guineas.

At the sale bidding was so brisk that I did not even raise my
finger; Agnew's paid 1,700 guineas for the painting and within a
year had sold it to the City Art Gallery in Bristol for a rumoured
£7,000. When Mahon catalogued the *Seicento* paintings shown in
the Royal Academy's Winter Exhibition of January-March 1960,
he had the gall to claim that he had recognised the authenticity of
the Cerano at the time of the sale – true enough, but so had I and
so too, no doubt, had Agnew's and the underbidder who had
made them pay so much for it (the price, a trifle now, was not
unreasonable for half a century ago); I wonder if he recalled how
paltry his bid had been.

The following sale, on Friday 6 June 1958, was another disaster,
but for very different reasons. The trustees of the Lady Lever Art
Gallery, Port Sunlight, had instructed Christie's to sell 175 paintings

and drawings deemed no longer suitable for the collection. In many cases they were right – a public gallery is no place ever to exhibit watercolours by Yeend King or Wynne Apperley, or paintings by Fred Appleyard and Edmund Monson Wimperis, but in with works by such forgotten minor painters were others of serious interest by painters whom we now hold in high regard. Half a century ago most painters on the heights of the Victorian Olympus had so tumbled in fashion as to be worth very little money, but trustees should make decisions to discard – and acquire – only on the basis of quality, never on fashion. These trustees shed twenty-nine drawings and two oil paintings by Burne-Jones for less than £600, an important sketch by Leighton for his *Cimabue* for 110 guineas, a Waterhouse *Siren* for 28 guineas, and a minor Alma-Tadema for 230 guineas – this last passing into the Allen Funt Collection that in a single-owner, single-artist sale at Sotheby's Belgravia in 1973, only fifteen years later, sold for £3,600;[20] it must now be worth some £360,000 and thus, by the trustees' false criteria, well worth having in Port Sunlight.

Even old Alec had recognised that unless at least a handful of less unfashionable pictures were included in the consignment the sale would be embarrassing for both Christie's and the trustees; thus *The Violet's Message* by Millais at the tag end of his Pre-Raphaelite years, and *A Bowl of Flowers* by Fantin-Latour, at 800 and 9,000 guineas, accounted for more than half the sale's total. The importance of this auction has been the use made of it since 1988 (when the matter was first raised by government) as proof that for museums and galleries to de-accession works of art is to court disaster, for that was also the year in which the Fantin-Latour reappeared at Christie's and new trustees of the Lady Lever thought they should re-acquire it, only to be far outbid at £950,000, pretty well exactly a hundred times the sum given for it thirty years before.

---

20   This sale, of thirty-five paintings by Alma-Tadema for a total of £235,000 marked the re-establishment of his reputation as a serious painter.

At least the discards of the Lady Lever were given the chance to survive in private hands; on the first morning of his employment at the Victoria and Albert Museum in 1960, the junior curator Lionel Lambton was bidden by the museum's Board of Survey to light a bonfire in a dustbin in an inner courtyard, and up in smoke went Richard Redgrave's design for a mural in the House of Lords, forty copies of Raphael's Roman frescoes, an unrecorded number of designs to scale for stained glass windows and other decorations by Burne-Jones (too difficult to store) and an unspecified quantity of Victorian artefacts.

*   *   *

During the summer break, when there were no sales, the pace and pressure lessened and at last Vic Heather left – but the comparative serenity was shattered by Patrick's causing for me a crisis that was both moral and professional. Amongst a range of property accumulated by the Rolls family, the Barons Llangattock of The Hendre (an old house preposterously renovated in the mid nineteenth century as a mock Tudor mansion) and 6,000 acres of Monmouthshire, scheduled for sales in the winter, was a book known as *The Llangattock Hours of the Virgin*. In this property Patrick took a proprietorial interest, not through cousinage but cars, for the third son of the second Baron was the Charles Stewart Rolls of Rolls-Royce and something of an heroic model in his daredevil activities. He also had the interests of the picture department in mind, for he thought that were the fourteen full-page illuminations extracted from the book and sold as paintings, they would provide the core of an important sale. As a book it should automatically have been sold as a book, but Patrick physically nabbed it, brought it to my room, told me to cut out and catalogue the fourteen and then pass the carcass to the book department.

I had never had such a thing in my hands. The illuminations were obviously by several collaborating painters, all more or less derivative from Jan van Eyck and, in my critical view, of indifferent quality as paintings. To me, the value of the volume, still in its original mid-fifteenth century binding – distinguished enough in the binder's mind for him to have signed it Liuinus Stuuaert me Ligavit and inscribed it A Gand (thus giving it a binding date of 1448–1458, the illuminations a little earlier) – lay in its condition, undisturbed since then, and here was I, in the mid twentieth century, about to disturb it, indeed to wreck it. I bearded Patrick in his room upstairs and was appalled by his rage; reminding me that I was an inexperienced employee and he a partner in the firm, he ordered me to do as I was told – he even used the phrase 'I order you . . . ,' and clinched the argument with the threat that he, if I refused, would do the job himself.

Bill, to whom I immediately went, shrugged off my plea – Patrick, it seemed, had been responsible for securing the Llangattock property and he, Bill, had no idea what undertakings and agreements had been made. In the end I went to Peter Chance, told him that I thought that breaking the book would be bad for Christie's reputation, proposed that the proper thing to do was to offer it as a perfect book with the reserve that Patrick might think the total value of the illuminations if sold separately – even to offer it as one lot in a sale of paintings (not such a silly idea, for two of the three dealers who eventually formed a consortium to buy it were the art dealers Edward Speelman and Marlborough) – and think again if it failed to find a buyer. I even said that I would feel compelled to resign if the integrity of the book were to be destroyed, and were this to be the chosen course, I would, as a last resort to save it, report the matter to *The Times*. Peter thought Patrick's proposal butchery (his word), assured me that it would not happen and took the Hours from me. It did not happen, and on 8 December 1958, as a book, lot 191, the Hours were sold for the world record price of £32,000. Christie's held that record for two days, and then it was trounced at Sotheby's by another book of hours from the collection of Dyson Perrins, Joan Seddon's uncle. *The Llangattock Hours*, after languishing in the trade for some years, returned to Flanders and are now in the Bibliotheque Royale, Brussels.

The bruising encounter with Patrick, his determination to put me in my place as his inferior and employee, was gentled a little by an invitation to the Congress of Art Historians in Paris in September, a reassurance that my academic work over the last ten months or so had been recognised. Bill encouraged me to attend, arguing that though I was not so soon entitled to any leave my presence in Paris might be good for Christie's – and this was good for me as Christie's paid the bills. By chance encountering Jill whom I had not seen since we had left the Courtauld, I was within days both dismayed and disappointed to learn that she too had secured an invitation (so much for what I had assumed to be recognition of my scholarship) and wanted to arrange our travelling together. In retrospect I should not have been surprised – she was later to intrude (there is no kinder word for it) on journeys to Albania, Turkey and even Liverpool. We stayed in my mother's old hotel, walked everywhere, attended seminars on every aspect of French art – two, memorably tedious, on the influence of seventeenth-century French architects on the formal buildings of late nineteenth century Roumania and Canada – and went to formal dinners, first in Malmaison and then in the newly restored Versailles, where the flamboyant curator, Gérald van der Kemp, had been responsible for much restitution of furniture and other artefacts lost to it after the French Revolution. Most of this he did through the Versailles Foundation established in New York with the assistance of his rich American (second) wife, Florence Harris, attracting huge donations from Rockefellers, Huttons and Lauders, with Rothschilds and Wildensteins not far behind. I liked him in spite of his overwhelming ebullience and self-esteem, and knowing that Christie's were searching for a major European figure (with, of course, social connections at least as much as expertise and experience of the art Market) to represent the firm in Europe, on my return to

London I suggested that he might be a suitable candidate and negotiations did, indeed, begin. I was never told why they failed but I suspect that van der Kemp was so far from Christie's idea of a gentleman that Peter and Patrick could not stomach him; instead there was the far greater good of his taking on, in the later 1970s, the restoration of Monet's estate in Giverny.

For me the special pleasure of the jaunt to Paris lay in renewing my friendship with Michel Laclotte who took Jill to be a sure sign that my puppy-dog days were over; I did not disillusion him. Through him I met the vivacious and very useful Roseline Bacou, then curator of drawings at the Louvre, who later let me loose on everything in her cure. I also met Carlos van Hasselt, then a curator at the Fitzwilliam but soon to become head of the Netherlands Institute in Paris and, for the rest of our lives, a fine and affectionate friend. He in turn introduced me to John Woodward, Keeper of Paintings at Birmingham City Art Gallery when that was a post of international stature, a brilliant judge of paintings but too unassuming, companionable and on the tipping-point of his descent into alcoholism. Poor John, he later became an Ancient Mariner from whom all friends fled, for he told, repeatedly, the same tales of, misfortune to explain his downright pennilessness, tearing trousers and raincoat to prove that he'd been mugged and now needed just enough money to buy a ticket back to Birmingham 'and for a taxi to Euston too, if you can spare it.' He was my first encounter with the condition – it was later to overtake Bill – and for a while, believing him, I gave him money, but when one day, by then uncertain, I took him to Euston, just as I was about to buy another he showed me his return ticket and broke into miserable sobbing.

In October Bill went to America. In a letter to my mother I complained of so much work that not only had I not been to Windsor for some weeks, but had found it necessary to go into Christie's at weekends to keep up with the flow of pictures to be catalogued – a state of affairs that was to prove more or less permanent for years. In Bill's absence, Alec, by then retired but mistakenly retained as a consultant, had taken it upon himself to resume his old responsibilities; I observed that 'All would be well were it not that old Sir Alec is the most difficult and most dishonest old idiot, and I have to do as he tells me.' He disliked Jewish dealers; to the Leggatts and Agnews he kow-towed, but were the Herner family who owned the Hallsborough Gallery to bid successfully at auction he'd knock the lot down to 'Ballsborough' in crude allusion to their borrowed name; and when I suggested that we should show a Parmigianinesque painting to Lili Fröhlich, an expert in the field, whose full surname was Fröhlich-Bum (pronounced Boom), his scorn for all the middle-European art historians who had fled from Europe in the 1930s and become dealers because there was nothing else to do, was expressed in his near-screaming repetition of 'Bum, bum, bum – what can anyone called Bum tell me?'

We crossed swords too over a decent still life by William Somerville Shanks – of whom I had never heard and nor, I suspect, had he; bright in colour and briskly painted with evident panache, I wanted to include it in a sale, but Alec did not. Argument was terminated in his usual way – repetition in increasing volume. 'Somerville Shanks? Somerville Shanks? That's not a good selling name' – introducing me to a ludicrous means of establishing the market value of a painter's work. In our worst encounter there was an additional element to his hostility in that, as he put it, I had caused mortal offence to Freddy Turner. At first, as I had no idea who Freddy Turner was, Alec's tirade was incomprehensible, but as it wore on in language that I had not heard since my first weeks in the army, I realised that Turner was the stout little man I had found on Christie's doorstep an hour earlier when returning from lunch, sending away a man with a large painting. At a glance I knew that it had qualities to be found in Mola and Testa, near contemporaries of Poussin, and intervened – tactlessly no doubt, but I wanted to save the picture rather than the face of the idiot rejecting it with assertions that it was too large and too dark to be worth anything, suggesting that it might find a buyer at Bonham's 'but it ain't good enough for us.' The idiot, however, was Freddie Turner, and Freddie Turner, old Alec spat at me, was his brother-in-law and had been valuing pictures for Christie's for more than forty years – hot dinners and short trousers too came into the argument. When I told Bill of the episode, apologetically, for Freddie was his uncle, his response was that he had indeed been Christie's travelling valuer up and down the country and 'God knows what damage he has done.' The rejected picture did turn out to be by Testa.

At much the same time I had an offer from Robin Fedden of the National Trust offering me a post that covered Dorset, Somerset, Wiltshire and Gloucestershire, with a flat in Dyrham Park and a starting salary of between £800 and £1,000 a year. After an interview, Robin, who was later my next door neighbour and a friend, confirmed the offer in a letter and this – double my salary at Christie's and more with the flat – I took to Peter asking how I should resolve the difficulty. His response I took to be a promise: it was that he could not immediately match the offered salary, but would, in the new year, reach some way towards it (in the event he almost doubled my starting salary), and that if the firm prospered I should be made a director within four or five years.

For me the main event of the autumn was the sale of the Skippe Collection of Old Master Drawings, scheduled for 20 and 21 November 1958, a field of connoisseurship and collecting in which even Patrick realised I had the better of him and he did not interfere, though he may have had something to do with securing the sale much earlier in the year. John Skippe, 1742–1812, much travelled in Italy, was an amateur painter now best known for trying his hand at the rare skill of making woodblock prints in colour (chiaroscuro woodcuts), mostly after Parmigianino, in the manner of Antonio Maria Zanetti; but he also amassed some eight hundred drawings, mostly by Italian hands, varying so widely in quality that his judgement was evidently uncertain. In 1939 A. E. Popham (Arthur

Ewart – but Hugh to his friends), who had been Assistant Keeper
of Prints and Drawings at the British Museum since 1912 (Keeper
1945–53) and was widely regarded as a scrupulous connoisseur and
art historian, compiled a manuscript catalogue in exquisite writing
small and clear. I had nothing to do but collate comments and
corrections that were the consequence of another decade of scholarship and brooding, adjust this to a pattern that was a compromise
between Christie's customs and my wish to reform them, and
hope for his approval. Great man though he was and often gloomy
of expression, nothing about him froze the impertinent tyro to his
bones – as did the unbearably lofty manners of Pope-Hennessy and
Kenneth Clark – and the thin and solemn face that seemed so
fifteenth century and Eyckian could occasionally be persuaded into
a slow smile. In 1958 it was difficult to believe that he had joined
the Naval Air Service on the outbreak of the Great War and been
shot down at Gallipoli, then to transfer to the Royal Flying Corps,
in which he had known Joan Seddon's father. It was difficult too to
imagine the tall, gaunt, slow-moving figure sailing and playing
tennis, for at sixty-nine or so, scholarship had bent his back and
bowed his head, and there was scant evidence of a muscled body
within his tired old suits. But until his death in December 1970,
whenever I knocked on his Islington door to show him some
scrap that I thought might have relevance to the great corpus
of Parmigianino's drawings[21] that were his last and longest pre-
occupation, I sensed a smile behind the seeming melancholy and
warmth in his slow and drawling voice. Never impatient, he
could nevertheless be remarkably wry, dry and ironic.

I also found myself in charge of prints – engravings, etchings,
drypoints, woodcuts, mezzotints and aquatints. This I had not
expected. Prints are not only an old man's field, for connoisseurship
depends on decades of experience, but are better fitted to the mind

21 A. E. Popham: *Catalogue of the Drawings of Parmigianino*, 3 vols, New
Haven and London 1971.

of the philatelist than to the spirit of the man who rejoices in colour and the brushstroke. The print man must know every detail of the beginning and the end of a print's development, the successive adjustments to the plate that make one pull minutely different from another (or occasionally, as in the case of Rembrandt, a sweeping change); he must know about the nationality and makes of paper, the width of margins from inches to mere thread, about too much and too little ink, and about all the other factors that make one print worth ten times the price of another, though the images are, to the sane man, identical. It was Christie's long-established custom to sell unframed prints, watercolours and drawings in whatever packaging they came, described as 'A parcel of . . . ' counting their number the only attempt at cataloguing. From this carelessness I had, as a schoolboy and as a Courtauld student, some benefit, occasionally bidding 3 guineas (and once 5 guineas) for parcels in which there were as many as a hundred sheets of paper, assuming from the price that nothing was of any individual value. Now, in charge and expected to make reforms, I inspected incoming parcels and put aside everything that I thought might reward investigation. Patrick dismissed the idea as a waste of time, but Bill allowed me to pursue it. But under whose tutelage? There was no one in Christie's to whom I could turn, but at Colnaghi's, the Bond Street dealers in prints and drawings from whom I had, when I was in the army, bought a Zanetti woodcut and a fine Castiglione etching, there was Arthur Driver who manifestly knew a thing or two, a moody bloke with a hefty working-class chip on his shoulder. When I put my problem to him he had the good grace to send me to Harold Wright who had recently, at seventy-three, retired from the firm after more than forty years as head of the print department. It was Wright who gave me the foundations of almost all that I know of prints and who opened my eyes to the post-Whistler generation of British printmakers – Strang, Cameron, Blampied, Smart – as well as knocking sense into Dürer and Rembrandt. He dined early – as old men do – and well into 1959 I spent many later evenings with him working our way through his orderly solander boxes, the annotated *catalogues raisonnés* on his shelves and his own unpublished manuscript catalogues, taking instruction from him. In his way he was as generous with his experience and scholarship as Blunt and Wilde, but where they revealed the spiritual best of things, he interpreted nothing, but acquainted me with the facts on which judgement could be made – this print is better than this because . . .

*   *   *

When the year came to its end it was time for summing-up. I had hardly set foot in Windsor and the promise of a four-day week so that I could, had been broken in such a way that I knew it to have been nothing better than a good intention. Another blow to possible scholarship had been a visit from Ben Nicolson, editor of the *Burlington Magazine*, specifically to tell me that as I had joined the trade, he could publish nothing more from me (nothing more? – one Shorter Notice and then nothing more?) – not even if it were connected with my work on Fontana which I knew would turn up all sorts of unpublished bits and pieces. This was a bitter blow, for I thought (and was right to think) that Christie's might be the source of all sorts of unknown paintings that for the sake of other art historians ought to be published in the *Burlington*, for Christie's catalogues were then not much seen beyond the trade and we very rarely published illustrations.

Christie's had become my world – yet not even the whole Christie's, but a picture department that was only part of it, riven between Bill and Patrick, held together by John Hancock; I had made little impression on it, my scholarship had been only haphazardly applied and I had become successor to Vic Heather, wasting my time putting together sales of ghastly and near worthless pictures when I should have been writing catalogue entries that drew attention to the rarity, beauty and particular or art historical interest of the better pictures that we sold. We were overwhelmed with bulk and should have taken much more care with paintings that had quality, but Patrick regarded Christie's as a clearing house for the trade at all its levels rather than an ally of museums, serious collectors and the nation's heritage, and any attempt I made to write the kind of note that I had written for the Stoskopff was at once deleted.

Of the rest of the firm I knew virtually nothing other than the bare bones that Jo Floyd was head of the furniture department, Guy Hannen was in charge of objects of Vertu – both by virtue of family relationship – and that Arthur Grimwade, brilliant silver expert, had no such connections and had achieved his worldwide eminence through enthusiasm and scrupulous hard work. With Patrick, these were the Young Turks of the board – and not nearly Turkish enough. The Old Guard was still represented – by Jo's cousin, Sir Harry Floyd, and Guy's father, Gordon Hannen, both of whom always carried neat leather cases but appeared to do no work; Sir Harry, rarely seen, was said to turn up in King Street once a month to collect his stipend in cash, but in his, Gordon carried bottles of gin and tonic – I once saw the case open and it was indeed neatly compartmented to prevent bottles and glasses from rattling. He tippled all day and when he set off for his homeward journey from Paddington was more or less plastered – his death on the concourse there, run down by a train of luggage trolleys, a Pooterish calamity, was the cause of grim and cynical laughter among Christie's lower employees.

My one friend was John Herbert, son of that colossus of the Thirties, A.P. Herbert, who had joined Christie's on the same day as I to invent and nurture a press office that could turn failure to advantage – as was his immediate task with the El Greco. John was surprisingly bumbling for a man of thirty-four, far too easily disconcerted by Christie's too frequent occasions for dismay. Constantly astonished by the uncomprehending arrogance of the directors, he was wily enough to become, through a fluke of circumstance, one of their number within a year. An absolutely honest man, he was incapable of what we now call 'spin,' and half a century later could never have been even an office boy in his now devious and unscrupulous profession. It was characteristic of him to drive a Citroën Six, a hopelessly old fashioned and under-powered but utterly engaging car of the Thirties – Patrick drove an Aston-Martin DB2, Jo a Jaguar 2.4, and Peter an R-type Bentley.

In asking myself if I really wanted to stay with Christie's, I realised that I had learned a phenomenal amount about painters of whose work I would otherwise never have heard, that there were periods and genres of painting in which the trade merrily traded – Style Maples, for example (to be pronounced as though it were French), the kind of paintings that went well with the 'Louis Quince' furniture sold by that once eminent emporium to devotees in St John's Wood – but of which the art historian knew nothing, and never would. Of these there were no monographs and the only reference books on Christie's shelves were an ancient set of Bénézit's eight-volume *Dictionnaire*[22] (they possessed neither Thieme-Becker nor the Vollmer Supplement)[23] and a broken-backed copy of Graves' *Dictionary*,[24] an alphabetical list of every painter who had ever exhibited in England, but as it was published in 1901, it was useless for the twentieth century. To learn anything of Benjamin Williams Leader and his crude imitator Dan Sherrin (the old drunk in the horse trough at Whitstable) one had to work at either Christie's or Sotheby's and piece together scraps of information randomly acquired – and those of us who took minor painters seriously made, by doing so, some contribution to the scholarly esteem in which some are now held – Atkinson Grimshaw and Albert Goodwin, Hercules Brabazon Brabazon and Alma-Tadema are all examples who have risen from nothing to being the subjects of monographs and exhibitions.

22   E. Bénézit: *Dictionnaire des Peintres* . . . , Librairie Gründ 1910.
23   U. Thieme und W. Becker: *Algemeines Lexikon der Bildenden Kunst* . . . , Leipzig 1907 and later.
24   Algernon Graves: *A Dictionary of Artists 1760–1893*, London 1901.

But much of what I saw at an average rate of a hundred a day was irredeemable rubbish and offered so little intellectual and aesthetic nourishment that I harboured a Communist dream of appointment as a Commissar of the art market with absolute power to order the destruction of crotcheted landscapes by E. J. Niemann, glossy flower paintings by Cecil Kennedy and Davis Richter, pretty farmyard friends by Walter Hunt and the jolly carousing cardinals exquisitely achieved by Giuseppe Signorini and Alessandro Rinaldi that ought to have been wry and subversive, but were not. All these horrors were worth substantial money then (and far more substantial now) – good selling names, as Alec had it – but there was not a scrap of merit in them, yet there were dealers in decent premises in St James's who sold nothing else and would turn away a Titian were one ever offered them. Did I want to devote my life to these? Were they really a rewarding match for the Claudes and Poussins with which I had dealt at the Royal Academy or the Canalettos I had catalogued for Munich? With the unrelenting pace at which Christie's turned over the thousands of pictures delivered in a month, they depended on what I already knew in the important art historical fields that I had studied as a student and as I had been given scant opportunity to deepen my knowledge, it seemed inevitable that in this conveyor-belt world I too would sooner or later make mistakes to match the El Greco and Cerano.

It was, however, a much smaller thing that almost tipped me into resignation – a Christie's ritual. One of the benefits of employment was the Luncheon Voucher – a slip of paper entitling the bearer to food worth three shillings (fifteen pence, or seventy-five over the week) at any café that would take them – that is very few in St James's, the territory of the great and exclusive London club and of such restaurants as Wilton's, Overton's and Prunier's. In practical terms it meant scrambling for a seat in The Bonbonnière, an Italian café in Duke Street used by the slaves of the art market, the lowest forms of salesman life, the packers of parcels and collectors of purchases, the commission agents who never betrayed the skeletons

in their employers' cupboards and every itinerant workman un-
fortunate enough to have employment in the neighbourhood. At
the Bonbon the rule was to share tables and shuffle seats, order
quickly, eat quickly, pay and go, for only by packing us in and
throwing us out could the ever-smiling Italian family that ran it
keep their prices down to a level that made the Luncheon Voucher
a viable bill of exchange. I found this subsidy humiliating and
would much rather have been paid a few more pounds a year. But
even more humiliating was the Lady Bountiful business of the
Christmas bird and bonus. The bonus was supposed to reflect,
according to our status in the firm, the profits of the year, but these
were so low − even dipping into loss, we were told − that the
envelopes distributed by the company secretary, Charlie Puddifoot,
on the eve of the Christmas break, contained so few banknotes as
to be insulting, particularly as news was leaked that the cash came
straight from the pockets of the poor suffering directors. And
then − the final straw − there was Ridley Leadbeater's circus at
the Front Counter, the distribution of Christmas birds to every
member of staff.

Ridley had a stake in a smallholding or poultry farm near nether
Basildon and had a contract with Christie's for the delivery of
perhaps a hundred geese and turkeys labelled with our names, but
in no discernible order, alphabetical or departmental. This disorder
led to bad temper, even panic, and was not helped by Ridley's
taking off for lunch at the Ritz − another ritual − with one of the
many dealers to whom he gave favours, returning glassy-eyed.
Frith could have painted *Christie's on Christmas Eve* as a pendant to
Paddington Station or *Derby Day*, and the performance, thoroughly
Victorian, perfectly encapsulated the hierarchy of the firm, the
lordly directors on the stair looking down on the scramble as
though the staff were terriers rat-catching in a barn. I wonder if any
of them ever noticed Ridley snatching opportunities to grope the
upturned bums presented on these occasions? He was an inveterate
but butter-would-not-melt groper of both boys and girls behind

his counter, his favourite trick the vicious jabbing of a pencil at the anus of a boy leaning forward to attend a visitor – an idiotic thing to do when most of them were the close relatives or godchildren of directors; even Charlie Allsopp, later Lord Hindlip, whom on his joining Christie's in 1962 I immediately (and rightly) identified as a future chairman of the firm, was the victim of Ridley's anal poke.

From these small things I learned exactly where in the hierarchy I stood. There had been other indications. With Vic Heather's departure, Frits Lugt, fastidious collector of old master drawings and scrupulous keeper of records, offered me half a crown to do what Vic had done for years – set aside for him a catalogue of every picture sale inscribed with prices, the names of buyers and any other information gleaned on the day. Dealers offered me a fiver to ensure that paintings were included in sales no matter what Patrick of Alec might think of them, another fiver to place a picture half way through the catalogue, another still to tweak the attribution, and I swiftly learned that behind Christie's grand facade ran two economies – the upstairs theatre of the saleroom with a suave director playing auctioneer, and downstairs the black economy of staff so poorly paid that they depended on the tips and bribes that so easily came their way. Was this why Vic Heather had for forty years endured the foul mouth of old Alec? – it explained why, until the very day of his retirement, he insisted on putting the catalogue entries in order, disrupting any logic that I had tried to introduce and determining in which sales pictures should be included; this, until his job was mine, I had attributed to some arcane wisdom of ages, but once I had his desk, the possibility of doubling my income was immediately apparent. In resisting that temptation I became unpopular with the many dealers whose regular delivery of paintings by the dozen provided background for the few from private sources that might revive the gloss of Christie's reputation. Bill, who continued his father's custom of being close to dealers of the old guard who had no premises but simply bought from country shops, auctioneers and old ladies on whose doors they knocked (hence the term 'knocker' for the itinerant dealer) and sent their accumulated bulk to Christie's to apply attributions and make profits, received many complaints of my arrogance.

Was it to please these that I had deserted not only the scholarship of art history but the theology that might have interrupted it? Was being something of a buffer for Bill when Patrick bullied him to be my career? Had I in eight months made anything of the mark I had been led to believe Christie's expected of me? To all these questions there was the same unarguable answer. Mulling over them with my stepfather, he counselled caution with the questions 'Have you learned anything?' and 'Is there more to learn?' – and to these the answer was equally unarguable, but opposite. 'In that case,' said Robert, 'stay with them until you are giving more than you gain from the experience.'

*   *   *

And what other life did I have in the later months of 1958? I went to Mass as regularly as ever, drove to Castle Hedingham frequently enough to mow my mother's lawn and take Penny for long walks through the Gainsborough landscapes that then lay between the village and Sudbury, seven walking miles away, though at thirteen she was getting old for such a distance. Mignon Frossard replaced my mother as companion at the opera; I saw a good deal of Baby Helen who had graduated in the summer and been appointed Philip Troutman's assistant as Keeper of the Courtauld Institute's collection, and began a long friendship with Richard Hughes-Hallett, one of my immediate contemporaries at the Courtauld, largely because I had moved to within three minutes walk of his family's house in Allen Street, Kensington. This move, to the basement of 16 Phillimore Place, the house in which Kenneth Grahame wrote *The Wind in the Willows*, brought me back to the heartland of my childhood, the churches of Our Lady of Victories and the Carmelites still familiar though rebuilt since the war, the High Street very much the same, the ground floor food department of John Barker's, where I had so often queued for rations during and after the war, quite unmodernised, some of the old staff still behind the counters – particularly the pink giant of a butcher who always gave me a tit-bit for Penny when she was with me, for dogs were then allowed in food shops.

The house belonged to Mrs Cecil Chesterton, the sister-in-law of G.K. Chesterton, who in 1927 had achieved admiring notoriety by establishing, with some advice from my stepfather, a hostel for homeless women (it still exists, as the Central and Cecil, in Waterloo Road). The basement was gloomy but the ceilings high, and white and ice-blue paint were my response. I asked John Critchley, my equivalent in Christie's furniture department, for advice and he told me to drive along the old road to Bath and haggle in the junk and antique shops, never paying the price asked. This I did, but instead of furniture found a painting that I could not afford – as Berenson once said, 'One look is enough if concentration is absolute.' The dealer, Frank Smith, whose wife kept a little china shop at the north end of Church Street Kensington, let me pay half the price with a promise to pay the rest within a year. It has lasted well. I have it still. As for furniture, friends gave me cast off chairs and an ottoman, Mignon gave me her spare piano, and I slept well enough on the floor for some months. Years later, long after his death, Frank Smith stared at me from the window of the Fine Art Society – a portrait painted by Maxwell Armfield – and I bought it, an act of purest sentiment.

Joyce Smith once told me a tale that I treasure. She had a tiny scrap of landscape acquired with a parcel of porcelain and put it in her window with a price tag of £3, just to get rid of it. Imagine her dismay when Graham Reynolds, author of the catalogue of all the Constables in the Victoria and Albert Museum, came into the shop and bought it without a word – had she, for nothing, let slip a masterpiece? Some days later he was back; 'I'm afraid I don't think this is by Constable,' he said, 'may I return it and have my money back?'

CHAPTER 12

Further Misgivings at Christie's

In one of the dead days between Christmas 1958 and the New Year break I was called to the Front Counter to talk to a young man who had brought nothing to show Christie's and who made little sense to Leadbeater, but who would not be sent away. To me he seemed in so emotional a state that he could hardly explain his errand, but slowly it emerged that he was offering the remaining contents of John Minton's studio, the proceeds of the sale to be given to the Artists' General Benevolent Fund. Prolific painter, illustrator and designer, melancholy Minton, compelled by a weight of miseries beyond relief, had committed suicide in January 1957, convinced that he was exhausted as an artist. He has since become a romantic hero, and his work is indeed burdened with romantic notions of anguish, haplessness and wistful longing. Consumed with tenderness when confronted by young men, his portraits have a telling truth about them, and it was the subject of one of these who stood before me; Minton was born on Christmas Day 1917 and we were talking of him and his work two days after what would have been his 41st birthday.

I met Minton only once, late in the Autumn Term of 1956, by the coincidence of our leaving a party at the Royal College of Art at the same moment, to which I had been invited by Keith Townend, an architecture student in whom I had found a kindred aesthetic spirit while we were training to be subalterns. I was stone cold sober, he very very drunk: I walked with the shambling, lanky, anguished man almost draped about my shoulders, to his home in Apollo Place, World's End, and, not knowing what to do with a famous artist almost old enough to be my father, would have left him on his doorstep had he not so obviously needed help beyond the door. I saw him to his bed, tugged off his clothes, turned him onto his side in a foetal position and drew up the blankets; his silent response was to indicate a card on the side table – 'Mr John Minton has removed from 5 Shaftesbury Villas W8 and is now installed at 9 Apollo Place SW10. Tel: FLA 0433.'

Like many of my generation of schoolboys, I had been compelled to read Alain-Fournier's *Le Grand Meaulnes*, slipped into the Higher Schools Certificate syllabus by some benign old queen, and had used as crib an English translation illustrated by Minton, conveniently published in 1947. To a romantic adolescent the sub-text of both the book and the illustrations was patently the puppy love of one boy for another, and this, of course, is the clue to much of Minton's work. He was an unrequited homosexual, the fifth former in love with the prefect, the boy in love with the man, the skinny with the muscular and stocky, the educated man with the never educable ignorant, the refined with the rough and tough, and, most miserable of all, the homo- with the heterosexual. 'What one paints and what one is are inescapably interwoven' said Minton in 1940 – as true of Leonardo da Vinci and his pretty boys, Rubens and his plump women, and of Lucian Freud whose paintbrush crawls into a woman's crutch with the insistence of a caterpillar into a cabbage heart, as it was of himself.

With the exception of the war years, Minton's adult life was spent in an atmosphere of sexual persecution, the trials of homosexual miscreants so notorious – Wildeblood, Montagu, Gielgud (for whom Minton had designed sets for *Macbeth*), Croft-Cooke and naughty old Ian Horabin among them, the judgements so prejudiced and the penalties so extreme that both the police and the law sank deep into disrepute, their very bigotry at last stimulating the liberal attitudes that brought about reform, though not until long after Minton's death. His sexual isolation, however, might not have mattered quite so much had he not felt even more isolated in his work. From the beginning he had been a painter of people and places, communicating an elegiac mood or romantic narrative, drawing on a peculiarly English thread that reached from Samuel Palmer's Shoreham to the Wales of Graham Sutherland. He was too graphic an artist ever, as a painter, to respond to the growing demand for abstract art, for bravura brushwork that when cold might or might not mean something, and had no patience for the contriving painters of St Ives. He tried his hand at it, even, under a false name, exhibiting abstracts as a jape, but this only confirmed his contempt for facile non-figurative art.

The material from his studio was delivered at the very beginning of 1959, accompanied by the same young man, who told me that a painting of a Michelangelesque male nude imposed on an abstract pattern was the canvas on Minton's easel when he died. I wanted to make a fuss of these sad remains, to publish in the catalogue a note on Minton explaining who he was and what he had done, even to hold a wake of sorts when the pictures went on view to which his students and fellow tutors at the Royal College would be invited – but nothing of this was to be. Patrick, probably recognising the homo-eroticism of the subjects was appalled – 'We don't do studio clearances' – and, having bullied me for committing Christie's to the sale, allowed it to take place only because the benefit to the AGBI could be seen as a justification for selling such contemporary rubbish. Without beat of drum or funeral note the paintings were hurried into a sale on 20 February 1959, tucked into a catalogue that was already prepared for the printers, and John Minton slipped into three decades of obscurity.

Had Patrick allowed me to treat the studio clearance as an exhibition we would have had not only, in art historical terms, a decent record of Minton's work in the months before his death, but almost certainly greater insight into his distressingly turbulent state of mind. The most significant indication of this was the painting on his easel at his death; bought by Lord Stanley of Alderley for 12 guineas, he paid for it but did not collect it and within weeks instructed Christie's to get rid of it. In the sale on Friday 17 July I gave myself a birthday present and bought it for 3 guineas. Half a century later it rewards me daily, hanging in my dining room, the first of a small collection of Minton's drawings and small paintings.

The Minton episode confirmed the haplessness of my situation in Christie's. Brought in to make changes and, above all, to raise the scholarly level of the catalogues, I was at every turn frustrated and I got little help from Bill who, never combative with Patrick, always let him have his way – over the Mintons his only contribution to the argument was 'Well, we've never sold contemporary art.' Sales were categorised as Important or Highly Important if paintings or their owners were thought to merit such terms, but the run–of–the–mill sales, the weekly attempts to clear the warehouses, were given the portmanteau title 'Ancient and Modern Pictures and Drawings,' and were a jumble of parcels of unframed prints and drawings on trestle tables and framed oils and watercolours on the walls, occasionally three rows of them reaching almost to the ceiling, with auctioneers competing to beat the record selling-rate of 120 lots an hour. As for the catalogues – these were no more than identification lists and offered no evidence of research, scholarship or expert opinion; if Ellis Waterhouse had thought a canvas quite certainly by a French follower of Caravaggio and just possibly by Trophime Bigot, this was regarded as perversely obscure and the simple listing as Caravaggio was preferred, with no note that he had looked at it with interest. Bigot was, in the 1950s, known only to a handful of scholars and years might have passed before I had proved or disproved Ellis's point, but simply by raising it another shred of evidence could have been brought into the open. Such shreds very rarely were.

Ancient and Modern was, to me, the title of a hymnal and seemed ridiculous in the context of a vigorous art market in the middle of the twentieth century. I suggested that we should dispense with both it and the haphazardly mixed sales that were the bulk of our turnover, by the very simple device of separating paintings into categories of period, nationality and type, colour-coding their covers and setting up independent sales devoted to watercolours, prints and old master drawings. When I proposed the term *genre* for nineteenth-century paintings of pretty children, immaculate farm animals and carousing cardinals, Patrick said 'I don't know the meaning of the word' and left the room. Bill was rather more receptive and, tentatively, the reform began and Ancient disappeared from our vocabulary. Genre was not a term ever used by Christie's for what Baudelaire described as 'oeuvres charmantes dans les regions moyennes du talent,' and we settled, for a while at least, on *Narrative*, for almost every nineteenth-century picture told some sort of story.

The one advantage of the old system was that if a consignment was a big mixed bag of paintings, drawings and watercolours of all ages, all were sold in one sale – one entry in the books, one sale catalogue to the owner, one cheque. With my meddling the department might now spread the consignment over half a dozen sales and the increased work caused administrative confusion and delay with which John Hancock and I could not keep pace – and it was thus that Ian Lowe joined the department in April 1959. Tall, erect, elegant, impossible to ruffle and slightly mysterious, Ian was utterly dependable. At Oxford he had been awarded the prize that honours Laurence Binyon, poet, playwright, translator of Dante, art historian, authority on the arts of China and Japan and slave in the British Museum for forty years; this was to encourage students to study works of art abroad and Ian's chosen subject, born of pan-European travels in long vacations as an undergraduate, was the baroque and rococo art and architecture of South Germany and Austria. This, studied for a year, brought him close contacts with the grandees of the Ashmolean and Victoria and Albert Museums, and with Brinsley Ford, the most eclectic gentleman scholar of his generation (he was born in 1908), the writer of some 300,000 words on the history of the

Grand Tour[25] and generous mentor to every young man who consulted him on the art and artefacts of the eighteenth century. At the V&A Ian had spent the six months from September 1958 editing the *Notes on Italian Monuments* bequeathed it by Margaret Longhurst, the formidable Keeper of Architecture and Sculpture who, in 1938, had been one of the two who were the first women to be given such high appointments there. It was the commendation of her successor, the ebullient Moley, Hender Delves Molesworth, an early enthusiast for the baroque of central Europe, that convinced Peter Chance that he should appoint Ian to the picture department; there Ian hoped to expand and consolidate his scholarship; as with me, his hopes were thwarted.

Ian relieved me of much of the basic chore of cataloguing. For this the tools provided were a spotlight on a long flex, white spirit in demijohns and rolls of cotton wool with which to swab it onto paintings obscured by varnish that had grown dark and opaque with age or, worse, that had 'chilled' – that is, turned greyish-white. Under the heat of the spotlight the white spirit evaporated fast and we had only seconds in which to discover signatures and dates carved in the bark of trees or hidden in the shadow of a dock leaf. With well over a hundred pictures the daily target unless I was present to thin them out on their arrival, we had at most four minutes in which to write a 'manuscript' – that is, on half a foolscap sheet, a record of ownership, correspondence and any information the vendor had supplied, notes of measurement and materials, the subject, signature and date, and if these last could not be found, a suggested attribution. Interruptions from the Front Counter, telephone enquiries and the visits of such necessary friends as Ellis Waterhouse, reduced the four minutes to three and two as we worked at breakneck speed. I could never keep my writing

25 Unpublished other than in short articles and the invaluable *A Dictionary of British and Irish Travellers in Italy 1701–1800*, compiled from his archive by John Ingamells, Yale 1997.

small and neat enough and so imported my typewriter – Ian's, however, was perfect for the task and wonderfully legible. That Christie's gave him no time to learn but merely turned him into a drudge, was in part my fault, for I should have seen, that as with me for the past year, all that was wanted by Bill and Patrick was another Vic Heather – and that I was determined not to be, but it was far from a suitable role for Ian.

He was far more disciplined than I and had nothing of my emotional involvement in the firm – he stuck to the hours of business, but I stayed late and sometimes returned after dinner knowing that in two uninterrupted hours I could achieve as much as in a working day; of these interruptions Ian was later to observe that with the public and other members of staff, I 'was not a master of the gentle word, nor of the encouraging gesture.' Ian disappeared for proper lunches, often collected by superior officials from the Ashmolean or Fitzwilliam who had announced themselves to Ridley at the Front Counter, unaware of the mock-grovelling charade that would then be performed in our office; never once was he seen where the humiliating vouchers were the currency. He spent weekends away, we knew not where, for he never boasted of the social connections that meant so much to the directors – Patrick always let it be known if he thought I'd be cowed by the, for me, unattainable grandeur of his. And fearlessly, he took holidays when he wished – fearlessly, because we were expected to fit in with Patrick's plan for absences to fly his Spitfire, race Remus, his famous Alfa-Romeo, and play with a fabled Napier that he claimed to have been (*pace* Rolls-Royce) the best car in the world (at times the most expensive, the marque – defunct by 1924 – was particularly popular with Maharajahs). I envied Ian's aplomb in these small confrontations; I always gave way, but he did not. One way and another we both took more than our allotted three weeks, but my breaks were always combined with work for Christie's and at random times, and in most years I took nothing that could be described as a conventional holiday. My only glimpse into Ian's private life was his purchase of a painting by Denis Wirth-Miller at a charity sale one evening; at the time this was bewildering, but now that Denis is perceived as a significant presence in Francis Bacon's life and art, I recognise the far-sightedness of it.

On 20 March 1961 Ian succumbed to glandular fever; early in April he flew to Rome to convalesce because Mary Howard, to whom he proposed on 30 April, was there; and early in May, returning to Christie's after a long excursion across northern Italy, he resigned. Glandular fever and the journey brought about this turning-point; with time to think he realised that work at Christie's was a useless grind and that work in a museum would better suit his temperament; he had learned little, and that little was in barren fields in which he had no interest, perfectly illustrated by the paintings of Alfred de Breanski, in the later nineteenth century and beyond a prolific exhibitor of anaemic sub-Barbizon (and worse) landscapes, the greens glaucous, the brushwork loose, the flamboyant signatures enormous, the Franco-Russian name his father's fraudulent invention. Within a year or so Ian was happily appointed an assistant keeper in the Ashmolean. We remained in touch, partly through Joan Seddon, more through Hecate, a whippet born to one of Mary's bitches – born to order, indeed, for I had said 'If ever you have a perfect blue bitch pup, call her Hecate on her pedigree papers and let me have her.' Ian and Mary brought her to me on 24 October 1967, a tiny creature to hold in one hand and keep warm peeping from my jumper.

With Ian's departure from Christie's, the height of the season upon us, I was in despair at the prospect of another bout of basic cataloguing in the airless cellar with Jock and Les for company. I was also ill with a malfunctioning kidney that required surgery and some time away for recovery. David Barclay, then a failing Courtauld student, was brought in. I had known him for some years as the friend of a girl student at the Courtauld, good-looking in a Young Conservative sort of way, a kind-hearted blameless boy, infuriatingly inhibited and proper, heir (it was said) to a grandfather's fortune made from the mass manufacture of sanitary towels, and rich enough to be among the first to have a Triumph TR2, the rare AC Aceca and the monstrous Facel-Vega. He had long wanted to work for Christie's, thinking it a suitable setting for a gentlemanly life, and to delay the day when he might seek my help in applying for a job, I had urged him first to learn something of art history by going to the Courtauld. To my astonishment he was accepted there. This had not been my intention; I had assumed that he'd be found wanting and, abashed, would then seek some other career, relieving me of the duty to tell him my harsh opinion that he'd not be fit for Christie's. David was not in any sense academic material and it became clear that there was no point in his sitting longer at Blunt's feet at precisely the moment of Ian's leaving Christie's. It was the worst possible coincidence. Through Ellis Waterhouse, Anthony knew that Ian was leaving and it has always been my belief that he saw the chance of easing David out of the Institute and into Christie's, the boy's declared ambition; without a word to me, they commended him to Patrick.

David was an early example of a Courtauld student who knew nothing of the Old Testament, nothing of the New, nothing of the legends of the saints, nothing of Greek and Roman myth and history; this is common now, the consequence of modern education systems that hold such background cultural foundations in contempt and see no use for them, but David was educated at a public school where these traditions had not quite faded – he, however, always incurious, had simply let them wash over him with no osmosis taking place. Looking at pictures, he recognised nothing, and correcting his catalogue manuscripts took more time than initiating them myself. The end came after six months or so when he described the subject of a seventeenth-century Dutch panel, not as Christ with the Pilgrims on the Road to Emmaus, but as Three men going for a Walk in a Wood. What happened then was described by John Herbert as a clash of personalities. It was nothing of the kind. It was an ill-tempered and abusive tantrum expressing feelings so intense that the words could never be withdrawn. Wholly justified, the manner of it was inexcusable.

John Morrish replaced David early in 1962. He too had a private income from a family business with which, in middle age, he had become disenchanted, and this enabled him to work for Christie's for a pittance. Quite how he joined the firm I can no longer recall, but his interest in art was in no way informed and his useful social contacts were even fewer than mine. Thin, spare, red-haired but greying, bearded and bespectacled, he looked both scholarly and shrewd – useful attributes. When one particularly dominant woman visitor to the Front Counter dismissed my arguments against the authenticity of her Rubens with 'Young man, I don't believe a word you've said; bring me someone older,' it was John I sent to her and he, instructed what to say and how to say it, sent her on her way, contented in the belief, not that she had a Rubens, but a painting so investment-worthy that she'd be foolish to sell it. I was to find John's dissemblings – 'Do you really need to sell it? It would be wiser to hang on until you have some pressing reason to let it go. Gosh, aren't you lucky to have this!' – much easier weapons to wield than the blunt truth.

John was also responsible for inventing Lawrence Bastard. Christie's had for many years sold old Dutch paintings of indifferent quality as by an unrecorded painter whose name had been suggested by Daan Cevaat, a friendly dealer from Holland whose advice old Alec Martin had occasionally sought, and I accepted this attribution when, often enough, it was suggested by Bill or Patrick for some kippered interior with drunken peasants, though my usual response to artists not recorded in Thieme-Becker was that they had never existed. But then Cevaat, kind to the new boy, dropped in to tell me to stop using it, for the name was not that of an artist, but Dutch slang for the penis. Lawrence Bastard, however, was not a trick but a necessity. A landscape some six feet wide was sent in by a solicitor closing an estate. Not signed but evidently English and from the 1930s, it was more than competent, but none of us recognised the hand, nor did any ancient Royal Academician or member of the New English Art Club. The solicitor grew impatient – the sale of the picture was delaying the settlement for which the heirs were clamouring. John and I looked at it yet again and still we were completely stumped. 'It's a bastard,' said I, to which John responded with 'That'll do – think of a Christian name.' And thus was Lawrence Bastard born. The painting was bought by Pulitzer, a small dealer in High Street, Kensington, who advertised it as the masterpiece of a genius too little known, and any who shared interest in it were given an entirely invented biography. We used his name again and again until we were in danger of constructing an oeuvre, and he spawned both Laurent Batard and Lorenzo Bastardo; soon David Carritt was to invent Van Esserbel for Netherlandish still lives of doubtful quality and innumerable variations on De Cock and De Haas.

Older than Patrick, John eventually found his bullying difficult to tolerate, exploding with futile incoherent rages. Increasingly restive, he thought first that he might leave to become an art dealer of some sort, for almost total ignorance was obviously never a barrier in that business, and then, to accumulate capital for it, there was his mad plan to dig for diamonds in West Africa for a year or two. He left early in 1964 and disappeared.

It was Ian who found his replacement, Noël Annesley, an Oxford undergraduate whom he had encountered in the Ashmolean; bearing in mind his own disappointment at Christie's, his commendation was diffident. I interviewed the boy over supper in Phillimore Place – a supper that he later described as a cruel test, for it consisted entirely of things eaten with the fingers. Though he had nothing to bring to Christie's and I realised that in the beginning it would be, for him, a crash course in distinguishing geographical origins and five centuries from each other if he were ever to be able to tell a Rembrandt from an Ingres, I liked his oddly

Outsider

hapless air, his modesty, enthusiasm and willingness. Interviews with Guy Hannen and Patrick followed (Patrick characteristically kept him waiting long after lunch at White's), and within ten days I was able, on Guy's instruction, to offer him the post, starting in September. He was a good choice: Christie's at first shaped him, but when, surprisingly early in his career, the imbalance reversed, he contributed much to its reshaping into what it now is some half century later.

*   *   *

On 1 May 1959, when I had been with Christie's for fifty-one weeks and Ian had for two, we witnessed an event that was to give Patrick absolute supremacy over us. It was a Friday, the day on which sales of paintings always took place, and this, as it included a consignment from the Marquess of Northampton, was a sale described as of Fine Pictures by Old and Modern Masters. Bill Martin was in the rostrum; liked by dealers, sympathetic to amateurs unused to the pace of the auction room, and above all, persuasive on behalf of private vendors when the bidding stalled at a point when the reserve could be reached with just another bid or two, he was a better auctioneer than most of his fellow partners, occasionally humorous, always well-tempered and, never tempted into a record-breaking pace, a little slower. At lot 149, twenty lots before the end, he slowed to a halt. His eyes unfocused, he seemed to gaze into a distance far beyond the opposite wall of the octagon, his mouth opening and closing in slow motion – and then he collapsed, more or less held in place by the confines of the rostrum, but falling backwards from it when the door was opened by the sales clerk. Within seconds, it seemed, Jo Floyd was in his place briskly concluding the sale while Bill, carried out of sight, deeply unconscious, the victim of a cerebral haemorrhage, lay waiting for an ambulance.

He was for weeks in the Middlesex Hospital, and for many evenings that early summer I walked from Christie's to Mortimer

236

Street to find at his bedside, not Margery his wife, nor Penny his daughter, nor Gregory his son (then a keeper at the National Gallery), but Beatrice West, his mistress, an uncomely woman broad of hip, her bespectacled face porcine, her possessive manner that of a practised termagant. Almost three months passed before, very tentatively, he returned to work; as he could make no decisions, bring in no business, remember no painter's name, I had to carry him and, as best I could, protect him from the manoeuvrings of Patrick who, during his absence, had unquestionably been the head of the department and was determined to remain so. Bill hung on at Christie's until forced by his partners to resign at the end of 1962, the worst year ever for the firm with so substantial a loss – for which Patrick was far more responsible than he – that he got very little for his shares and spent the rest of his life in near penury.

As he faded, there were some who still respected him, among them Paul Getty who, on a whim one Friday, spent 500 guineas on a large and handsome copy of a landscape by Hobbema. Bill and I had had some trouble with this painting, for it had been brought to us by Jack Harris, a dealer whose usual stock was would-be *dix-huitième* French furniture but who could never resist gambling on pictures; he drove a Mercedes 300SE when this was still a flashy and vulgar thing to do. He knew Bill well enough to insist on his seeing him at once, refused to accept his view that the picture was only a later nineteenth-century copy, rejected the same view from me, and insisted that we sell it with a reserve of 500 guineas, a figure we thought far beyond the realms of possibility. Bill, as usual, gave way.

It was this that Getty had bought without even knowing how it had been described in the sale catalogue; he had simply dropped in with nothing but curiosity in mind, had seen the picture from the back of the octagon and, hearing the bidding falter at what seemed an absurdly low figure for so handsome a thing, had joined in until he reached (unknowing) Harris's reserve. 'What have I bought?' he asked as his factotum followed him into Bill's room, carrying the landscape. 'Oh my Gawd!' was Bill's response. He then told Getty the whole tale. Getty turned to me: 'Do you think it's a copy?' And when I said that I did, the factotum, at some signal from his master that I neither saw nor heard, slammed the canvas down over the back of a chair. With a serene 'Good day,' Getty and his man then left the room, the farce so exquisitely executed that I wondered if they had performed it many times before.

*　　*　　*

Ian's dependability made it possible for me to take a long break in the early autumn of 1959. I had managed to spend enough weekends in Windsor to justify a jaunt to Rome to look at buildings by Fontana, and by chance – for neither Bill nor Patrick could read any European language (Patrick pronounced every foreign painter's name with such exaggerated Churchillian ignorance that I wondered how Berenson had endured his presence at I Tatti) and all foreign correspondence to the picture department fell to me to answer, letting me gather enough requests for visits to plot a route to Rome through France, returning through Switzerland and Germany. Hans Backer, Christie's representative in Rome, had also set aside some clients for me to see. Bill, indulgent as ever, sent me off for as long as the journey might take, instructing me to keep all bills and claim repayment on my return.

I took Baby Helen with me. We had seen a good deal of each other since her graduation and so flirtatious had we become that I had to tell her the truth about my sexuality – to which her response was of the 'never mind, it's not important' kind. I now had to raise the matter again, for thinking it immoral to charge Christie's for feeding and sheltering her on the journey, we planned to camp where we could and stay in the cheapest hotels, both of which might bring us into the sort of proximity that in normal circumstances might reasonably end in companionable conjugation. Thinking it folly to tax the reliability of my old Wolseley by driving it to Rome, I hired a Morris Minor Traveller – an oak-beamed thatched cottage kind of car — and into it we packed decent clothes for the inevitable formal occasions on the way (and certainly in Rome), my camping things and, I thought, the tent that Helen had agreed to bring.

Our route was dictated by my responsibilities to Christie's, but the pace was deliberately leisurely, and though it was the second week of September, the blazing sun as we crossed the Channel encouraged us to make for Le Touquet, swim and laze the rest of the day, spending the night in nearby camping-site on the edge of Meaulnes, a village too small for the map, where, to our delight, we found the school announced as the Lycée Alain Fournier. I erected my tent while Helen appeared to rummage in the car. 'Where's yours?' I asked when mine was up. 'I haven't brought it.' Her smile, demure, seraphic and direct, was enough to tell me that this had been deliberate and I was briefly furious. I could not pretend that my tent was too small for two — it had housed four on its last journey to Italy — nor could I compel Helen to sleep in so small a car as the Minor; it was a moment for very plain speaking. In a letter a week or so later I told my mother that 'Helen is a delightful and amusing companion: all the French call her Madame — I suppose they think her my wife.' And so, indeed, they did, in spite of our passports, and put us into double beds in which we lay like brother and sister, in perfect innocence; only in puritanical Switzerland, weeks later, did a Calvinist hotel clerk, examining our passports, question our relationship and object to our sharing a room.

We spent some days in Paris before driving south to beyond Clermont-Ferrand where, in a small hunting-lodge, I found a sketch by Rubens. Jubilant, we spent that night in an inn named Le Lion d'Or in the village of La Chaise Dieu, tucked up in the deepest of feather mattresses. Then there was a man in Avignon with a fake Simone Martini to be seen — and never have I been so badly bitten by mosquitoes; and after more things to inspect in Nîmes and Arles and Aix, we had freedom to laze and swim at Fos-sur-Mer and Rayol before setting off more purposefully for Rome.

There, Helen recalls, I kept on saying 'I've seen it all before' –
but I had not and it was familiar only from closely-studied photographs. In the first days of October I made ecstatic notes on Tivoli,
Frascati and other beauty spots in the Campagna – 'wonderful,
wonderful, all so very close to Claude.' Rising early to see before
breakfast churches that seemed accessible only during early Mass, I
walked myself to a standstill; Helen, made of tougher stuff, did not
quite collapse, but I did – every bone aching, every sinew so stiff
that I could not, one morning in our pensione, put weight onto
the first foot out of bed. There was too, the daily worsening attack
of fresco neck, the failure of neck muscles to return, unaided by a
helping hand, the head to its normal position after looking at
painted domes and ceilings. Hans Backer required my services for
several days, swanning about the city in the beautiful Lancia Aurelia
coupé that he was far too small to drive, and far too timid too; most
of this work was a waste of time, an exercise in diplomatic flattery,
but one errand stopped me in my tracks, for as soon as the door of
the apartment opened, I saw over the owner's shoulder, a beautiful
Modigliani portrait of a young woman – reward enough and more
for my journey, though not its objective, for what I was really
there to assess was a wretched copy of a Caravaggio.

On our very first evening in Rome we bumped into Anthony
Blunt, staying at a nearby albergo almost as humble as our pensione,
and had the first of many dinners with him in a restaurant at which
he was evidently known. Within spitting distance of the Pantheon,
it was the haunt of local families and workmen, cheap and simple,
and there – never having been in his company without professional
reason – I saw an astonishingly different Anthony, warm, funny and
engaging, for with the master-pupil relationship set aside he became
an older brother or young uncle. Helen, by then contentedly
established as Philip Troutman's assistant in his new post in charge
of the Courtauld collections, he treated as an equal. Of course we
talked about Fontana, but not even the constant frustrations of that
project affected the new chemistry.

Further Misgivings at Christie's

A month after leaving London we began the return journey, pausing in Arezzo, Bologna and Parma before the long haul over the Alps. Jubilant that I had found two important paintings for Christie's to sell, with the words 'I hope these are not too much,' I laid notes of my expenses on Puddifoot's desk. Within the hour he came, I thought to reject them as too high with 'I can't accept these.' 'Oh Puddy,' I said reproachfully, 'they are what I spent.' 'I know, but when the auditors see how long you've been away and how little you've charged, they'll start questioning the directors' expenses.' I do not know how he got the sum, adjusted to almost £1,000 unsupported by bills, past the auditors, but he assured me that it was still well short of what Patrick would have spent and that I must never undercut him by so much again. On a trip to Switzerland the following year I based myself in the Baur au Lac in Zürich.

I wrote to Monsieur Joly in whose hunting-lodge I had identified the Rubens, explained in detail my certainty that it was an autograph sketch, proposed that it was worth a considerable sum and asked him to send it to London for sale. When it arrived, Bill was uncertain and Patrick dismissive. I was instructed to show it to Michael Jaffé, then already well on his way to becoming the most published expert on Rubens and, by constant self-declaration far the most important. A prominent post-graduate student at the Courtauld Institute in my first incarnation, he then occasionally appeared in a black leather jacket and tight pale blue jeans, and it was said by Francis Hawcroft (one of his peers and later Principal Keeper of the Whitworth Gallery, Manchester) that he haunted Hyde Park at night in search of sadistic sex. Of this raffishness there was not the slightest hint – the professorial Jaffé was as exquisitely suited and overcoated as his city banker ancestors when he came to see the sketch hanging in the large and well-lit room that I had been newly given at the top of the main stairs. Now stout, his corset creaked as he bent to peer into its grisaille subtleties. Within seconds he turned to me with 'Why do you waste my time?' and went on to say that he could see in it nothing to support an attribution to Rubens, that it was not even by a pupil or close follower, and left. Blushing with chagrin, I told Bill. He suggested that I should say nothing to Patrick, who had probably forgotten the matter, but return the painting to Joly with an apology and an offer to pay all the charges involved in sending it to us.

A second blow swiftly followed. Hans Backer brought the Modigliani to London and showed it to Bill. It was, I suppose, not unreasonable to want an opinion more authoritative than mine – if wrong about Rubens, on whose work I still hankered to work for a PhD, I could be wrong about anything – though I doubt if he knew that forgeries of Modigliani had been made within five years of his death in 1920. He asked Oliver Brown to come and see it. Oliver was head of the Leicester Galleries, long established just off the south-east corner of Leicester Square, a firm that for more than half a century had dealt in contemporary French and British art – it had, for example, been first to exhibit a complete set of bronzes by Degas (in 1923) and landscapes by Kokoschka (in 1928). A Leicester Galleries label on the back of any painting is still regarded now, some forty years after the business closed, as a guarantee of quality, and I must argue that the firm, in constantly mounting exhibitions – the first one-man shows in Britain of Van Gogh, Cézanne, Matisse, Picasso (1921) and Klee – did more in its heyday for the education of the British public than the two absurdly celebrated exhibitions arranged by Roger Fry in 1910 and 1912, *Manet and the Post-Impressionists* and his *Second Post-Impressionist Exhibition.* Into his seventies, wobbly on his pins, profoundly deaf and given to uttering at the end of every sentence an interrogatory 'What?' in a throaty voice gurgling with accumulated spittle (inherited by his son, Nicholas), Oliver made an unconvincing show of expertise with the Roman Modigliani – 'I never met the man . . . I never gave him a one-man show . . . there are a lot of forgeries about . . . you must ask someone else . . . show it to Pfannstiel in Hamburg . . .'

Further Misgivings at Christie's

Arthur Pfannstiel was, in 1929, the author of the first monograph on Modigliani and had ever since – though it was hardly an illuminating book – been regarded as an authority. Over a very wintry weekend in November I took the canvas to him. On the Friday evening he could not make up his mind, asked me to leave it with him and invited me to dinner the following day. On Saturday evening he still could not make up his mind; we had dinner, accompanied by his wife, and stayed late into the night in a telephone-table bar in the red light quarter. In such bars one sits at a numbered table either making calls to young women at other numbered tables or receiving them – my inexplicable discomfort caused the Pfannstiels much amusement. Back at their flat I was again asked to leave the Modigliani with them and, happy enough to spend another day prowling the museums of Hamburg, I agreed to pick it up on my way to the airport on Sunday evening. This I did, and still he would say neither yea or nay. I sensed that he wanted a fee and had earlier called Bill, but he told me not to offer payment and to refuse if asked for it – 'We never pay for expertise.' From Pfannstiel's obviously impoverished circumstances I could see that he needed to earn whatever he could, and when at last he suggested a fee, found it painful to repeat Bill's mantra; that he had not condemned it was of no help to me when reporting events to Patrick, who with some relish told Backer to take it back to Rome.

In fairness, I could see that the promise of a fee might well corrupt an expression of opinion and, by and large, it was sensible to ignore most certificates written on the backs of photographs, as was then the custom of the day. Max Friedländer, an ancient art historian whom I much admired and whose *Landscape, Portrait and Still Life* had consoled me as a subaltern, abjured almost all his late certificates; those written before 1933, he told me, were his true uninfluenced opinion, but after being forced by the Nazis to leave the Berlin Gemälde Museum of which he was Director and in which he had worked since 1896, he wrote certificates for cash. Lavish with praise, these were often for Jewish owners, the victims

243

of forced sales, in the hope that Nazis would pay more for poor pictures with wonderful certificates; for Party Members, for whom he was compelled to write certificates for nothing, he wrote in such hyperbolic terms as might prompt the shrewd reader to realise the truth. I was soon to learn that American experts on Impressionist and Post-Impressionist painters, writing aesthetic or art historical assessments rather than certificates, expected to be paid as much as five per cent of the price realised if pictures were sold with their support.

In December 1962, among the Shorter Notices – those snippets of art historical information that are so valuable to other scholars but too slight to be the subject of a full-scale article – the *Burlington Magazine* published *An Ecce Homo by Rubens* and gave the painting a full page illustration. It was Monsieur Joly's sketch. As the writer of the note was only Marcel Röthlisberger, an art historian not known as an expert on Rubens, but on Claude, I assumed for a moment that in treading on an alien field he, like me three years before, had made a serious error of connoisseurship, but then I read the first line of his text: 'I am grateful to Professor Jaffé . . . for having most generously helped me with this note.' He went on to remark on its 'excellent, fresh preservation, the handling suggests that it is entirely by Rubens. It can be dated just before 1620 . . . it is not an engraver's model . . . Whether in painting this sketch Rubens was thinking of a large painting (which was never executed) remains an open question.' These were exactly the points I had made in my letter to Joly in 1959.

My stomach clenched at this proof of Jaffé's foul play. If Röthlisberger brought the sketch to his notice, he must have recognised it as the panel he had seen earlier in my room – he had a photograph and knew the owner's name – and should, with such a change of mind, have done the decent thing and ensured that I knew of it. My supposition is that he did change his mind but preferred to hand the discovery to Röthlisberger, 'most generously' helping to write the note with his own name prominent in the first line rather than relegated – as is customary – to a footnote in small print far below.

Within a year or so I saw the Modigliani again. The Italian owner, disappointed to the point of distaste, had sold it for nothing to an Italian dealer; he in turn had sold it to a Lebanese – the Lebanon was, in the 1960s, at peace and a centre of great wealth – and he had at once taken it to Pfannstiel; with his wholehearted confirmation of its authenticity, it returned to Christie's. I wrote him a reproachful note; his response was that he had not so much changed his mind as confirmed it – scant consolation for me.

There were experts in whom Christie's could absolutely trust; there were others whom we could not, knowing them to be rogues, but they were nevertheless acknowledged to be expert in particular fields and buyers expected us to consult them; and there were experts who fell into both categories, either concurrently or over time. Teddy Archibald, of the Maritime Museum at Green-wich, and David Piper, of the National Portrait Gallery, were indefatigable in their rounds of the London auction rooms early every Monday morning and could always be drawn into the warehouse to see paintings set aside for them, giving their opinions freely; Ben Nicolson, expert on Caravaggio and all his followers, was one of a number of scholars and academics with particular interests on whom I regularly called; and I kept notes of all Courtauld students working for higher degrees whose subjects and the market place were bound to coincide. All these gave us scrupulously honest help and advice, their quid pro quo the benefit of seeing things first and often of seeing them in the very short interval between their emerging from and returning to obscurity.

Of the known rogues, most were French. In Paris, Paul Pétridès held sway as sole agent over the uncannily prolific Maurice Utrillo, in his reclusive dotage a painter of increasingly wretched suburban views. For a full decade after the painter's death in 1955, his widow, Lucie, was involved with Pétridès in the certification of forgeries, many of which he included in the five-volume catalogue raisonné that he began to compile in 1959 (published in 1974). As an *Expert près la Douane* his certificates were legal documents, proof absolute that paintings were authentic, often supported by Lucie's 'recollections' of having seen her husband at work on them, but I was one of many put in the awkward position of feeling in our bones that we were dealing with forgeries, yet, certified as genuine, we could not refuse to sell them. Almost as often, it seemed, we dealt with this situation in reverse – that is, with genuine paintings that had a provenance reaching back to some respected German (and Jewish) dealer in the 1920s but could not be sold because Pétridès, though in charge of Utrillo only since 1937, refused to recognise them; one particularly sour example of this malpractice was the Utrillo belonging to Mrs Lisa Gurr (originally Goehr), the collector (by inheritance) whose generosity so enriched the Museum in Leicester with twentieth-century German paintings – this had an impeccable Flechtheim of Düsseldorf provenance even including the bill paid by her father, but this did not influence Pétridès.

Many years after my involvement in the art market had ended, after a case in 1979 in which he was found guilty of forging documents, Pétridès was sent to prison for three years; accused of issuing false certificates, dealing in fakes, misusing the title 'expert' and acquiring paintings from the Nazis during the Occupation, he was at last stripped of his right to issue certificates. All this, however, will be forgotten – if not already so – and his mendacious catalogue raisonné, seeming important in bulk and binding, will live on to support in perpetuity the hundreds of fakes commissioned by its author.

Alexandre Ananoff, less flamboyantly culpable, escaped with nothing worse than a damaged reputation. This silver-plated self-appointed expert on Boucher and Fragonard, much the same size and shape as Peter Chance and as immaculately presented, burst into my room one day and, having told me who and what he was, dumped on my desk a folder of drawings to be included in a sale. I leafed through them with misgiving, overwhelmed by the presence of the man. The papers were of the period, but the fringe damages seemed recent and deliberate; the images were possible for the eighteenth century but were, I thought, by a recent hand copying figures from paintings, and the drawing techniques, bold and crude, were of the twentieth century – one drawing, signed and dated 17FB22 (when Boucher, at 19, was employed as an engraver after Watteau) was absurdly coarse. But who was I to argue with the greatest expert in the field, who was I to refuse to sell a dozen drawings by these great *dix-huitième* masters, signed, dated and certified? I went to Bill, and at the mere mention of Ananoff he groaned. I went to Francis Watson and he uttered a strange high-pitched sound that was both snort and yelp. And when next I saw Ananoff, I was vigorously accused of ignorance, impertinence and malevolence.

With such downright dishonesty it was comparatively easy to deal, but with betrayal it was not. Philip Pouncey, Deputy Keeper of Prints and Drawings in the British Museum, was another regular visitor, as much interested in obscure and unattributable paintings as in the drawings I was supposed always to show him, but after hearing too often his quip that 'an attribution a day keeps depression away,' usually uttered when the artist proposed was too recondite ever to be checked, I began to lose my trust and think his cleverness one-upmanship. I lost trust altogether when a beautiful drawing by Jan Brueghel, the only decent thing in a wretched sale that I had had to pull together, flopped. Bumping into Hans Calmann, a dealer in old master drawings who would have been engaging had he not been quite so overbearing, wilful and dismissive, I asked why he and almost every other dealer in the field had sat on their hands and let it be bought for nothing. 'Ah,' he said, 'You didn't know? Pouncey wanted it, and he warned us off with the threat that he'd never again give us help if any of us thwarted him.'

There was a worse betrayal, more calculated, directly personal. Lot 71 in the sale of paintings on 19 June 1959 was a *Road to Calvary*, attributed to Polidoro. I had catalogued it as indubitably by Polido Caldara da Caravaggio, a short-lived labourer in the Vatican under Raphael, an unfettered and idiosyncratic mind, an imagination dark and never genial. This remarkable rarity I showed to Pouncey. He disagreed. His immediate and very strong reaction was that this appalling daub, grotesquely unrefined, had nothing of Polidoro's qualities to commend it; I felt compelled to downgrade it to mere attribution, and, as nothing but a fumbled copy, made no mention of its obvious links with an altarpiece in Capodimonte.

The bidding stopped at 48 guineas (£50.40) and the picture was bought by F. T. Dent, a dealer notorious for buying trifles unconsidered and disdained by other dealers. The sum was so much lower than I had expected – a tenth of my annual income – that I immediately asked him if he would sell it on to me for a small profit. 'Can't do that, my boy, I bought it on commission.' Ten years later, by which time I had left Christie's and Pouncey had become a leading director of Sotheby's, he asked me to dinner, and as a pre-prandial treat showed me his treasures. Of these the most astonishing, the most shocking indeed, was the Polidoro over one of his many mantlepieces. I did not stay for dinner. I did not speak to him again. It was he for whom Dent had acted on commission. He stole from me some small credit as an art historian, stole credit from Christie's, a firm that trusted and admired him, and in his deceit, stole from the owner of the painting. After his death his estate sold it to the National Gallery for £500,000; as Assistant Keeper there for eleven years he must have known in 1959 what a valuable addition to the national collection it would be, but instead of going hot foot to Trafalgar Square to tell them what had been discovered, he kept it to himself.

Buried in Christie's archives there is, I hope, a brief corres-pondence with Picasso that I should, perhaps, have kept. I sent him a photograph of a drawing that had been greeted with suspicion, for it was an isolated offering from a vendor of whom Christie's knew nothing and who could supply no provenance, but I felt it worth pursuing. The photograph was returned, the word FAUX scrawled large between diagonal lines across it, with a signature. This, from Picasso himself, should have been the last word, but I was still puzzled and spent hours leafing through material in the Courtauld Institute until I found it reproduced in, I think, a *Cahier d'Art* of 1934. I wrote again. I wish I could recall precisely Picasso's answer – it was a French equivalent of David Carritt's favourite apology 'Hey Ho! Silly me.'

*   *   *

David Carritt did not join Christie's until January 1963, but it was in 1959 that John Herbert began to campaign for the board to appoint an internationally known expert to join the picture department and David was their eventual choice. That there was such a campaign made it clear that no one on the board – not even John, whom I had thought my ally – thought of me as an expert in that sense, though it would have been easy enough to build on the scholarly connections I had made in France and Germany before I joined the firm and that I was keeping in good repair. Instead, I was the drudge who dealt with weekly sales, occasionally retrieved from the troglodytic conditions of the warehouse to perform clever parlour tricks. Peter Chance took me with him to Ireland to make a valuation of the paintings at Birr Castle, Offaly, the home of the Earl of Rosse, an old school friend (it was on many such old loyalties that the prosperity of Christie's had come to depend); Anne Rosse, his wife and earlier the mother of Anthony Armstrong-Jones, said of me to her husband when I was midway through the task, 'Oh darling, dear Mr Sewell is saying such darling things about our pictures,' but such esteem was not enough to make me seem, even in Peter's eyes, an expert. Nor was my saving a very different situation first thing another morning, when he whisked me off in his Bentley to placate a west country nobleman whose Van Dycks Patrick had just valued for insurance at enormous figures, sending the bill in a scale related to the total sum, not realising that the portraits were copies made when Duveen had bought the originals at the beginning of the century. It was my job to save Patrick's face and keep the client's business. This I did by praising the quality of the copies, by attributing them to Pierre Coulette, Duveen's most skilful forger (to put no fine point on it), by praising the original frames that lent such weight to the deception – themselves worth many thousands – even by saying that the household wear and tear of open fires and tobacco smoke had given them a patina of age that any expert might think dated back for centuries; but throughout this placatory dissimulation I was aware of an odd protocol – I was there, not to speak to his lordship, but to tell Peter what to say, which he did with an even more conciliatory gloss and a dozen Chinese whispers that I could not correct. Between us we left this heir to bogus family portraits with the impression that his copies were infinitely superior to the originals – Van Dyck, when all is said and done, I said, was only a fashionable hack – reduced the bill to nothing and saved the day, but I remained puzzled by the business of my being the oracle but somehow socially unfit to talk to noblemen. There were to be other valuations by Patrick to redeem, other noblemen to whom I was deemed unfit to speak, even occasions when Christie's partners were asked to lunch but their dogsbody sent off to the local pub to fend for himself.

I had, however, begun to find my independent feet in the field of drawings by old masters, an area of connoisseurship in which Patrick could not even pretend to have an eye. In this I depended very much on the help of a trade that was largely in the hands of dealers who had earlier been art historians or were, at least, trained in the discipline, scholars of Austrian and German-Jewish origin who traded from their homes and occasionally mounted small exhibitions at the Alpine Gallery in South Audley Street. A few of their more fortunate peers had joined the Warburg Institute or taught me at the Courtauld, and I was immediately at ease with them, their knowledge and their judgement; apart from the Old Bond Street firm of Colnaghi's, then under the saintly wing of James Byam-Shaw (their match in scholarship), they were the only dealers in any area of the art trade in whom the innocent might put his trust. All are now gone, and the few who remember them have left too late the worthy business of recording their brief presence in London in the decades between *c.*1935 and *c.*1975 when they exercised so civilising a presence on the trade.

Herbert Bier (1905–1981) was the quiet and unassuming grandee among them; with work at the Kaiser Friedrich Museum and the Alte Pinakotek behind him, he came to London in 1935 – earlier than many who fled the Nazis – and was able to establish museum contacts here and in America that bore fruit after the war when he dealt at the highest level. Incapable of deceit, he was a man whom both the inexperienced collector and the callow employee of an auction house could trust. Hans Calmann (1899–1992) was in every sense his opposite; tall, broad-shouldered, blustering, he was so often given to standing over me like a vulture, telling me that I was mistaken in an attribution when I knew absolutely that I was right, that I was confused – that is until I realised that this was nothing but a ploy to make me miscatalogue a drawing, not for his advantage, but for malicious fun. He bought many good drawings and made huge profits, but was deeply flawed in his obstinate belief in his own attributions; for these he had no foundation in scholarship but attempted to browbeat the relevant experts into supporting them – and woe betide any who offered him the slightest support out of politeness, for even the most grudging 'I suppose it might . . . ' would be used as wholehearted agreement. This manipulation brought him into many conflicts and at the end of his life few art historians, museum curators and fellow dealers had much respect for him, though they might like him as a man, enjoy his hospitality and feel for him over the death of his son John. It was a wry thing that he so frequently voiced contempt for homosexuals and accused all Englishmen with being tainted by the vice, yet it was John's promiscuous homosexual activity that brought about his violent death near Avignon in April 1980.

Of Lili Fröhlich (she at last dropped the hyphenated -Bum), at the pathetic other extreme of this group, my fond memories are oppressed by guilt. Older than the others – her magnum opus on Parmigianino was published in 1921, and in 1959 she may well have been eighty – tiny, bent, her notable nose enlarged with age, and her command of English (learned too late) slipping away from her, she tottered round sales with the help of a stick, encumbered by a huge handbag that made leafing through the folders and solander boxes hazardous for the drawings they contained. And there's another thing – Christie's, until I joined the firm, showed drawings in flimsy paper folders and I had to beg them to commission stout folders and solander boxes as a conservation measure. Lili never bought anything on the day of an auction, but took small shares of things bought by friends on her advice. When I first knew her, in her gloomy flat on Parliament Hill she held a small stock of intriguing drawings that I could take back to Christie's, but after a while everything she had was recently familiar and my visits became infrequent. After one long gap I telephoned Peter Claas, the dealer in drawings who had introduced us, and suggested that we go together. 'Oh. Didn't you know?' he said.

There were, perhaps, a dozen others eking a living on the fringes of this market, dependent on the vestiges of scholarship founded many years before, decent, civilised and sad. They were part of the overwhelming influx of Central European culture in the later Thirties that bore fruit during and after the war in chamber and orchestral music, opera, theatre, literature, philosophy, the visual arts and critical argument that so transformed, enriched and enlivened our native cultural activities – a cultural revolution now utterly forgotten by those who command the wilful mediocrities that are the BBC and the Arts Council, the very institutions in whose hands the arts then flourished, affecting and enhancing all our lives. With so much continuing emphasis on the horrors of the Holocaust, it has slipped from our minds that in this unintended consequence the Jews who escaped the Nazis and came here, gave us a second Enlightenment.

With new solander boxes in hand, as early as July 1959 I put together a sale built largely on my vigilant sorting of miscellaneous consignments, but it also contained the properties of three people whom I knew – so much for Alec Martin's jibe 'We know you've no social connections.' John Brophy, the father of Brigid Brophy and himself a writer, was an indefatigable collector of drawings, most of them worthless rubbish, but with careful dredging it had been possible to assemble a handful that shamed neither him nor me. Frida Brackley, the devoutly Christian granddaughter of Ludwig Mond, the industrialist whose bequest to the National Gallery ranged from undoubted masterpieces to irretrievable wrecks, had inherited part of his small collection of drawings. Sitting by her bedside – she was always in bed when I dashed up to Blakeney from Castle Hedingham to see her – I wondered if she had ever walked the short distance to Walsingham, for its nearness to this pilgrimage site had been her reason for buying so ordinary a house. I also found it difficult to believe that she needed the little money that her drawings would bring, for, like her grandfather's pictures, many were not what they had been thought to be – but she was in a constant state of anguish about her wealth (or lack of it – I never knew quite which) and seemed to relish the torment of betraying her grandfather by shedding the last scraps of his collection for more prayers and candles at the Shrine of our Lady to which, emotionally, she had become umbilically attached.

The third of my contributors to this humdrum sale was Dr William Crofton who owned a sketchbook by Domenico Becca-fumi to which I had been alerted by a note in the *Burlington Magazine* in December 1957. I bearded him in his huge house in Regent's Park, hoping that he might have other treasures. He did. The walls of hall, stairs, passages and every room were crowded cheek-by-jowl with canvases that pretended to be by Corot,

Constable and Turner. The Corots were uniformly glaucous, the Constables were impastose masses of dark green, and in every one of the supposed Turners a sunset shrieked in flaming agony. Not one was genuine and I dared not ask how one collector could have been so utterly seduced by three forgers – for all the Corots were by a single hand and the Constables and Turners by two others – and yet not be suspicious of the improbability. Amongst all this the intriguing sketchbook was a lost soul. It was also something of a disappointment (as Beccafumi so often is); incoherent in date and subject, the studies undoubtedly by Beccafumi interspersed with a few by other hands, I was not wholly convinced that it was even a sketchbook in the conventional sense and thought it a gathering of sheets bound, perhaps posthumously, by a pupil or workshop assistant – the binding pages offered no clue.

Crofton did not want to sell it – 'I'd rather sell a Constable or Turner.' I asked what he thought it might be worth and £1,500 was his answer – I had the impression that he had snatched this figure from the air as an absurdly demanding price that would put an end to the discussion. I accepted it as his reserve and then asked if I might separate the pages and sell each separately if everyone agreed that it was a compilation rather than a sketchbook once held in Beccafumi's hand. He was horrified, but I sensed that he was warming to the idea of selling it – 'Sell any of your paintings and you'll have to re-hang your walls,' I argued, 'sell this and no one will notice.' At last I came away with it, though I feared that he might change his mind – and he did, but only by raising his reserve at the last minute on the morning of the sale, to £2,000. In the event, Agnew's bought it for 4,800 guineas, a trifle over £5,000, and some years later broke it up for an exhibition from which they sold it page by page.

It was far from an important sale, though that term was used in the title of the catalogue; nevertheless, it was important for me, for in the wake of the Skippe sale it proved that Christie's could have an independent specialist department in old master drawings and, subsequently, in English drawings and watercolours, in nineteenth-century works on paper, and in prints. No one thanked me for it and Patrick was never to let go of his conviction that he was as much in charge of these as of every other aspect of the picture department. My Latinity is now frail; even so, I perhaps do Terence no injustice in translating a quip from his *Adelphoe* as 'never is anyone more unjust than the ignorant.'

CHAPTER 13

Abandoning God

There was in 1959 a change in my life far more important than
any happening at Christie's – a change essential for my sanity.
Deliberate observation of my religious duties had continued since
my graduation in spite of my then immediate change of course,
for I was by no means certain that the change was permanent, but
it was as a dry discipline, scarcely spiritual and much troubled by
my sexuality. One Sunday morning in the spring, however, on
my way to Mass at the Carmelites in Church Street, a little early, I
walked on and into Kensington Gardens by the passage through
York Place, and there I challenged God. A sudden inspiration,
there is no other word for it – I challenged him to give me a sign
of some sort. In a one-sided conversation I told him that he had
had my physical chastity (insofar as anyone else was involved) since
I joined the army more than seven years before, that I had willingly
given it in the expectation of becoming a priest, though I had
found chastity of the imagination impossible to achieve, and that
this, now more turbulent than ever, was separating me from the
Church. I sat on a bench on the Broad Walk and let pass the hour
of Mass. I wandered through the arched espaliered trees of the
sunken garden, familiar from my earliest childhood, recalling lines
from Francis Thompson's *Hound of Heaven*, a favourite poem as a
boy, and compared his conviction that he could not escape the
hound, with mine that the Dog of God had lost my scent. I
returned to Phillimore Place with no further thought of Mass and
have not since been a communicant.

Oddly disappointed not to have had a Pauline revelation, not
even the staying hand of an angel vouchsafed Abraham, there was

no obvious step to take. Homosexual activity of any kind was illegal and 'importuning male persons', a common offence much reported in newspapers, meant immediate social disgrace and, quite probably, loss of employment. I knew that there were pubs and drinking clubs with queer reputations, but not their names and whereabouts; and I also knew that there were the streets. That night I walked the length of Church Street idly inspecting the windows of antique shops. Exactly as I thought I might, with an exchange of glances I caught a man and took him home. Older by some years he was quickly efficient, but I doubt if it was much fun for him; for me the business was less erotic than mechanical and left me profoundly disappointed, asking myself if this could really be the alternative to chastity. By chance, a few days later, on the New Books shelf of the local library I found a novel by James Courage, *A Way of Love*. I can recall nothing of the plot, only that it was for its time a liberating tale suggesting that homosexuality could indeed be more than just the sexual acts. I wrote to him. He asked me to tea on Saturday, and to this mild man, elderly, precise, I said enough to make him think I wanted him to pimp for me – to which his response was 'Well, your golden years have passed you by.' He did, however, introduce me to a pretty youth whose golden years had not, but undressed, from his belly-button almost to his knees he was coal black, for the climax of his recent induction ceremony as an apprentice printer had been the dunking of his buttocks in a vat of ink. After all my years of abstinence, to have a willing boy in my hands should have been an explosive release, but I found the aesthetic disruption sexually unmanageable. Years later much the same thing happened when undressing a butch little toughie, only to find him clad in a woman's scarlet underclothes. Courage then introduced me to an Australian boy of my own age with whom I had some shared intellectual interests, but for whom my pent-up affection was far too demanding – unlike me, he was not wholly queer and eventually married and had children; we perfectly illustrated lines (slightly paraphrased) from Cavafy (Rae Dalven's translation was reissued yet again in 1959) – 'the consummation was lacking that must be intensely desired by both – we were not both equally given to deviant sensual pleasure. I alone it had utterly mastered.' I owe him something for his tolerance and much more for what he did for me beyond his bed, for he lived in Hampstead and his introducing me to his friends there led directly to lifelong friendship with the photographer John Vere Brown and, through the intersection of queer circles, to something approaching friendship with Keith Vaughan, the painter.

The most important instrument of my metamorphosis from celibate to whore was Eric Bewsey. Eric, a civil servant two or three years my senior, was wholly at ease with his sexuality and neither blazoned nor concealed it. Devoutly sensual, sex was for him as necessary as food and drink and he was as expert in finding casual partners as he was in preparing delicious simple suppers. I was one of his mistakes. After a few minutes on his bed he said 'You've got the flattest belly in the business, but you're hopeless.' He then undertook my sexual education: he would give me, he said, precisely three months to learn everything he could teach me of sex between men, every trick, every practice (though some of the more arcane now popular had not then been devised), disrupting every conventional notion of what is passive and what active, separating pleasure from love, distinguishing the satisfaction of sexual desire from emotion. Whatever I might think of these things I must learn that they are done and might one day be expected of me – that indeed, I too might expect them. This course of instruction was a roller-coaster of nights on which I reached from ecstasy to disgust, that taught me a great deal about my body and, by extension, the bodies of those with whom I might find myself; and I learned that sex ranges from tenderness to violence, from the short and sharp to the night long, from the security of the bedroom to the thrilling risky business of doing it while standing up in a canoe, and that the opportunist must make his opportunities. Eric was abashed by nothing; his preference was for the long, slow and tender at home with the body beautiful, but if a uniformed policeman in a dark alley was available, then this was a dish most fiercely spiced. Three months to the day the teaching ended and never again did I share a bed with Eric, but our friendship lasted until he fell in love – promiscuity is no bar to that – and he dropped us all to depart with his lover to New Zealand. His London friends were largely literary and, as is the way of these things, I subsequently slept on many a bed of letters before moving on to freedom.

Letters intersected with the arts and parties given by both offered opportunities to intersect with the men of pursuits and interests who were their friends and lovers, current and discarded, cutting across all barriers of class – indeed, the barriers were for some the erotic stimulus for sexual relationships. Three young men living in the rambling basement of Christabel Aberconway's house in North Audley Street held parties almost every Saturday of which she must have known, though perhaps, as a celebrated hostess between the wars and the mistress of Samuel Courtauld, she was amused to see how little had changed in this peripheral department of the demi-monde. Jack Harriman, one of Eric's friends, troubled about his sexuality and desperate to cast aside his doubts, was another regular party-giver in a mews cottage near Portman Square, miserably surrendering to alcohol when all his guests paired with each other and abandoned him. To these gatherings we were expected to take a bottle of wine for immediate consumption and a friend to exchange for the night. Much the same entry fee was charged at not quite so frequent orgies in Emperor's Gate and Little Venice. At these the sexual activity was immediate, common, multiple and public, and beginning at once, might last till morning; at one of them, in Little Venice, there was a posse of London Transport staff and for weeks after I had assignations with a bus driver on the 46 route that meant my waiting at a particular bus stop for him to whisk me off to the terminus in Wembley; at another there was a policeman based in Hyde Park who, infatuated, entertained me throughout the summer with theatre tickets given gratis to his station – never opera, always musicals or Saturday Night at the Palladium – until, with relief, I broke the contact by going to Rome with Helen.

In all this there was always considerable risk and yet not once was there a betrayal of which I am aware – though betrayals there must have been, for these circles reached across London and beyond (as any casual visitor to the old Turkish baths of Greenwich and Bermondsey must have known). There were too the contacts made in the open, effected with nothing more than a glance, a turn of the head and a pause in the stride – all so easy once one had the knack. The easiest place for this was the street, any street a happy hunting-ground, but it worked in a bus queue too, scanning the oncoming walkers, and in the Underground or walking the aisle to descend from the top deck of a bus. At weekends museums and galleries were the encountering points, none better, even on a fine Sunday afternoon, than the free-standing glass cases of the V&A. One exhibition there, of Italian Bronze Statuettes in 1961, produced a particularly rich crop of casual lovers, and I realise now that the exhibition catalogues that crowd my bookshelves are as much reminders of such episodes as records useful for the jobbing art historian. With so much sex so easily available, I wonder if Eric Bewsey was the God-given sign for which I asked. Meanwhile Helen, for three years so important in my life and wholly unaware of all this, though made miserable by my deliberate detachment, was offered a job at an American university that led to a jolly husband, three boisterous sons and half a lifetime in the Boston Museum of Fine Arts. We are still friends.

*   *   *

On 10 July 1959 the Arts Council's exhibition *The Romantic Movement* opened at the Tate Gallery – just short of a thousand exhibits (Arts Councillors now should look at such a great national and international event and compare what the Council achieved in the past with its current futile and transitory exhibitions). I recall it not only for its marvellous self, but for two episodes associated with it – the opening of the case in which Delacroix's *Massacre at Chios* had been sent from Paris, and my second encounter with John Vere Brown. I had been asked by the authorities at the Louvre to be present when the great Delacroix was delivered and to check its condition. To my surprise the painting had been taken off its stretcher, rolled, and slotted into a long coffin of a case, the lid of which had been nailed down, not screwed, as one might expect; as this was prised away it was clear that some of the nails had not been driven their full length into the sides of the box, but had curved inwards, in some cases perforating the canvas. Two days later I was again at the Tate when a restorer from the Louvre came to inspect the punctures and, if possible, execute a running repair; this he did with tiny pellets of malleable wax applied with a palette knife and moulded to comply with the surrounding textures, a temporarily effective method that I had not been taught in my brief weeks in the Courtauld Institute's technology department. When I saw the painting again a year later, I could discern no trace of these small damages.

I had a season ticket to the exhibition – ten shillings, fifty pence – and was there the day after first meeting John Vere Brown, for whom I had at once developed a powerful dislike at dinner with the Australian boy, and to whom I had been pretty abrupt before leaving early. John – a painter who wanted to be a portrait photographer and a photographer who wanted to be a landscape painter – was a slightly Quasimodo figure with the head of a late ancient Roman emperor and a voice that combined the pseudo-cockney affectations of the Edwardian beau with the mew of a cat and the shriek of a parrot, larding his language with fuck and its derivatives as often as any illiterate workman. It was this voice that I heard from many rooms away: he was with his elderly mother, tiny and profoundly deaf, to whom he was explaining paintings with such extraordinary sympathy that my dislike was overturned. I apologised for my misbehaviour, and that apology laid the foundation of a close and lasting friendship – not entirely unruffled, but always repaired after a spat – that enriched both our lives until his death in 2000.

It was indirectly through John – intersecting circles again – that I met Keith Vaughan, a distinguished painter whose innumerable lightly abstracted compositions of male nudes, singly and in various contiguities, were as lightly homo-erotic – so lightly indeed that most who purchased them hardly noticed the probabilities they deftly camouflaged. His small drawings in gouache particularly stated his sexual preference, their honesty gently pleading their cause without blatant propaganda. Many grew from the haunting imagery in his mind's eye as well as from studies of a younger lover for whom – unfairly – his affection turned to hate, Ramsay McClure, one of his students at the Central School in 1948, whose large rounded skull is instantly recognisable even if his puny body has been idealised to heroic proportions. Ramsay he made utterly miserable, but through mental cruelty rather than any putting into practice his sadistic fantasies, and I, over some months, had to comfort the weeping man (though I always saw him as a boy) with long-drawn hugs. For one of these episodes – in which it seemed they might destroy their strange and strained relationship and I had whisked Ramsay away for a chaste weekend – Keith gave me two prints by Picasso, the subjects ballet boys, that I believe were things of some early influence. I drifted out of their lives after I left Christie's and had little time for anything other than building a new life of my own; Keith, stricken with cancer, committed suicide in November 1977, and Ramsay died, as much of misery as anything, four years later, his life destroyed by love. I learned from them that love can be extraordinarily cruel and destructively submissive, that love of a sort can remain long after the sexual interest is extinguished, and that lovers can be lovers for years without ever understanding each the other's needs and wants – Keith was both a sadist and a masochist, tormenting himself with whip and thong while longing for a victim, but Ramsay was neither and did not know how to gratifyingly respond. Only in Keith's confession that he spent two thirds of his waking hours dwelling on sexual matters, did I find some reassurance.

In 1959 I launched into a life of such promiscuity as might suggest that I was making up for the golden years that had passed me by, for the opportunities lost in the arid years of denial, but it was sheer intoxication with the sudden ease of it and the abandonment of guilt. It was not unusual to pick up a companion on my way home – Cléo de cinq à sept, so to speak – to have had a fuck one way or the other and be home having a bath by seven, then to go and see my current lover (duration three days to three weeks, perhaps), and on the way home to pick up someone else with whom either to have a quickie before bed or take home for the night – which usually meant another perfunctory fuck first thing in the morning. Throw in a few Jack Rabbit weekends and all this might amount to a thousand fucks a year and easily a thousand sexual partners in a quinquennium. Now, when both times and I have changed, my first thought when seeming strangers begin a conversation with 'You won't remember me, but . . . ' is that half a century ago we had a sexual encounter that meant more to him than me – but the blankness of my mind is only another bout of the prosopagnosia with which all my life I have been cursed, the face-blindness, the near inability to distinguish one face from another when out of the context in which it is familiar.

It was at a party early in 1961 that I met Peter Norris, a young Canadian poet; tall, his skin so pale it was as though it had never seen the light, his eyes a startling dark blue, his curly hair a reddish gold well short of ginger, at twenty-four or so his beauty was androgynous, Pre-Raphaelite. He let slip that he had just parted from a much older man, a Greek racing driver named Embiricos of whom I knew, though only because in 1939 he had been the famous owner of a famous Bentley of that period, an astonishing aerodynamic Bentley by Pourtout, a great Parisian coachbuilder who in this car anticipated the post-war designs of Enzo Ferrari. It may seem odd, but there was a certain frisson in taking on the boyfriend of Embiricos. There was also risk – though not of some vengeful Aeschylean tragedy with me the victim; their parting had left Peter emotionally damaged, unstable, difficult, even inconsolable – and he was, too, a poet, given to unaccountable disappearances into himself – but his ethereal beauty was reward enough for me as he lay sated in the lamplight that drifted in from the street, for me he was Endymion. Our friendship did not end until his death in the 1990s, but our relationship as lovers came to a sudden and appalling halt when, late in 1961, at a party given by Richard Hughes-Hallett, he slashed his wrists. Richard's flat was a rambling basement round the light well of a small block in Palace Gate, and through the bathroom window two boys who had gone into the well to smoke saw Peter and the blood; gatecrashers, they did not know whose flat it was and rather than waste time it was they who broke down the door, they who, with me, knelt on the floor and tried to stem the blood until an ambulance arrived.

In St Stephen's hospital I stayed with him until I was sure that he would survive and then returned to Richard's flat, intending to deal with the mess, but other than the shattered door-frame there was no trace of it. The boys who had seen Peter's attempted suicide had sluiced and mopped the bathroom and were still there, for the party was still going strong.

One, Sicilian, spoke only very broken English, but fluent French and German, and after a helter-skelter conversation in any language in which we knew the words, I was, if not enchanted, then mightily amused. He was not handsome; tall and almost fair-haired, he did not even look Italian – an ancient Norman strain, perhaps. He came from Taormina and was the very last of a line that had governed the town for a thousand years before the unification of Italy and the new nobility of Victor Emmanuel II displaced the old in 1861. The Marchese Corvaya was then dispossessed, the Palazzo Corvaya became municipal offices, and the family moved to an unpreposessing villa on the city's edge and faded into bleak obscurity; that Marchese was Claudio Corvaya's great-grandfather, a lesser Lampedusa leopard.

When Peter Norris's physical wounds were sufficiently healed, he returned to Canada to fall into the hands of a good woman and write bad poetry. Claudio moved into his place. It was, at first, an almost casual relationship, its irregularity forced on us by his employment with CIT, the Italian state tourist agency, always dashing back to Italy or being shunted off to Spain and Switzerland (he spoke as perfectly as Hochdeutsch the Swiss guttural corruption, Schweizerdeutsch), leaving me to be promiscuous. Perhaps because of these partings, the enmeshing of our lives was so slow that we did not realise how strong our loyalties and longings were becoming. With Phillimore Place his pied-à-terre, it seemed quite rational to take him to Castle Hedingham to equally enchant my mother – 'Isn't he hateful,' they said to each other when I was difficult, laughing and hugging. For seven years we were to be content.

*   *   *

When my stepfather died in May 1962, leaving my mother penniless, I was determined that she should stay in her house in Castle Hedingham because I could not bear the thought of losing my freedom by bringing her back to London to live with me. I was, however, under notice to leave Phillimore Place because Mrs Chesterton had died in January and the house was to be sold, but this, after some months of misery and misfortune, brought me a stroke of luck. I found a small Pooterish house near Westbourne Grove for £7,000, which, with a mortgage and lodgers I could almost afford – the necessity for lodgers compelled the exclusion of my mother. An American PhD student at the Courtauld lodged in what he described as the *piano nobile* sitting room, an art student took the small back room on that floor, Claudio and I occupied two rooms on the first floor and John Morrish the third, finding his

Blackheath house inconvenient for working at Christie's; we all shared the bathroom and the kitchen. It was hell. In addition, in the long half year that we were there, burglars broke in three times, my car was vandalised as often, and the Westbourne River (the source of the Serpentine in Hyde Park), long buried in a crumbling conduit beneath the house, twice invaded it through the basement floor. I was in despair when luck came in the shape of a middle-aged couple who knocked on the door one Sunday afternoon and asked if I had just moved in, or might be leaving, so dishevelled looked the house. Whatever their reasons for offering me £14,500 on condition that I was out within a week, I did not question them and did exactly that, paid back the mortgage and returned to Phillimore Place when I learned that for the sake of Mrs Chesterton's housekeeper-companion the house had not been sold and might not be for some time.

I had profited by seven years of my salary in as many months and for the first time felt at ease in the worldly world of Christie's; moreover, I could afford to keep my mother in her house and thus retain my treasured independence from her. Pious, banal and silly things are said about the relative unimportance of money. To me my puny profit was a fortune; it freed me from penny-pinching and my total dependence on my income from Christie's; it let me buy books and catalogues and begin to establish the working library that was to become the essential tool of my career as an art critic; it allowed me to travel without always having to key my journeys to work for Christie's, to fly my car over the Channel and dash to exhibitions in France, Germany and the Low Countries, and it bought and maintained the succession of slightly flamboyant cars in which I then took foolish pleasure, Daimlers of some age and character. With most of it wisely invested, that ludicrously small sum of money changed my life. From the grim prospect that had confronted me on Robert's death I was, within a year, released.

CHAPTER 14

Christie's in the Doldrums

It could be argued that in the early months of 1960, with Bill's perhaps unexpected return to Christie's, the *status quo ante* should also have returned, but this was made impossible by the planned sale of a collection of seventeenth-century Dutch paintings consigned from Holland by the ageing Dr C. J. K. van Aalst. This was the only important sale on the firm's horizon and Patrick had assumed absolute command of it, effectively side-lining Bill who had neither the energy nor will to assert his position as head of the department. Among these paintings was one by Rembrandt of the goddess *Juno*, an allegorical portrait of a woman too handsome to be Dutch, dark-eyed and full-lipped enough to be Italian, an ermine cloak over her broad shoulders, held there by jewels too fabulous to be anything other than theatrical junk from the property boxes that we know he kept. For this Patrick instructed John Herbert to tell the press that the expected price was £100,000 or so – then still an astonishing sum. Though naive reporters were impressed, the mocking scepticism of the trade roused their misgivings and when they turned to Bill he characteristically expressed his honest doubt. Asked by an *Evening Standard* reporter what I thought of it, I said that it had been so crushingly relined that Rembrandt's distinctive impastose brushwork might be discerned more easily on the back of the relining canvas than in any surface that we could see, which resembled ancient and well-polished linoleum – true, but I should have remained silent.

In the event on April Fool's day, the bidding dried up at £50,000 with most of us convinced that Peter Chance – the head of the firm lending his lustre to what he had been told was a most important sale – had not received a single bid from anyone in the room. Though other paintings in the sale did well, the embarrassment caused by the failure of the *Juno* before the television cameras and reporters assembled by John Herbert was damagingly public; Patrick, of course, showed not the least sign of humiliation. My feeling was that he had rushed into the sale for Christie's short term benefit and had not given van Aalst the advice that he should. The *Juno* was in a condition widely thought acceptable between the wars but not a generation later; the flattening of brushwork caused by relining could not have been reversed, but the canvas should have been stripped of its glutinous varnish to remove a veil from Rembrandt's robust and daring handling of paint, to let the whites startle with their freshness and reveal the subtleties of colour lost in the darkened tonal gloom. Even in the hands of the most conscientious restorer this surface treatment would have delayed the sale only by two months, and there might well have been some benefit in scheduling it late in June, traditionally the high point of the saleroom season. There is another possible explanation for the flop, concealed from us by van Aalst but known in the trade – that *Juno* had already been offered to museums and art dealers in Holland as a national treasure and that no deal had been done, for in those days, when significant paintings were by no means rare, none was more tarnished than one that had been traded but not sold. Years later, cleaned more or less as I wish I had been able to suggest, it now hangs in Los Angeles, an undoubted treasure of the Hammer Museum, worth every penny of Patrick's estimate mutiplied two hundred times.

In May, Bill – still the boss I had to ask for leave – let me escape to Paris with Anthony Blunt for the opening of his great and unprecedented Poussin exhibition at the Louvre, a gathering of 120 paintings, 120 drawings and one sculpture in wax. I drove him to Paris. Earlier in the year I had blown the engine of my old Wolseley attempting to maintain 70 mph on the new M1 – conrods through the engine block, the most dramatic and catastrophic of failures –

and had replaced it with an eight year old Daimler Special Sports, a very pretty drop-head coupé built by Barker that waffled along quite happily at speeds mortal for the Wolseley. I was intrigued to notice that Anthony had no reaction to anything that I or any other driver did, nor any to the rare epicyclic gearchange and pre-selector lever on the steering column that invariably intrigued drivers aware only of synchromesh and crash gearboxes; this convinced me that he could not drive, yet in my first incarnation at the Courtauld we all knew the tale of his driving a yellow Railton – a car as fast as it was rare – to Rome, and abandoning it, boiling, in a traffic jam just within the Porta del Popolo. I observe in passing that in the Beaulieu Motor Museum there is a photograph of a yellow Railton mud-plugging in the 1938 Cambridge University Automobile Trial, with Donald Maclean at the wheel.

In mid afternoon we reached the Louvre and scampered upstairs to the exhibition of which the scholarly purpose was to establish a chronology of Poussin's work with which all interested scholars could broadly agree, the early years of his development long a matter of uncomprehending and often spiteful controversy. Miranda Carter, author of Anthony's one biography,[26] has it that he had for several weeks been in Paris supervising the hanging of paintings lent by museums in East Berlin, Dresden, Leningrad and Moscow, none of which he could have seen since 1939, and from Florida and California, perhaps never seen, as well as those familiar in western Europe and the less distant museums of America. I must argue the contrary; for Anthony to abandon the Courtauld Institute in weeks so close to Finals would have been a selfish dereliction of responsibility of which he was not capable. I have no doubt that he played some theoretical part in planning the hang, but am convinced that he saw it in its finished state for the first time when we arrived that afternoon. We had been there only for seconds when he muttered 'I was wrong' – and again and again he was to

26 Miranda Carter: *Anthony Blunt: His Lives*, 2001.

mutter it. Michel Laclotte was responsible for the final hang and we saw it in the company of Germain Bazin, Charles Sterling, René Varin and Jacques Dupont, worthies all and all well pleased with it, though Anthony was not. He was the victim, as are so many art historians, of hypotheses based on photographs and reproductions, notes and memories, when none of these can readily be checked against the original paintings – the Poussins from Russia, for example, he had seen only once, and briefly, in August 1935, a quarter of a century before. He had written so much, lectured so much, that even the French were prepared to surrender Poussin to him, Poussin their most intellectual painter, yet here in Paris he was confronted with the failure of his eye, the instrument of connoisseurship that can instantly demolish not only a hypothetical chronology, but one seemingly securely documented: I am not the first to believe that when connoisseurship is in conflict with a document, the sensible art historian believes his eye. The immediate necessity, however, was that Anthony should shrug off his anguish, for this was almost a French state occasion and a bold front was required for the speeches, lectures, toasting and formal dinners that would follow. It was my first experience of his ability to switch into another character, that of a man thoroughly at ease with the enthusiasm of others.

In spite of its flaws it was a great exhibition, the foundation of many leaps in Poussin scholarship of which Anthony should have been allowed to make the first. It was his intention to publish a revisionary commentary on the Louvre catalogue, but, returning to a Courtauld Institute on the brink of Finals, he had more immediate responsibilities. Denis Mahon, however, had none to prevent or delay his publishing his observations. Mahon, an art historian of independent means, was almost single-handedly responsible for reviving in England the reputations of seventeenth-century Bolognese and other Italian painters despised by Ruskin as 'art-weeds' and the 'scum of Titian,' and by Roger Fry as painters 'whose expression of sentimental and melodramatic emotion provides a slope down which the imagination glides without effort . . . '[27] He was not quite alone in this, though his admirers maintain that this is so; Ellis Waterhouse, John Pope-Hennessy, Blunt and Wittkower were in the vanguard too, but the difference between Mahon and these older peers, now all dead, was that he was a free spirit unencumbered by the obligations of employment in any museum, gallery or university with anxious students sitting at his feet. The other major distinction that set Mahon apart was the powerful instinct (and the funds to support it) that drove him to acquire paintings by any painter who became a new enthusiasm – in later life as true of Poussin as of his first love, Guercino, the painter with a squint – and it was in opening his collection to students that he influenced their taste and demonstrated the inadequacies of the National Gallery.

Mahon had gone to the Poussin exhibition in the spirit of enquiry, expecting to find that the arguments over the order of paintings executed in the early years – *c*.1624–*c*.1633 – had been resolved; instead, he found what he later described as 'a hotchpotch' so fundamentally and obviously flawed that he could not allow it to stand unchallenged. Though not at this stage recognised as an expert on Poussin, that is what he became, overnight, when his observations appeared in the July issue of the *Burlington Magazine*. That these were in print so soon was tragic in their consequences for Anthony, only a handful of whose friends knew that he was desperately anxious to publish his own new thoughts on the chronology but could not give them priority over his students at the end of their third year. Mahon, however, considered it a matter of great importance that the debate should begin before the exhibition closed and the paintings were dispersed. A kinder spirit would have waited.

The debate was increasingly unkind on Mahon's part and it was not pretty to see Anthony, whose life had been so occupied by Poussin, inexorably usurped by the persistent (some might say malignant) Mahon. For me, having heard that plaintive murmur 'I

---

27 Roger Fry: *Transformations*, 1926.

was wrong,' it was a wretched business, knowing that if only
Mahon had waited for six months, giving Anthony time to deal
first with his academic duties, they might never have been so
seriously at odds in their conclusions, their guarded friendship
destroyed. Things went from bad to worse and disputes over
Poussin reached far beyond the exhibition. Mahon had been kind
to me as a student and at Christie's I had sometimes been his
errand boy; I liked him and his occasionally Puckish humour;
worse, I thought him nearer the mark than Anthony, and Anthony
too, I am convinced, in some respects thought so, but was, not
surprisingly, grudging with the admission. This was unusual –
but then the circumstances of the challenge had been acutely
disagreeable; in the course of any normal argument Anthony
would, if convinced, generously concede, even to a student.

Anthony's memory was not infallible – as was evident in a later
squabble with Mahon who, in 1964, had bought a painting in a
sale at Sotheby's that he believed to be an early Poussin. I was not
privy to the row that developed over whether Anthony had seen
the painting rather than only a photograph before doubting its
authenticity, and more's the pity, for I know that he had and that
his memory betrayed him. In the summer of 1963 the painting
was in the window of a shop in Pimlico Road owned by Geoffrey
Bennison, an outrageously camp interior decorator and dealer famous
for his sharp eye. Edward Lucie-Smith, then more celebrated for his
poetry than as an art historian, made me dash in a taxi to see it.
Grubby and obscured by darkened varnish, I wondered, without
conviction, if it might be by Andrea di Leone, Poussin's Neapolitan
follower, but it was Poussinesque enough for me to drive Anthony
to see it that same evening. We looked long at it in good late
daylight and came to no definite conclusion. That a year later he had
no recollection of our doing so is perhaps not altogether surprising,
for in April 1964, convinced of his guilt as a spy for the Russians, the
interrogations of MI5 began. Again Mahon was right; the painting is
now accepted as an early work undoubtedly by Poussin, but I am

inclined to dispute the date, c.1627, proposed for it; indeed, the dating of Poussin's paintings before 1624 when, at the age of thirty, he settled in Rome, and for the next decade, are to me still almost as much a matter for dispute as they were when Mahon and Blunt began their quarrel in 1960, for so many lost paintings have been rediscovered to give a shadowy idea of his work before he went to Rome and thus reshape our notions of the early Roman years.

With Anthony usurped from his position of primacy among Poussin scholars – for Mahon's assault achieved no less a consequence – the way was open for further erosive attacks in 1979 when he was exposed as a spy, attacks by the press whose false logic had it that he was flawed in all aspects of his life and work, attacks even by many in some way attached to the Courtauld Institute who could see some professional advantage in playing jackal. Miranda Carter (op. cit. p. 434) quotes just the kind of gleeful tale that was circulating in the Institute, in this case of a very small painting of *The Agony in the Garden* that he owned but had attributed to a follower or imitator, identified as autograph well after his death – I can still hear the exultant sniggering. The truth of that matter is that I bought that picture on his behalf and he knew unequivocally what it was. He knew too exactly what was under his nose when I brought back from Florence the fine preparatory sketch of *The Martyrdom of St Erasmus* for an altar in St Peter's, a canvas that, if not exactly lost, had by 1963 been quite forgotten. At Dover, Customs men had gone so far as to take the tyres off my car in their search for drugs (though why their suspicions were roused I could not fathom), but in the canvas under a blanket they showed not the slightest interest. For me, finding this Poussin was an exultant experience that, but for Claudio, would not have come about, for I had driven to Italy to see other pictures proposed for sale at Christie's and he had come for the ride. It was April and the spring was glorious after what, in the early months of 1963, had been a dreadful winter with temperatures so far below freezing-point that a burst water main had levelled the street outside the house under ice so thick that for weeks we could not distinguish the pavements from the road. In Switzerland, in Villeneuve, I had identified two wonderful bozzetti[28] by Piazzetta for altarpieces in Venetian churches – the consequence of an 'if you ever find yourself near Vevey, do drop in' conversation, and was in jubilant mood until I reached Milan; there, however, the collection that was my real objective proved to be of the sort of dregs that Christie's reserved for end-of-season sales when bargains were to be had by the bad Italian dealers who had contributed so much to this accumulation of rubbish. We escaped within hours rather than the projected days and, with time in hand, drove south to Florence where Claudio had cousins with whom we could stay. It was through these and a wearying round of lunches and drinks with a decaying nobility whose titles were as moribund as his, that we encountered the Poussin. In spite of its ghastly subject – St Erasmus tied down in agony while his intestines were wound onto a roller – I was enchanted by the vigour and freedom with which this large sketch was painted (it is a metre tall) and was at once convinced that it was by Poussin in an unusually easy mood. Significant but minor differences from the altarpiece for St Peter's proved its primacy over the larger work.

For some months it hung in my room at Christie's. Anthony's immediate response was absolute conviction; others were equally convinced; but when, at last, the time came to include it in an auction, I ran into difficulties. I could not catalogue it without quoting its full provenance and that would identify the owner who had no permit to export for sale what might well be regarded as an Italian national treasure – my driving it to London without the necessary papers had been quite outside Italian law. Christie's had thus to return the painting to Florence and trust the owner to initiate the proper process for export. He did not; instead, using my

28   A bozzetto or modello is a more or less final preparatory sketch in oils for a much larger painting; when the terms are used for sculpture the material is usually terracotta or plaster.

valuation, he saved himself the commission on the sale and all associated expenses by selling it to an Italian dealer who, in turn, sold it to one of the most eminent dealers in New York, and in 1972 the National Gallery of Canada announced its acquisition.

Later in 1963 Anthony identified another painting by Poussin, belonging to Duncan Grant who had bought it in Paris in the 1920s without quite knowing what it was. *A Landscape with a Man pursued by a Serpent* is related to a very much larger variation on the theme in the National Gallery. It is not absurd to say that Anthony fell in love with it – his desire to own it was as much emotional as intellectual; this he confessed to Duncan with 'everything I own I would exchange for it.' He was thus confronted by the moral problem of the man who is both the expert and the would-be purchaser, resolving it by asking for valuations from three experts in the market known to both Duncan and himself, deciding in advance that he would pay the highest estimate. Both Colnaghi's and I fitted this description and without collusion arrived at £12,000 as a fair figure between willing buyer and willing vendor if no commission or other expense came into play. I have no idea how Colnaghi's arrived at their figure – mine was based on the far larger sum I had suggested as a reserve for the *St Erasmus*, a painting almost twice the size. The third estimate came from Tomas Harris, a flamboyant dealer long retired to the comforts of Majorca but known to Anthony before the war – and perhaps not known at all to Duncan; his significantly lower figure can be attributed to his being out of touch and it was ignored. Duncan was pleased enough with his £12,000 (then enough to buy a decent house in middle Kensington) – but Heaven knows what he did with it, for Charleston, the house that he had shared with half the denizens of Bloomsbury, increasingly ragged and dilapidated year on year, remained as cold and damp as ever, often with so little evidence of food in it that I and Joseph McCrindle (a mutual friend and collector of Duncan's work) made a point of dropping in on him with assortments of smoked tit-bits and things in tins and jars that he need not cook, whenever we were weekending in Joe's cottage in Winchelsea – a custom from which, in the mid-seventies, we were sternly deterred by Paul Roche, Duncan's self-appointed guardian.

Joe I encountered in 1962. Checking the auctioneer's book of a sale of drawings in which all reserves and prior bids were recorded, I saw yet again the name McCrindle among the bidders, his bids wildly high and absurdly low. 'Who is this idiot?' I asked John Hancock – to which the answer was 'A nice American – but he knows nothing about drawings.' I took him to lunch at Prunier's and gently told him what I thought of his bids, suggesting that I might help him be nearer the mark; some days later he asked me to dinner at his house in Edwardes Square – a chaotic affair in which a hired cook produced and served everything in the wrong order, Bruce – a disorderly Labrador – settled on a weighty American lesbian for his sexual victim for the evening, and assorted aspiring writers, both hetero and homosexual, played games of vain one-upmanship beyond my understanding. It was, nevertheless, the beginning of almost half a century of friendship.

As an American, Joe lived in London as much as the taxation authorities allowed, his friends as conscious of his absences as of his presences, for the emptiness of the first was as noticeable as the fullness of the second. He belonged to a generation of old money and the Social Register, a New Yorker whose grandmother – a profound influence – lived in a whole house on Fifth Avenue and saw to it that, through private tutors, he spoke French, German and Italian as idiomatically as English, and learned to box, dance and play the violin – for none of which disciplines had he any talent. She owned an ocean-going steam yacht and in the long summers of the Thirties Joe sailed alone – but for the crew and his tutor, Lanning Roper (later a great gardener) – to fashionable Europe and once to the Near East; what can it have meant to a boy of eight to be on the wilder shores of the old Ottoman Empire? At eighteen Grandmama gave him a Duesenberg, the very best of American cars, as his runabout at Harvard, and there he studied law.

This he had neither the wish nor the need to practice. His loves were literature and art. He conceived, and for two decades subsidised and edited, *The Transatlantic Review*, a magazine in which the early strivings of scribblers were published, stepping-stones to fame. For more than twice as long he supported the careers of young painters and collected paintings and drawings by old masters, for which he had an instinctive rather than an educated eye; only Eric Hebborn, the notorious forger, abused his trust and fell into both categories. Never vain, as his collections grew in importance, he could not see that the friendship of museum curators was often nothing but mainchance flattery – as, indeed, was the interest of so many of the elegant young men who dined with him.

At dinners with Joe the American novelist rubbed shoulders with the English academic, the literary agent with the art dealer, and staunch friends with the latest favourite boy. Joe was a romantic giver, successive boys unromantic takers who left him with unhealing hurts. In friendships not disturbed by sex he was formidably loyal and generous.

Strokes eventually disabled his stout form, restricting him to New York. His last visit to London was in a wheelchair; he could neither speak nor feed himself, but nevertheless we lunched in what had long been a customary restaurant, another fond friend feeding him as might a mother a big baby. Between us, conversation with Joe was by proxy, so to speak, widening eyes his only contribution. When we parted, having juggled the wheelchair into a taxi, there was a long and telling pause, a holding of the gaze, for we both knew that we'd not meet again. What can a man do in a circumstance for which there are no words? A fumbled hug. A graceless kiss. In July 2008 he was altogether gone, his absence his permanent memorial.

* * *

By far the most important matter in which I was briefly involved in 1962 was the Royal Academy's sale of *The Virgin and Child with*

Outsider

Saints Anne and John the Baptist, by Leonardo da Vinci, known as *The Leonardo Cartoon* or simply 'the cartoon' – cartoon used in the sense of a full size final preparatory drawing for a painting – now in the National Gallery. Late in January, Humphrey Brooke, secretary to the Academy, who had become something of a paternal friend during and since my work on *The Age of Louis XIV*, gave me a furtive lunch in one of his clubs, after which he asked a question that explained his attempted *sotto voce*. A big man, often noisily exuberant and always voluble, his was the whisper and furtiveness of the stage farce, and when I got the gist of it so did every other man in his long earshot. He wanted to know what I thought Christie's might get for the cartoon if we were given it to auction. This it was impossible to answer. Few drawings by Leonardo are not in the captivity of impregnable collections and this cartoon, the last stage in the planning of a major painting (never executed) before the first stroke of the brush swept onto the panel or the canvas, must surely count more as an unfinished painting than as a drawing, and be priceless – Humphrey, however, was at that stage thinking of it as a drawing and had thus approached me rather than Bill or Patrick, both of whom he had known rather longer. I hazarded a guess that £1,000,000 might be a starting figure for debate, stressing the importance of a shrewdly judged reserve in case major museums might agree to pool resources or not compete; I also said that if the cartoon were to be sure of a foreign buyer, it would have to be at such a price as to make refusing an export license quite impossible. Humphrey then swore me to secrecy – no sure decision had been reached, it might not happen, and no one at Christie's was yet to learn of it. Feeling slightly sick and at the same time intoxicated – to sell so wonderful a thing would be a mighty coup – I returned to work. Should I tell Bill, who always found discretion difficult? Should I tell Patrick, who was likely to dismiss the possibility as absurd or at once storm the Academy? I did neither; instead, after two days of brooding I telephoned Jacob Bean in New York, the wonderfully urbane and gentlemanly

Curator of Drawings recently appointed at the Metropolitan Museum, less than a decade my senior in age but a lifetime in Jamesian sophistication, whom at that stage I knew only through Michel Laclotte and Roseline Bacou at the Louvre, where Jacob had been a voluntary assistant in the Cabinet des Dessins. I asked him – hedged about with ifs, buts and supposes – Humphrey's hypothetical question; and his response – 'Two million dollars and beyond' – I relayed at once to Humphrey, whom I knew in my bones had probably asked half a dozen others in the market.

I do not quite know the subsequent course of events in what was to become a fractious and distasteful squabble between the Academy, the government, the fundraisers who came into play and a population that did not care a hoot about something called a cartoon – about which newspaper cartoonists were making pretty fierce fun. These developments, traumatic for Humphrey, triggered another bout of the manic depression from which he suffered – in the end he only wanted a conclusion, any conclusion, to a decision that had brought him and the Academy only opprobrium, scorn and notoriety. That decision had been to sell the cartoon. When I learned that there had been written valuations from James Byam Shaw of Colnaghi's at £750,000, from Geoffrey Agnew of £500,000 to £600,000, and from Peter Wilson of Sotheby's the assurance of a reserve price of £850,000, I knew the secret was out – and must have been out for some time – and needing no longer to hold my tongue, I told Bill and Patrick of my small part so far. My preliminary estimate of £1,000,000 had been tempered by Jacob Bean's 2,000,000 dollars – then just over £700,000 – and I felt that a firm estimate of £1,000,000 should be confirmed, vaguely supported by the gloss of Jacob's 'and beyond'. Bill was dismayed by the unprecedented figure; Patrick, on the other hand, was more dismayed that I, not he, had been consulted by Humphrey and at once, exactly as I thought he might, rushed off in a rage to beard him in the Academy with a higher bid than Sotheby's. In the bearding he was right, but the rage, I suspect, undid him. Humphrey was at least as large as Patrick and well able to rage back. Patrick, on his return, forbade me to have any further conversations with Humphrey. A sale through Sotheby's was then announced.

This was greeted by an outcry from the great and good and the Academy backed down, agreeing to sell the cartoon to the nation at what to all sane men was by then the bargain figure of £800,000 – that sum to be raised by an appeal to the public; if the appeal failed, then selling it at Sotheby's – where Peter Wilson had raised the proposed reserve to £1,000,000 – became inevitable, as did the certainty of a foreign buyer. Patrick's father, Lord Crawford, the public face of the National Art Collections Fund and thus of the campaign and public appeal, was unrelentingly bitter and disparaging in his expressed view of the Academicians and their folly; would he have been more amicable, I wondered, had the sale been scheduled at Christie's, the firm at which, through his influence, his son had become a partner?

On 16 March the great and good gathered to initiate the public appeal and determined that the cartoon should go to the National Gallery as a painting not yet begun, rather than to the British Museum where the nation's drawings are housed. Two weeks later it was taken to Trafalgar Square so that the public could more easily understand and respond to the rattling of begging-bowls. Response was slow and grudging; on the last day of the appeal, 31 July, after four full months only a very little over half the sum had been donated, but the government then contributed £350,000 and the NACF the rest, and the cartoon remained in the National Gallery. No one came out of it well; the Academy was damned for greed and blackmail and the government for failing yet again to establish a reasonable means of protecting the heritage – as is still the case. The only consolation for Christie's was that Sotheby's was not given the sale.

Within a year, however, on 26 March 1963, I did have a drawing by Leonardo in a sale. Captain John Noel, descended from the

Earls of Gainsborough, Noel their family name, still using his military rank forty years after his resignation from the army, came into Christie's with Mary, his unlikely wife-cum-housekeeper as fat as he was thin and every ounce a peasant. I knew him very slightly through a much younger officer in his regiment, recently disgraced, who, when keeping an occasional eye on his ancient aunt (and hoped-for inheritance) declining in the cathedral precinct of Canterbury, looked in on him in his Kent cottage not far off. As Nigel was certainly queer (hence the disgrace – something about being buggered over the barrel of an antique cannon) and John Noel, though born in 1890, in his early seventies seemed to be still consumed by a romantic passion for George Mallory, the lost hero of the 1924 Everest Expedition, I assumed that he too was queer and Mary merely a convenience. I was wrong; Noel was twice married and had a daughter by Mary, but whenever he spoke of Mallory – which was often – his eyes filled with tears that I mistook for those of a sometime lover (and Mallory, often said to have been the most beautiful of men, is now thought by many to have been at least bi-sexual). He was quite the last man I expected to ask for me at the Front Counter, shabby of dress, with a drip from his nose and any passing thought that he might once have been a gentleman, banished by the even shabbier bulk of Mary, yet he had with him two small drawings some 110 by 80 mm, one on a mount inscribed *Leonardo da Vinci*, the subject a grotesque caricature of a bald old man in profile, the other so benign an observation of a nutcracker male profile that the old man seemed quite beautiful.

The provenance of both reached back to the collection of the Earl of Arundel early in the seventeenth century, from which the Leonardo drawings in the Royal Collection came, but when I took them to Popham – so much regarded as the expert that I was bound to be asked by every serious enquirer 'And what did Popham say?' – his opinion was that only the grotesque was genuine, dismissing the other as by an imitator; he had a point, for the direction of the shading lines indicated beyond argument that the draughtsman was right-handed – but it was, nevertheless, the more beautiful scrap and I advised him not to sell it. But he did, two years later, at Sotheby's, for £750. For the grotesque Christie's got him 14,000 guineas, a sum quite large enough to relieve the impression of penury and discomfort given by the circumstances in which he lived – but whatever benefits the drawings brought, they must have expired long before his death in 1989, just short of his centenary.

*   *   *

At much the same time as the Leonardo Cartoon became our focus of interest, Christie's were called in to arrange a sale from the remaining contents of the studios of Augustus John, forced on his family by death duties. As a student I had taken to what became the lifelong habit of falling asleep with the wireless on, to be wakened in the morning by the early news bulletin. On Tuesday 31 October 1961 a voice announced John's death, two months short of his eighty-fourth birthday, and the President of the Royal Academy, Charles Wheeler, delivered a touching eulogy that ended with the phrase 'Truly, he could draw like a God.' I could not explain then, and cannot now, why I felt such an emotional wrench – bumping into him in Bertorelli's as a student in search of a cheap supper (soused herring and boiled potatoes) was not enough to call acquaintance and yet the news had for me something of the sense of loss felt by half the nation on the death of Princess Diana. A few months later, nothing (other than securing the Leonardo Cartoon) could have pleased me more than being despatched to Fryern Court, the John family house at Fordingbridge, in which he had lived and worked since 1927, late in the decade during which genius slipped away from him.

It was, as so often with life at Christie's, a job to be rushed; the sale was an important stage in settling the estate and perhaps an even more important event in our increasingly meagre calendar, but choosing what was to be included in it was far from straight-forward, for wonderful drawings had been eaten away by extra-ordinary moulds in black and brilliant pink, hundreds of canvases scattered between three studios were filthy with the ingrained dirt of decades and hung about with the webs of spiders whose crumpled corpses nestled behind the stretchers, and panels from his very early years were scuffed and scratched. Some paintings were as good as any of their various periods; others, unfinished, he had halted at a stage acceptable enough to the aesthetics of the Sixties; to others still he had returned after decades of wondering how to continue and had ruined them with revisions in a wholly different style. One particularly beautiful full-length portrait of a young woman, three-quarter life-size, almost completed in 1900 or so, he had very recently attacked with altogether cruder brushes and cheap paint, inspired to do so by a postcard of a painting by El Greco pinned through the canvas to the stretcher. To sell paintings and drawings in such conditions would have suited the trade well enough, for dealers can always see through dirt and damage and, as a rule, profit greatly from their remedying and improvement by uninhibited restorers – Kahnweiler's exploitation of Cézanne's studio leavings a warning to us all – but most private buyers are deterred by flawed condition, and it was to these and particularly to John's diminishing generation of admirers whom I thought this sale would have immediate appeal. I discussed the problem with Sir Caspar John, eldest son of Augustus, a relaxed and rather jolly Admiral of the Fleet and First Sea Lord who had inherited his father's libido, and we agreed on a crash programme of cleaning and repair; we also agreed that he should put this to Patrick so that he, in turn, could put it to me – 'What a splendid idea – why didn't I think of it?' to be my spontaneous response.

The drawings I took to Doreen Lewisohn, the most modest and most scrupulous of restorers specialising in works on paper, a tiny, bird-like, bicycle-riding wit, living and working in the smallest cottage in St John's Wood. Though born in London in 1916 she was, through her wider family, in many ways thoroughly Viennese, after the *Anschluss* a neighbour briefly familiar with Freud and witness of his departure, even assisting the formidable housekeeper of Berggasse 19 who kept inquisitive Nazis at bay while she packed the master's treasures for transport to Hampstead – if only Doreen had kept a diary . . . Her first venture was into the design of furniture and that her only comfortable chair was often mistaken for one by Breuer gave her constant pleasure. She then became the world's only expert in the repair and conservation of antique globes, but for this arcane skill there was scant demand and she drifted into the related field of works on paper, with which she was so sensitive and deft that her interventions could rarely be identified. Of her one rival in London this could not be said and by the adjective 'Drescherised' we all knew exactly what was meant – a ruined drawing on bleached paper into which the faded ink had sunk and from which much chalk, charcoal or pastel had been flushed away. Once Doreen's skills had been enlisted by the Fitzwilliam Museum, she became so involved there that she moved to Cambridge and was appointed conservator for works on paper. I adored her for daring to attempt the seemingly impossible, her gossip, and for her diligent kindness to my mother with whom she had some kindred spirit, never neglecting to see her on her not infrequent visits to London. Of her work on the 115 drawings included in the first Augustus John sale there was not a trace and, though some had lost their freshness from exposure, most were as fresh as on the day they were executed.

The paintings were dusted down by Joan Seddon. I had selected 68 that were both fair to his reputation and required least work to prepare – except for a vast unfinished canvas, some four by twelve metres, neither stretched nor framed, intended as a Canadian War Memorial, potentially magnificent but halted in 1919 (though Lord Beaverbrook was still angling for it as late as 1959), that we hoped might be bought by a Canadian museum (in the event it went to a private collector in Chile who, it was later rumoured,

Doreen Lewisohn at work in her studio; she was so deft with her hands that she could peel a banknote in two

Doreen Lewisohn

Drawings and watercolours restorer at the Fitzwilliam Museum in Cambridge

DOREEN LEWISOHN, who has died aged 83, was an expert in the conservation and restoration of drawings and watercolours.

After studying with Willem van Oort at the Rijksprintenkabinet in Amsterdam after the war, she set up as a conservator of drawings and watercolours in London. To begin with, she worked mostly for dealers, among them Yvonne ffrench, Hans Calmann and Annely Juda.

She always maintained that her professional breakthrough came when Brian Sewell, then working at Christie's, the auctioneers, recommended that she be given the Beauchamp Album, containing 166 drawings by the 18th-century artist Giandomenico Tiepolo, to

take apart and restore before its sale in 1965.

By then she had also been commissioned to work on some of the Old Master drawings at the Fitzwilliam Museum in Cambridge. When, subsequently, the Area Museums Service for South East England was set up, she was appointed the conservator for works of art on paper and moved to Cambridge to work full time at the Fitzwilliam, remaining there from 1975 until her retirement to 1981.

Doreen Ina Lewisohn was born in London on July 25 1916 and went to Mrs Spalding's school in Queen's Gate. She went on to study interior design and furniture making at the Central School of Art and before the Second

World War travelled widely in America and Mexico.

During the war she worked for the War Damage Commission, where her duties included bicycling round London every morning and reporting back to her chief on which buildings he should go to inspect for damage.

With the return of peace, she spent a time studying picture framing and then went to Florence to study gilding with the Ceis. She also spent several months in Rome, with the art historian Eve Borsook, in addition to the spell in Amsterdam.

After retiring from the museum world, Doreen Lewisohn continued in private practice for several years. Observers noted how adept she was with her hands, and

the quick, effortless way in which she would remove the backing of a drawing. To amuse her friends, she would sometimes peel a £5 note in two.

Small, thin and bird-like, but possessing great vivacity and spirit, Doreen Lewisohn was an excellent raconteur and had a keen sense of the absurd. She was completely without side and made friends with all sorts.

Though frugal, she was always elegantly dressed. At home, in somewhat chaotic surroundings, there was modern furniture, some of which she had made herself. She always wrote her letters in brown ink on blue paper, and she rode her bicycle around Cambridge until she was more than 80 years old.

Doreen Lewisohn's obituary from the *Daily Telegraph*, March 2000

commissioned its adaptation to celebrate the victory of Bernardo O'Higgins over Spanish forces at Chacabuco in 1817, establishing a new republic). Joan had a year before dealt with an emergency repair to an extraordinary still life of flowers that we had catalogued as by Francesco Guardi. I thought it a fake, but this was a period when Guardi had been expanded far beyond the painter of Venetian views by the recent discovery of huge rococo illustrations to Tasso's *Gerusalemme Liberata* and by Antonio Morassi's public-ation of a batch of similar still lives as genuine early works. Our example fell from the west wall of the octagon – the wall that always spelt misfortune – late on a Friday afternoon and was raggedly pierced by the back of a chair; scheduled to be on view first thing on Monday morning, something had to be done. Joan, then new to Christie's, came at once – the brutal hacks in service to the art trade, to whom Bill and Patrick always turned for help with our not infrequent accidents, turned them down. The proper course was to reline the canvas but for that there was no time; instead, we closed the tears with discreet stitches and joined the broken threads of an improbably coarse canvas with an invisible adhesive, masking these repairs with paint to match the broad brushing of white pigment that appeared to 'dust' the reverse of the canvas (for which there was no obvious genuine reason). On the following day Joan restored the damaged flowers in tempera and when the picture was returned to the wall no one could see that it had been the victim of a very recent accident. Some fool paid 11,000 guineas for it. Over the next few years so many Guardi flower pieces increasingly inferior in quality appeared that Christie's were compelled to refuse such obvious fakes; they migrated to the lesser auction rooms, Phillips, Bonhams and Knight, Frank and Rutley, and when there the prices eventually dropped to £100 a pair, the fakers turned to mock-Montgolfier ballooning pictures. There was at the same time a flood of mock-Guardi drawings, hundreds of them, small and unambitious, given the suggestion of age with spots of mould immediately recognisable to any housewife (though not to art historians) as the dust of Nescafé blown onto damp paper.

Taking into account the amount of work to be done by Doreen and Joan the date of the John sale had been scheduled as late as we dared, 20 July 1962, for by tradition the last Friday of July was the end-of-season sale in which we cleared the warehouse rooms of paintings that had failed to reach reserves, been forgotten, or were too embarrassingly bad to show unless hung at least three deep on every wall – a bargain-hunter's paradise. The room was crowded and inexperienced amateurs were slow in bidding, but the total slowly mounted to £99,645 – rather more than we had expected when we considered the steep decline that the old boy's reputation had suffered for almost forty years. I produced a rotten catalogue; it had no note on Augustus as once the white hope of British painting, but by 1962 neglected, even forgotten, by the old establishment of his day, and unknown to the new; it had no notes on sitters, friends, family, time, place or meaning; nor did it recognise what an important document such a catalogue should be, a record, a memorial, a work of reference. But that was how Christie's was at that time – a catalogue entry was mainly for identification purposes so that Jock, Les and the other porters were quite sure that they were putting the right number on each lot. There was too the long-drawn business of my stepfather's dying; he had held his own until the beginning of the year, but then the cancer accelerated and I took to dashing to Castle Hedingham on weekday evenings, and the repercussions of his death at the end of May coincided with the final preparation of the catalogue for the printer.

With Peter Chance in the rostrum, performing with his usual élan and warmth, it was the most successful sale of the season. Perhaps relieved that so unpredictable an event had exceeded all expectations, he celebrated after lunch by giving a job to a boy who wanted one – no ordinary boy, but a boy tall, loose-limbed, flopsy and passably handsome in a very English way. At £6 a week (and Luncheon Vouchers), the Hon. Charlie Allsopp joined the

Front Counter to endure Ridley Leadbeater's pokes and prods for a trial period of a year. I took one look at him and predicted that this dyslexic, shambling, trustful and innocent golden retriever of a boy would one day be Christie's chairman – and was right; to see him in Peter's company was to see the older man in love – not the lustful physical love with which I was now familiar, but pure unquestioning adoration.

Eleven months after the first John sale there was a second. On 21 June 1963, 110 drawings and 63 paintings made the wretched sum of only £33,405, clear evidence that the market had been flooded, yet this, in terms of diversity and invention, as well as decline, was far the more interesting sale, particularly among the drawings, revealing moments of improbable achievement; lot 117, for example, a life-size study of a *French Peasant Youth* from the first decade of the twentieth century, would not be shamed in the company of a Blue Period painting by Picasso, John's very near contemporary. The catalogue was designed to match the first, but was a marginal improvement. The choice this time was far more difficult. Twenty-one wonderfully handsome academic nudes, male and female, from John's years at the Slade, had been eaten away by mould, losing their feet, and had to be stabilised and patched by Doreen – restoration was impossible; and for the paintings we established a studio for Joan in one of the few warehouse rooms with a rooflight. Hers was an Augean task but she carried it out with great sensibility and I dogsbodied for her as much as I could. On a day that I had wholly set aside for her, John Maxon, Director of the Art Institute of Chicago, came to see if by chance I was free for lunch; never less than dapper, he expressed surprise to find me in a porter's apron, sleeves rolled up, arms black with dust, surprise changing to dismay when I introduced Joan with 'This is Joan Seddon, here to clean the Johns' – in American slang Johns are lavatories.

On the afternoon of Friday, 19 April 1963, it was just as well that Joan was on the premises. A vast painting by Edward Burne-Jones,

The Sleep of Arthur at Avalon, was delivered to Christie's for sale the following Friday. I had had to catalogue it blind, so to speak, from drawings, bibliographical references and ancient photographs, and was anxious to know how much in error I might be. More than six metres wide and nearly three high, this enormous composition was a too personal, spiritual and emotional exploration of himself and a romantic mythological past with which he identified so closely that one may well see it as his *Parsifal*, which occupied Wagner twice the seventeen years that Burne-Jones spent on Arthur. Sentimental, anguished and morbid, reeking with the odour of sanctity, it underwent more significant re-composing than even Picasso's *Guernica*. No one had seen it since 1933, the centenary of the painter's birth, other than, on the outbreak of World War II, to remove it from its frame and stretcher, to roll it, and put it in a stout box some half-metre square and three metres long (much as Delacroix's *Massacre* had been twenty years later); in that box it stayed, unseen, until it reached Christie's.

The lid unscrewed, a myriad spiders scuttled from the box; gently we unrolled the heavy canvas on the floor of the lofty anteroom where it was to hang and dusted away the mass of webs and other arachnid detritus that obscured it. How could we display so large a canvas without a stretcher? As a tapestry on a tapestry bar, I decided, but none we had was long enough and all we could do was procure a six-metre length of timber; with the canvas tacked to it by the raw edge that had formerly folded over the original stretcher, it was hauled up the wall with a dozen of us supporting it to ensure that the inevitable inverted curvature was kept as open as possible. It worked, and for the first time for thirty years, eyes feasted on the masterpiece. The canvas, however, was much weightier than any tapestry.

Peter Chance strode in to see it, pink, silver and immaculate; he strode to its very centre and within a pace of it, and at that moment the weight of the canvas began to tear it from the bar. Poor Peter reached to press it against the wall, but the avalanche could not be halted, the canvas ripped away, curled forward and enclosed him in its vastness. Instead of standing still, he panicked, fought his way out of the belly of this whale more dishevelled than his wife had ever seen him first thing in the morning, and the canvas lay face down, a crumpled heap. When we reversed it (no mean feat) and flattened it, we saw the consequences – flaked paint lay thickly on the floor, the whole width of the canvas where flowers fill the foreground, the area of heaviest initial impact, was extensively damaged, and widespread random damages elsewhere reflected Peter's efforts to escape.

Joan and I had until Monday morning, when the picture officially went on view – at most some thirty working hours we thought – in which to camouflage the injuries. Lying on cushions on the canvas, Joan began work at the top, and I, on my knees, began at the bottom on the easier business of repairing the more or less crudely painted flowers. Thirty hours were not enough and we worked through the night on Sunday.

During the week of the sale not a word was said by anyone. Did no one notice how much of *Arthur at Avalon* had been damaged? And if they did, did they assume that the damages were old? When, on the following Friday, the painting was bought by the museum in Puerto Rico, it was relined, cleaned and stretched before being framed and installed in a specially constructed room – did none of the experts responsible for these procedures not notice how much of the paint was new? Forty-five years later when the painting returned to England to spend a year in the Tate Gallery, I could identify very few of Joan's interventions, but was appalled by the crude quality of the irises, bluebells and forget-me-nots in which I had a hand.

*   *   *

Even though the second John sale was a disappointment, there was still more to do for Caspar, for there remained at Fryern Court over a thousand drawings and some four hundred canvases, all of which had to be valued for further discussions over tax. Many of the drawings were early, small, irregular in shape and dirty, but in their inventive and intriguing subjects they were precursors of major paintings and thus of value to future art historians, were there ever to be any attracted to study so minor a figure (for that is what Augustus had become), but in commercial terms worth nothing in so saturated a market. Other drawings, later, sketchier, scrappier or evidently discarded (even scribbled over), were not only worth nothing, but would always be virtually worthless in commercial and art historical terms. As for the canvases, a handful – of which the figure on the easel with the El Greco postcard was an example – were worth preserving as art historical documents, but the rest, the bulk of them failed portraits, were fit only for scraping and re-use; this I proposed for the benefit of students at the Slade, but this was deemed impossible (it was not – as I later proved with more than fifty of my own paintings, between heart attacks in 1995); I then suggested that they should be destroyed rather than expose John's reputation to further ridicule. The tax men disagreed; pointing to the sales, they took the view that every canvas and scrap of paper had a value and must be taxed. I argued that to preserve the value of works already sold, those remaining at Fryern must never escape onto the open market – a view as incomprehensible to tax men as the ludicrous idea that one of our duties was to preserve John's reputation by not preserving works that he, by retaining them for decades, had ensured should never be seen by the public. I spent many days at Fryern Court and grew fond of Dorelia, devoted mistress, muse, wife and widow to Augustus, at 81 more truly beautiful than any portrait he had painted of her in her sensual twenties. Setting aside drawings that I was sure were not by Augustus, but muddled with his, I asked her opinion. 'I'll ask him,' she replied, took the drawings from me and left the room. Some minutes later she returned with 'No, they're not.' When I told Caspar what had happened he chuckled – 'She asked her wedding ring – on a thread, you know.'

Matters were not finally settled until Dorelia's death in July 1969, aged eighty-six and still wistfully enchanting. Caspar, still the Admiral, wrote me an oddly nautical note – 'She managed it very well and had a peaceful passage out . . . the end of an era and a generation.' On her estate yet more tax had to be paid – £25,115 – and what was left in the studio was again a matter of dispute with the authorities, resolved by a block sale of over a thousand drawings to the National Museum of Wales; the museum bought the remaining paintings too, but of these there were only 110, 'nearly all unfinished or rejected portraits, mostly later than 1920,' according to the Keeper there, A. D. Fraser Jenkins, in 1978. So many decades later it is now safe to say that Caspar took my advice and burned some three hundred canvases. To Joan he gave a wonderful small early painting on panel of the highest quality, the very best of Johns, and to me a random handful of drawings, among them some mould-rotted academies that had lost their feet – more work for Doreen Lewisohn.

*   *   *

Of Charlie Allsopp I had no fear, for his obvious destiny was remote from my ambition – I simply wanted to head a department of prints and drawings without losing my toe-hold among the better paintings, no matter what their date and school, and in this Charlie had no hope of treading on my heels. David Carritt was an entirely different matter, ushered in to do what I had never been given time to do and likely to deprive me of the only thrilling aspect of my job, the identification of masterpieces. He was charming, generous and witty, his quips as deadly as stilettos, his broader humour crude, lewd and often bluntly homosexual – after his corruption of Sir Geoffrey Agnew (notoriously vain and boastful) and his mournful crew to 'Geoff and the Agonies, the Bond Street Pop Group,' we none of us could take those bullies seriously, and his having to explain to an uncomprehending Patrick what he meant by a 'pork injection' (his euphemism for the act of sodomy) was a moment of pure farce. Nor could Patrick chuckle with the rest of us at David's Monday morning gossip of obliging frustrated heterosexual young men picked up outside the Hammersmith Palais late on Saturday night and whisked back to 120 Mount Street – though Patrick himself, reputed to have seduced most of the secretary girls in the directors' flat in Christie's attic (intended only for emergencies) was not above letting slip hints of his own sexual prowess; David, I suspect, told some of his stories simply to provoke Patrick's puritanical distaste for everything sexually divergent. Often David's nonchalant audacity in divulging not only his own escapades but those of others in the art world, was the only thing that could break the oppressive mood imposed by Patrick when, as a group, we were inspecting the latest batch of paintings. As an aside it is worth recording that sex in Christie's was as much downstairs as up; in the carpet warehouse there was regular brothel business at lunchtime, with the senior porter in the department guarding the door and taking the entrance fee from below-stairs staff wishing to conjugate with a working girl or two on the heaped treasures of the Silk Route. And how, in this context, can I omit Bill Spowers, 'The Major', the dapper, dashing and diminutive Australian, at some time of the Grenadier Guards and the Parachute Regiment, who joined the book department in 1960, presumably for what must have been to him mere pocket money? Apparently Croesus rich, when offered the car registration plates WS1 to WS6, Bill bought the lot, and then bought cars to match them, among them a silver Gullwing Mercedes, a pale blue Rolls-Royce Silver Cloud drop-head coupé and an open Bentley Continental. He also bought a flat above Prunier's, ostensibly to use after working late (he lived in far off Windlesham, minutes away in any of these cars), but its principal purpose was as an afternoon bolt-hole to which to repair with whichever Christie's girl he had in tow as his *Cléo de trois à cinq*. According to gossip, his penis was wondrously disproportionate.

David Carritt joined Christie's in January 1963 at seven times my salary with expenses and privileges accorded only to the partners – of which he was soon to become another. To the wider public he was a man who had for four years been the art critic of the *Evening Standard*. To Christie's partners he was the man who, as a private dealer – that is one working without a gallery or other business premises – had made a remarkable series of discoveries, among them paintings by Caravaggio, Dürer, and Guardi. To the art trade he was tainted as a partner in a leading auction house (as John Herbert, his chief advocate, should have known would be the case) and wary dealers were suspicious of him – leopards and spots, they thought. To Peter Wilson of Sotheby's, an almost equal wit, he was 'a rat *joining* a sinking ship.' Scholars too were suspicious; Francis Watson, who had for so long known the whereabouts of the great Tiepolo discovery that David was to make in 1964, had not thought the paintings missing, and fizzed with rage – a matter of different generations, I suppose – and the Dürer, now in the National Gallery, was and still is, disputed, increasingly to boot. As for the Guardis – four huge canvases (the largest 2.5 × 4.5 metres) and four narrow upright filler panels – these were the illustrations to *Gerusalemme Liberata* that he, with Patrick O'Connor, Curator of the then moribund Hugh Lane Gallery in Dublin, but more widely known as a thoroughly unscrupulous dealer-cum-restorer, had identified, lending authority to the recently forged flower paintings and precipitating the fierce argument as to whether all these sudden extensions to our knowledge were by the celebrated Francesco Guardi, his elder brother Antonio, or both combining in the family workshop. Of this discovery we shall never know the whole truth; the bare facts are that these paintings had been part of the decoration of a once great house overlooking Bantry Bay, near Cork, and that in 1956 O'Connor had paid a mere £12,000 for them, had rolled them face in (a dreadful thing to do – it cracks the paint and abrades the cracks), and to make them look like nothing more than rolls of old canvas found in a barn, covered them with some foul adhesive, stable straw and dung that might deter customs officers from their curiosity, and sent them to London. The point at which David came into play is uncertain; Mrs Clodagh Shelswell-White, descendant of the 2nd Earl of Bantry, who brought them from Venice in the early nineteenth century, might well have been foolish enough to let him into Bantry House, but I doubt if the big, blustering and boorish O'Connor would have been given that courtesy for knocking on the door.

Patrick was the son of Andrew O'Connor (1874–1941), a not undistinguished sculptor born in Massachusetts and trained in Paris, who had settled in Ireland in 1932; unlike his father he underwent no formal training – indeed, no perceptible education of any kind – and his conservation and restoration methods were not short of brutal. Anne O'Connor, his American wife and my engaging friend, never wavered from her version of the tale that David saw the paintings in situ in the house and said nothing to the owner, but went to O'Connor to see if he would do the dirty work of paying as little as he could and exporting them to London. They should, as part of independent Ireland's Georgian heritage, have remained in the house of which they were a significant embellishment; as a public servant of sorts threatened with the possibility of imprisonment in Ireland for his part in the deceit, O'Connor fled to Palm Beach and set up his studio as a restorer to the local millionaires who adored the sight and sound of him. The four large paintings and one upright were bought by Geoffrey Merton and, in 1960, exhibited at the Royal Academy;[29] the last sentence in the catalogue entry offers no more information than 'The identification of the series was made by Mr David Carritt.' Seeing them as tainted, Merton subsequently sold them and they, together with the remaining three upright panels (at first retained by O'Connor) are now dispersed at points between Copenhagen and California – but Dublin is not one of them.

29 *Italian Art and Britain*, Royal Academy 1960, Nos 457, 460, 462, 465 and 466.

My first encounter with David had been much earlier, and by proxy, in my first incarnation at the Courtauld Institute. In the attic room in which I then chose to read and write there hung a marvellous painting by Caravaggio, a temporary loan to the Institute's collection, to be removed at a moment's notice and thus to be greedily and urgently absorbed. Facing the window, it caught the long warm rays of the autumn sun and sang of things languid and sensual of which I knew nothing but sensed much, for it seemed to touch part of my nature, then half recognised. When I should have been writing essays on Filippo Lippi and Tino da Camaino, instead I sat and gazed, enthralled, enchanted, transported, at the four indolent boys who inhabit Caravaggio's *Una Musica*, making the music of the love song rather than in praise of God – very different putti from those of Donatello and Luca della Robbia. One day the wall was bare, the canvas packed and flying to New York, the Metropolitan Museum having paid for it the then enormous sum of £20,000. Years later, driving David from Chatsworth to spend the weekend with Lord Faringdon, he told me the circumstances in which he had discovered and identified the Caravaggio that had for so many weeks occupied my mind and eye. As a small boy, at Rugby, he had become insatiably enquiring about paintings by old masters and, when the opportunity occurred, had used his intuition, wit and charm to knock on the doors of likely houses; with success, this impertinence became habitual. In such a house, in remote Cumbria, in the hamlet of Maulds Meaburn, midway between Barnard Castle and Carlisle, the property of Surgeon Captain W. G. Thwaytes, he found himself – though no longer a boy but a young man of twenty-four – in the captain's bed, the subject of ancient naval custom and, looking back through the arches formed by two pairs of thighs, glimpsed, upside-down from this angle, the four boys making music. I cannot recall whether David kept his counsel until the captain's energies were spent or whether he brought the proceedings to a sudden halt with the disconcerting cry 'Look! Look! A Caravaggio!'

David did more than sing for his supper; he brought the painting to the attention of Denis Mahon, who published it in *Paragone* and the *Burlington Magazine* in January 1952. In 1953 Bernard Berenson and Roger Hinks included it in books, and Roberto Longhi too acknowledged it, followed by Walter Friedlaender in his catalogue raisonné of 1955 – thus did David not only draw the attention of the great and good among art historians to a wonderful unknown painting, but establish himself as a new and very clever eye. For my part I owe him the particular debt that my few weeks in the company of *The Musicians* (the title given it by the Metropolitan Museum since 1953) resulted in a treasured awakening, an undimmed passion roused.

David in his first few weeks at Christie's showed – quite rightly – every sign of impatient boredom with the bread and butter paintings inflicted on all of us in the almost daily catalogue-checking sessions in the warehouse, but his presence did not result in the expected sudden influx of masterpieces, and the financial years of 1962–63 and 1963–64 ended with a loss of £6,000 and a puny profit of only £11,000 – not even enough to pay David's salary and expenses; in surveying the later year Peter Chance tersely observed that paintings by old masters had been in noticeably short supply. From a weekend in Milan David returned with a supposed Raphael in his overnight bag, confronting us with the irreconcilables of public auction and illegal export from a very prickly country of origin. I said I thought it a fake; David pointed to obvious recent restoration as an indication of authenticity – 'Oh that old trick,' I replied, having too often seen the deliberately clumsy repair of a deliberately damaged forgery. We went together to the technology department of the Courtauld Institute where Stephen Rees-Jones without hesitation damned it as a dud. David then had to spend another weekend in Milan, running the gauntlet of customs officers (the painting was later the subject of a fierce Italo-American squabble). He was often away; he had only to begin telephone conversations (quite knowingly) with 'David here . . . ' for the wealthy and noble of all Europe to offer him a bed – he said it was his 'little trick,' for 'David here . . . ' were always the opening words of the Duke of Windsor when he telephoned and David could pitch the timbre precisely – 'Imagine their surprise when little me turns up.' From his overcoat pocket one morning he drew the Dürer that he had identified in 1956, *St Jerome in the Wilderness*, and we discussed its possible sale; as I doubted the attribution then, and do so still,[30] and he himself had become less convinced, he returned it to its owner. In 1996, long after I had left Christie's and twelve years after David's death, quite unaware of our doubts, Christie's sold it by private treaty to the National Gallery for £10 million; in recent monographs on Dürer it has had intriguing treatment – acceptance, illustration without comment in the text, omission without explanation and, most recently, well-argued rejection.[31]

David could not even claim a part in securing for sale five important paintings from what little was left of the Cook Collection – a great nineteenth-century accumulation of old masters that in the curatorial care of old Maurice Brockwell had remained intact until 1939. In 1940 – a year in which the National Gallery, the National Art Collections Fund and the government were hardly in a position to object to the third baronet's decision to sell what was once one of the greatest treasures in the land, *The Three Marys at the Sepulchre* by either Hubert or Jan Van Eyck (without the divination of a medium the painter's identity will be for ever a matter of dispute), left for Rotterdam and the Van Beuningen collection; this was the first of the dribs and drabs that during and after the war eroded the collection to pay death duties and settle the demands of disgruntled wives, the prices invariably wretched. As Sotheby's in June 1958 had sold 156 paintings by

---

30 See *National Gallery Report 1996–97*, p. 14, note 1, where, curiously, my rejection is recorded.
31 Katherine Crawford Luber, *Dürer and the Venetian Renaissance*, Cambridge University Press 2005.

old masters for the insignificant sum of £64,668, it is not surprising that when Sir Francis Cook and his seventh wife decided to sell a handful of the remaining fifty, they called Peter Chance to their tax exile in Jersey – and with him went Patrick to hold his hand and David to lend a little gaiety to the occasion. The great prize was Rembrandt's *Portrait of Titus* as a child of perhaps seven, an enchanting and affectionate study, the handling of paint wonderfully broad for less that four square feet of canvas, and for this alone we expected to raise ten times the total of the Sotheby sale seven years before.

When it went on view on the afternoon of Friday 12 March 1965, I saw that not only had the gilt frame been chipped, leaving a white scar, but that the canvas had been punctured. Careless handling was a constant problem at Christie's; old Jock and Les were as tender as they could be, but once the pictures left their domain downstairs, any fool could handle them – there was no training of any kind (and woe betide any whippersnapper like me who dared to tell an upstairs porter how to carry precious fretted frames or support the fragile paper of unmounted drawings) and more porters were instinctively careless than were careful. Joan Seddon was nowhere to be found, nor was Ivor Jones, an able restorer for the Fitzwilliam Museum whom I trusted and always used when Joan was not available. As none of the partners was about – they had all seen the Cook pictures hanging in the directors' flat, by then converted into a private viewing room – young *Titus* was removed to my room while I tore home in a taxi to collect what tools I needed, Barbola paste, dull brown stains and gold wax for the frame, and for the painting, a patching material in case I could not persuade the broken threads of canvas to rejoin, my smallest spoon-shaped palette knife and, in the hope of a perfect match with Rembrandt's impastose paint, my cherished tins of brown shoe polish, evaporated, stiff and cracked, that when applied with the palette knife would have the dull gleam of old varnish.

Barbola paste and shoe polish survived unobserved their week of

ohn Herbert with Rembrandt's *Portrait of Titus*

Mr Norton Simon scowling at Peter Chance during the dispute which arose as a
esult of his special bidding arrangement during the sale of the Rembrandt

intense scrutiny, and when, the following Friday, as lot 105, *Titus* ended the sale, it was to the American collector Norton Simon for 760,000 guineas (2,234,400 US Dollars) – but it is less for this record price that the event is remembered than for the confusion over the bidding that resulted in its first being knocked down to a rival bidder, Marlborough Fine Art. Norton Simon was entirely responsible; a cautious man, he wished to be present at the sale but did not want to be seen bidding; nor did he trust anyone to bid for him; he therefore gave Patrick, though Peter was to be in the rostrum, written instructions that in the heat of the moment it might be impossible to recall. Minutes before the sale these were verbally simplified to 'When I'm sitting, I'm bidding; when I stand up, I've stopped.' In the event, from 300,000 to 650,000 guineas he bid openly and ostentatiously by calling out his bids, then dropped out of the bidding and made as though to leave the room while others took the bidding further; he then returned to his seat. Bidding faltered at 740,000 guineas, but Simon did not respond, and only when Marlborough was declared the buyer did he leap to his feet and invoke the original nonsensical instruction to Patrick which ended with, in the case of his having resumed his seat and raised his finger 'he is continuing to bid until he stands up again.' There was uproar – the press and television crews could not understand what was happening and though we were all on our feet, few of us on the ground could see. I seized one of the tiny gilt chairs brought in for great occasions and stood on it – and still could not see; but when I stood on my toes and could, the cane seat gave way and I dropped through to the floor, shackled about the knees, keeled over against my neighbour and toppled him and half a dozen others, adding farce and helpless laughter to the mayhem.

Perhaps the best thing David did for Christie's had nothing to do with discovering a masterpiece but, within months, to suggest that the firm's great weakness lay in the fields of Impressionism and later developments in painting, urging that a dedicated specialist should be brought in. This was undoubtedly true, and in spite of Sotheby's trouncing us again and again with such pictures, something of the old prejudice embodied in Alec Martin – 'this 'ere filth', as he once put it to Anthony Lousada, the firm's lawyer – still clogged the arteries of Christie's. In 1958, in Paris, at the Congress of Art Historians, I had been sought out by a mischievous old dealer named Paul Botte to see a painting bearing the inscription *Georges de la Tour*, we sat beneath it in his dining room while we ate white sausages, boudins blanc, and for the first time I heard the inevitable joke. I said I thought his picture a preposterous fake, quite new (in the 1980s it was to draw me into a disagreeable controversy), but was forgiven and we became friends. It was Botte who in 1962 called me to Paris to see Georges Renand and his collection on the Quai Bethune. This was one of the great thrills of my life, one that I recall every time that I go to the Courtauld Galleries now, for there, in a tiny room in which hang eight oil sketches on panel by Georges Seurat, I recall the long day spent in Renand's company as one of revelation, of my beginning to understand the workings of Seurat's aesthetic mind. My notes, if they survive, are buried deep in Christie's archive vaults and my recollection is now insecure, but it is that Renand had at least an equal number of such sketches, and it was the sale of these that he proposed. The panels – as was common for Seurat – were all within a fraction of 6 × 10 inches (or 10 × 6); most were horizontal landscapes, but at least one was a study of a standing female nude; all were steps towards a loose pointillism, in a touch that was lyrically free, before the freezing of the rigid formula. I was enchanted. He wanted a sum in francs that divided into an average of £9,000 each, and I agreed that this, with some flexibility to take into account connections with major finished paintings (or their absence), should be a running reserve. To Botte I promised, in my excitement, an introductory commission half a per cent above the customary two.

My exultation died within two minutes of my telling Patrick; nor, in these last few months as a partner, was there support from Bill. Both were appalled that I had agreed such a price. I pointed out that Sotheby's had sold a similar sketch for the Tate's great *Bathers at Asnières* for £12,000 four years before, but this they seemed to think had been achieved through evil genius – this was a period when rivalry with the ever more successful Sotheby's had become a manic loathing and mistrust that poisoned many decisions. They were intransigent. My arrangements were, to my humiliation, cancelled, the sale did not take place, and Renand's sketches began to dribble into the trade; the last left in the collection were finally dispersed through the Parisian auctioneers Drouot in 1987. All these years later I wonder why I did not plead with John Herbert for support, for he surely, as an advertising man, would have understood how this most distinguished private collection could have been promoted to bring the firm success – but then John was never brought into any departmental discussion, never informed of what made a painting or its collector important, but merely presented with very basic information and left to get on as best he could. Looking back on my years at Christie's, time and again I see what fools we were, how naive, how complacent and how blind.

Telling him my Renand tale may have lent strength to David's determination that someone should be brought in to cover this field, in which he had no strengths and I had very few, and he suggested David Bathurst, then working for the Marlborough Gallery. This second David, as the future Viscount Bledisloe, had all the social connections Christie's could desire – Eton, Magdalen, the 12th Royal Lancers, cricket and the Cresta Run – and I am inclined to argue that, hardly noticed by Patrick, he was, with the comfortable increase in Impressionist business that his presence brought, far the most important single force in Christie's revival at a time when the firm was all but moribund. He was fortunate in that the idea of departments within the picture department had already been established, though only mine – of drawings and prints – had a clear identity and independence, while the rest were not yet the subjects of specialists but areas in which we all had a hand, even, to begin with, David's Impressionist department. Poor soul, even he was the victim of the basic cataloguing system in which we all gathered to look at every picture – and perhaps just as well at that early stage; as a large and flashy watercolour was drawn from the stacks, David began read his catalogue note – 'Raoul Dufy, *Venus rising from the Waves* . . . ' a list of American dealers' labels providing a respectable provenance. 'It's a fake,' I said, 'It can't be,' the response. Telling Jock and Les to remove it from its frame without damaging the labels, I said that a bosh shot at the composition would be found on the reverse, smaller, less bold, and scribbled over with a brush loaded with blue wash, and, moreover the paper would be a full imperial sheet bearing an English water-mark. I had recognised it as one that I had made for Alan Harverson in my last year at school – 'What would you like for your birthday?' I had asked, 'A painting by Dufy,' his answer. When Christie's were disinclined to sell a painting a reason was usually offered – the value too small, the market uncertain, the condition too poor – but of these for my Dufy none was plausible; what can David have written to the New York dealer who had confidently gone to the expense of consigning it to London?

Christopher Wood, who was to become widely acknowledged as an expert and dealer in Victorian art and artefacts, also joined Christie's in 1963 – not a boy for whom I much cared. After his death in 2009 a close mutual friend asked me the reason for my lifelong coldness towards a colleague who had done so much to revive respect for the nineteenth-century Olympians of English art and, having held my tongue at the time and ever since when accused of envy, I felt some relief in at last telling her the reason for it. It was well into 1964 before Christopher felt certain of his place in the picture department; his degree in art history at Cambridge under Michael Jaffé was not much of a recommendation and what we still needed was another Vic Heather to slave over the paintings in which neither David nor I were interested – and this, after some bullying by Patrick, was the mould in which Christopher seemed willing to be formed. I thought him admirably scrupulous – until his father gave me lunch and made a proposal. From Christopher he had learned that setting aside paintings for particular sales did not please clients whose need for a sale was urgent; how would it be, he asked, if he offered to buy such pictures and banked them for a year or two before selling them at Christie's who would lose nothing by the delay? It would mean setting up a business in which my partnership was essential. I think my refusal to have anything to do with it meant that this shoddy notion was still-born, but I was never certain that this was so; I was, moreover, angered by the assumption that I could be drawn into the deceit and my trust in Christopher was never recovered.

*   *   *

With Bill Martin's almost unnoticed departure and the arrival of the unruly Davids, it seemed to lesser hands in the picture department that there must have been a recriminatory upheaval among the partners of the board, Patrick its victim, for in the proper course of things he should have been acknowledged as our supreme Gauleiter, but was not. Perhaps Peter Chance and the others had seen through his ignorant bluster and had realised how useless he was, useless in exploiting his social connections, useless in what the army called 'man management,' and useless in almost every question of identification and attribution. Guy Hannen, who hardly knew the back of a picture from the front, suddenly announced himself to be the department's administrative head, its real authority, and at once we had to contend, not only with our own feelings in the matter, but with the evident animosity between our two directors, relieved only by the farce of their throwing open my door, often within minutes, to proclaim each his supremacy over the other – 'Yes, Patrick . . . Of course, Guy.' Had the board had the courage to rid themselves of Patrick, Guy's shrewd ability to respect and trust his employees, allied to his instinctive sense of order, would have made him the best head the department ever had.

CHAPTER 15

Dénouement

I should have recognised the threat embodied in David Carritt's joining Christie's, for he, like me almost five years before, had been invited to join the firm to improve the status of the picture department, and it was inevitable that the aspect of my work that I most enjoyed when I had time to do it adequately – research – would pass to him. It did; and when, eventually, he was disinclined to do it, he requested, and was given, as his assistant, his friend Willie Mostyn-Owen, a wealthy landed intellectual who for seven years had worked with Bernard Berenson and wonderfully resembled the loftier English Grand Tourists recorded in caricature by Thomas Patch; his salary immaterial, he can only have been persuaded into the job as a remedy for idleness, David's merry company his real reward.

I had last had a holiday in 1961 – a long haul round Spain and Portugal with John Croft, a painter of exquisitely judged hard-edged abstracts and a civil servant in the Home Office, whom I had met through Richard Hughes-Hallett (we all lived within spitting distance). 'What,' enquired Richard of him on the day he intro-duced us, 'are you working on at the moment?' in so very much a polite tea-time tone that I was absurdly surprised by the reply – 'Oh, an outbreak of sodomy in the approved schools of Wales.' Our weeks away were a test of stamina over appalling roads, thwarted by floods, burnt by the sun and twice the victim of road accidents when we were stationary – my pretty Daimler could hardly have been more rent and torn had it been in Guernica in 1937. I remember crossing the Bay of Biscay in a storm so wild that every inch of everything on the boat that could provide a perch was occupied by a migrating bird. I ate goat for the first time in Oviedo. With cold clarity I remember the nausea and anger induced by the bull fights that we saw in Seville, though determined, in the spirit of enquiry, to endure them to the end. Compostella sowed the seed of curiosity in its great pan-European pilgrimage. Cordoba and Granada put flesh on the work I had done with Professor Bargebuhr. And in Barcelona, where we stayed with Joe Baker, a devil-may-care American friend of John, there was the thrill of meeting an ancient warrior from the Civil War, El Campesino the name by which he went, riding out of the darkness on an antique motorbike, and back into it when he had done with us, his appearances as much a danger to us as to himself were the Guardia Civil to become aware of them. The first thing I did when I returned to London was to buy Hugh Thomas's book on the Spanish Civil War, published earlier that year to great acclaim, to find this of Valentin Gonzalez, El Campesino: 'Today he is in Brussels allegedly forming an army to invade Spain.'

There had been no break for me in 1962, a year too crowded with my domestic and financial problems to even think of taking a holiday, but the following summer, deposed by David Carritt, as it were, with every French museum celebrating Delacroix on the centenary of his death, I began a trawl on 4 July during which I saw more than three thousand of his paintings, drawings and watercolours, and concluded that never had a major painter done himself more mischief in the production of so many ill-considered minor works. I was back in London for no more than ten days before a real holiday began with the great exhibition of *Piedmontese Baroque*, an overwhelming accumulation of sculpture, painting, architecture and artefacts my prime objective. I set off with Robbert Gras, a Dutch psychologist of eventually considerable academic eminence, with whom I had had a foolishly fierce affair, though its burning-out had left us friends. Genoa, Naples and the far south were also our objectives and to some extent we achieved them, but by the time we reached Cape Palinuro, then a deserted beauty spot well south of Paestum, I was so troubled by the heat that we had to flee still further south and climb into the hills of La Sila, where I lay for several days like a gaffed haddock. There was, I suppose, some small point in seeing Cosenza and Catanzaro in impoverished decay, and Matera when most of the rock houses were still in use, and there was certainly much at which to wonder sadly in Lecce, a baroque Turin in small that had irreversibly crumbled since Ellis Waterhouse photographed it in the early Thirties (a gift of his photographs prompted this detour into Italy's heel). No memory is more deeply etched than our sleeping, just for the romantic heck of it, in the magnificent ruin of Castel del Monte, the architectural marvel of a hunting lodge built for the Hohenstaufen Emperor Frederick II, begun in 1240, thirty miles due west of Bari. I wish that we had slept in the temples of Paestum too, for they were then equally uncluttered with railings, souvenir stalls and hotels and seemed as wistfully Ozymandian as they were when first revealed to the Grand Tourists of the later eighteenth century.

Within a month of my return I was off on another crucial journey – one booked and paid for by Christie's while I had been in Italy, and the only move the firm ever made to improve my education and contacts. The Museums Association had organised a jaunt to east coast America so that interested members could meet their peers at all points between Boston and Washington, and I was to go with them. Roy Strong, then still in his infancy at the National Portrait Gallery, and I were far the youngest and kept each other company in evenings and situations that might otherwise have been deadly dull; together we lost something of our innocence in a bar in Baltimore where young women without knickers danced among our glasses while we gazed upward, aghast in my case, gloating in Roy's, at what we had never seen before. It was also my first real exposure to pornography – far beyond the smutty photographs of Paris and the army – readily available in both pictorial and literary forms among the newspapers of almost every bookstall on the streets. In addition, it was an invaluable experience to see, often out of hours, the astonishing riches gathered in what were essentially private, provincial and comparatively new museums densely packed over much the same distance as separates Edinburgh from London. I did not know it then, but this journey was the first foundation of the life that I was to lead when I left Christie's.

Back in England there was, almost immediately, a day in Paris – one of many mad jaunts demanded by Austin Bradfield-England, a strange emaciated little man whose few front teeth were so large and far apart that his mouth was a distraction in any conversation. Fascinated by paintings, he was frequently in Christie's to offer things that he had seen in Paris, where he lived, and on his travels in Switzerland and Italy, but both Bill and Patrick had ignored him; I, in my naivety, had not and swiftly had been woven into his web to discover that his contacts were by no means contemptible and that he should have been taken seriously. The trouble was that his appearance in old and grubby clothes that had never been of quality (least of all his hats) matched neither his double-barrelled name nor his talk of masterpieces – but the paintings and clients he introduced were almost always worth the journey. He lived in a succession of hotels with half a dozen telephones and made a fortune by buying and selling the cargo of oil tankers in transit, content to take a percentage profit too meagre for any ordinary broker. He had neither property nor car, ate frugally in back street restaurants, and his only extravagance was a string of boys from the less joyful pages of a Genet novel, one of whom, unknown, eventually murdered him. On this occasion I was to see a *bozzetto* for an altarpiece by El Greco; this involved an early morning flight from Heathrow, breakfast with Austin, lunch with two disagreeable Spaniards and tea with a young and astonishingly handsome Portuguese (though his legs were too short), who claimed ownership of the painting, an exquisitely impetuous sketch on panel. Try as I did, I could not bring the discussion to a close, but when I stood up and said that I must leave to catch my plane, not only was the reserve figure suddenly agreed but I was asked to take the panel with me. I asked for something in which to wrap it, but neither paper nor cloth was to be had and I set off with it under my arm, certain that I would be stopped by a customs officer. And I was. 'What's this?' he asked. 'An El Greco,' I replied – at which, with 'This idiot thinks he's got an El Greco,' he held it aloft for other officers to see; they laughed, and my inquisitor let me pass, shaking his head, with an expression of sad sympathy that said 'Poor sod. Poor deluded sod.'

At the very end of the year, recognising that for months I had not been to Windsor and that my work on Fontana had run into the sand, I surrendered him or had him taken from me by Anthony Blunt in a stern and unforgiving mood – both perhaps, though I am sure of nothing other than the blow to my hope of recognised scholarship. Fontana had been part of my life for six whole years, a leitmotiv through all my jaunts to Italy, but Christie's had never let me have my promised four-day week and I had failed to complete my work by the end of 1963. I spent a sad day in Windsor with Anthony and Aydua, explained what I had done and not done, and have never since returned – to do so would be too painful.

*   *   *

Nineteen sixty-four began with yet another journey, first to Rome and then to Sicily, where Claudio had rediscovered a half-length portrait by Bronzino that had once belonged to his family. Though not quite by Bronzino, it was a perfectly decent portrait of his period and type and made the journey well worthwhile – which was more than could be said of the paintings accumulated in Rome by Hans Backer, Christie's resident representative there, a man with great expertise in porcelain but no eye at all for paint on canvas. The Bronzino's owner, a local countess (half the inhabitants of Taormina seemed claimants to a defunct title), drove me as far up Mount Etna as was possible with a Volkswagen Beetle in deep snow, our mad intention to have a picnic, but the Beetle jammed its nose into a snowdrift at a point where we could both see and

Dénouement

hear red streams of lava sizzling all round us, a sight infinitely more frightening and beautiful against the snow than any Vesuvius has offered in my lifetime, and single-handedly manhandling the car through what seemed a thirty-three point turn with a hapless and hysterical Contessa at the wheel, was a strenuous matter of some urgency.

Above and behind the Roman theatre of Taormina I had a more melancholy encounter. Claudio took me to meet an old man living in a featureless shack with a marvellous and often painted view towards the sea; his skin saurian, his back and joints bent and broken, his worn clothes far from clean, he welcomed us in a form of Italian that I could hardly comprehend – a patois into which Claudio slipped easily and merrily. To my disagreeable 'What are we doing here?' his answer was a mysterious 'Wait and see – this will take time.' It was worth the wait. Until the old man passed me one, I did not notice the heaps of glass photographic plates that lay in a dark corner of the room – and when he did, I knew at once why we had come. I held to the light an image typical of Wilhelm von Gloedon, a German photographer born in 1851 who in his early twenties had settled in Taormina. There he photographed the local boys, sometimes merely naked, more often embellished as though they were the catamites of ancient Rome enacting mildly erotic *tableaux vivants*. As paintings, his compositions were very much of their time in academic circles, but of pubescent boys rather than the lower ranks of obscure female divinities and virgins; but these were photographs, with none of the subtleties that classical painters introduced, and their abundant penises were almost always on their way to or from tumescence. I thought of Oscar Wilde, Max Reinhardt, Richard Strauss and the notorious performance of *Salome* in which the enthroned Herodias stroked to erection the naked negro boys at either hand while Salome tossed aside her seven veils.

In 1939, eight years after von Gloeden's death at 75, Mussolini's police, on grounds of obscenity, destroyed what they could find of his work; during the German occupation, more still were destroyed in 1944; but this old man, now unrecognisable as one of the olive-skinned pubescent boys, had saved the residue. It is one of the most profound of my regrets that I did not do what I wanted to do if the old man agreed – that is, transport the plates to London for inclusion in a sale. Now it would be possible and I can imagine the razzmatazz that would be attached to it, for the blatantly homosexual imagery would be set aside for the sake of von Gloeden's place in the history of the photograph, and absurd prices would be paid by grave collectors and institutions of high seriousness for whom erotica of this kind is no more than an abstraction; but I knew in my bones that were I to propose it only David Carritt would support me and that I should not risk humiliation at the hands of a disgusted Patrick.

The most important event of the year was the death of 'Old Spencer-Churchill' (Captain Edward George Spencer-Churchill) who had long before inherited the remains of the some 1,500 pictures that, accumulated in the early nineteenth century, had formed the once celebrated Northwick Park Collection; an impression of its status is quickly gained in the National Gallery where Botticelli's *Portrait of a Young Man*, Raphael's *St Catherine* and Annibale Carracci's *Quo Vadis?* are all of Northwick provenance, but its status in my day was much diminished. I and every other young man in Christie's had from time to time stayed in that great ugly house, starved of food and frozen to the bone in winter, charming the old man into specifying in his will that his collections should be dispersed by Christie's on his death. This exercise in charm may have been easier for those interested in antiquities, furniture, books, manuscripts and the applied arts, but for me it was difficult, for old Spencer-Churchill was less interested in his inherited paintings by Guercino, Reni, Rosa, Jordaens, Gentileschi and the elder Brueghel's family than in what he called his 'rescues.' Seduced by the conviction that he had a discerning eye, for years he had haunted Christie's for paintings obscured by chilled varnish or damaged beyond reasonable repair, and had had them 'revealed' as masterpieces by restorers who without scruple were able to find precisely what he hoped to find. In truth, for paintings he had no eye at all – indeed, by the time I knew him, into his eighties, his eyes were so rheumy that he could hardly see, with discernment or without it.

To his dreadful death at eighty-eight on 24 June 1964 (caused by his inability to turn off the scalding hot water in his bath), Christie's reacted with indecent haste. Under Patrick's command we descended on the house, directors, experts, secretary girls and porters, catalogued everything as best we could – which was not well – and physically emptied it. It was a period of intense slavery, my sleep broken every night by the noise of rats scrabbling for soap in the adjoining bathroom. There was very little light relief. Bill Spowers tried water-skiing on the lake, Charlie so mis-managing his speedboat that it overturned and sank. I tried to demonstrate the pile-driver on Annabel Hoyer-Miller, one of the more substantial young women employed by Christie's; accusing me of being puny she had challenged me to this all-in wrestling manoeuvre in which, holding the ankles of one's adversary, his (in this case her) head is driven into the floor of the ring; I managed to turn her topsyturvy but could not lift her free of the floor to complete the exercise. A bout of rather more close-knit wrestling with Charlie ended with our tumbling in a tight bundle of limbs all the way down Northwick's grand staircase; and I also discovered the knack of tearing telephone directories in half. If all this seems absurdly irresponsible, our excuse was the tension brought on by the unrelenting pressure of our work there, at a time when television had introduced the whole nation to the gladiatorial pleasures of professional wrestling.

The Northwick sales did not begin until the following year, the first of the Old Masters on 28 May 1965, the second on 29 October, and the last on 26 February 1966. In spite of the time in hand, the catalogues, appallingly muddled in school and date, were a disgrace to anyone with a sense of order and a claim to scholarship, but the decisions were entirely Patrick's in the hope that the first sale might break, if not individual records, the record for a sale total (it did not). The tiny Fra Angelico, some eight inches square, of *The Dream of the Deacon Justinian*, was, for example, catalogued as unarguably by him, though I knew it to have been disputed since at least 1919 and felt that we should have included some discussion of the matter in the catalogue entry – as had been the case when I first saw the painting with Michel Laclotte (who knew more about Fra Angelico than any of us) in the Manchester exhibition of 1957;[32] Patrick, however, laid down the law and that was that – an opportunity in which David, Willy and I could have lifted our sale catalogues to an unprecedented level of honest scholarship was denied us, and old Vic Heather could have done what we did.

*   *   *

In 1957, Charles Merrill Mount, a young American, published a biography of John Singer Sargent, fifty years earlier the most fashionable portrait painter in London and New York. That the book was not a success should have surprised nobody, for with the Great Depression of 1929–33, followed by World War II, international art markets had collapsed and Sargent's swagger portraits were worth less than their ornate frames. By 1957 there were haphazard indications that the market for Impressionist painting was reviving, but this did not include Sargent and Mount's book on him was doomed to be remaindered.

Even so, it established him as something of an authority. In his preface Mount paid tribute to a long list of the institutions – the Royal Academy, the Imperial War Museum, the Metropolitan Museum and others – that had let him loose in their archives, and to the great and good of private patronage and the art market, establishing his credentials as a diligent enquirer; he let it be known

32 *Art Treasures Centenary*, Manchester Art Gallery 1957, p. 1, No. 1.

that he had had help from Sir Alec Martin, Sargent's friend who had prepared the contents of the painter's studio for posthumous dispersal; and the preface ends with 'I cannot forget . . . the kindness and help of the artist's sister, Violet Ormond, with whom I spent evenings plunged into a world known only to the two of us'. Here then was a man who knew all the right people, a man to whom the art market might look if ever it needed an expert on John Singer Sargent.

In 1964 Mount walked into my office at Christie's with a bundle of watercolours by Sargent. 'Gosh,' I said – or something of the kind – and 'Whoopee' too, no doubt. He had found them, he said, in the forgotten collection of an old lady in Dublin, now in need of money. They were of landscapes, mostly small, loose in handling, not quite of the quality one might expect, but in 1964 Sargent was still a dead and buried artist and no one of my generation had seen much with which to form a value judgement. Christie's sold them for prices between £200 and £1,100 – prices high enough to suggest, perhaps, a revival in the market. Mount came back with more – another gosh, another whoopee. But when he appeared a third time, the watercolours were so bad and smelled so fresh that I took them to Peter Chance, with whom Mount had struck up friendship, and demonstrated why I thought them slapdash forgeries.

We had what can only be described as a row; I was overruled and on 13 November 1966 Christie's sold nine more watercolours as by Sargent, authenticated by Mount, for £3,700 – the sort of money that would then have bought a decent mansion flat in Kensington. As Mount's watercolours were bought by Agnew's, Newman, Maas, the Fine Art Society, Charles Jerdein and other reputable London dealers, and sold by them to American dealers of equal reputation, it is not altogether surprising that Peter felt justified in ignoring my lone dissenting voice, but in 1967, when an American dealer cast doubt on those that he had bought, alarm became widespread. A panel of experts, one from Sotheby's, a keeper from the National Portrait Gallery, the librarian of the

Boston Athenaeum and a director from Christie's who had been glad enough to sell them, inspected as many of Mount's water-colours as could be recovered and, wisely after the event, con-demned them all as 'dreadful' and 'awful' forgeries.

Mount not only defended his reputation against what, with some justification, he called 'these Johnny-come-latelys,' but asserted that he had, through his assiduous work, 'created the present interest in Sargent.' Of this there is no doubt and it is a wry thought that without Mount's putting his forgeries into Christie's, the revival of interest in Sargent might not have occurred until much later – it is to Mount's credit that for genuine Sargent watercolours we must now think in five and six figure sums, though there is now no doubt that Mount's discoveries were by Mount himself. Many of them survive, stashed away among the stock of the duped dealers, waiting for the moment when, Mount forgotten, they might more successfully be reintroduced to the market.

In the early stages of his deception I was completely gulled by Mount, yet at much the same time I came to the conclusion that Eric Hebborn, then not notorious as a forger of old master drawings, was a cheat and had deceived me with several that I had catalogued and put in sales. An able draughtsman and painter in outworn English academic traditions (so able indeed that as a student at the Royal Academy in the mid-fifties it was he who was trusted to restore the Leonardo *Cartoon* when it was damaged by scalding water spurting from the bleeding valve of a radiator – or so he claimed), in his two years of a scholarship at the British School in Rome he met Ellis Waterhouse and, infinitely more important, Anthony Blunt, through whom I met him, and whose flat in the Courtauld Institute was in later years to become his London *pied-á-terre*. As a student at the RA he, and others, were, in the lane leading from Burlington Gardens to the students' entrance, canvassed by George Aczel, the most blatant of restorers to the trade – and, incidentally, the restorer most employed by old Spencer-Churchill – to earn pocket money as his assistant. Aczel was one of several trade restorers used by Christie's until I joined the firm, and in turning nothing into something he was no exception – only in his flagrant openness about the old Dutch landscapes he produced (Wynants a specialty) did he differ from the others. Early in my first months at Christie's I witnessed Geoffrey Agnew – a man so arrogant that he did not care that he was heard – having a 'What can we make of it?' conversation with a restorer in Albemarle Street, and am sure that this rotten streak ran right through every level of the trade. Later, having discovered that the studio of Campbell Mellon – the most obscure of painters of the Norfolk scene – had remained untouched since his death in 1955, I brought its contents to Christie's, where his small plein-air sketches on panel fetched remarkably high prices; for years after, a Duke Street dealer who bought only a couple of pairs, was never out of stock, so adept was his restorer in imitating them.

It was from Aczel that Hebborn learned the basic business of restoration forgery and its camouflage. Turning to drawings – the field in which Eric most made his name – John Minton was his first victim (even to employing one of Minton's models) and Augustus John his second, and from these he moved to old masters as rare and eminent as Bellini and Mantegna, as big and generally desirable as Piranesi, and as improbable as Corot and Pissarro. Setting up a business as The Pannini Gallery, he issued an illustrated catalogue from which Joe McCrindle bought a large landscape by Pissarro, on which I expressed doubt, but eventually surrendered on the grounds that it was so improbable that such an attribution could never have been made unless supported by external evidence, now lost; then Anthony asked me to drop in one evening and I met the man himself, saturnine, dark, bearded and persuasive, and I was shown drawings that he wished to sell at Christie's.

In spite of Anthony's apparent backing, I was not convinced, yet on the other hand, without more than mere suspicion, how could I reasonably refuse? I cannot now remember what I agreed should be included in a sale, but the receipt given him by Christie's on 1 May 1963, reproduced in his autobiography[33] as evidence of my gullibility, is not in my handwriting, nor does it bear my initials – as would have been the case had I seen him or the drawings at the Front Counter. But then Eric was much given to errors of fact, as was demonstrated in detail in one scrupulously researched review:[34] according to 'an old memorandum' he claims that he saw me at Christie's on 2 June 1966 and for supper on 13 June 1966, but I was at Chatsworth on both dates, and had severed relations with him for ever in October 1964, for I was by then absolutely certain that he was forging both drawings and paintings.

Of this, proof lay in a portrait by Sickert. The sitter was Cicely Hey, a painter who acted as Sickert's model in the 1920s; it was recognisably of her but corresponded with none of the five known portraits; Eric had sold it to Joe for a *prix d'amitié* and I had thought it, though ugly, not a foolish acquisition – but then I caught Eric *in flagrente*. I had been in Malta for a few days, looking at Caravaggio's *Beheading of John the Baptist* in the Co-Cathedral of St John, talking to John Gauchi, the director of the museum in Valetta, and being stoned in the Governor-General's limousine – independence for the Maltese was then a matter of furious argument – and as it had been impossible to make contact with Eric by telephone, I simply turned up in the middle of the afternoon at his rambling apartment in the Piazza Paganica. There the door was opened by Eric's lover, Graham Smith, and over his shoulder, framed at the end of a long view through an enfilade of rooms, stood Eric at his easel, working on an identical portrait of Cicely Hey; when I reached his studio there was a third on another easel, possibly the original from which Joe's was copied – at least that is what I was led to believe when Eric said 'You can only really learn from copying,' adding that he

33 Eric Hebborn: *Drawn to Trouble*, Mainstream 1991, p. 155.
34 Gertrude Prescott Nuding: *Hebborn the Fake, The Art Newspaper*, December 1991, p. 16.

had been in love with Sickert since his earliest days at an art school, but only now could afford to buy one. He did not at that point know that I knew Joe. When I told him that I did and thus knew of three identical Cicely Heys, he did not argue or rebuff; I still do not know if any of them was by Sickert himself – certainly, if one is genuine, it does not appear in Wendy Baron's catalogue raisonné.

We parted on bad terms. I told him that there would be no point in his ever again consigning drawings or paintings to Christie's, for I would not hesitate to reject them even if, grudgingly, I thought them genuine – for he had, I believed, played the stale trick of mixing evidently old and genuine drawings of small value with his far more ambitiously attributed forgeries. He responded that he could manage well enough through Sotheby's and Colnaghi's. Within months, however, of my leaving Christie's in 1967, he consigned two drawings that caused something of a rumpus, one by Pontormo, the other by Castiglione,[35] each of which sold for 1,400 guineas – too much for duds, not enough for the real things. When the catalogue became available, Hans Calmann, who had bought dozens of drawings by Eric and sold them to the most eminent private collectors and museums (as had, Eric claimed, Agnew's and Colnaghi's), at last alerted by some common factor in them all no matter what the date or nationality, demanded that I 'do something.' 'I can't,' I replied, 'I no longer work at Christie's. I cannot interfere.' I had some sympathy with his outrage, but greed had blunted his perceptions and he had chosen to ignore the gossip that was running through the trade, of which I knew because while I was still at Christie's I had had conversations with a number of dealers – particularly with Regina Slatkin and Helene Seiferheld, of New York, the first to express their doubts to me – all of whom suspected or knew that they were Eric's dupes, and had been able to assure them that since October 1964 he had been warned off and nothing of his has since been accepted for sale.

35 Lots 139 and 140 on 26 March 1968.

I had, of course, to tell Anthony that he too had been gulled by Eric, if only in the careful indiscretion of his giving C/O Blunt, 20 Portman Square, as his London address. Aghast at the tale of three identical Sickerts, he told me that he had already begun to wonder how quite so many distinguished drawings had fallen into Eric's hands in quite so short a time, but he did not do what he should have done – cut short their association and forbid Eric's presence in Home House – he merely asked him to desist. I suppose the infatuation was too strong – the sentimental longing of an older man for a younger, never physical, is a much tougher thing to break than a sexual relationship. Anthony was then betrayed by his partner, John Gaskin, a shrewish kept woman of a man, greedy for money, who, carefully schooled by Eric, became his agent and delivery boy, taking drawings into Bond Street dealers, letting it be thought that the attributions had the blessing of Anthony, even that they belonged to Anthony, too shy to let it be known that he needed to sell his private collection. It was a wretched betrayal and it did Anthony great harm in 1979 when many supposedly expert dealers were happy to talk to the press about the part that Gaskin's bandying his name had played in countering their intuitive suspicion of drawings by then thought to be by Eric.

The events of the winter of 1979–80 brought Eric to the fore to such a degree that I was forced to defend him in the sense that he could not possibly have drawn all the doubtful drawings attributed to him, so great their number, their styles and mannerisms so diverse that there was nothing of the common character that, in retrospect, had in the 1960s, been so evident across the board. In 1981 we exchanged not unsympathetic letters on the effect that the exaggeration of the number of his forgeries was having on the reputation of the trade, but I refused to see him and renew what he called our friendship. In January 1996 Eric was murdered, his skull fractured by so brutal a blow that his death must have been intended. On this ugly crime the Roman police expended very little energy. His lover in the 1960s, Graham Smith, long since

Dénouement

discarded, appeared on my doorstep some weeks later to pour vitriol on his memory. He too had written an autobiography[36] using the same obscure publisher – a nauseating book that perhaps corrects a few of Eric's lies and offers credible glimpses of Anthony's unhappy life with John Gaskin; those intrigued by this important and largely successful example of art forgery in the later twentieth century should read both lives in tandem, for together they offer an account that is neither wholly mendacious nor close to the whole truth.

*   *   *

In the spring of 1965 David Carritt returned from a weekend jaunt with an album of drawings in his pocket, found in an idle hour in Earl Beauchamp's library in Madresfield Court, Worcestershire. It contained 167 drawings by Giandomenico Tiepolo – enough to provide me with a whole sale if detached from the album and sold separately, as David had already arranged. The date of the sale was fixed on 15 June 1965, immediately putting me under pressure with the catalogue. The first step was to take a photograph of every sheet in the album so that we had a record of every drawing and inscription. The disbinding of the album was then entrusted to Doreen Lewisohn, so too the necessary minor restorations – she was later to claim this task, rather than the repairing and cleaning of the drawings by Augustus John in 1962–63, to have been 'her professional breakthrough;' and mounts had to be cut so that the chances of clumsy handling were reduced while the drawings were on view before the sale. As both these procedures involved the long absence of the drawings, I had to write the catalogue from the preliminary photographs – no bad thing, as it happened, for I developed German measles and was banished from the building by Guy who seemed to think half the secretary girls might be pregnant. I drove to Castle Hedingham and retired to my bed

36   Graham David Smith: *Celebration*, Mainstream 1996

with photographs all about me, grouping them by subject and making what notes I could from memory. As a matter of courtesy, when I recovered, I informed James Byam Shaw, of Colnaghi's, the only real authority on Giandomenico Tiepolo, that I had pillaged his book for guidance,[37] and showed him the photographs; he was the first outsider to see the drawings when they returned from the mount-cutter.

The last lot in the sale was the binding of the album – a sad little relic but of interest for the bookplate of Horace Walpole (a most distinguished previous owner) and the inscriptions, one of which is possibly by Francesco Guardi (Giandomenico's uncle) who seems to have had the drawings for sale individually at prices from 15 cechini (sic) to 22 lira, presumably to Grand Tourists. Now, of course, I regret the disbinding, for we could have learned from the original folds which two drawings were on the same sheets of paper and thus intellectually as well as physically connected, and whether the album was a random gathering or, as I now suspect, prepared for the removal and sale of individual sheets, and merely a convenient means of storing and display. A French inscription gives the number of drawings as 162, an English as 166 – but the number photographed and for which I wrote a catalogue entry was 167. The announcement of the sale roused overwhelming interest, particularly among Italian dealers, and it became necessary to arrange viewing facilities before the manuscript of the catalogue had been sent to the printers. Intended to be a substantial work of reference this was the fattest catalogue issued by the picture department in my time, and we made a particular effort to provide illustrations of a higher quality than ever before, using matt paper and a semi-photogravure technique that proved hopelessly unsubtle in distinguishing grey inks and washes from those in brown. As for the text – it was not bad for its time, but when I think what could and should have been made of it, the idea that a thing so

37 James Byam Shaw: *The Drawings of Domenico Tiepolo*, Faber 1962.

intellectually meagre could ever be a work of wider reference is laughable.

The course to the sale total of £87,260 – then a sum remarkable enough to figure in the records for the year – should have been direct and smooth; Doreen made an exquisite job of the disbinding, cleaning and repair, and newly separated in their mounts the sheets gained a high seriousness and presence that, crammed into the album, they had lacked; and Noël Annesley, who had had to hold the fort while I recovered from the debilitating attack of measles, had so much command of the logistics that I was content to let him stay in charge. The logistics, alas, included the early viewing arrangements, early in which one drawing was stolen – we thought, through process of elimination, by a pair of Italian dealers. Guy, administratively in charge of us, was furious, justifiably so, for it was far the most important of the drawings, not only in its subject, *The Apotheosis of San Giacomo Giustiniani*, in which it was directly associated with a painted ceiling in the Doge's Palaca, Genoa, of 1783 – from which we could perhaps assume a *terminus post quem* for binding the album (the *terminus ante quem* already established by Guardi's death in 1793) – but in its lending focus to six other drawings more loosely connected with that ceiling. In its detailed finish I thought it more likely a *ricordo* than a summary of pre-liminary ideas, but I hoped nevertheless that it would be bought by the Metropolitan Museum, New York, where there is a fine preparatory modello in oil on canvas – certainly it was the drawing for which I expected the highest price. There was panic when a count revealed that we had lost a drawing; as the binding recorded 166 drawings as its contents, Guy could not at first see that one was missing, but Doreen, the mount-cutter and the photographer had recorded 167, and I had written the longest entry on this drawing and in an index of subjects the other six had been grouped with it – a physical check left no doubt that it had been removed. Guy as good as accused Noël of taking it, so nearly reducing him to tears that in his defence I sparked a terrible row that, with Guy's logic of 'Well if it wasn't Noël it must be you,' diverted the accusation of theft to me. Never was there a darker, bleaker moment in my life at Christie's – seven years of loyal slavery rewarded with suspicion.

I could not afford to alienate Guy. In spite of his maddening habit of jingling change in his trouser pocket while he watched us vet incoming pictures, in spite of his total incomprehension of the ways in which our minds worked and the speed of their working when answering the unasked questions 'Who painted this and is it any good?', and in spite of our regarding him as superfluous, even an impediment, unlike Patrick he had the good sense or good grace to laugh at the puerile jokes that both relieved our boredom and restored our concentration – in that, at least, he understood us. I knew that I needed him as an ally, not an enemy, if the picture department was ever to escape Patrick's time-worn atavistic strong-hold and if prints and drawings were to become a separate department under my direction. He could tell, he said, when I was nearing the end of my tether because my nostrils flared like those of a rearing horse, and I dare say they flared in the row over the stolen Tiepolo – of which the one reward had been Noël's stout loyalty to me (indeed, I felt that he would have sacrificed his job for me). It was too much to expect an apology from Guy but he made amends soon after by inviting me to spend a night at his house in Berkshire – and rather jolly it was, with hardly a word said about Christie's, but I felt that underlying the jollity and the domesticity of washing dishes was something in the nature of a War Office Selection Board. There was always something inscrutable about Guy, something of the cobra hissing before the strike, something of the school prefect sticking to the rules, something of the teddy bear – and I could never predict his reaction. Standing with him and Patrick at the bottom of Christie's main stairs late one morning, waiting to set off on an errand with David Carritt, we were all surprised to see him begin a slow descent with arms outstretched, one before and one behind, the palms of both hands upturned.

Dénouement

'What the hell do you think you're doing?' bellowed Patrick. 'Oh,' said David when he reached us, unperturbed, 'I just thought I'd come downstairs in the Egyptian style.' Guy was as much consumed as I with laughter.

My relationship with Patrick worsened in the autumn of 1965. I was called to New York by Robert Lehman, the banker, most of whose collection is now housed in its own wing in the Metropolitan Museum, though in constantly toying with the idea of selling things, he kept curators, dealers and auction houses alert and in attendance. On an earlier working journey he had allowed me to see his drawings and I knew that his was a summons for which I should drop everything in my diary and get onto a plane. I understood him to be, in New York, the client of Eugene Thaw, a powerful dealer of considerable physical presence, from whose character the gods had omitted modesty and candour. In London he was Hans Calmann's client and he, with indiscretion born of vanity, let it be known that Lehman thought nothing of spending £25,000 on a single drawing – indeed, I am inclined to think that he was at heart as much influenced in favour of a purchase by its outrageous price as its exceptional quality. He died in 1969 and was seventy-four or so when he made the telephone call to me. 'Young man,' he said, 'I am calling you because you are the only professional visitor to my collection who did not offer to be of service, did not leave me a card.' Unlike the others, whoever they were, I had simply looked at the drawings, envying them, learning from them, and my note of thanks, though written from Christie's, had been just that – thanks.

In one sense only was it an easy week – Lehman knew the market price of everything. He did not work on the stale principle still in force at Christie's that it was the auctioneer's business to establish a basic figure on which the dealer could make a handsome profit; to him the buying price at auction was exactly the same for the dealer, the collector and the museum, and it was the auctioneer's job to get that price, to establish at the moment of sale the highest price that could be paid, whether by a museum (the end of the line in any series of transactions), by a private collector who, by the nature of things, could only own his possessions for a comparatively short while, or by a dealer who could no longer expect to make an immediate and huge percentage profit. I had some sympathy with his view, for I too thought it foolish to hand dealers a hundred per cent profit on their auction bids, but at Christie's this was heresy. So Lehman and I worked on his heretical principle when we discussed the reserves to be placed on the drawings he had all but decided to sell. At the very end of our negotiation he asked 'Now what are your terms?' Terms for ordinary vendors were a ten per cent commission on the selling price and a charge for illustration in the catalogue; if the business had been introduced by a dealer, lawyer or other intermediary, two per cent went to him and Christie's did the work for eight. I sensed danger and offered a commission of eight per cent with no other charges. 'Not good enough,' he said, pointing out that he was offering the most important sale I had ever mounted, openly lending his name to it (pure gold in the influence that this might have on other vendors), and that, as a banker, he never settled on the first offer. To my response that I had conceded as much as I could and that any further reduction in our charges could only be negotiated by a partner in the firm, his retort was volcanic, beginning, if not with the monkey and the organ-grinder, something very like it, mounting in discourtesy until I found myself in the street. How much of it was theatre, I could not judge.

I returned to London on the first plane I could catch and went straight to Peter Chance – a mistake, but Patrick I thought would do no more than pick up the telephone and speak *de haut en bas* when humble pie was necessary, and Guy might just not understand what was at stake. Peter did understand, but what I wanted – that is Patrick's prompt despatch on a diplomatic mission to New York – did not come to pass. Instead, I was hauled into Patrick's room and roundly bollocked for having first spoken to Peter – and then the death knell – 'No old Jew in New York with a handful of drawings is going to tell me how Christie's should run its business.' Patrick did telephone Lehman, but the opportunity to sell his drawings was lost, leaving me angry, disappointed, bruised. It was not the first such mishap: almost exactly the same course of events had happened on a previous journey to New York when Judge Untermeyer, a supposed 'old friend of the firm,' had shown me paintings and drawings, but his were too unremarkable to merit hefty concessions from Christie's and his behaviour more measured; even so, I should have learned from it that in America, without the status of partner or director, worse trouble might confront me.

*   *   *

In January 1966 I bought my third old Daimler, built nine years earlier and cossetted by an owner who had his coat-of-arms blazoned on the rear doors. Big, beautiful and rare but at the bottom of the market (for new Daimlers were by then indistinguishable from Jaguars and the great old name on its way to oblivion), it was mechanically much the same as any Daimler built thirty years before, but it carried a very pretty close-coupled saloon body by Mulliner, of which it is said that only twelve were built. Under its long bonnet lay a lazy and whispering 4.5-litre six cylinder engine that settled down to cruise quite happily at 80 mph and was perfect for German Autobahns. I also bought a house, a large, ugly, late Victorian monstrosity in Barnes, fronting what proved to be the intolerably noisy Castelnau (once considered a good address, alas by then considerably run down), but with an open view at the back over a reservoir that is now a wetland for wild birds. It was a rash decision far from wise, compelled by the sudden sale, at last, of 16 Phillimore Place, but if needs be was large enough to house my mother too; meanwhile, it could pay for itself with lodgers.

Within a week of buying the Daimler I was off to Germany in it with Ulrich von Artus, the very bright, very shrewd and very German (blonde straight hair and a flawless skin the colour of a butter biscuit) apprentice at the Front Counter, working without pay for the experience, the son of a friendly art auctioneer in Frankfurt. His father had a string of contacts with whom he felt unqualified to deal. It was my first acquaintance with the under-world of the post-Nazi art market; two full decades after the end of World War II, paintings without provenance were creeping onto a market where questions were not asked. Occasionally, in London, paintings were brought to Christie's that I recognised from pre-war museum catalogues and these we always made every effort to restore to the institutions from which they had been removed, though sometimes they had been de-accessioned on the grounds of degeneracy, *Entartete Kunst* the great scandal of the Nazi art establishment in 1937,[38] and the new owners often had every right to them; with old masters and nineteenth-century paintings it was a very different matter and with this wave of material consigned to a small local auction house in Frankfurt – and, I later learned, to many others of its ilk – I sensed confusion between genuine ownership and the consequences of forced sales to Nazi collectors in the Thirties. After I left Christie's my link with Ulrich and his father was to bring me into direct contact with the most unpleasant, perhaps even evil, of men in the art market.

There was a second unpaid apprentice from Germany working on the Front Counter, Jens Wollesen, son of an antique dealer in Bad Oeynhausen, a big, tall hobbledehoy but intellectually a far more interesting boy than Ulrich, who eventually became a dis-tinguished specialist in Trecento art and a professor at Toronto University – an odd coincidence when I think how close I came to a post there in 1957. As he lodged with me in Castelnau I was a close observer when he fell into a dog-like infatuation for Yvonne tan Bunzl, the daughter of a wealthy Austrian family, who had just

38   See Peter Adam: *Arts in the Third Reich*, Thames and Hudson 1992.

begun to make her presence felt as an adventurous dealer in old master drawings. It was the only time that I have heard the moans and groans of unrequited adoration; he was eighteen, she I guessed to be in her mid-twenties, but the gap in sophistication was far greater. Eventually, without too clumsy an excuse, I introduced them and left him to get on with his fawning. The sighs continued until, at last, she let him take her to dinner; then, aware of her wealth, I made sure that he had cash enough wherever she might want to go. It was a salutary lesson; almost every penny of the cash consumed, and very late, he had to walk back to Barnes with not so much as a chaste kiss of encouragement. He burst into my bedroom to curse and swear at his expensive disappointment, and then made an unpolished offer to get into my bed. This I refused. It was not that I resented playing second fiddle to Yvonne; it was that I cared too much for him, patently heterosexual, to let him go through the anguish of guilt, denial and self-doubt that might well be the consequence of such a one-night stand when simple masturbation with Yvonne in mind was so evidently the wiser release of his frustration. Late in August, shortly before the end of his apprenticeship, we spent a riotous week in Landsberg-am-Lech and Munich looking at more old masters that might be sold at Christie's, our evenings spent in the manly pursuits of eating too much and getting very, very drunk.

Three whole weeks in June and July, as well as many odd days after, were spent at Chatsworth working on a valuation of the drawings collected, largely, by William Cavendish, the second Duke of Devonshire from 1707 until his death in 1729. In 1966 it was, and – in spite of major depletions through subsequent sales at Christie's – is still the most important British collection of old master drawings outside the Royal Collection and the British Museum, to which so many of its treasures have been transferred. Many drawings had been exhibited both singly and in large groups in this country and America, and these had been properly catalogued by A. E. Popham and James Byam Shaw; other scholars had noted their observations and attributions on the mounts, among them Johannes Wilde, Jacob Bean and Philip Pouncey, and to these David and I occasionally added ours; and with Tom Wragg on hand – Chatsworth's Librarian and Keeper – with not only the typescript catalogue written by his immediate predecessor, Francis Thompson, but his extraordinary recollection of what every worthy visitor in his time had said, though not written, we were not short of information. Tom was an unlikely Keeper in that he was a local Derbyshire lad of no conventional education as an art historian, with no command of foreign languages, and nothing about his dress or manner to suggest that he was anything other than a downtrodden collector of weekly sixpences for a Life Assurance Company, his raincoat perfect for the flasher. He was, however, greatly respected and much loved. I had known him since *The Age of Louis XIV*, as it were, and he had been much in evidence at Christie's in June 1958 when twenty-four paintings were sold from Chatsworth as part of the settlement of the 10th Duke's death duties (I am amused to find, scribbled in my copy of the sale catalogue, a list of art books bought that week – £45 spent on twenty-one, ranging from Denis Mahon's *Seicento Theory* at £3.10 to fifteen shillings for the catalogue of the Lotto exhibition in Venice in 1953, this last still with the bookseller's note, 'Pile. £45.' My salary then was £8 a week).

'D. Carritt & B. Sewell come back tomorrow to continue valuing the drawings and prints. It's a scream watching them work, I'll keep my imitation up my sleeve & will try & perfect it tomorrow. I love them both (rather) . . . ' So wrote Deborah (Debo), Duchess of Devonshire, to Nancy Mitford on 27 June 1966.[39] My weeks spent at Chatsworth, partly with David, partly with Noël Annesley, looking at drawings and cossetting whippets, were among the happiest of my life and full of laughter. We giggled helplessly as

---

39   Charlotte Mosley ed: *The Mitfords – Letters between Six Sisters*, Harper 2007.

Dénouement

Debo decided that she would entertain James Rorimer, Director of the Metropolitan Museum, to tea and give him tomato sandwiches made with fruit grown from seeds, not planted, but spontaneously growing in the Chatsworth sewage – and then let him know that this was so. We giggled helplessly a lot.

In the dead days of late July and August the support work for the Chatsworth valuation continued in London, the rummaging through exhibition and collection catalogues, books and photographs, to confirm or adjust attributions, the checking of auctions at Sotheby's and elsewhere, uncovering prices recently asked by dealers in a rapidly rising market. Others took holidays but my nose was to its grindstone, not only in this enjoyable chore but in the daily grind of the department and the preparation of sales for the autumn season. My week away in Bavaria with Jens only increased the pressure, but I knew that on Friday 16 September I should be off and away again – with nothing to do for Christie's – to Spain with Claudio, partly to fill gaps in my journey with John Croft five years before, and partly, having with him followed the pilgrimage route to Compostella across the north of the country, to rejoin it at Burgos and return to England along the route from Bordeaux to Paris.

Ten days or so before I left, urgently assembling manuscripts (as raw catalogue entries were impertinently called) for a sale catalogue while the printer and Guy hovered at my shoulders, a boy from the Front Counter came into my room holding part of a split panel in each hand, laughing as he told me that 'some woman' had insisted that it be seen by an expert. I simply said 'Don't let that woman leave the building – don't,' and continued shuffling manuscripts. 'What is it?' said Guy – to which, my nostrils no doubt flaring, my deliberately infuriating answer was 'Guy, you've ordered me to finish this catalogue, and finish it I will. Then I'll tell you what it is.'

It was a sketch by Rubens in preparation for his *Samson and Delilah*, now in the National Gallery but then, if known at all, thought lost. I knew it only from an engraving by Jacob Matham seen years before, but the picture itself had never been reproduced in any monograph and I had some reason to believe that it had been destroyed in British bombing raids on Hamburg. For this my source was Ludwig Burchard (1886–1960), a devoted scholar who had since 1922 been compiling a catalogue raisonné of paintings by Rubens, to whom I had been sent by Johannes Wilde when I first thought of Rubens as a subject for a PhD. His *Corpus Rubenianum* was then a vast amorphous mass of notes, papers, tentative publications, photographs and memories – and remained so at his death (even now it is still in course of publication); no one ever knew more of Rubens, but overwhelmed by what he knew, he could organise almost nothing for publication.

It was thus with great excitement and enthusiasm that I told 'some woman' what she had brought in. I learned later that she had already been to Sotheby's and to the National Gallery which used, on Wednesdays, to hold an open day for enquiries and often shed persistent nuisances by sending them on to nearby Christie's for second opinions and valuations. 'I've just been to the National Gallery and they said this is a Rubens (or Raphael, or Rembrandt)' was always a bad beginning to a consultation, but on this occasion it was I who began the conversation with no ifs, buts and caveats about the attribution.

I left for Spain with Claudio, and in my absence John Herbert released to the press an announcement that David Carritt had made another astonishing discovery – the preparatory *modello* for a great painting by Rubens long believed lost, *Samson and Delilah*. David was photographed holding it. I dare say he was blameless. The press release was concocted by Patrick and his naive intention was to publicise David's thaumaturgical abilities in the hope of invitations hither and yon to discover other masterpieces long unrecognised – a break from the firm's tradition that it, rather than any individual within it, made discoveries. The *Daily Telegraph* made most fuss, so much indeed that someone in Christie's sent the editor an anonymous note asserting that his report of the affair was nonsense and that it was I who had identified the Rubens. When, on 17 October, I returned from Spain, it was to a raging accusation of disloyalty from Patrick who had assumed me to be the author of the note. I had no idea what he was shouting about and did not know how to respond. The note could have been sent by anyone in the department, indeed by almost anyone in the firm, for the tale of how I had driven the grin from the face of the boy on the Front Counter and kept Guy fretting in anticipation for a quarter of an hour was the gossip of the day, but it could not have been sent by me, driving long and fast to Cordoba. I suspected Patrick's secretary, Julia Lucas, who had earlier been mine; we were fond of each other and both resented the way in which, recognising her ability, intelligence and the perception that enabled her to compose letters as though I had written them myself, he had broken our partnership.

I had been away for four full weeks – time enough to brood, and between the delights of Granada, Toledo, Madrid, the Escorial, Segovia, Burgos and points between and north, I had contemplated leaving Christie's. It had become too rarely a happy place to work. My initial role had been scuppered by the ghost of Vic Heather and the department's dependence on a workhorse, blind, ignorant and unambitious; what connoisseurship and scholarship I had been able to add had now been usurped by David – not his fault and my resentment was never directed at him, but at Guy and Patrick who were puppet-masters to us both; the difference was that I had been asked to join the firm before they had defined what I was to do and be, and that their having later discovered the definition, they applied it instead to David. My second role, discovered by me for myself, the builder of a department of prints and drawings independent of the picture department, had been frustrated for fully five years since I had proved that it could be done. And now, this melancholy much in mind, I was confronted by Patrick in a poisonous rage that he had sustained and nurtured the full length of my absence.

I had a busy week. There was a month's correspondence to read and a month's cataloguing to check – though Noël had proved to be a shrewd and sensibilitous pupil. There was, too, a mad dash to Wales in my diary – a journey promising a Van Eyck that in the event proved to be a worthless copy of Van Dyck's portrait of *Thomas Wentworth with his Secretary* (one of hundreds). Driving gave me yet more time to think about Patrick and work at Christie's that was now turning me into little better than a travelling salesman; it was a time when few people had access to a camera, before the invention of the polaroid and when owners wrote descriptions of their paintings, the words of this Welshman so lyrically poetic that his Eyck-Dyck became a late medieval masterpiece. I did not expect another *Arnolfini Portrait* – that was too far beyond the bounds of chance – but the description of a man holding a letter, seated before a rich cloth-of-honour, could have been of a portrait by Memling later in the fifteenth century, or even by a sixteenth century German hand, and 'the family tradition that it is by Van Eyck' was tempting. There were no other pictures of note in the house and I returned to London empty-handed.

Was this to be my life? – a life of largely fruitless journeys in hope of a discovery or two with which David would be credited? Was I to be not even the replacement for Vic Heather now, but the new Freddy Turner (old Alec's ignorant brother-in-law), always on the move, always alone at night in cheap hotels or at the mercy of bed-and-breakfast keepers? Still brooding, I spent the weekend at Castle Hedingham, saying nothing of my mood – easily managed with so much to say of Spain and pilgrimage. The following week I drove to Hull to advise on the insurance value of paintings in a proposed loan exhibition, and then on to Newcastle to inspect the stock of two dealers who regularly consigned paintings in bulk to Christie's. One of the paintings I saw in Hull was by Kate Coughtrie, *Remembrance*, and I telephoned my mother to ask if she had any recollection of it or had played some part in it. It was on the long slog back to London in the dark that I decided to talk to Peter Chance.

Dénouement

In the first week of November I asked Peter to give me a few uninterrupted minutes. I told him that working under Patrick had from the very start been difficult, but that with Guy too in charge of the department matters had worsened in the sense that I had to contend with the competition between them. I recalled my difficulties in America and our loss of the Lehman sale. I explained that the market for old master drawings was driven by American collectors and dealers, and expressed the opinion that without a dedicated director we could never play any part in it other than second fiddle to Sotheby's where, even though they had the year before taken Philip Pouncey from the British Museum to add expertise to that department, Richard Day, its workhorse, younger than me and far less experienced, had been made a partner and director. I reminded him that on the three occasions when I had been approached by the National Trust, the British Council and an American university collection with offers of a post, he had urged me not to go, reiterating and reinforcing the promise made at my first interview with him in 1958 that I would eventually be appointed a director. Those offers should have reassured him that I was worth having in his employment. 'This time I have not been offered another job. I am not being tempted to leave by any outside prospect. But I am no longer happy here, and for this the only remedy is my being able to talk to Patrick on equal terms.'

'Give me three days,' he said, 'I'll talk to the others.' He took a little longer. In mid afternoon on Wednesday 9 November 1966 he called me to his room. 'I'm afraid it's no. It's Patrick.' I had no alternative but to resign; I had, perhaps, been too frank and talked myself into a corner — certainly that is how I felt — but to retreat from what had been something of an ultimatum would not only have been humiliating but would have put me in an abject relationship with Patrick. I had long said to myself that I should be settled in a career by the time I reached thirty-five and I expected to spend the rest of my working life at Christie's, but the extraordinary peak of happiness and contentment in the first part of the year had been wiped out by the affair of the Rubens sketch, which I had not even been allowed to catalogue, and I felt that I had been eliminated as effectively as a dissident Russian general from a photograph of Stalin.

I told Peter that I would leave in three months or on completion of the Chatsworth valuation, whichever was the sooner, and returned to my room wretchedly downcast – a mood that turned to hurt, anger and absolute resolve when David Carritt came to see me. He told me of the meeting of his fellow directors at which my joining them had been discussed. All but one had been in favour, but the decision had to be unanimous. Patrick had objected, and objected in such terms as had humiliated David – 'We've got one homosexual on the board; we don't need another . . . ' Other directors, when confronted, confirmed that this was so. So there it was; my knowledge, experience and dogged devotion counted for nothing because I was queer; even, illogically, my uncomplaining exploitation when knowingly packed off to spend a night or two with any titled Old Etonian who had a picture he might sell if enchanted by a pretty boy, counted for nothing; in Patrick's view I was contemptible – and that was to be the lurking elephant with us for the next three months or so.

As Chatsworth, like refurbishing the Forth Bridge, proved to be a matter that dragged on for decades, resulting in spectacular sales under Noël Annesley and acutely embarrassing misjudgements by the British Museum, 9 February 1967 was officially the day of my departure. In the event, my life at Christie's both fizzled out and fizzled on. While completing that part of the Chatsworth valuation for which I was responsible, I took on nothing new that could not be completed within a day or two and inexorably became what in my army days was dubbed the spare prick at the wedding. Half a dozen times, both before and after Christmas, Peter took me to lunch and tried to persuade me not to leave, 'You don't have to go' always his refrain. His charm and sincerity were persuasive – but how could I weaken when I knew that he had concealed from

Dénouement

me Patrick's 'We've got one homosexual on the board . . . ' My only misgiving was for Noël; for a year or so I left him my reference books on the prints of Dürer and Rembrandt – the essential keys to any that he might have to catalogue – and from time to time slipped back to look at drawings with him, but towards the end of 1967 this no longer seemed necessary, so much had his confidence grown, and my occasional visits dwindled away.

In spite of Patrick, leaving Christie's was painful. The longest episode of my life – longer than school, the army or the Courtauld Institute, it had been a period of continual growth in knowledge and experience, of constant opportunity, though I felt that I had given the firm as much as it had given me. And I was leaving it, not because I had exhausted its resources, nor because it had exhausted mine, not for any professional advancement, but because I was damned for being queer.

Coda

If a man's life is indeed the biblical term of three score years and ten, then mine was half done, but, far from Dante's predicament when writing of that midway stage - 'Nel mezzo del cammin di nostra vita' - I was neither lost nor terrified. I had told very few within and without the firm that I was about to leave Christie's, I had made no plans, I had not even done what afterwards I learned that 'everybody did' – that is take a copy of the client list and of subscribers to the relevant catalogues – and my future was uncertain. I was, however, overwhelmingly aware of a sense of freedom. All my life I had been under the control of others, parents, priests and mentors, or at school and in the army one of many in a large group with a common and disciplined aim, but now I had the opportunity to do, if not entirely what I pleased, then at least to find work that I enjoyed and to pursue it at any pace I chose. There were false starts and the discovery that avenues were closed, but I had more friends that I had realised; America and Europe became happy hunting grounds and in my travels I saw not only great museums and galleries, but many forgotten, obscure and rarely visited by Englishmen, constantly widening and complementing my knowledge. Dali was for some years my friend, Warhol an occasional acquaintance across a smoke-filled room, Bacon a sometimes petulant and demanding neighbour. I rode the moors of Derbyshire on a docile gelding and was nourished by the solitude; I took my skis to Norway and was delighted by the flight of ptarmigan; I learned, if not to climb them, to clamber about in mountains and cherish isolation; and for fifteen years or so, summer and winter, I quartered Turkey in pursuit of Greek, Roman, Christian and, particularly, Armenian monuments. No scholar gypsy could have been happier.

Now well beyond my second half I ought, at eighty, like old

King Cole, to be a merry old soul content with Burgundy and 'baccy. Instead, I chose to write this book, partly because so many friends have begged me to record such matters as the working methods of Hercules Brabazon Brabazon, and the survival into the mid-sixties of Baron von Gloeden's photographic plates, but more because it may reassure readers not remotely interested in art, particularly young men in times far more enlightened than mine, that it is not quite the end of the world to be a bastard or queer. At eighty I have felt far more able to be candid than at sixty, and even what-the-hellish about matters in which candour may still shock, in the hope that my survival may help others to survive.

I have had one small difficulty with language: buggery was the common word for sodomy when I was young and, as the Oxford English Dictionary has it, 'in decent use only as a legal term;' now used quite comfortably in almost all the exclamatory and idiomatic senses listed by the great Eric Partridge in his *Dictionary of Slang*, to today's ear the word seems blunt and brutal in its sexual sense. Those as intrigued as I by etymology will understand my clinging to the word for the sake of its period feel when writing of my early years; if there is a sequel to this book I shall, no doubt, as the transition is now absolute in vulgar parlance, use the verb *to fuck* for the very same activity.

Index of Artists

General Index

General Index

National Gallery 15–16

Nicolson, Benedict 217

Noel, Captain John 280–2

Northwick Collection 310–12

Oman, Charles 183

Petrides, Paul 245–6

Pool, Phoebe 60–1

Pope-Hennessy, Sir John 182, 186, 271

Popham, Arthur Ewart 214–15

Pouncey, Philip 247–8, 333

Rees-Jones, Professor Stephen 160–2, 296

Rigden, Jil *see* Allibone, Jill

Robbins, Professor Lionel 116

Röthlisberger, Marcel 121, 244

Rokoko, Die Welt des (exhibition) 182–4

Romantic Movement, The (exhibition) 260–1

Rostal, Max 57–8, 62

Ruhemann, Helmuth 160–2

St Gabriel's Singers 66–8

Scott-Elliot, Aydua 171, 174, 181, 194

Seddon, Joan 154, 162–5, 232, 284–91

Sewell, Jessica (mother) ix, xii, 1–16, 102–4, 194, 265, 308

Sewell, Robert (stepfather) 24–35, 40, 58, 65–6, 223

Sorabji, Francina 150, 154

Spencer-Churchill, Captain Edward George 310–11

Strong, Sir Roy 183, 306

Suez Crisis 100–1

Troutman, Philip 151

Victoria and Albert Museum 209, 260

Warburg Institute 114; and note 116

Warlock, Peter *see* Heseltine, Philip

Waterhouse, Professor Ellis 137, 198–200, 228, 271, 306, 314

Watson, Sir Francis 183, 293

Whinney, Dr Margaret 112, 115, 137–8, 142

White, Professor John 118, 123–4, 131

Whitstable ix, 10, 11, 18, 25, 26

Wilde, Professor Johannes 112, 118–20, 157

Wind in the Willows, The 11, 223

Wollesen, Professor Jens 326–7

Wood, Christopher 302–3

Wright, Harold 216